Wyoming Range War

Wyoming Range War

The Infamous Invasion of Johnson County

John W. Davis

University of Oklahoma Press : Norman

Also by John W. Davis
Worland before Worland (Worland, Wyo., 1987)
Sadie and Charlie (Worland, Wyo., 1989)
A Vast Amount of Trouble (Niwot, Colo., 1993; Norman, Okla., 2005)
Goodbye, Judge Lynch (Norman, Okla., 2005)

Library of Congress Cataloging-in-Publication Data

Davis, John W., 1943–
    Wyoming range war : the infamous invasion of Johnson County / John W. Davis. — 1st ed.
        p.   cm.
    Includes bibliographical references and index.
    ISBN 978-0-8061-4106-0 (cloth)
    ISBN 978-0-8061-4261-6 (paper)
    1. Johnson County War, 1892. 2. Johnson County (Wyo.)—History—19th century. 3. Cattle trade—Wyoming—History—19th century. I. Title.
    F767.J8D38 2010
    978.7'3501—dc22

                                                          2009041237

The paper in this book meets the guidelines for permanence and durability of the Committee on Production Guidelines for Book Longevity of the Council on Library Resources, Inc. ∞

2 3 4 5 6 7 8 9 10

Contents

Illustrations

ALL P = PORTRAITS unless other P W/CAP

FIGURES

MAP

Preface

I grew up in Worland, Wyoming, and from a very early age have had a thing about history. Worland is the seat of Washakie County, created in 1913. Before Washakie County, however, there was Johnson County, and between 1881 and 1897 the eastern part of what is now Washakie County, including the site of most of present-day Worland, was in Johnson County. (At first, Johnson County extended to all the land east of the Big Horn River, or roughly the eastern half of the Big Horn Basin.) The automobile trip from Worland to Buffalo, the county seat of Johnson County, is only ninety miles. From Worland, a traveler first goes through badlands—desiccated, eroded, yet colorful country—before coming down into the Nowood River valley and the storybook setting of the town of Ten Sleep. From there, U.S. Highway 16 crosses the Big Horn Mountains, rising more than five thousand feet to Powder River Pass, through remarkably varied mountain country. Then the road winds down the east slope of the Big Horns into Buffalo. I've made this drive at least a couple hundred times and have spent a great deal of time in and around Buffalo; I feel I know the area well.

Given my weakness for history, I've naturally been interested in the Johnson County War. What constitutes the "Johnson County War" has never been strictly defined, but the name refers generally to murderous episodes beginning in late 1891 and culminating in the full-scale invasion of the county in April 1892 by twenty-five big cattlemen and their top hands, along with another twenty-five hired guns. It was an amazing event, the subject of movies, seemingly countless articles, and something on the order of ten books. Only recently, though, during the course of research for my book, *Goodbye, Judge Lynch*, did I give serious thought to writing about the Johnson County War myself.

In preparation for *Goodbye, Judge Lynch*, which reviews the development of the criminal justice system in the Big Horn Basin from 1879 to 1909, I spent a great deal of time going through early records in various courthouses. At the Johnson County courthouse (surely the neatest old courthouse in Wyoming), I came across one item after another that related to the invasion. That 1884 landmark is full of musty, yellowed handwritten records made by and about such fabled characters as Frank Canton, Red Angus, Robert Foote, and Fred Hesse. Within the county commissioner minutes, land records, assessment records, and court files, I kept running into information I'd not known about before. I thought all these items were wonderful and found them stirring. In fact, they inspired me, taking my simmering interest in the Johnson County War to a boil.

The Johnson County Library has an excellent collection of Johnson County War items, and I decided to review it all. The first thing I learned was that the amount of material about the invasion is overwhelming, and after spending months going through the principal writings, I came away with the unsettling feeling that I knew less about the event than when I started. Writers on both sides of the conflict were highly emotional, leading them to present adversarial and mutually exclusive accounts. As well, virtually all of the writings strongly focused on the sensational violence that occurred in 1891 and 1892. Most of the authors had been personally involved in the invasion; they had little interest in historical context but, rather, wanted to defend an agenda. These writings are profound influences skewing the historical record. Of course, much of what I've described is true of almost all celebrated legal causes, but unlike most such events, no trial followed the events of April 1892, no full and balanced presentation in a courtroom to sort out fact, fiction, and hyperbole. Instead, the "presentation" of evidence related to the Johnson County War was made almost completely in various public forums, very much outside the scrutiny of cross-examination.

Another factor affecting the accuracy of the reporting of the invasion was that most writers were not people from Johnson County but folks from the outside looking in, primarily invaders or those associated with them. The invaders were especially good at getting their story out, and their allegations have set the terms of the debate. (Even Asa Mercer's incomparable polemic, *The Banditti of the Plains*, is a response to the big cattlemen's contentions, addressing the event from the perspective of citizens of Cheyenne.) The invaders' version of the Johnson County War, however, is surely the most suspect viewpoint. It was forwarded by men in a whole lot of trouble who desperately wished to justify their actions.

I looked hard for a satisfactory critique of a number of the key allegations made by the invaders. According to them, Johnson County was an outlaw society dominated by cattle thieves whose allies held all the important public offices, making convictions for cattle theft all but impossible to obtain. The men who rode north from Casper, Wyoming, in April 1892 insisted that their invasion was therefore justified, along with the summary execution of seventy men in Johnson, Natrona, and Converse counties, including alleged rustlers, a sheriff and his deputies, county commissioners, a newspaper editor, and at least one leading merchant. It seemed to me that to get to the heart of the Johnson County War, these allegations had to be closely scrutinized.

Somewhere in the middle of all my musings and readings, I reviewed an excellent article by Sheridan County historian John McDermott about the historiography of the Johnson County War, and it helped to focus my thoughts about the invasion. McDermott made the point I've been discussing above, that almost every writer about the Johnson County War had little concern for historical context. He noted that broad areas of inquiry had been neglected, areas that could shed light on the validity of the versions of accounts from the participants in the Johnson County War. McDermott was referring to such things as the contemporary newspaper reports, the Johnson County court records, and land records. I agreed with him wholeheartedly.

In my other writings, I've made extensive use of local newspapers, and I believe they are invaluable to understanding the times in which tumultuous events took place. In the late nineteenth and early twentieth century, when there was no competition from radio, television, motion pictures, fax machines, telephones, or the Internet, local newspapers from emerging small towns were highly detailed chronicles, telling, with some notable exceptions, virtually everything. People in those tiny, isolated communities were intensely involved in the lives of their neighbors and wanted to know all they could about them. So, on the pages of the *Worland Grit,* for example (the newspaper I know best), the tiny frontier town comes to life, as a reader learns about what buildings and homes are being constructed, what businesses are being opened, what goods those businesses are selling and to whom, who went to the dance last Saturday night, who is marrying whom, who is having a baby, who got in trouble, who got hurt, who is sick, who visited whom and what they are all talking about, and how just doggone wonderful it is to be in this garden spot of Wyoming and maybe the whole United States. As great luck would have it, the majority of the issues of the newspapers published in Johnson County from 1883 through 1895 are extant.

Only one complete issue of the *Buffalo Echo* is available, however— the first one, published in August 1883. But all the issues of the *Big Horn Sentinel,* published from September 13, 1884, to October 19, 1889, are on microfilm, as are all of the issues of the *Buffalo Bulletin,* beginning in October 1890, and several early issues of the *People's Voice,* published after May 28, 1892. These issues are contained in five microfilm rolls in the Wyoming State Archives in Cheyenne, and I asked the people in that office to make duplicates for me. I started going through each roll, using a simple but efficient microfilm reader installed in my basement. It took me six months to make one pass through the five rolls and another six months to index and collate them. After completing this long but invaluable exercise, I felt even more reason to agree with a comment by Owen Wister about the *Buffalo Bulletin* (published in the May 26, 1892, *Bulletin* when he ordered a one-year subscription): "It seems to me to reveal more satisfactorily than anything I have seen the real state of things in your community." The reader of this book will have to make the final judgment about the value of the information developed, as it is interwoven throughout the book. Suffice it to say that I was surprised, even startled, by what I learned. The perspective of Johnson County people in the late 1880s and early 1890s was starkly different from what has been presented in virtually all the published writings. Johnson County citizens proudly focused on the progressive community they had created and the splendid prospects of Buffalo, their attractive county seat. The occasional theft of cattle in the remote corners of the county was not a central concern, at least not until very late, almost into 1892.

I spent a lot of contented hours in nooks and crannies of the Johnson County Courthouse, looking for documents prepared by Johnson County residents over a century ago, searching the court files at the clerk of court's office and the land records at the clerk's office. This information is highly reliable, because most of it was compiled before anyone dreamed of an invasion of Johnson County. Such basic information, coupled with contemporary newspaper reports, provides essential data against which writings and opinions can be tested and, since it does not suffer the taint of some human being's desperate need to twist facts, can usually be considered more trustworthy than the information in the numerous personal accounts forwarded after the invasion. For instance, the official records and newspapers are invaluable to address whether the principal activity of the residents of Johnson County was the building of family farms and ranches, or whether the county had the trappings of a rogue society collaborating with criminals who were stealing large cattle ranchers blind. Such papers can help to show whether the responsible authorities were intimidated by a criminal element (or, worse yet, were actively abetting criminal activity) or, on the other hand, were doing their best to discharge their duties.

In the course of my research, I learned that the Johnson County Library and the court records in the Johnson County Courthouse are not the only places holding period documents relating to the invasion. The Jim Gatchell Memorial Museum in Buffalo has made a concerted effort in recent years to draw together various collections of invasion information, including many items not found elsewhere. Its Tom Tisdale Collection contains some especially valuable information. The American Heritage Center in Laramie also contains valuable information, such as the Fred Hesse Collection.

As I stated above, the Johnson County War has not often been presented from the standpoint of those who lived in the county. It is true that there are extensive accounts from two county residents, and they would normally be given special weight. Ordinarily, such accounts would be expected to be fairly reliable, but these two—by Jack Flagg and Frank Canton—are diametrically opposed. Jack Flagg was a man deeply involved in all the ugly events of 1892 and wrote extensively about them. He has been dismissed as overly partisan, however. The writings of Frank Canton, the sheriff of Johnson County between 1883 and 1887, have been given more credence. Canton was a man in a position to know the whole truth about Johnson County's experiences, and his judgments upon the people of Johnson County are damning. His credibility, or lack thereof, is a crucial consideration when trying to reach reasoned conclusions about Johnson County in the nineteenth century. In this connection, Robert K. DeArment's book *Alias Frank Canton* was a revelation to me, providing information about Canton not addressed or considered in any of the books about the Johnson County War. DeArment's book prompted me to critically examine and investigate a number of Canton's declarations. Another eye-opener was George W. Hufsmith's *The Wyoming Lynching of Cattle Kate,* because it so convincingly demonstrates how efficiently disinformation was generated and disseminated out of Cheyenne in the late nineteenth century. This perspective, in turn, was a major help in selecting the most supportable conclusions among the cacophony of competing assertions relating to the invasion.

As might be apparent, the overall approach I settled upon was to present the Johnson County War from the viewpoint of the residents of Johnson County, while reconsidering and reevaluating all the evidence relating to the event. The event has become so encrusted with distortions and obfuscations that it is crucial to look closely at the community in the 1880s (which, fortunately, was an interesting time), and to use the events and the established character of the community as an anchor to the plausibility of claims in the 1890s. I concentrate on ten remarkable men who came to Johnson County early, were deeply involved in the community from the time they arrived, including the traumatic events of 1891 and 1892, and most of whom left writings that vividly present their experiences and attitudes. They are Frank M. Canton, William Galispie "Red" Angus, Charles H. Burritt, Robert N. Foote, Jack Flagg, William J. Clarke, Horace R. Mann, Gustave E. A. Moeller, Fred G. S. Hesse, and John R. Smith.

I gave special weight to information supported by contemporaneous documents when the reporter (in the broad sense) had no motivation to distort the record. I also gave special credence to what lawyers call "admissions against interest"—that is, statements made by involved parties that are directly contrary to their interests. These include later writings of people such as Dr. Charles Penrose and William C. Irvine, the statements of Hiram B. Ijams to George Dunning, the writings of Robert David, as well as John Rolfe Burroughs's *Guardian of the Grasslands,* an official history of the Wyoming Stock Growers Association. Burroughs can fairly be said to have accurately stated the positions of the association, at least at the time of publication (1971) and earlier. I was skeptical of statements without contemporaneous support and more than skeptical if such statements were made by someone with a motive to distort. This approach meant a drastic reordering of the weight and value of some famous items of evidence.

I believe that a full presentation from the point of view of the residents of Johnson County has never been made—that is, one that primarily relies on the everyday experiences and perspective of local people, as well as their accumulated information. In many instances, such as court proceedings and real estate transactions, Johnson County citizens had legal duties to accurately record information, and in still others, such as the reporting of news, they felt a responsibility to provide accurate information to readers. To state the obvious, Johnson County people were directly and personally involved in community events, so I believe their viewpoint is presumptively the most valid, especially for the times before the populace became excited (roughly, December 1891, following the assassinations of two local men). I do not take the position that such information should escape scrutiny, however, nor that information supplied from December 1891 onward is invalid. Such later information, though, should be subjected to a higher level of scrutiny than information compiled earlier by disinterested people. Even after December 1, 1891, though, Johnson County people still had the best vantage point. Joe DeBarthe, the editor of the *Buffalo Bulletin* in 1891, wrote these cogent remarks in the December 24, 1891, issue: "We are in about as good a position to know the real facts as anyone, and a great deal better than many who are writing foolish articles against the rustlers from hearsay and guesswork."

I also kept other concepts in mind, seeing them as working hypotheses. McDermott made the point I allude to above, that virtually all the writings about the invasion overemphasized the violent events of 1891 and 1892, presenting the Johnson County War as an exciting anachronism, a brief and anomalous explosion of frontier violence that quickly abated. But I've concluded that this explosion of violence was no more an isolated event than are the earthquakes and volcanoes along tectonic plates. Those spectacular phenomena get all the attention, but they occur because of the pressure of whole continents. The Johnson County War, too, was much more than brief pyrotechnics; rather, it was one of the events in which the profound American friction that had been building throughout the second half of the nineteenth century surged to the surface. I believe that the Johnson County War was of a piece with the 1886 Haymarket riot, the 1892 Homestead strike, and the 1894 Pullman strike; they were all points of explosion stemming from deep conflicts permeating American society. At a time when the entrepreneurial class entertained enhanced notions of its power and prerogatives, the federal laws allowing unrestricted use of public lands invited ruinous competition for the settlement and use of those lands. I also came to the paradoxical conclusion, however, that although it was very likely an episode of violence like the Johnson County War would occur somewhere within the intermountain West, Johnson County was one of the least likely settings for it. I believe the invasion would never have happened but for the involvement of a few men of odd and unfortunate character.

During the nineteenth century the United States changed from an agricultural society to an industrial one, and the change did not come easily. As an agricultural society, America was remarkably democratic, as Alexis de Tocqueville described it the early 1830s. De Tocqueville found a middle-class society, dominated by Jefferson's "yeoman farmers." It was the product of a land-rich country that, at least after 1820, quite deliberately employed a policy of ready distribution of land to ensure an egalitarian nation controlled by the governed. That policy was continued into the second half of the nineteenth century, as Congress passed legislation such as the famous Homestead Act of 1862 and the Desert Land Entry Act of 1877. Remarkably, though, in the second half of the nineteenth century, the democracy described by de Tocqueville came under threat.

After the Civil War, the trend toward a more urban society accelerated, and the power of great corporations grew enormously. As the country became less rural, though, labor was more and more subject to control by capital, to the point that the division between labor and capital became increasingly rigid and workers were in danger of being permanently ground down. Concepts such as Spencer's social Darwinism—a thinly veiled justification for the exploitation of workers—gained currency. At the same time, the availability of free land, that great safety valve that had so long protected Americans of modest means from an over-robust capitalism, lessened. After 1890, Frederick Jackson Turner even declared that time of opportunity to be over. It was not, though. Despite the lack of a clear frontier demarcation, there were still places in which the barrier separating labor and capital was not carved in stone, places where people could find good, productive land and start building their lives their own way. One of those places was Johnson County, Wyoming, an area that was unusually well-watered, with fertile acreage along streambeds, coupled with generally moderate weather. But, unlike the settlers in most other new lands in the United States, some settlers in northern Wyoming encountered fierce opposition. The story of the Johnson County War is the story of that opposition and how it all worked out.

Wyoming Range War

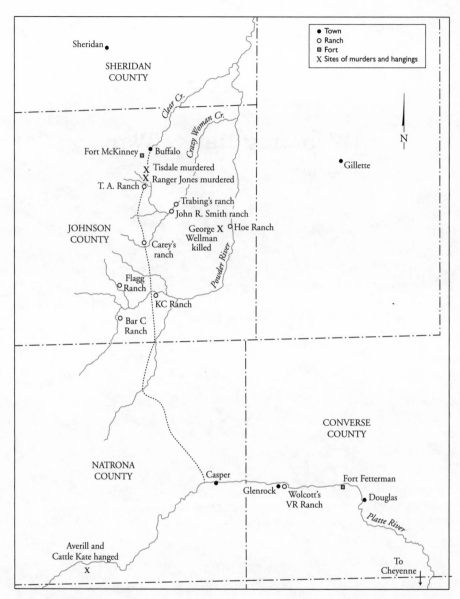

Sheridan •

SHERIDAN
COUNTY

Clear Cr.

Crazy Woman Cr.

Fort McKinney ☐ • Buffalo

X Tisdale murdered
X Ranger Jones murdered
T. A. Ranch ○

○ Trabing's ranch
○ John R. Smith ranch

JOHNSON
COUNTY

George X ○ Hoe Ranch
Wellman
○ Carey's   killed
ranch

Powder River

Flagg
○ Ranch
○ KC Ranch

○ Bar C
Ranch

• Gillette

N

● Town
○ Ranch
☐ Fort
X Sites of murders and hangings

CONVERSE
COUNTY

NATRONA
COUNTY

Casper •

Glenrock • ○ Wolcott's
VR Ranch

Fort Fetterman ☐
• Douglas

Platte River

Averill and
Cattle Kate hanged
X

To
Cheyenne

North-central Wyoming

Prologue

In 1891 and 1892, northern Wyoming witnessed a series of shocking and murderous events, which have come down to us as the Johnson County War. These happenings staggered the people of Wyoming and were made all the more bewildering by sensationally inaccurate newspaper articles that drowned out the reports of Johnson County citizens—the people directly involved in the events. Many volumes have been written about the Johnson County War, but the story has never been told from the viewpoint of the people in the community where the War occurred. This is that story.

CHAPTER ONE

The Beginning

About three miles east of Buffalo, Wyoming, there is a turnout off the westbound lanes of Interstate 90, just before the interstate reaches the Big Horn Mountains. The turnout overlooks Buffalo and the valley surrounding the town, and it presents one of the great vistas in America. In April and May the valley can be as green as Ireland, and the mountains loom over Buffalo like giant snow-laden skyscrapers; it seems that half the sky is filled with the majesty of the Big Horns. Deep-green timber starts almost at Buffalo, rising until it meets the tundra of the high peaks. Those high peaks are topped by Cloud Peak, floating 8,500 feet above Buffalo. Buffalo, with a population of fewer than four thousand people in the 2000 census, snuggles in the middle of this scene like a New England village.

Buffalo has been the seat of Johnson County, Wyoming, since 1881, when the county first began operation and the town was growing up as an adjunct to a frontier army post. Buffalo's peaceful and pleasing setting today makes it hard to believe this little town was once the center of a happening that, as T. A. Larson wrote, "ranks as the most notorious event in the history of Wyoming."[1] It was called the Johnson County War, it happened more than a century ago, and within Wyoming the very mention of Johnson County still calls up a time of infamy.

What is now Johnson County was originally created as Pease County by the territorial legislature in 1875, a time when settlement, and thus organization of the county, was impossible—the entire northeastern

quarter of Wyoming was then set aside as unceded Indian territory.[2] Nevertheless, the legisture found at least one use for Pease County and Crook
County, which together comprised most of the Indian territory. An unpopular judge, William Ware Peck, was "sagebrushed" by the Wyoming legislature when legislators assigned these unorganized counties as his district,
thereby ensuring he had no trial court duties, presiding over only sagebrush.[3]

Pease County was a remarkable domain. It was roughly one hundred
miles by one hundred miles, extending south from the Montana border
and from the Big Horn River on the west (in the Big Horn Basin) to
the Powder River on the east. It encompassed virtually the entire Big
Horn Mountain chain, which meant that the area was unusually well
watered, especially along the base of the Big Horns. The eastern slope
drains numerous streams between the Powder River on the south and
Tongue River on the north; every few miles a traveler crosses a stream,
usually flowing clear mountain water.[4] A lot of water meant a lot of
grass, and the grazing in the shortgrass prairie east of the Big Horns was
as good as could be found in Wyoming. The resources were practically
limitless; to name only two, the Big Horn Mountains were full of timber,
and the eastern part of the county was full of coal.

Until the spring of 1877, the northeastern quarter of Wyoming
remained the realm of the Sioux, the Cheyennes, and the Arapahoes.[5]
The warriors of these tribes were fearsome; under Red Cloud, they
drove whites from the Bozeman Trail (the "bloody Bozeman" ran
north and south along the eastern base of the Big Horn Mountains). Then,
a few years later, when led by Crazy Horse, they checked General George
Crook at the Battle of the Rosebud, preventing him from joining Alfred
Terry and George Custer. These tribes were finally worn down by U.S.
forces and confined to reservations.

The United States, to assure that the tribes that defeated Custer would
stay put, decided "to surround these Indians with a cordon of posts."[6]
In 1878 Captain Edwin Pollock of the Ninth U.S. Cavalry was given
orders to select a site for a fort along the Bozeman Trail.[7] On July 18,
1878, Captain Pollock laid out a military reservation centered on Clear
Creek, where that stream first emerges from the Big Horn Mountains.

All of this meant not only that Pease County was open to land settlement but also that there were opportunities for entrepreneurs who wished
to service the substantial needs of an army post. During the year 1879

the name of Pease County was changed to Johnson County (in honor of the U.S. attorney for the Territory of Wyoming, who had just died),[8] and entrepreneurs did arrive and set up shop at a site just downstream from the new fort, which was named Fort McKinney.

Buffalo's earliest years must have been truly boisterous, judging by the comments of T. V. McCandlish, the editor of the first newspaper published in Johnson County, the *Buffalo Echo*. In its inaugural edition, issued on August 2, 1883, McCandlish provided histories of Buffalo and Johnson County. He first discussed the establishment of Fort McKinney and then described the beginning days of the town growing up near the fort: "On the banks of Clear Creek was soon gathered as rough an element of humanity as a frontier settlement is usually blessed or cursed with. During the years 1880 and 1881, the town was the scene of many deeds of violence." McCandlish added, however, that after 1882 the citizens of the town, bolstered by the addition of "a few more energetic and peace-loving citizens," determined that law and order would "reign supreme." The editor proudly pointed to a number of developments that showed that Buffalo was no longer a wild and lawless town. These included two large general merchandise stores, as well as "a Bank, six saloons, two hotels [one was the Occidental Hotel], two eating houses, one livery stable, barber shop, . . . dentist's office, blacksmith and wagon making shop, shoemaker's shop, meat market, lumber yard, court house, school house, etc."[9]

Buffalo was never a very large town during the 1880s and early 1890s (population: 1,087 in 1890), but it was active.[10] Although the inaugural edition of the *Buffalo Echo* is the only extant issue of a Johnson County newspaper from before September 1884, it provides an invaluable window into the community, a detailed early portrait of Johnson County and Buffalo.[11] The most striking thing about this newspaper (shared by subsequent newspapers in Buffalo) was its faithful reflection of the outlook of the entire community. These people were utterly excited by their prospects, by the adventure and challenge of building a wholly new society in a wholly new place. For example, in one *Echo* article the writer proclaims that the arrival of a railroad was "an assured fact," that Buffalo was "destined to become the principal city of Northern Wyoming," and that within a few years Johnson County would "have double the population of any other county in the territory."[12] Perhaps this attitude should not come as a surprise, because a selection process was at work here. The people drawn

Frank Canton with his horse Fred. Courtesy of Johnson County Jim Gatchell Memorial Museum.

to frontier towns such as Buffalo, including newspaper editors, were young, ambitious, and optimistic. Those who did not share their enthusiasm and energy had been left back home.

Johnson County had a full complement of officers in 1883, including E. U. Snider, Johnson County representative to the territorial legislature; James M. Lobban, probate judge and county treasurer; Nathaniel G. Carwile, county clerk; H. S. Elliott, county attorney, and Frank M. Canton, sheriff.[13]

Even among the ambitious and active young people in Johnson County, Frank Canton stood out. He was a proud, tough, and ferociously efficient peace officer, traits that very early earned him the admiration and praise of the large cattle interests in the area. He was thirty-three in 1882, almost six feet tall, and slender. He was a good-looking man who seemed to have many friends, but Johnson County people had conflicting feelings about him. His personality was so strong that it seemed that his mere presence caused people anxiety; he intimidated men with only a look.[14]

In his autobiography, Canton stated that in his entire four years as sheriff, from 1883 to 1887, he returned every writ and indictment issued by the courts of Johnson County, and "not a single return showed 'not found.'"[15] Given the terrain over which he had to operate, and the character of some of the young men who inhabited it, this boast seems highly dubious, but if any Wyoming sheriff could have done this, it was Frank Canton.

Canton had arrived in Johnson County in 1881; he told people that he had been born in Virginia and educated there. He said he then had come west to Missouri in 1861 and to Colorado with his father in 1868, where they engaged in stock raising southwest of Denver. He also reported that he had relocated to Montana, where he was in the stock business with one William Jamison. In 1877 he went to Cheyenne, and in 1881 to Buffalo, where he was hired by the Wyoming Stock Growers Association as a detective.[16]

As the county seat, Buffalo was the center of legal activity in Johnson County, and early on, attorneys arrived in Buffalo and began the practice of law. They prosecuted and defended the criminal cases forwarded by Frank Canton and other sheriffs, and they engaged in an active civil practice. These attorneys appeared before Judge Jacob Blair, who had been Johnson County's only district judge since 1881 and would remain so until the spring of 1888.[17] Blair lived in Albany County (in Laramie City), which formed part of the southern boundary of Wyoming, but the district over which he presided included Johnson County, which was part of the northern boundary of Wyoming. Twice a year, just before the beginning of the spring and fall judicial terms in Johnson County, Judge Blair had to make the very long trek from far southern Wyoming to far northern Wyoming and, for several weeks, preside over criminal and civil cases. He did not seem to mind this twice-yearly sojourn, and various public pronouncements through the years show that he favored the northern part of his judicial district; it was Blair who coined the term "bouquet county," referring to Johnson County. Blair was a popular figure in Buffalo, unusually so for a district judge, and the simplest explanation is that he liked Buffalo and Buffalo liked Judge Blair.[18]

In 1883 five attorneys were practicing in Buffalo, including Charles H. Burritt, who was, without question, the leading figure in the Buffalo bar during the 1880s and early 1890s.[19] Burritt was from Manchester, Vermont, and had received a splendid education, first at Middlebury College and then at Brown University. This was unusual for the time; most men who would be lawyers simply read law in an established attorney's office and took no college courses at all. Burritt began practicing law in Michigan in 1876, when only twenty-two, but for some reason he left Michigan and came west, working first as a sheepherder and then as a

Justice of the Peace.

Charles H. Burritt, attorney at law, with
signature. Courtesy of Johnson County
Jim Gatchell Memorial Museum
(portrait); records of the Johnson County
Clerk of the District Court (signature).

foreman. He arrived in Buffalo in the spring of 1883, was a deputy sheriff
for Frank Canton for four months, and in 1884 was elected a justice of
the peace.[20]

Burritt was a tall, confident man. Early Johnson County records contain
numerous original documents with his bold and elegant signature. Burritt
dressed well, being "always garbed in black frock coat, neatly fitting vest
and striped trousers." He quickly and firmly aligned himself with the monied
interests of the county, including John H. Conrad and the larger cattle
corporations.[21] He also made enemies, one of whom was Robert N.
Foote, who was described as Burritt's "staunch opponent" and was no
friend of Burritt's clients.[22]

Robert Foote was one of the leading merchants in early Buffalo. He
had been the sutler at Fort Halleck (near Rawlins, Wyoming), but he moved
to Buffalo in 1882 and established a general mercantile store there. His
principal competitor was John Conrad and Company, another dealer in
general merchandise and a client of Burritt's.[23] Foote was an older man
by early Buffalo standards, being one of the rare persons over fifty, but
he fit right in because he reportedly had a lot of get-up-and-go. He

Robert N. Foote. Courtesy of Johnson County Jim Gatchell Memorial Museum.

seemingly had his fingers in every aspect of the life and economy of Johnson County—land, livestock, merchandise, crops, public affairs, and public service. Foote was an impressive figure, a man who, according to those who wrote about Buffalo's first hundred years, was "never to be forgotten as long as there is a Buffalo, or a Johnson County."[24] He was born in Scotland in 1832—he never lost his pronounced Scottish brogue—and he was a strong-minded man. He conveyed a striking presence, well described in *Buffalo's First Century*: "Anytime he appeared on the dusty streets of Buffalo, he was attired in top hat, Prince Albert coat, and striped trousers. He was, moreover, an object of tonsorial magnificence with his long white beard carefully combed, and his footwear highly polished. And he never appeared without his fine walking stick, which he handled with deft and natural ease."[25]

Foote ran a main-street business, but Buffalo had other businesses, not quite so respectable, businesses that catered to some of the baser needs of the soldiers of Fort McKinney. One man who was deeply immersed in such businesses, but who would nevertheless rise to prominence in Buffalo over the next ten years, was William Galispie "Red" Angus. Angus was only thirty-three in 1883 (he was born the same year as Frank Canton, 1849). Like many men in Buffalo at that time, Angus had already lived an eventful life. His family located in Kansas in 1856, when the territory was in the worst throes of a nasty guerrilla war over slavery, an ugly harbinger of the Civil War. In 1862 Angus demanded that he be allowed to enlist in the Union army, though he was only twelve years old, and he was allowed to do so as a drummer boy. When discharged in 1865, he was just fifteen but had served in several campaigns.[26] After he left the army, he worked as a freighter in western Kansas, when such an occupation was considered "hazardous employment." Several tribes (principally the Cheyennes but also the Arapahoes and the Lakota Sioux) were active in the area and hostile, and Angus was in Fort Wallace in 1867 during its harrowing siege.[27] In October 1868, Angus enlisted in the Nineteenth Kansas Volunteer Cavalry, which participated in a campaign against the Cheyennes. Angus was discharged in April 1869, and though it might seem that he had filled a lifetime quota of excitement, he did not thereafter seek a quiet life. He first resumed freighting between Kansas and Oklahoma, then worked for three years in Texas (apparently as a cowboy), spent a year as a teamster in Guatemala (he later told "vivid" tales about the country, its people, and a revolt he witnessed), and returned to the United States by way of California, working there for two years as a cowboy and a teamster. In 1880 he arrived in Wyoming, driving a herd of cattle. He first alighted near Prairie Dog Creek in the northern part of Johnson County but then relocated to Buffalo in the spring of 1881.[28]

W. G. "Red" Angus. Courtesy of Johnson County Jim Gatchell Memorial Museum.

Red Angus had red hair (hence his nickname) and was "slightly shorter than average." He was a likable man, but although usually easygoing, he possessed a strong temper. It was said that his courage was without question.[29] In Buffalo he became part of the Laurel Avenue and saloon crowd—"Laurel Avenue" being the red-light district in Buffalo. Indeed, Angus was referred to as the "Mayor of Laurel Avenue," and his first wife had been a prostitute in one of the brothels.[30] He also had run-ins with the law. *Territory v. Angus* was the first criminal case filed in Johnson County, Wyoming, in which Angus was charged with assault for pistol-whipping a man. He was tried on July 12, 1882, convicted, and paid a fine of $80 and $5 in court costs.[31]

Fort McKinney may have been the primary economic force in Johnson County, enabling Red Angus and many others to make a living, but cattle raising was a close second, one that supported a great number of cowboys and a few rich men. Observing that Buffalo sat "on the dividing line between the vast stock raising territory on the south" and the agricultural country to the north, the *Buffalo Echo* contended that the country to the south was not suitable for agricultural pursuits but was ideal for grazing.[32] The newspaper did not explain why only the northern part of the county was suitable for agricultural pursuits, but it was certainly true that big companies running cattle dominated the southern half of the county, while smaller family outfits, raising crops and small herds of cattle, dominated the northern half.

Both of these groups spotted opportunity early and came into the country soon after the land became accessible. Large corporations, exceptionally well funded, pushed cattle into southern Johnson County almost at the same time as Fort McKinney was erected on Clear Creek (1878 and 1879) and began running massive herds. They did so not on privately owned land but on the public domain, land owned by the United States, theoretically by each and every citizen. In 1878 and 1879 that was every last acre in Johnson County, but the big cattle outfits in southern Johnson County, whether or not they held legal title, occupied and monopolized huge chunks of land, vastly more than they could ever legally claim, asserting rights under fictitious legal theories such as "range rights" and "accustomed ranges."

To obtain private title to land in the county, it was necessary for people to make a claim under one of several land acts, such as the 1862 Homestead Act or the 1877 Desert Land Entry Act, and to thereby obtain a deed from the United States, referred to as a "patent." The earliest patents issued for Johnson County show the settlement patterns in the north and south. Of the first thirty patents issued for land in Johnson County, twelve were for lands on streams such as Piney Creek and Rock Creek north of Buffalo, and with one notable exception (Francis E. Warren), they appear to have been filed by small operators.[33] Another fourteen individuals received patents on lands south of Buffalo and northeast along Clear Creek, and several of these people—Fred G. S. Hesse was the most prominent—were associated with much larger outfits.[34] The remaining four men lived in or immediately adjacent to Buffalo, including John Conrad.[35]

Fred G. S. Hesse's claim was his own property, but he had a particularly close connection with a large cattle company.[36] Hesse was English, born in Essex in 1852. He studied law for a time and then traveled to the United States in 1873, where he worked for various cattle outfits, finally settling in Johnson County in 1877. He was a stern, competent, and diligent man (he was called "a man of great ability and great rigidity"), and in 1879, when he was only twenty-seven, he was hired by Moreton Frewen as foreman of the huge Powder River Cattle Company, then

Fred G. S. Hesse as a young man. Courtesy of Johnson County Jim Gatchell Memorial Museum.

the biggest outfit in Johnson County.[37] Frewen reported in 1883 that he held 39,000 head of livestock, counting horses.[38]

One of the reasons Frewen chose Hesse as foreman was that the two shared a similar background. Hesse was not from such prominent British stock as his employer, but he did come from a solid middle-class English family.[39] Hesse and Frewen shared a dismissive attitude toward their cowboys (many of whom, in turn, disliked their English employers). Frewen once said, "Being a gentleman is much against one here, as in the colonies generally," and Hesse probably agreed with the sentiment.[40]

The patronizing attitudes of English gentlemen toward the locals were not confined to their hired hands but extended to owners of the smaller ranches. Not all of the outfits south of Buffalo were big corporations; a few smaller operators had come into the country even earlier than the large cattle corporations. Most notable was John Randolph Smith, always referred to as John R. Smith. There is no indication of early conflict between Hesse and Smith, but their personalities were fundamentally different. Hesse was, throughout his life, a businessman; Smith was a frontiersmen. The nineteenth century in America was turbulent, and many men in Johnson County had experienced that turbulence, but of them all, Smith may have had the most amazing life story. Only a few months after the Civil War began, he had enlisted in an Indiana regiment

John R. Smith. Courtesy of Johnson County Jim Gatchell Memorial Museum.

at age seventeen. He was with Grant's army at the Battle of Champion Hill in Mississippi and at the siege of Vicksburg.[41] After the war he went west, freighting for a living.[42] At Fort Laramie in 1867, he met Little Dog, a Cheyenne Indian, and for a time traveled with him, his wife, and his beautiful daughter. Many years later, Smith wrote about his many experiences and described colorfully such things as how the Cheyenne pursued, killed, and processed buffalo, as well as how he escaped the clutches of Little Dog, who wanted him to marry his daughter, whom Smith acknowledged was very appealing.[43]

Late in 1867 Smith came north to what became southern Johnson County and engaged in a series of skirmishes with Sioux, Cheyenne, and Arapahoe warriors.[44] In 1868 he bought an interest in the Horseshoe Ranch along the old Oregon Trail, but in March of that year he and six other men were attacked by Crazy Horse, leading a band of Lakotas. A battle raged for three days, until Smith's group, then down to four, made a desperate truce and escaped with their scalps and little else.[45] Smith then relocated to the South Pass mines, where over the next two years he was involved in other Indian fights. In the middle of all this, Smith married, but in 1875 he sent his wife and children to the safety of Ohio and did not bring them back to Wyoming until 1878. During that interval, in the spring of 1876, Smith traveled to northern Wyoming and joined General Crook's column (then part of the spring 1876 offensive in which Custer and his troops were wiped out at the Little Big Horn) as a scout and freighter.[46] After leaving Crook's command in 1877, Smith took up a homestead on the Middle Fork of Crazy Woman Creek, just upstream from Gus Trabing's road ranch. Over a few years, he constructed what has been referred to as the first irrigation system in Wyoming, one with long ditches that finally reached his homestead in 1884.[47]

Smith was well respected in the area, and when Johnson County was to be organized, the territorial governor appointed him and two other men as acting commissioners. They in turn established voting places and ordered an election for the first county officers, which took place on April 19, 1881.[48]

By 1883, after a rough couple of years, the citizens of Johnson County nevertheless fervently believed in the promise of the place they had chosen as their home and were working hard to make the town and county a model among Wyoming communities. And yet, only a few years later, this tiny Wyoming county found itself the subject of sensational national press stories that painted Buffalo in very different terms. The town was described as a raw and brutal haven for "range pirates" and as "the most lawless town in the country." In 1891 and 1892, Buffalo was declared to be under the control of criminals so maliciously confident that they had begun naming big cattlemen to be put to death. It was asserted that in Johnson County the sympathy for cattle thieves was so forceful and deep that its citizens refused, no matter how clear the evidence, to honor their oaths as jurymen and bring in a conviction for cattle theft. As a result, it was stated, there were "enormous depredations" of the cattle holdings of the large cattle outfits.[49]

All this heated rhetoric from 1891 and 1892 would seem to indicate that Johnson County had wholly faltered after its promising beginning. By 1892, charges and countercharges were flung about with such abandon that it seems impossible to know whether this was true, impossible to separate the convenient and bold lie from the simple truth. But the citizens of the county had calmly collected objective information about Buffalo and Johnson County between 1884 and 1891, a period when no one could have conceived of the heated charges of a later day. Indeed, the best way to know the true character of the community is to look carefully at the candid reports by local people about themselves before they could have known of the later allegations against them. There is a great deal of material available to do this—from weekly publications of a local newspaper to the county clerk's land records and the criminal case files held by the clerk of the district court. And from these sources, a clear portrait of Buffalo and Johnson County can be drawn.

CHAPTER TWO

The County Grows as the *Sentinel* Watches

On September 13, 1884, the *Big Horn Sentinel* began publication and reported on local events every week during the ensuing five years of its existence. The *Sentinel* issued its first edition from Big Horn, twenty-five miles north of Buffalo. Thirteen months later, however, editor E. H. Becker moved the paper to Buffalo. The *Sentinel* was hardly a sophisticated journal, but it covered a remarkable span of topics, offering Wyoming Territory and the world to those in Johnson County who took the time to read it. The paper told of the death of the French novelist Victor Hugo, of Hiram Maxim's machine gun, and of the very pretty Lady Randolph Churchill, whose sister was married to seasonal Johnson County resident Moreton Frewen.[1] It published articles about issues confronting Congress and the attack upon the McCormick reaper works in Chicago by "socialists and anarchists" who favored an eight-hour workday.[2]

The people of Johnson County also read of the dark side of America in the 1880s, about an endless litany of lynchings, seemingly a new one or two every week, atrocities that had somehow become woven into the fabric of normalcy. They were told, for example, of the lynching of a man accused of murdering his family in Kansas, of two men hanged in Choteau, Montana, for horse stealing, of the lynching of two men in Tennessee who were "members of a well-known band of robbers," of "a negro who criminally assaulted a white woman" at Charlotte, North Carolina, and of a "negro named James Hathorn," who allegedly attempted to rape a little girl in Trinity, Texas.[3] Editor Becker was not at all bothered by the numerous extralegal killings he reported; he commented favorably upon such actions on several occasions. When writing of horse thieves who escaped lynching in Montana by coming south, he noted that they would meet the same fate in Wyoming. "Their bodies would make beautiful ornaments," he wrote, "for the cottonwood trees along the banks of our pure streams when the frost has told its tale and has stripped the summer garments off everything that showed a mark of summer."[4]

But the primary focus of the newspaper was Wyoming and Johnson County. The biggest event of 1885 was the agricultural fair, the first of its kind in Wyoming. All through the summer the fair seized the attention of Johnson County, and when the time finally arrived in September, there was feverish excitement.[5] The Sentinel's report of the event made it clear that the people of the county had done it up right. They awarded premiums for the top items in virtually every category displayed at the fair, including livestock, poultry, mechanical items, field products, vegetables, dairy products, cookery, relics and curiosities, minerals, and needlework.[6]

The fair showed that Johnson County was forging into mainstream America, but other happenings reminded Buffalo people they were not living in what they frequently referred to as the "effete East." On several occasions, bands of Crow Indians came through Big Horn, to the immense interest of the white residents, none more so than awestruck young boys who followed them about the town. Commenting on one such visit, the Sentinel observed: "The town has been full of Crow Indians for two or three days, and the small boy can be heard on every street corner attempting the articulation of a jaw-breaking word of the Crow lingo."[7]

New men were rising to prominence in the county, and the Sentinel wrote about them. One was an Englishman, William J. Clarke. By 1884, Clarke was secretary of the local Republican Party and president of the Johnson County Stock Growers Association, although he temporarily suspended his efforts on behalf of this association when he returned to Huddersfield, England, for the winter.[8] For several years after 1884, local newspapers carried reports about Clarke, who was described as "young, intelligent and well liked."[9] Perhaps because of their shared English roots, Clarke became friends with Fred Hesse, and he was also closely associated with other big cattlemen, such as John Conrad. Clarke formed a livestock company with Conrad, known as Conrad and Clarke, and Clarke actively participated in the firm. He continued his involvement in the local stock growers association until 1892, as well as the Wyoming Stock Growers Association, the powerful organization that counted virtually every big cattleman in Wyoming as a member.[10]

In 1884, Horace R. Mann, generally known as H. R. Mann, was the deputy clerk of court, a position he had held for at least two years.[11] In modern times, a person holding such a job usually does so exclusively and does not pursue another occupation. Not so in 1884 Buffalo. Throughout 1884 and 1885, the *Sentinel* carried an ad for "Hinkle and Mann, Real Estate and Abstract Agents," and stories within the newspaper showed the firm extensively involved in the sale of real estate and land claims.[12] ("Hinkle" was J. D. Hinkle, one of the five practicing attorneys in Buffalo.) Land claims were being submitted by people all over the county, and Hinkle and Mann made out filings for claimants (including for Mann himself and for his wife, Minnie). Mann made at least one trip to Cheyenne "in the interest of a number of parties holding desert claims in this section."[13] Other news stories indicate that he was representing companies before the Johnson County commissioners.[14] In later years, he acted briefly as the editor of the *Sentinel*, and his writings were usually well presented, thoughtful, and thought provoking.

Mann was elected Johnson County clerk of court in 1884, and he hired a deputy, G. E. A. Moeller. Like Mann, Moeller was intelligent, well-read, and an excellent writer. His background was different from Mann's in other ways, though. Gustave Ernest Albert Moeller was born in Germany, and his pathway to Buffalo was by way of the United States Army—he was assigned to Fort McKinney and helped build the fort. He left the army in the late 1870s and homesteaded on French Creek. He had been married, but his wife, Anna, died in 1884. Moeller was a musician, organizing and leading choirs and accompanying them on the piano. Like many of the early residents of Buffalo, he had a connection with Frank Canton, having been a clerical worker for the sheriff.[15]

In 1884 and 1885, marriage was a major topic for the people of Johnson County. The place was filled with zestful young men and women, and they made connections. Editor Becker, who was articulate and ardent, liked to write about the romances and marriages in Buffalo and Big Horn. When young men came to Big Horn to court the young women of the town, Becker was sure to comment upon it. And when a marriage occurred, he would positively trumpet it. So, on October 18, 1884, Becker happily reported the marriage of attorney Charles Burritt to Clara Wheeler, "a charming young lady of Laramie City," and a month later he was able to report the marriage of G. E. A. Moeller to Clara Works, of Buffalo.[16] When Sheriff Frank Canton married a local girl, Annie Wilkerson, in January 1885, the newspaper carried three items about the marriage. It took place at Miss Wilkerson's parents' home, and the best man was the mayor of Buffalo, H. A. Bennett, described as "Canton's intimate friend." Becker teased the groom: "Canton got married and, instead of setting a good example, has had a terrible effect on young folks, about a half dozen looking at getting married."[17] Later that year the paper reported the marriage of W. J. Clarke, although not held in Johnson County. Clarke left Buffalo for New York City, where he met his bride when she arrived from England, and they were married on December 8, 1885.[18]

One reason there were so many marriages is that the young people of Johnson County were so active socially, as witnessed by all the dances. On October 18, 1884, the *Sentinel* announced two big upcoming dances, one in Sheridan, a new town about ten miles north of Big Horn, and one in Big Horn. In writing about the ambitious ball in Big Horn, Becker offered a felicitous phrase, that "the bright eyes of laughing girls will be the center of interest."[19] The Sheridan dance, for which two hundred invitations had been sent out, was held on November 1, and the "grand ball" in the new courthouse in Buffalo only two weeks later was said to "eclipse any similar affair ever given in Northern Wyoming."[20] These big dances were not the only ones held in northern Wyoming in November; throughout the month there were "hops" at private residences in Big Horn and Sheridan.[21] All this gaiety was finally too much for a local clergyman, who delivered a sermon about dancing, in which he "handled the subject without gloves, directing his remarks particularly to many of his young friends in the congregation." The *Sentinel* observed, however, that those members of the congregation "have paid little attention to the speaker's remarks, as they have since given a number of hops in town and vicinity."[22]

From marriages came children, which were seen as a blessing, but a qualified one. Infant mortality in the late nineteenth century was high, and some of the happiest events too soon descended to the worst anguish of people's lives. In August of 1885 H. R. Mann went to Cheyenne, and he was surprised by the happy news that in his absence his wife had given birth to a baby boy.[23] But not a year later, the infant, after first "lying near the point of death for several days" and then appearing to recover, had died at the age of eleven months and fourteen days.[24] Even greater tragedy awaited Mr. and Mrs. Robert Foote. When the Foote family visited Omaha in November 1885, their two youngest children died of diphtheria and were buried there. When they returned to Buffalo, fears were expressed that the Footes might have carried diphtheria with them from Omaha, but Drs. J. H. Lott and John Watkins visited the Foote home and concluded that all necessary precautions had been taken to prevent an outbreak in Buffalo.[25] The Manns and the Footes were not alone in their grief. Through 1885 and 1886, another six small children in the county died, a terrible toll from a population of only about two thousand people.[26]

Despite the most wrenching losses of their lives, the young and resilient people of Buffalo and Johnson County kept working hard to improve their community. In March 1885 the *Sentinel* declared that "Buffalo will have a boom this year," citing the building of two churches, a $15,000 schoolhouse, and a brick block containing the John Conrad and Company store.[27] Indeed, all of these things did come to pass in 1885, just after the completion of a project bigger than any of those mentioned, the construction of a new courthouse. The *Sentinel* published comments about Buffalo that had appeared in the *Laramie Boomerang* in January 1886: "What town of 800 can boast of a $35,000 court house and a $15,000 school house, which taxpayers call a mere bagatelle? Yet Buffalo has both and $6,000 has been subscribed for a church?"[28] One sour note was the land situation in Buffalo proper. The townsite was owned by Mrs. Julia Hart, widow of a former commander of Fort McKinney. Mrs. Hart was seen as difficult and rapacious and was heartily disliked.[29] Her high prices were declared to "work us a greater injury than any other evil that might be cast upon us."[30] The general interest and ambition about acquiring land, however, certainly did not abate.

The *Big Horn Sentinel*, like any good newspaper, tried to publish items of interest to its readers, and most of its weekly issues 1884 to 1886 contained at least one article about some aspect of claims for public land. Every issue contained several notices in which land claimants announced their intention to make final proof for the right to receive title to the land on which they had staked their claims. Each notice was usually printed only six times, but there were plenty of new names to supplant those who completed the publication requirement, so that the number of notices appearing in the *Sentinel* steadily rose from six in the October 25, 1884, issue to fourteen in the May 8, 1886, issue. The interest in acquiring public land had persisted despite difficulties that had arisen since March 1885, when Grover Cleveland was inaugurated as president. Concerned about land fraud, Cleveland had appointed a land commissioner who scrutinized all new applications; Commissioner William A. J. Sparks was almost as disliked by the people of Buffalo as Julia Hart.[31]

No subject so consumed the ambitious people of Johnson County as the coming of a railroad. In the late nineteenth century, connection to a railroad was the one essential for the continued growth and prosperity of a community. Towns not close to a railroad were referred to as "inland" towns, the same term used to describe a backward place with no access to water. The presence of a railroad ensured a connection to the entire U.S. economic system, the most vibrant economy in the world. Without a railroad, a nineteenth-century town could never be deemed a success, and the people of Buffalo were acutely aware of that.

Talk of a railroad began in 1883 and by 1885 had become a drumbeat.[32] In July 1885 came news "that a railroad would shortly be built from the Northern Pacific to the Big Horn country."[33] In August reports were received of railroad prospects across northwestern Wyoming, and in October the *Sentinel* published an especially hopeful article, saying that the Chicago and Northwestern would construct "at once" a railway through northern Wyoming.[34]

None of these stories was ever followed by a train pulling into Buffalo, but it seems there was no rumor so insubstantial that it would not be printed in the *Sentinel*. If anything, the number of railroad stories increased in frequency into the late 1880s.

But Johnson County people did not sit around while waiting for a railroad to arrive; they attended to business. The running of the county was the biggest activity (except, of course, for Fort McKinney). The county assessor appraised the values of property (principally livestock) scattered throughout Johnson County, a process that led to constant complaints. The county treasurer collected and disbursed the taxes, and the county clerk established and maintained a repository for land records, marriage records, and the records of the county commission. It was the operation of the justice system, though, that took the most time and energy; it involved everything from peace officers and attorneys to courts and jails. Wyoming had a system of justice courts, and there were justices of the peace all over Johnson County, including G. E. A. Moeller, H. R. Mann, and Charles Burritt. These courts handled minor matters, but when a more serious criminal matter was charged, the first proceedings were held in justice courts, then went to the district court, for which there was only one judge.

The performance of the criminal justice system in Johnson County during the 1880s and early 1890s later became the subject of intense comment and scrutiny, and a close look at this system from its beginning is instructive. It is hard to pinpoint the exact number of serious criminal cases prosecuted in the earliest years of the county, because even though all the records of the clerk of the district court are available, many of the files are incomplete. Through 1885, however, about one hundred criminal cases had been filed, with about eighty of them representing separate events.[35] In at least ten of those remaining cases, no action was taken beyond the initial filing, probably because the defendants left the territory. In even more cases, the records simply show a dismissal, though not the basis for it. This is common for any criminal docket; cases are dismissed for any of several legitimate reasons, such as transfer to another jurisdiction, prosecutorial errors, factual development showing conviction unlikely, or changes in law.[36]

The criminal docket during this period shows a representative group of crimes, such as assaults, grand larceny, stealing cattle (a species of larceny), stealing horses, and homicides. Other offenses included burglary, larceny by bailee, the sale of liquor without a license (John Conrad was charged with this offense), bad checks, and fornication (charged against Nettie Wright, among others).[37] The most common offense, by far, was larceny, whether involving horses or mules (ten charges), cattle (nine charges), or other kinds of personal property (nine charges). Also common, with eleven charges, was some variant of assault, ranging from simple assault and battery (a misdemeanor that the district court saw in the form of appeals from a justice court) to assault with intent to commit murder. There were four homicide charges.

The prosecution of crime in Johnson County in the early 1880s was a difficult proposition, and there were an outsized number of acquittals. Of those first hundred or so criminal cases, about twenty-six went to trial, resulting in about sixteen convictions and ten acquittals.[38] There is no apparent pattern among the convictions and acquittals; that is, some people were acquitted for the same offenses for which others were convicted. Of the acquittals, two were for cattle theft (there were three convictions), three for a variant of theft of horses (there were at least seven convictions), and one for manslaughter (there was a conviction for murder); the remaining acquittals were for furnishing liquor to jail mates, grand larceny (stealing a saddle), fornication, and burglary.[39]

The biggest problem with the prosecution of crime in Johnson County, Territory of Wyoming, was detecting an offense in the first place. Although there was a concentration of people around Buffalo, the remainder of the residents of the county were widely distributed within a huge and complicated domain, which ranged from the Montana line (forty miles north of Buffalo) to country below Powder River (about sixty miles south), and from the banks of the Big Horn River near what is now Thermopolis, Wyoming, to the banks of the same river almost one hundred miles north. Centered in the middle of the county were the Big Horn Mountains—beautiful and majestic, to be sure, but extremely formidable obstacles, especially in the winter, and especially at a time when no motor vehicles, airplanes, railroads, or even effective telegraph lines existed in the county.[40] Unless a crime took place near Buffalo, Sheriff Canton would probably not learn of it for days, even weeks. Then, when he did learn of a crime, it might take days to get to the scene, while evidence (including the statements of witnesses) might be scattered and compromised. If a crime occurred in the Big Horn Basin in the winter, Canton would have had to wait until spring (no deputy resided in that area until 1888). That is almost surely the reason why, among the first fifty criminal cases in Johnson County, none can be identified as having been committed in the Basin, although crime definitely occurred there, and the great majority of charges were for acts committed within a few miles of Buffalo.[41]

When a crime was committed at a place not far from Buffalo, Sheriff Canton was dogged in his pursuit of suspects. Harry Anable and a cohort, Jack Knight, made the mistake of stealing three mules and two horses near Buffalo (two of the horses were those of Anable's employer, S. W. Hyatt, who was soon to move to the western slope of the Big Horn Mountains) and drove them west over the mountains. In its September 27, 1884 issue, the *Sentinel* noted that Canton was after Anable and Knight and would likely overtake them, because "Canton is not much of a man to 'monkey' with them once he gets started."[42] Sure enough, Canton got his men, who must have been shocked when he found and arrested them in the Nowood country, just west of the Big Horn Mountains; the suspects were returned to Buffalo, found guilty, and sentenced to three years in prison at Joliet, Illinois.[43] This crime was one of the largest thefts of livestock during Canton's tenure as sheriff (most of the thefts of horses were single animals, and all but one of the charged thefts of cattle during Sheriff's Canton's service between 1882 and 1885 were of "one head of neat cattle"), and he no doubt wanted to impress the voters for the fall 1884 election.[44] He apparently did so, as he won reelection in November 1884 by 770 votes to 557.[45]

Such a competent sheriff probably made more arrests and collected better evidence than a less able officer. But the number of acquittals was still high. As good as Canton was, there were distinct limitations to what he could do, and these were manifest in cases of cattle theft. It is a far different thing to engage in the hot pursuit of horse thieves than to solve a cattle theft in the Big Horn Basin discovered, say, two months after the event. In 1885, Johnson County had 171,150 cattle, or about 17 per square mile.[46] Given about two thousand people in the county, this meant that for every five square miles there was an average of one human being and 85 cattle. The human beings, though widely distributed, were not located randomly, but mostly were in towns and along streams, whereas the cattle were purposely scattered to every corner where they might graze. There is little evidence of systematic cattle theft during Canton's four years as sheriff, nothing reported in the newspapers, nor any charges to indicate any such activity, but in any population some individuals are going to commit crimes, and the temptation was surely magnified by the relative safety of grabbing a cow or a calf here and there.

Every year the cattlemen of Johnson County suffered large losses from weather and predators, typically measured in the thousands of animals, and the loss of a few cattle from theft usually would not even be detected.[47] But now and again one of the owners or one of his trusted employees would come across evidence of a cow having been killed, rebranded, or transported to the control of another person and would insist upon prosecution. Then the legal difficulties would begin. Grand larceny of livestock may seem like a simple crime but, in fact, demands proof of each of several stringent elements. It had to be established that an animal, of a value of at least $25, owned by another, was taken and carried away, with intent to steal.[48] The value of cattle was strong at the beginning of the 1880s, peaking in 1882, but then started downward in 1885, and in 1886 the average value of a range cow was only about $16.[49] This meant that conviction of the theft of a cow could produce a conviction only for petit larceny, a misdemeanor; the maximum penalty was six months in jail, but the maximum was usually not given.

It would seem a straightforward matter to prove that an accused stole another person's cow, but in practice it was not at all straightforward. Except in rare cases, the only way to identify a range cow as owned by another was the brand. In many instances, however, an animal had no brand. If it was a calf, it would go to its mother, making identification possible. Sometimes, however, a calf had no mother (the famous "maverick"), or in some cases there was a mother, but she had no brand. Twice yearly, cattle owners held roundups, collecting their animals, branding them, and cutting out those to be sold, but this process was not always efficient, so that many cattle went unbranded. Attempting to collect 150,000 to 170,000 head of cattle scattered over 10,000 square miles of every conceivable kind of terrain could not be a perfectly efficient exercise. Even in modern times ranchers running cattle within fenced pastures of a few thousand acres frequently cannot find all their cattle. Another complication was that brands were not always clear indicators of ownership. Some were not properly applied in the first place. Some were purposely obscured, whether by thieves or by new buyers. Some were later the site of injuries. And a brand frequently fades over a couple of years.

Because of such factors, it was not uncommon for prosecutors to have difficulty proving that a supposedly stolen animal was owned "by another." Johnson County prosecutors very quickly ran into such difficulties, so that indictments were quashed, or acquittals resulted when ownership could not be proven.[50] In at least one well-known case Fred Hesse was unable to testify that an animal allegedly stolen from him was actually his.[51]

It was also hard to prove that on the open range an owner's animal was taken and carried away with intent to steal. If a range cow drifted out of her customary range (usually unfenced) to another man's range, that would prove little. If the cow was then gathered by a neighbor and placed in a corral, that might go further to prove taking and carrying away with intent to steal, but it would be thin proof. If the cow was rebranded, that might be considerably stronger evidence, but it could be rebutted by a showing that the first brand was obscured for any of a number of reasons.[52] Even the killing and butchering of such a cow might have little significance if the neighbor could show a plausible reason why he believed the cow was his (and therefore he had no intent to steal).

All of this was made even harder because of the difficulty of gathering evidence of any kind, good or not so good. Even assuming Sheriff Canton could accumulate what appeared to be evidence sufficient to obtain a conviction, he then faced the problem of getting it back intact to Buffalo for presentation at a trial, which could be held only during two brief periods of the year, the spring term and the fall term.[53]

Given the difficulties of proof, the patterns revealed by the criminal cases filed in Johnson County between 1882 and 1885 are not surprising. Americans believed in the presumption of innocence and the necessity to prove a defendant guilty beyond a reasonable doubt, and the people living in the frontier community of Johnson County, Wyoming, clearly abided by that principle. The Johnson County records from the early 1880s show simply that if a solid case was presented, a jury convicted. If a solid case was not presented, it would not.

CHAPTER THREE

A Fabled Winter and a
Spring of Bitter Division

The people of Johnson County strode with determination into the election year of 1886, even as they witnessed the onset of a savage winter that
greatly changed the economic landscape of their county. The merchants
in Buffalo did their best to forward the prosperity of the town. New
merchant Fred Hasbrouck engaged in a trade war with John Conrad, each
retailer running huge advertisements in the *Big Horn Sentinel* touting
his superior dry goods stock, and in 1886 Hasbrouck erected a two-
story brick block, despite the "fabulous figures" Mrs. Hart was charging
for lots.[1] Even Red Angus did his part toward boosting the economy. In
1884 Angus showed interest in law enforcement when he was appointed
a night watchman in Buffalo and elected a constable, but it was not long
before he began a serious commercial venture.[2] He and another man,
acting as "Angus & Robinson," began construction of a brick saloon on
Main Street that grew to two stories and incorporated "the finest
and coziest club room in the city," known as the Gold Room.[3] The
leaders of the town wanted to encourage construction, and several of
them formed a building and loan association; the officers and directors
included Nathaniel G. Carwile, Fred Hasbrouck, James M. Lobban, and
Charles H. Burritt.[4]

With a new brick schoolhouse and growing numbers of students,
the community's focus on schools was increasing. The *Sentinel* published
the grades of every pupil; there were twenty-six in the "Advanced

Department," taught by Minnie Wittington, and forty in the "Primary Department," taught by Mary Winters. Carroll H. Parmelee, a new lawyer in town from Cleveland, Ohio, was the principal.[5]

Certainly the biggest event of 1886, at least until the winter arrived, was the election of county officers. As usual, Frank Canton was the man talked about most. He still enjoyed support in Buffalo, but it was clear that most of the people of the community had lost their infatuation with him. He was too tough for a small town. Comments about his aura of personal power are especially telling. J. Elmer Brock, a local rancher, said that Canton had "yellow coyote eyes," surely not a compliment. Other people referred to how Canton would fix men with his "steely eye."[6] And it seemed that everyone in Canton's office was tough, that he set the tone and his deputies followed it. Chris Gross, a large Swedish man, was one of Canton's deputy sheriffs, and he was involved in at least two controversial actions around 1886. S. A. Iden, a prominent local man, slaughtered one of his own beeves, then failed to exhibit the hide of the animal, as state statute was asserted to require, and Gross arrested him. Iden was embarrassed and wrote a letter to the *Sentinel*, stating that he had no idea that he was supposed to haul the hide of his own cow around "on exhibition from market to market," or he certainly would have done so. He commented on the "unwonted zeal of that most enthusiastic officer, Gross."[7] The authorities tried to indict Iden, but the grand jury, apparently recognizing that the purpose of the law was to protect owners of cattle, refused to charge this owner.[8] As things turned out, the charge against Iden was the only case in 1886 involving cattle. Only thirteen cases were filed that year, in two of which indictments were refused. Of the remaining cases, there were six trials, with five convictions of at least one of the defendants charged (all grand larceny— three charges of horse theft and two for stealing a watch) and one acquittal (murder in the first degree).[9] It was reported that within the territory in 1886, there had been nine convictions in stock-stealing cases, two acquittals, and two dismissals for lack of evidence.[10]

Gross was involved in a second, far more serious incident, in which he sought to arrest a man named George Stevens for stealing horses. Gross arrived at Stevens's cabin on Spring Creek in the Big Horn Basin and announced the arrest. Stevens supposedly objected, and "hot words passed between Gross and Stevens, . . . which resulted in a shot being fired by Gross, the ball taking effect in Stevens' head, killing him instantly."[11]

Deputy Gross then threw Stevens's body over a horse and rode back to Buffalo in the dead of winter. A coroner's jury found that Gross was "entirely justifiable in such shooting," but two years later, after Frank Canton had left office, a grand injury indicted Gross for manslaughter. Gross was acquitted, but it was clear that many people in Johnson County did not approve of Gross and Canton or their rough methods.[12]

Some forty years later, Frank Canton wrote: "In 1886, I was strongly urged by the citizens of Johnson County to accept the office of sheriff for a third term. But as my little herd of cattle and my farm needed my attention, I retired to my little farm and moved out to my ranch with my young wife and little daughter Ruby."[13] This short passage seems innocuous enough, but it is filled with half-truths and gross omissions. Canton probably was asked by several of his friends and remaining admirers to run for a third term, and after the election he certainly did focus on his ranch south of Buffalo. The overall thrust of the above passage, though—that he stepped away from public service despite a clamoring public's demands that he remain—is a distortion.

As the election neared, newspaper stories in the *Sentinel* show that Canton was undecided whether to run for a third term. There were several inconsistent reports; at different times it was assumed that Canton would not run and then that he might and then that he would not, then he would, and, finally, that he would definitely not.[14] This was unlike Frank Canton; he was hardly an indecisive man. What explains his conduct and what the public did not know was that Canton was negotiating behind the scenes with the Wyoming Stock Growers Association for a very attractive position, to be the chief stock detective for the association in northern Wyoming. Canton was well suited for this job, as it entailed what he had been doing as sheriff: investigating criminal violations and garnering evidence for a prosecution. The offer for the job was not formally made until October 21, 1886. The decision to offer it was probably made considerably before that date, however, or at least Canton had reason to believe that a job would probably be offered him.[15]

There were reasons why Canton might hesitate to run for sheriff again, although it is understandable that he might be reluctant to give up the chance for the office, absent a better situation. A highly intelligent man (at least when he calmly evaluated a situation), Canton had to know that he had an uphill battle for reelection in 1886. He had won only 58 percent of the votes in 1884 and must have sensed that many in the community no longer approved of him. More than that, he surely knew there was a strong feeling in Johnson County in 1886 that no candidate ought to run for more than two terms. Indeed, the only two-term incumbent who ran for another term in 1886 was the Johnson County clerk, Nathaniel G. Carwile, who was extremely popular. Even the Republican opposition conceded that "in the main" Carwile had been a good public officer, although it declared that two terms was enough. Despite his popularity, Carwile was beaten soundly in the general election, 855 to 692.[16] The biggest omission in Canton's latter-day description of his service as Johnson County sheriff was his failure to admit that in 1888, when he did try to become sheriff again, he was overwhelmingly rejected.

The Republicans nominated E. U. Snider, a man said to be well-liked, especially by his own party. Snider was regarded as a pioneer, as shown by an article printed two weeks after the election, in which it was noted that Snider, John R. Smith, and Robert Foote were people who "came here with the first tide of white settlers."[17] Still, in the election he barely beat out John McDermott, winning by 787 to 748.[18]

After the election, the *Sentinel* commented favorably upon Sheriff Canton's service, stating, "A more efficient sheriff than Mr. Canton in the pursuit, detection and capture of criminals will not be expected."[19] It is hard to say, however, whether this reflected a broad consensus, or even the opinion of the ownership of the *Sentinel*, as it was written by Canton supporter Charles Burritt, who was editing the newspaper in E. H. Becker's absence.[20] Burritt's statement, though, does fairly reflect Canton's record. It was certainly Canton's own view of his time as sheriff; he had declared pride in his "remarkable record." Canton apparently bore no personal animus toward Snider and even wrote that Snider was "a good man and a big-hearted fellow," although Canton then declared that Snider was far too loose toward the criminal element, so that he "did not make a success of his office."[21]

At the time of the election, an early winter was setting in; November was a very tough month. The *Sentinel* wrote of harsh conditions throughout November, referring to such things as the difficulty of county commissioner William Richards coming to Buffalo from his home in the Big Horn Basin, to the heavy fall of snow and a cold snap that "revived the coal trade and brought out the sleighs with their merry bells," and, late in the month, to "heavy snows of wind, snow and curses" that were "a terror."[22]

December brought a short lull in the bad weather, inspiring the hope that the recent weather meant the range stock would get through the winter well.[23] Later in December and in early January, however, the harsh winter resumed with a vengeance. In early January, the stage ran into snow four feet on the level and encountered a blinding blizzard east of Buffalo.[24] The *Sentinel* stated that range losses had not been too severe so far, but that if conditions did not abate, the outlook was "anything but encouraging." The report added, "Unless a gentle Chinook pays us a visit, there is room to anticipate a heavy loss when the time comes to tally up at the spring round-up."[25]

There was to be no "gentle Chinook." Conditions in January and February 1887 were at least as bad as the horrendous weather of November and December 1886. On January 15 the *Sentinel*, after referring to the "almost ceaseless storms" of the winter, observed that range men were seriously alarmed.[26] They had reason to be alarmed, although there was a brief respite in late January. In early February, winter came roaring back, and the *Sentinel* stated that "a genuine cold wave struck this section last week" and spoke of all the cattle dying on the range.[27] It was reported that the temperature in Miles City, Montana (about 150 miles northeast of Buffalo), was 52 degrees below zero and that there was "heavy loss of live stock."[28] No one could know before spring how much damage the weather had caused, but the signs were ominous. Even in the previous summer, Johnson County citizens had dreaded the effects of a hard winter, because 1886 drought conditions were "burning up" what grass there was, leaving an overcrowded range dry and barren, and cattle vulnerable.[29] People's worst fears were becoming ugly realities.

The losses were not confined to range cattle. One man was lost in a blizzard near Buffalo, and his body was not found until March. The *Sentinel* published an article titled "Two More Victims of King Cold," about a man who froze near Stinking Water and another man who perished three miles from the Hoodoo Ranch, in the Big Horn Basin.[30]

After the winter of 1886–87 was all done, the *Cheyenne Daily Sun* described 1887 as "a year that is regarded as the most disastrous the territory has ever experienced"; indeed, most Wyoming people today would say that 1887 has never been topped.[31] But when the winter finally abated, Johnson County people, ever upbeat, looked hard for positives in the situation. At first they declared that the cattle losses were not nearly as bad as had been feared, maybe only 25 percent, and that the ferocious winter meant that the grass was going to be excellent in 1887.[32] But as all the news came in from Johnson County and the region, it became clear that the losses had been catastrophic, probably 50 percent of the range cattle in Wyoming and 75 percent in Montana.[33] The strongest evidence of the magnitude of the disaster was its effect on the big ranchers, the members of the Wyoming Stock Growers Association.

The cattle business, already plagued by low market prices, fell on "exceedingly hard times" after the winter of 1886–87.[34] April 1886 had witnessed the all-time high for membership in the Wyoming Stock Growers Association—443 members in good standing—but a year later membership had dropped to 365, and a year after that the membership had collapsed, to 183.[35] The association was so short of money that there was talk that it would go under, and drastic steps were taken to stretch the meager monies available.[36] Officers' wages were cut, as were even the wages of some of the association's prized range detectives, including Frank Canton. Canton was making the excellent salary of $200 per month ($40 per month was the standard wage for experienced cowhands), but in September 1887 he, along with other detectives, was asked to take a $50 per month pay cut.[37] Worse was to follow, as the association's Detective Bureau was closed down completely at the end of 1887, although Canton continued to be paid through March of 1888.[38] In May 1888, Canton was appointed a stock inspector by the Board of Livestock Commissioners. It is not known how much Canton was paid, but it must have been a comedown from his earlier wages, because in 1888 he became very interested in the sheriff's job in Johnson County.[39]

The most significant result of the hard times for big cattle was that they opened new ranges for settlers. The big cattlemen sometimes paid lip service to their tolerance of small operators, but such pronouncements were sheer hypocrisy. John Clay, a president of the Wyoming Stock Growers Association, was as smooth and careful a man as one is ever likely to encounter, but Clay sometimes let slip the profound anger of the big cattlemen toward settlers. About twenty-five years after his western experiences, he wrote about his life on the Wyoming range, and even from that distance he made references to the big outfits "being strangled by settlement," and the "deep-seated hatred between the cattlemen and the settler."[40]

This should come as no shock; the only surprise is that the big cattlemen would sometimes deny their attitude toward settlers. A settler who exercised his perfect right to 160 acres along a stream could significantly impair a big cowman's range; if several did so, the range would be lost altogether, as happened, for example, along Shell Creek in the Big Horn Basin. Without all that free rangeland, the operations of large ranches could not continue. As western historian Herbert Brayer has written, "To the large rancher extensive ranges were fundamental. His costs mounted as his ranges shrank."[41] Given that American land laws favored families and restricted settlement to relatively small acreage, the big cattle-men had taken a huge risk when they made the public domain the base of their operations, and then deepened the risk by piling cattle into the area. Using all available legislation, the most land a person could patent was 1,120 acres, a small fraction of the tens of thousands of acres used in the huge ranch operations of the big cattle outfits.[42] Human nature being what it is, though, the forceful men who put together the big ranches were not about to passively accept their fates. Fraudulent land claims by big cattlemen were common, as were methods such as illegal fencing and intimidation.[43] Land Commissioner William A. J. Sparks was unpopular because he slowed the processing of land claims by carefully scrutinizing all applications. But this posture reflected the Cleveland administration's conviction that large monied interests were choking off land from every-day citizens.[44] A similar sentiment led to a push to repeal all land laws but the Homestead Act.[45] In 1887 President Cleveland even issued a proclamation that a detail of a troop of cavalry was to be stationed in Cheyenne to assist local authorities in taking down fences of cattle kings that enclosed public domain lands.[46]

In 1886 and 1887, inquiries and investigations were undertaken by the Land Office and Congress because of complaints by would-be settlers that settlement was being obstructed along the base of the Big Horn Mountains. Charles Lindsay, seminal historian of the Big Horn Basin, summarized the situation: "The Granger complained bitterly that the country was controlled by large cattlemen, and that the big herds magi-cally absorbed his own small bands, that the round-up outfits put their employers' brands on his few calves, and finally that he was discouraged and intimidated when he took up land."[47]

During the investigations, a letter was provided to the Land Office, one from Fred Hesse to his ranch foreman. Hesse had sent his foreman "formal notice" that he was not to allow anyone "to stay at the ranch more than twenty-four hours, especially land jumpers," and the foreman was most certainly not allowed to let such people or their animals have any feed.[48] Hesse was faithfully reflecting the attitude of his employer, Moreton Frewen. In 1884 Frewen wrote Hesse and instructed him how to deal with a man who had settled on what Frewen felt was his range: "Split him like a rail . . . pull his fence all over the place and have the wire cut in short lengths. He is the kind of man to make an example of."[49] When, in March 1885, one settler arrived at a location about thirty miles from Frewen's ranch headquarters and tried to establish a claim, he was immediately visited by a group of English cowboys who announced, "You cahn't do that, you know, this is the Frewen brothers' cattle range." Even though this man had a legal right to settle, supposedly guaranteed by federal law, he moved on.[50] Sometimes the big outfits would allow a family to homestead but then would not permit it to run cattle. For example, early settler Albert Brock was allowed one milk cow, but each year its calf would be branded by employees of the big ranchers, to make sure that Brock "never got a start in the business."[51]

Not all the big ranches went out of business in 1887; some did quite well after the winter, but only by adopting new methods of operation. As George Rollins wrote in his doctoral thesis about battles over the control of the public domain, in order to survive they had to "swallow a bitter pill, the acceptance of the ideas and methods used by their most hated enemies, the settlers or farmers." Rollins was referring to methods such as running smaller herds over less land and putting up or buying sufficient hay to get through the winter.[52] But there is no doubt that the big rancher's ability to inhibit settlement was diminished after the winter of 1886–87, and that change in itself, following the waning of the power of big cattlemen, gives the lie to the assertion that big cattle did not frustrate settlement. One of the distinctive patterns of settlement in the Big Horn Basin was the large number of patents that followed a claim first asserted in 1887, as settlers (frequently cowboys who had just lost their jobs because their employer went broke or cut his workforce) staked out lands that had been claimed as part of a big outfit's range.[53] On the east side of the Big Horn Mountains, newcomers also moved in, including Jack Flagg and a young cowboy, Ranger Jones, who each settled on the Red Fork of the Powder River, in the far southern part of Johnson County. In 1888 Flagg added four partners: W. H. "Billy" Hill, Lew Webb, Thomas Gardner, and Al Allison.[54] All of them were soon blackballed by the Wyoming Stock Growers Association. Flagg attributed this to his purchase of cattle and taking up government land, a claim given credence by statements such as one by Maurice Frink in *Cow Country Cavalcade* (an authorized history of the Wyoming Stock Growers Association): "The big ranchers blacklisted those who thus came into competition with them."[55]

Despite all the efforts of the big cattlemen, the push to homestead land remained a powerful impulse among Wyoming people in the 1880s that would not be suppressed. The *Sentinel*, in May 1886, carried an article with an unambiguous declaration to the people of Johnson County:

> Get upon the land while there are free homesteads to be had.... Endure privation and loneliness, if need be, for the sake of being your own masters and of gaining a competence for your declining years, and the right to live without the favor of any man.... Escape when you can from the ranks of those who toil for hire. Their burdens are becoming more and more gallant. Be your own employer. Get upon the land.[56]

The *Sentinel* was surely preaching to the choir, telling its readers what it knew they already deeply believed and were acting upon. From 1884 to 1886 the number of land entries submitted to the Cheyenne Land Office had climbed from 2,923 to 3,512.[57] Indeed, the clamor for land was so great that a new land office was needed; this was discussed for some time, but finally a new office was opened in Buffalo on May 1, 1888.[58]

Not all was gloom and struggle in 1887; good things continued to happen in the county seat. Buffalo got a brewery and a flouring mill and began an electrical plant, while proudly announcing a slew of professionals—a dentist, two physicians, a "Hydrostatic and hydraulic Engineer and Surveyor," a mineral surveyor, and five lawyers (C. H. Parmelee, J. D. Hinkle, N. L. Andrews, Charles Burritt, and Henry Elliott).[59] Buffalo people were busy grading and filling Main Street, churning out bricks for new buildings, and building sidewalks, crosswalks, and footbridges.[60] The residents were intensely proud of their progressive little town; the *Sentinel* declared: "There is no town in the country that has a better future than Buffalo."[61]

A discordant note in all this pride, however, was the growing expression of discontent from the northern part of the county, accompanied by talk of splitting Johnson County at Massacre Hill (the site of the 1866

Fetterman massacre, about fifteen miles northwest of Buffalo). When rumors of a push for a new county first surfaced in early 1887, editor Becker immediately assailed what he viewed as a wrongheaded scheme benefiting only a few selfish people.[62] The principal thrust of his opposition was that division of the county made no sense economically, that it would produce higher taxes for both a new county and the old one.[63] Reading Becker's strong and visceral reaction, however, one cannot escape the feeling that his objections came from a deeper source than economics, that he felt those who advocated the division were attacking something precious in trying to break up Johnson County, a region with almost limitless promise.

In the fall of 1887, Becker acknowledged that a bill would be introduced in the 1888 legislature; he insisted that it should not be taken seriously. As the legislative session got closer, and the debate got even hotter, Becker adopted a sarcastic tone: "With a feeling of certainty that the division scheme will amount to nothing when the legislative body is approached upon the matter, the people of the southern part of the county can well afford to allow a few up north to amuse themselves with the subject."[64]

During this tense time, a candidate for the territorial legislature appeared in Buffalo, one J. D. Loucks of Sheridan, and the *Sentinel* noted that "he had nothing to say regarding the county division question." When the legislative session began, however, Loucks had a great deal to say after he was elected, as he forwarded and pushed a bill to create a new county to be named Sheridan, by splitting off the northern thirty miles of Johnson County. The *Sentinel* felt Johnson County had been betrayed; the paper had supported Loucks, but, Becker wrote, "we admit to being a victim of misplaced confidence in the man."[65]

The February 4, 1888, edition of the *Sentinel* was issued at the most feverish time in the debate; the issue included nine articles about the fight over division. The heat over the question was well shown by some of the stories, wherein editor Becker referred to the division bill as "the worst cutthroat measure that has come up in the Wyoming legislature in many years"; he also referred adversely to an issue of the *Sheridan Post*, stating that its pages "fairly bristle with accusations that the citizens of Buffalo are taking undue advantage of the weakness of the Town of Sheridan."[66]

Another theme that was sounded on February 4, 1888 (and would frequently be sounded thereafter) was that J. D. Loucks was representing

Sheridan and not Johnson County, that Johnson County really had no representative.[67] Becker's belief—that Loucks was a faithless servant—had merit. Loucks had been elected to represent the people of Johnson County, but instead of advocating the strongly expressed interests of the majority of the county's residents, he forwarded the agenda of those from his own area, Sheridan, and thus most of the people who had elected him were left without a voice. Worse, Loucks had concealed his intentions when running for office.[68]

As the division bill neared a final vote, people from Buffalo and Sheridan started threatening commercial boycotts against one another.[69] Becker declared that the people of Johnson County were "threatened with almost a life burden in the way of heavy taxation," and thanked the *Cheyenne Daily Sun* for supporting the county, in marked contrast to the Sheridan papers with whom Becker was bickering.[70] In the March 3, 1888, issue, the *Sentinel* editor was optimistic that the division bill would not pass, but just a week later, he had to announce the galling news that the bill had passed, even over a veto by Governor Thomas Moonlight.[71] Becker's bitterness toward Loucks reached its zenith, as he asserted that Loucks had sold his vote on the appropriations measure to get the county division bill through; he referred to Loucks as "a hypocrite of the deepest dye," one who would "trade his soul into hell to make a point in which dollars and cents are concerned."[72]

The passage of the bill, though, even over the governor's veto, did not end the battle. The legislature had adjourned before the veto and then reconvened to override it, raising questions about the legitimacy of the legislative action. Becker declared that the battle had only begun over the division bill, that "the conviction is growing stronger every day that the infamous measure will not stand a ghost of a show when the legality is canceled," and he observed that "he who laughs last laughs best."[73] In a subsequent article, Becker snidely wrote that the people of Buffalo were no longer alarmed that a division would occur, and the fight was, therefore, of little interest there. "We are now giving our attention," he announced, "to building operations and preparing to receive the railroad, which is more profitable than fighting dead issues."[74]

At first it seemed that Becker was absolutely right, that the Sheridan County bill would be thrown out. Chief Justice William L. Maginnis of the Wyoming Supreme Court issued an injunction restraining the commissioners of Sheridan County from organizing, thus allowing Becker to smugly announce that the county division fight "is now a thing of the past, the board of county commissioners having unanimously decided that it is a matter that threatens, to a great extent, financial ruin to Johnson County," and that the commissioners had "therefore obtained an injunction."[75]

For the next month or so, while the challenge to the division bill was being played out in the courts, the people of the old Johnson County and the new Sheridan County hissed and spit at one another. What was probably the low point was reported in the May 12, 1888, *Sentinel*. Becker stated that the Sheridan County supporters had reached "that stage only equaled by thieves, cutthroats and thugs." He reported that the editor of the *Sentinel* (Becker himself) had been hung in effigy in Sheridan and the "dummy thoroughly perforated with bullet holes." Apparently the people of Sheridan had noticed Becker's sarcasm.[76]

The court battle, however, quickly turned against Johnson County, as the injunction of Judge McGinnis was set aside, although the issue was still not quite final.[77] But then in July 1888 a new judge to Wyoming, Micah Saufley, rendered a decision that permanently set aside the injunction against the organization of Sheridan County. Sheridan County was allowed to be created, and the battle over the division of Johnson County finally ended.[78]

The dispute over the division of the county had been the most emotional issue in the short history of the county, the one about which the people of the area seemed to care the most. The editor of the paper was a diehard on the question, but by and large he was expressing feelings shared by most of the citizens of the southern part of Johnson County. They reluctantly accepted the result but knew they had lost the bright future of a united Johnson County.

Even before the big fight over county division was put to rest, editor Becker announced that he had purchased a newspaper in Billings, Montana (the *Gazette*), and would be leaving Buffalo that month (September 1888); C. H. Parmelee would take over as editor and manager of the *Sentinel*.[79] During his tenure, Becker had been a strong supporter of Johnson County, although his zeal too often descended into feuds, such as long battles with the county commissioners and Land Office officials.[80] Still, he was a vital personality who had enlivened Buffalo; it would be a different town in his absence. But absent he was, and just at a crucial turning point, the election of 1888.

Carroll H. Parmelee as a young
man. Courtesy of Johnson County
Jim Gatchell Memorial Museum.

Parmelee dived into his new duties, although he had certainly been
active in his community before this new assignment. He had been practicing law in Buffalo for about two years and was very much involved
in local theatrical productions (a review indicated that he was not a great
actor, but his faults were graciously overlooked by the audience[81]). Most
of his time, however, had apparently been spent as the principal of the
Buffalo schools. In October 1886 the *Sentinel* praised Parmelee, who
had just been appointed principal a month and a half before, saying that he
was a "thorough scholar."[82] As principal of the Buffalo schools, Parmelee
dealt frequently with Charles Burritt, then superintendent of the schools.
For instance, in December 1888, Burritt appointed a committee consisting
of Parmelee, John R. Smith, and W. H. C. Newington to draw up resolutions to present to the Wyoming legislature concerning the schools. That
report was filed a week later and seems thoughtful and well presented.[83]

The two Buffalo newspapers, the *Echo* and the *Sentinel*, had different
political postures at different times. In the fall of 1888 the *Sentinel* leaned
heavily in favor of Republicans; the *Echo* was identified as the Democratic paper.[84] Parmelee, who was an active and committed Republican,
got right into the thick of the election, supporting his party's candidates.

He took an inordinate interest in one Democratic contest, though: the selection of the Democratic nominee for sheriff.

E. U. Snider, the incumbent, chose not to run for a second term, though exactly why is not known. Despite Canton's statements about Snider, the 1887 and 1888 record of criminal prosecution was not that different from the years in which Frank Canton was sheriff. During 1887 and 1888, thirty-two separate cases were filed. Of these, eleven went to trial, resulting in nine convictions and two acquittals, although four of the convictions were for misdemeanors after felonies had been charged (such as simple assault when assault with a deadly weapon was charged). Of the four live-stock cases, all involved horses, much as in 1886. There were two convictions and one acquittal; both the convictions were of felonies.[85] As in previous years, the majority of the charges involved three or fewer animals. With one exception—the theft of twenty-nine horses in December 1886, when Canton was in his last month of office—there were never indications of large-scale theft in either the *Sentinel* or the criminal records.[86]

It does appear that there were more dismissals by the prosecuting attorney than usual, probably because of the presence in 1887 of an inexperienced county attorney, Edward C. Simpson. The other attorneys, such as Burritt and Parmelee, took advantage of this situation. Suddenly the files show several motions to throw indictments out because of technical complaints. The clearest example of a mistake made by Simpson was in a case against John Hopkins for unlawfully branding a maverick (the first such charge brought in Johnson County). Simpson filed an affidavit for continuance in the case, saying that he had not subpoenaed two witnesses because he erroneously understood Hopkins to have fled the jurisdiction. Hopkins turned up after all, but Simpson could not find his witnesses, who would supposedly testify that they saw the unlawful branding, and he had no evidence now. Apparently the witnesses were gone for good, because Simpson soon had to dismiss the case against Hopkins.[87] In 1888 Henry Elliott, a former county attorney, took over for Simpson, and from that point the files no longer show evidence of ineptness by the prosecuting attorney.

The interest in the race for the Democratic nomination for sheriff was not because of any perceived breakdown of law and order—at least as reported in the *Sentinel*—but because of the candidates, Frank Canton and Red Angus. Any event involving Frank Canton held a fascination, but here the contrast between the two men created high drama. On the one hand, there was Angus, the easygoing, likable bar owner closely associated with the Buffalo brothels. On the other hand, there was Frank Canton, the very model of an efficient sheriff. At least that is the way Frank Canton saw himself. Canton held Angus in utter contempt, saying that Angus was a man who had "lived in a saloon and house of prostitution all his life" and that "his associates are thieves and cutthroats of the worst type."[88] Most probably, Canton viewed the contest between himself and Angus (to be decided in the county Democratic convention) as absurd, that Angus could not be taken seriously when contrasted with a distinguished former officeholder with a "remarkable record."

If Canton had been inclined to look at Red Angus in a more objective way, though, he would not have taken his opponent so lightly. Besides being well liked (an important attribute in any election, but especially in a small, rural setting), Angus had shown leadership qualities. He had been active in the local chapters of the Odd Fellows and the Grand Army of the Republic, holding an office in each organization.[89] More significantly, in the early spring of 1888, Angus was elected to the Buffalo town council, and in May he was chosen as president of that board. The same month, the council elected him to be chief of the city fire department, a choice that the *Sentinel* deemed "a very good selection."[90]

It was certainly true that Angus had some unsavory associations, but would this offend the Democrats who would select their candidate for sheriff? This was, after all, the frontier community of Johnson County, Wyoming, a place with a good majority of men, many of whom frequented bars and houses of prostitution.

When the Democratic county convention convened, it was packed with Angus supporters "whose special purpose was to secure his nomination," and they swept Angus to the Democratic nomination over Canton by a vote of 24 to 7.[91] Frank Canton was shocked by the result.

Some men, when faced with crushing defeat, view the event, although perhaps only in retrospect, with insight and humility. Such men would accurately perceive that they should change their methods or that their talents might be more appropriate elsewhere, such as in a big city. For Frank Canton, this would have meant a recognition that people in informal, rural settings want law enforcement officers who enforce the law but who are not so zealous as to be viewed as persecuting their neighbors.

There was never a chance that Frank Canton would see the situation in this way. He immediately took great offense and looked to attack those who had offended him. The best evidence of this is a series of editorials by C. H. Parmelee. What seems likely is that after the Democratic county convention completed its work, Canton, perhaps accompanied by Charles Burritt and other supporters, talked to Parmelee.

Parmelee was more than happy to exploit differences between Democrats. In the October 20, 1888, issue of the *Sentinel*, Parmelee wrote that "the management of the affairs of the party had been taken charge of by a class of citizens whose influence, to say the least, would add nothing to the dignity or good name of the party." He added that this was a state of affairs "most strongly denounced by other Democrats." Further, noted Parmelee, "the fact remains that they owe their nomination and their support largely to a class of citizens who are too familiar with disturbances, justice dockets and jail records to recommend them."[92] In other words, Parmelee fully embraced the position of Frank Canton—that Red Angus was unfit to be sheriff, because he was part of the bar and brothel crowd.

Charles Burritt was among those attending the Democratic county convention (he was then the mayor of Buffalo and during the convention was nominated for territorial representative). In the *Sentinel* edition following Parmelee's first article, it appears that Parmelee is referring to someone like Burritt. The editor's previous editorial had offended some citizens, and in the subsequent issue he defended his position, saying that "some of the best Democrats in the city give expression to similar sentiments to those of our article, and which was, in comparison to ours, oil of vitriol to olive oil."[93] Parmelee was obviously enjoying tweaking Democrats, and he noted that a man who once ran for president of the United States had remarked: "I will not say that all Democrats are horse thieves, but I will say that all horse thieves are Democrats." Parmelee insisted that he was not going this far, but again emphasized that "the sentiments expressed in last week's *Sentinel* are the expressions of many Democrats right in this city" and that "it is all true and everybody knows it."[94]

So the selection of a new sheriff in 1888 started with a clear division (at least among Republicans and Canton supporters) between the reputable and the disreputable. In Frank Canton's mind, though, the situation went further. The Democratic county convention was held about three months after the homicide trial of Deputy Chris Gross for shooting a suspected horse thief. Canton was well aware of these charges against his former deputy (Canton was one of the two signers of the bail bond for Gross), and he surely saw the charge against Gross as an attack on himself and his service as sheriff.[95] Canton would have seen a link between the Gross trial and the nomination for sheriff. His conclusion from the county convention was not that the community was choosing Red Angus because they liked Angus more, but that the community had gone off course, that it was choosing wrong over right, favoring lawbreakers over the law-abiding, and, indeed, that the community favored rustlers and thieves over solid citizens such as his employers.[96]

In the general election, Angus won handily, 509 to 379.[97]

CHAPTER FOUR

Mavericks

In the years before 1889, only a few of the citizens of Johnson County (such as Frank Canton) perceived a great conflict between the owners of the large ranches in the southern part of the county and all the rest of the people in the county. By and large, the *Big Horn Sentinel* spoke positively about the big ranches and their owners and foremen.[1] Articles were published in which such things as illegal fencing and the uppity manners of the English gentry were criticized ("Milord" was a subject of satire), but there was no indication of serious disputes.[2] Nevertheless, though the people of Johnson County may not have known it, from a very early time big cattle owners and the great majority of the county residents were headed in starkly different directions.

In 1880, when a large corporation in Johnson County gathered its cows, bulls, and calves in the spring, it could be reasonably sure that every animal was owned by the corporation. When other owners brought cattle to the same area (as they were entitled to do), things became more complicated. The cows and bulls that had gone into the previous winter were usually easy to identify, because they were branded. But what of the calves born since the last roundup? Fortunately, establishing ownership of most of the calves was not a problem, because young calves usually stayed with their mothers, and the ownership of the mother could be ascribed to the calf. One final class of cattle, however, calves without mothers, posed a very big problem indeed. Calves could become motherless when cows died or when men separated a cow and her calf. There never were large numbers of the mavericks, as they were called—1,971 through-out the entire state of Wyoming in 1884, and 3,446 in 1886—but their numbers were enough to cause monumental difficulties.[3] Their distribu-tion presented a problem that nineteenth-century Wyoming men found impossible to overcome.

The obvious solution, to distribute the mavericks to cattlemen in proportion to the cows they had placed on the range, seemed never to appeal to the large cattlemen, although this procedure had been used in cooperative roundups.[4] Instead, large cattlemen, who during almost all the time between 1868 and 1892 had effective control of Wyoming legisla-tures, proposed rules that caused untold harm. These men acted through the Wyoming Stock Growers Association, of which virtually all of them were members. The original position taken by the association was forwarded by Thomas Sturgis, its secretary from 1876 to 1887.[5] In a report made in the spring of 1883, he submitted a proposal for the disposition of mavericks. This revealing document shows that, at least as early as 1883, members of the association held settled convictions that they were the only respectable members of the Wyoming cattle fraternity and that they were besieged by all the rest, who constituted an army of thieves. Thomas Sturgis assumed that any man (other than a big ranch owner) who ran his own herd of cattle had no possibility of ownership and must be a thief. John Clay embellished on this concept and postulated that the movement of cattle and cowboys from Texas had pulled in the "criminal, the thief and the indifferently honest," who constituted a majority of these small cattlemen.[6]

Sturgis declared that the appropriate policy for the distribution of mavericks was "presumptive ownership," a concept whereby the owner of the largest herd in a range was presumptively entitled to *all* of the mavericks found.[7] This meant that if a small cattleman held, say, 10 percent of the cows on a range, he was not entitled to 10 percent of the mavericks that turned up in the spring roundup; instead, any property to which he might have been entitled was confiscated by his larger neighbor. Sturgis was born into a well-to-do New York City family, and perhaps within his social class such a proposal was seen as fitting.[8] Certainly the British upper-class money interests represented within the association were not offended by his position, but it was bound to be extremely unpopular in the rest of a very democratic Wyoming. Nevertheless,

Sturgis's autocratic concept of the rights of rich men versus the rights of poor men ultimately carried the day and directly led to the Maverick Law passed in 1884 by the territorial legislature.

The stock growers association prepared for the 1884 legislative session by holding a special meeting in Cheyenne on November 9, 1883. The president of the association, Joseph M. Carey, issued a notice of the meeting, and his declaration of the meeting's purposes showed his firm attitude. The notice referred to the necessity of obtaining from all members "full details of all illegal acts (relating to stock laws)," of adopting "measures for the punishment of past crimes and the prevention of future ones," and of addressing "the maverick question and the suppression of brands started by irresponsible persons for the purpose of stealing stock."[9] Four resolutions were passed. The first endorsed and ratified the creation of a "Detective Bureau." The second created a "black list" of cowboys, the third declared that no member of the association was to employ any man who had his own brand, and the fourth (actually, four separate resolutions all going to the same topic) formulated the association's policy relating to mavericks.[10]

The bill that was passed in the territorial legislature gave the Wyoming Stock Growers Association most of what it sought; it bestowed complete control of the roundup procedure to the association and, with it, control over the distribution of mavericks. Mavericks were to be sold to the highest bidder by foremen selected by the association.[11] Jack Flagg, a man who worked as a cowboy in Johnson County during the 1880s, wrote a series of newspaper articles in which he discussed extensively the maverick law and the small operator's reaction to it. From Flagg and others, it is clear that the small rancher was bitterly angry about this new law, viewing it as class legislation that gave authority to a private organization consisting almost exclusively of rich men and shut out the little guy entirely. Anecdotal evidence indicates that this was usually the case when disposal of the mavericks was carried out under this legislation.[12]

The big cattlemen gave little weight to these complaints. Frequently heard was a response repeated in many different situations for several years thereafter—that if people did not agree with the position of the Wyoming Stock Growers Association, they were siding with thieves.[13] The Maverick Law was satisfactory to the big cattlemen, by and large. Sturgis complained that it was "cumbersome," but assumed that it could be amended in the future.[14]

There was a further corollary to the attitudes of big cattlemen in 1883, and it related to the judicial system. It was an article of faith that large cattlemen could not obtain convictions before any Wyoming jury, that not only were most small owners thieving rascals, but these unworthies were protected by their own kind who sat on juries.[15] In *Guardian of the Grasslands*, a sponsored history of the Wyoming Stock Growers Association, John Burroughs accurately stated the position of association members in the nineteenth century when he wrote: "The stark fact remained that, no matter how flagrant or how air-tight the evidence, *Wyoming courts simply would not convict the defendant in a cattle stealing case*" (emphasis in original).[16] Contrary evidence, such as the experience of Johnson County from 1882 to 1888 and that in the territory in 1886, was minimized and rationalized. Fred Hesse, when addressing the time before 1886, would, on the one hand, bemoan the inability to obtain convictions and, on the other, almost simultaneously trumpet the great efficiency of his close friend Frank Canton, saying that Canton had rid the county of cattle thieves between 1883 and 1886.[17] Hesse, when writing about "depredations" in the early years (apparently those that took place during Canton's service but didn't really count), would use phrases, seen time and again in other writings, about men charged with crimes being confronted with "the strongest possible evidence" but all being turned loose.[18]

The public records show mixed results during Canton's service as sheriff; while several acquittals were obtained, most charges resulted in convictions.[19] And the records also show that in 1887 and 1888, after Canton had left office, the majority of livestock theft cases likewise resulted in convictions.[20] Canton, however, when addressing this time shortly after his tour of office, spoke of horrendous problems with stock theft, writing in March 1888, "I have never known them to be so bold as at the present time." In his autobiography, Canton went further, stating that during this time "there was organized the most systematic and powerful gang of cattle thieves ever known in the history of the United States."[21] These statements are highly dubious; they are not supported in contemporary criminal records or newspaper reports. In fact, it seems their only sources were the declarations of big cattlemen and their supporters, a situation commented upon by regional historians.[22]

But surely Frank M. Canton, the prominent former sheriff of Johnson County, was entitled to a presumption of veracity. Then again, maybe not. For one thing, he wasn't even Frank Canton. That was an alias that he made up when he fled from Texas. He and his family did not come from Virginia either; in fact, all of his family history was made up. It is no exaggeration to say that his entire life was a lie. The truth was that Frank Canton was Joe Horner, a fugitive from Texas with an extensive criminal history there.

Attempts have been made to minimize Canton's criminal past—for example, Burroughs, in *Guardian of the Grasslands*, refers to Canton's involvement in an "escapade" when he was a teenager—but Robert DeArment has now thoroughly established the broad, deep, and disturbing roster of crimes committed by Joe Horner.[23] Between 1874 and 1879, when Horner went from age twenty-four to thirty, he was part of one gang or another, consisting primarily of Joe and his brothers, as they engaged in a prolonged crime spree.[24]

In early 1874 the Jacksboro, Texas, post office was burglarized; a safe was broken into and the contents removed. Henry Strong, a Texas lawman, was asked to investigate the crime, and he immediately suspected the Joe Horner–Bill Cotnam gang. In the course of his investigation he developed strong evidence against Henry Jones, "gang member and special pal" of Joe Horner. When Strong attempted an arrest, a fight broke out, and Strong shot and killed Jones.[25] As a result, several attempts were made upon Strong's life. Strong stated that "the Horner party have sworn to kill me" and that they had shot at him nine times in several incidents. Horner's gang never did get Strong, and he was an affliction to them until they were all put in prison.

In 1874, Joe Horner was charged with aggravated assault and battery against one Ed Harris and with two cases of cattle theft. The Harris charge arose out of a "ruckus" in a Jacksboro saloon; the cattle theft accusations were for the alleged theft of four cows, also in the Jacksboro area.[26] In October of 1874, Horner, while out on bail awaiting trial, got into another Jacksboro saloon fight, this time with two black troopers from Fort Richardson, Texas (Tenth Cavalry).[27] This incident erupted into a running battle with black soldiers, during which Horner shot one man but did not kill him and then shot and killed another man.[28] Horner was charged with only one count of assault for the crimes committed in this shooting episode, probably because of pervasive prejudice against African American soldiers.[29] That was certainly the feeling among Joe's relatives; Horner's family thought that his actions were heroic.[30]

In early 1875, Horner was charged with two more counts of cattle theft, so that in the February term of court he faced two indictments for assault and four for cattle theft.[31] The cases were continued and Horner was freed on bond, but in September one of his bondsmen withdrew his bond, meaning, as a local newspaper reported, that "the notorious Joe Horner was gobbled up by Deputy Sheriff Hartley" and taken to jail.[32] The charges against Horner were set for trial in February 1876. Instead of serving five months in jail awaiting trial for his various crimes, however, Horner served only a week, until September 13, 1875, when four men (probably three of Horner's brothers and fellow gang member Bill Redding) raided the jail and delivered him from his captors.[33]

September 13, 1875, was a watershed date for Joe Horner. Before that time, most of his crimes were apparently the product of impulse and too much drink. After 1875, however, Horner became an outlaw, making his living by breaking the law.[34] After the jail break, Horner and his gang committed a series of robberies and thefts in late 1875 and early 1876. The record is ambiguous as to murders; there were suspicions, but evidently no such charges were filed against Horner. The *San Antonio Daily Express* wrote about the activities of the gang during this time, saying, "Honest and peaceable citizens dread their presence as they do death. We might occupy this entire page of our newspaper in giving details of robberies, thefts and murders which they have committed, and even then not present one-half."[35]

The biggest job for the Horner gang was the robbery of a bank in Comanche, Texas, about one hundred miles southwest of Dallas. Horner, his brother George, and Bill Redding entered the bank with guns drawn. They took $5,500 and led the employees of the bank out into the street at gunpoint, but then released the employees, jumped on their horses, and rode out of town.[36]

Henry Strong had traced the gang to Comanche and went there because he was convinced that he was still marked for death by Joe Horner; Strong hoped "to nail the gang before Horner killed him."[37] Strong watched the robbery and then immediately contacted the local sheriff and asked for a posse to track the robbers. They were tracked for two hundred miles, until the trail was lost near San Antonio. Shortly thereafter, though, each of the gang members was arrested by sheriff's deputies in San Antonio. Joe was seized after he had just mounted his horse; he desperately tried to pull his pistol but was overpowered.[38]

Joe Horner was taken to trial in San Antonio on March 15, 1877, for the Comanche bank robbery. The jury took only twenty-five minutes to convict him, and he was sentenced to ten years of hard labor at the state penitentiary in Huntsville.[39] Only two weeks after his trial, however, Horner escaped, finding ways to saw through his leg irons and the walls of his jail. He stole some horses to make good his escape, and only a few days later he and an accomplice robbed a stage, stealing from the passengers and firing a shot close to one. They then cut telegraph wires, a tactic Horner frequently employed.[40] Soon, though, Horner and his accomplice were surrounded by a local group of men. After a gun battle, Horner surrendered, but the accomplice got away.[41] Horner was quickly tried and sentenced to another ten years in the penitentiary, to run concurrently with the earlier sentence. He made further attempts to escape, but his efforts were discovered; to make sure he was delivered to the state penitentiary, three officers were assigned to escort him there.[42] His various escape attempts explain some later events when Horner, as Sheriff Frank Canton, was in Johnson County. In 1885 a man named Bill Booth was convicted of murder in Johnson County. He made several attempts to escape, but time and again his attempts were quickly detected and thwarted by the sheriff. It was uncanny how Canton seemed to have a sixth sense for Booth's intentions and actions.[43]

During the trip to Huntsville, Horner showed no remorse for his crimes but boasted of his actions and spoke of escaping and committing more crimes.[44] The two years he spent in the Texas prison must have sobered him, however, considering the turn his life took in the future. He was a well-behaved prisoner, although the probable reason for his changed behavior was so that he could earn assignment to outside work gangs, from which escape was easy. In August 1879, Horner did escape from one of those work gangs and was never recaptured.[45] In 1881 he showed up in Johnson County, Wyoming (though not as Joe Horner), and on August 22 of that year was employed as an inspector by Thomas Sturgis of the Wyoming Stock Growers Association.[46]

Joe Horner's life changed dramatically, Indeed, after 1879 it seemed as if Joe Horner had vanished from the face of the earth. In his place, a new man arose, a man named Frank M. Canton, who would spend the rest of his life trying to bury the memory of Joe Horner.[47]

While Joe Horner may have been suppressed, Frank Canton was very much active and alive, a dominant presence. Heading into 1889, a pivotal year for Johnson County, it was the perspective of Frank Canton that carried the day, leading ultimately to the notorious and disastrous events of 1891 and 1892. It is hard to draw the line between what Frank Canton actually believed and what he sensed his employers wanted to hear (throughout the rest of his life he purposely allied himself with powerful men and embraced their causes), but however melded, Canton's declarations carried weight.[48] The historical record shows that time and again his employers eagerly accepted his opinions. These men were predisposed to accept Canton's statements, as shown by the territorial roundup and the Maverick Law the Wyoming Stock Growers Association procured in 1884. Indeed, during 1889 and subsequent years it seems that the big cattlemen in the association willingly and uncritically accepted any negative statements about other citizens of Johnson County and reflexively disregarded any contrary information. The explanation for this bias was the core conflict between settlers and the big cattlemen, centering on competition for land; it was so strong that big cattlemen were always willing to assign the worst motives to the settlers. The parallels that come to mind are opponents in lawsuits, people with opposite political positions, or even people at war. The commanding and overriding emotion was the "deep-seated hatred" about which John Clay wrote, the anger toward settlers (and anyone who supported them) who would come in and strangle the big cattle owners, destroying their ranges, their ranches, and their livelihoods. The consequences of these emotions are clear: because big cattlemen had no legal way to stop settlement, they zealously pursued a campaign against rustling.[49]

CHAPTER FIVE

Cattle Theft Charges

In 1889, criminal charges were filed in Johnson County that heralded heightened conflict between large and small cattlemen. The big early news in Buffalo in 1889, however, was the new water system, completed after testing the fire hydrants "one by one."[1] Buffalo people still held an abiding conviction that they were citizens of the most progressive town in Wyoming, and in 1889 the *Sentinel* reprinted two articles that validated their view. The Brighton, Colorado, *Courier* had referred to the countryside around Buffalo as "thickly settled with a go-ahead well-to-do class of farmers" and provided a glowing description of the town's excellent collection of retail establishments and civic improvements.[2] And an article in the *New York Tribune*, besides mentioning the civic improvements, had remarked about how well-read the people were, how well-educated their children were becoming, and how beautiful the mountains were that wrapped Buffalo in its "giant arms."[3]

It was enough to make the heads of Buffalo citizens swell. Praise from strangers, however, did not insulate the people of Buffalo from the vicissitudes of daily life. Personal tragedy struck Mr. and Mrs. W. J. Clarke in April of that year. Mrs. Clarke's brother, William G. Robinson, went boating at Lake DeSmet, and his boat capsized. Robinson clung to the boat while his companion ran for help three miles distant; when the companion returned, however, he only found the boat, not Mr. Robinson. An extensive search was undertaken, but the body was not found until about a month later. The Clarkes ran a statement in the *Sentinel*, declaring deep appreciation for their neighbors: "We desire to extend our thanks to the people of Buffalo and vicinity who have so promptly and unstintedly rendered us their aid and assistance in endeavoring to recover the body of our brother William G. Robinson. In our hour of need have they assisted us and we trust that in their time of trial we may be able to return some aid to them."[4] The last sentence in this card of thanks seemed to signify that W. J. Clarke, though not an American, had bonded with the people of his adopted community.

As always, however, after tragedy life goes on. Indeed, the people of Johnson County seemed more industrious than ever. The pages of the *Sentinel* in April, May, and June of 1889 were full of land application notices. On May 4 the *Sentinel* printed about thirty notices, on May 11 about thirty-five, and thirty-eight on June 1.[5] About three-quarters of these notices related to the Richards ditch project, which involved the digging of a canal on the west side of the Big Horn River, around what is now Worland, Wyoming. It seemed like a big move onto the land, but apparently few if any of the people filing these notices actually set foot on the land they claimed. There were allegations that the Richards project was just a land grab, exploiting a loophole in the Desert Land Act that allowed a claim without residence.[6]

It was not until May 1889 that signs of serious trouble began to arise in Johnson County, ominous indications that must have given thoughtful residents pause. The *Sentinel* reported on May 11 that "cattlemen have offered rewards aggregating $22,000, for the conviction of any person for stealing, unlawfully killing, defacing, or altering brands of their live-stock."[7] A week later, the *Sentinel* printed an editorial, probably written by H. R. Mann (who had taken over from Parmelee as editor), in support of these rewards: "[They] will make it more profitable to give the gang away than it is to stand with it. Startling developments are very likely to occur in the near future. . . . This manner of depredations on our stock interests is becoming alarming and the officers should show their ability to control these violations of law."[8]

This article was followed by an advertisement that ran in every edition of the *Sentinel* for about three months:

> $1,500 reward: We the undersigned agree to pay the sum of $1,500
> for the conviction of each and every person caught stealing,

unlawfully killing, defacing or altering the brands of cattle or horses, belonging to any or all of us anywhere. Also for the unlawful branding of mavericks on our respective ranges.

Murphy Cattle Co., Powder River Cattle Co. (Fred Hesse), Pratt & Ferris Cattle Co., Peters and Alston, Des Moines Cattle Co. (Holland and Pfeiffer), Wm. Harris, Wm. Heywood, Conrad & Clarke, Wyoming Land and Cattle Co. (W. R. Holt), Frontier Cattle Co. (Horace Plunkett), Stoddard and Howard Live Stock Co.[9]

The offering of such a huge reward was an aggressive move by the big cattlemen, since the whole subject of rewards related to livestock theft was controversial in Wyoming. In December 1887 the *Sentinel* had run an article about how Cheyenne newspapers were exposing the unscrupulous actions of detectives of the Wyoming Stock Growers Association, who were trumping up charges so they could get the $250 reward authorized under the 1884 Maverick Law. The 1889 reward offer was not just huge but vastly disproportionate. The average range cow in 1889 was worth only between $15 to $20; the cattlemen were offering a reward that was about seventy-five to one hundred times the value of the item stolen.[10]

The big cattlemen were deadly serious about prosecutions for cattle theft, though. In late June 1889 an unusually large number of new criminal cases were filed and tried (these were probably the "startling developments" referred to in the May 18 editorial). The 1888 grand jury, whose foreman was none other than H. R. Mann, may have contributed one of these, *Territory v. McDermott*, but the remainder of the indictments and trials came from the June 1889 grand jury.[11] A total of thirteen indictments were issued against thirteen different men for theft of cattle, the theft of three horses, and the unlawful branding of mavericks on seven different occasions. All of these offenses were alleged to have been committed in May and June of 1889.[12]

What was happening here? Until May 1889 there was not the slightest hint in any public records of big problems with cattle theft in Johnson County. No stories in the *Sentinel* had proclaimed anything such as "Ranchman Decries Theft of 200 Head" or "Bandits Make Off with 80 Cows Owned by Big Cattle, Inc." If such events had occurred, the *Sentinel* would have announced them in big headlines.[13] It is notable that even when counting all the various charges pressed by cattlemen in

1889 (the year of the most livestock charges by far), the total number of animals allegedly taken by the thirteen men charged was only twenty.

Johnson County, in general, had a reputation as a law-abiding place. District judges sitting in Buffalo had commented upon this, speaking of the "comparative infrequency of crime in your midst" and noting that Johnson County "is the most law-abiding portion of Wyoming which I have been in."[14] Perhaps these comments were just gracious remarks to please the home folks, but it is unlikely they would have been made had Buffalo a reputation for extensive crime.

The editor of the *Sentinel*, despite having one of the best listening posts in the county and having declared that there were "alarming" depredations, had no personal knowledge of such events. This is shown from an editorial published in September 1889 that addressed cattle theft, in which H. R. Mann wrote, "If the crime is growing more prevalent, as it is claimed it is . . ."[15] Clearly, Mann did not know whether cattle theft was growing more prevalent, but he was being told by some people that it was.

"Some people" probably included Fred Hesse and Frank Canton, who were always ready to ascribe the worst to other citizens of Johnson County. Still, something beyond the ordinary seemed to be riling up the big cattlemen of Johnson County in 1889. Cattle theft, however, was probably not the principal source of their agitation. The sharp increase in land applications in 1889 may have upset those in Johnson County who were trying to monopolize large tracts of land. Even more significantly, the cattle industry continued to perform poorly, and this surely contributed to big cattlemen's perspective about the importance of cattle theft. Dr. Charles Penrose, one of the members of the 1892 invading force, later acknowledged that after the winter of 1886–87 and the market downturn, "stealing became relatively of more account" and "was the final misfortune on top of others."[16] Fred Hesse, when writing a relative in late 1889, said that the cattle business in Wyoming had proven to be another "South Sea Bubble" for English investors (a 1720 financial disaster), who were all quitting the business (eighteen had left the country in the last fifteen months). Hesse indicated that he was one of the few who could not leave or that at least he "must wait for a better time."[17]

Most significantly, when new, assertive settlers started pushing their way into southern Johnson County in 1887 and 1888 and challenging the control of the range by the big outfits, those running the big operations saw it as a considerable threat. The bullying tactics of Frewen, Hesse, and others had backfired. The more cautious men, the men with families who felt they had something to lose, had been chased off. But this meant that land remained open to settlement, and more tenacious men, who would not be chased off, came in. The most prominent among them was O. H. "Jack" Flagg.

Handsome Jack Flagg was a big, confident, contentious man, and a bit of a rogue. He liked women, gambling, and whiskey, and he refused to be pushed around.[18] Born in 1860, he was the son of a prominent couple in Charleston, Virginia (later West Virginia). Supposedly he could trace his family line to Robert E. Lee. With the coming of the Civil War the family fortunes slipped, although Flagg's father was able to send him to the Charles Town Academy, from which he graduated. Shortly thereafter, at age seventeen, he left West Virginia and headed west.[19] Flagg first went to Texas, where he worked as a cowhand, and then gradually moved north until he arrived in Johnson County in 1882.[20] In 1886 he was active in the strike called by Wyoming cowboys after their wages were cut. The Wyoming Stock Growers Association voted to blacklist the leaders of that strike (so much for the notion that the sole purpose of the blacklist was to combat theft), although it is not clear whether the association actually carried out this edict, nor whether Flagg was listed among the strike leaders.[21] When Flagg bought his own brand and homesteaded some land on the Red Fork of the Powder River, however, he ensured that he would be blacklisted—and he was, in the spring of 1887.[22]

Flagg had purchased his brand from W. E. Hathaway, and it was known as the Hat brand. Flagg bought a few cattle in 1886 and a few the next year, hardly unusual for that time; virtually every man who was not prohibited by a big outfit ran his own small herd. In 1888 Flagg sold interests in this outfit to four men, W. H. "Billy" Hill, Lew Webb, Thomas Gardner, and Al Allison, all from Texas.[23] The historical record does not reveal the form of the consideration, but it most probably involved horses and cattle owned by each of these men; the five owners probably pooled their livestock. Back in 1884, the Wyoming Stock Growers Association had resolved to blacklist any man who had his own brand, and that was the association's prompt response for all four of Flagg's new partners.[24]

The difference in this case was that the men of the Hat brand were not about to slink into the shadows; they simply brought in their own wagon for the roundups. In 1888 Flagg was prominent in the spring roundup. He got into a rousing fight with Mike Shonsey, who was then foreman for the CY, owned by Joseph M. Carey and one of the biggest outfits in Wyoming. All indications are that he won the fight but secured Shonsey's enduring hatred.[25] The fight—a nasty affair in which Flagg struck Shonsey repeatedly with his riding quirt—arose because Flagg accused Shonsey of "blotching" one of Flagg's cows—that is, burning over Flagg's brand to establish his employer's brand.[26] When he called Shonsey down, Flagg unequivocally declared that he was not going to allow anyone on the range, even the biggest of cattlemen, to treat him unfairly.

It is not clear exactly what the connections were between Jack Flagg and Fred Hesse back in 1887 and 1888, but there is no question that these men very early despised one another. As one historian of the Johnson County War put it, Flagg and Hesse "were enemies to the knife."[27] Their private and public writings are full of nasty comments by one about the other. Hesse wrote about "the gang," meaning Flagg and his associates (which apparently was the source of the phrase "the gang" used by H. R. Mann in 1889), and asserted that after 1886 Flagg was responsible for "enormous depredations."[28] Flagg, in his writings, accused Hesse of stealing horses and cattle from his neighbors and his employer, and he railed about Hesse's "arbitrary and domineering ways."[29]

Frank Canton (Joe Horner) also had a personal grudge against Jack Flagg. In 1887 Canton, probably influenced by Hesse, wrote that Flagg "is Crooked" and contended that Flagg set up on Red Fork for the purpose of establishing a rustling business. Flagg surely knew of Canton's views and in 1888 got a chance to strike back. Flagg was active in Democratic Party politics in Johnson County and was one of the principal men who pushed for Red Angus for sheriff.[30] When Flagg's candidate crushed Canton, Canton had one more reason to hate Flagg.

The primary sources for Hesse's allegations that Flagg was responsible for "enormous depredations" are Hesse and Canton, and the bald statements of neither should be accepted without corroboration. This does not mean, though, that Flagg and his compatriots never stole cattle or branded mavericks. J. Elmer Brock was a knowledgeable and impartial observer, and his statements should thus be given weight. Brock wrote that the Hat brand represented "the leadership of the cattle rustler element." With the discernment of hindsight, he wrote: "Men, ordinarily honest, stole cattle from the big outfits and did not consider it dishonest, but an act justifiable in a war of classes. Men of this type later became leading citizens and were respected even by their former enemies."[31] Put another way, if Jack Flagg or one of his partners saw an opportunity to brand a calf from a cow owned by Fred Hesse, and they could get away with it, they would not hesitate to do so. Men such as Flagg, Webb, and Gardner, however, did not come to the country to steal cattle. They were there to realize the promise of the frontier, to build their lives their own way. Conflict with the big cattlemen arose when they were frustrated from doing so.

Hesse did not like the men of the Hat outfit to be involved in the roundups. In 1887 and 1888 some of the men associated with big outfits helped Flagg, including Lee Moore, who surprisingly let him buy some mavericks, and Ed Spaugh. Spaugh was the foreman of the EK Ranch, and he committed the heresy of letting Flagg and his associates bring a wagon to the roundup (the big cattlemen wanted no one on roundups but members of the Wyoming Stock Growers Association—one more manifestation of the big cattlemen's conviction that only they were legitimate). One of the usual consequences of being blacklisted was that a cowboy could not even participate in the roundup, could not even protect the few cows and calves he might own.[32] Flagg alleged that Hesse later got Spaugh fired. Given Hesse's long and close relationship with Horace Plunkett, the English manager of the Powder River Cattle Company and an owner of the EK Ranch, and George W. Baxter, manager of the American Cattle Trust and most probably the man who fired Spaugh, the allegation is likely valid.[33] But in 1889 Jack Flagg was not going to allow Fred Hesse to keep him from participating in the spring roundup. Flagg, Lew Webb, Tom Gardner, Al Allison, and Billy Hill were all there, a tough group of men who boldly insisted on their rights. In 1893, after the dispute between big and little cattlemen had exploded into violence, Hesse alleged that the men of the Hat brand "spent much time just before the round-up, branding mavericks and big calves, which they held away from their mothers." Hesse added, "As they had the men working for the outfits terrorized, the reps were afraid to report what was going on."[34]

All of the 1889 maverick charges were against Flagg and his associates, growing out of the Hat brand's participation in the spring 1889 roundup and the anger of the big cattlemen over the audacity of Flagg, Webb, Allison, Gardner, and Hill. Flagg denied that he or his partners had violated any laws, and when he was arrested, Flagg's take on the situation was that the big cattlemen knew they had no case against the Hat brand but still tried to press criminal charges.[35] Each of the bonds for the men charged was set exceptionally high, even though all but one charge was for a misdemeanor, apparently to keep the defendants in jail and punish them whether or not they were convicted of a crime, and perhaps to keep them off the range during the fall roundup. But all were able to achieve bail and were released.[36]

The Hat brand men were probably the principal target of the big prosecutorial push in 1889, but the more serious charges were against other men. Three felony charges of cattle stealing were brought against men for the theft of cattle owned by one of the big outfits—that is, one of the outfits offering a $1,500 reward for the conviction of anyone stealing their animals. The large reward served as a strong incentive to seek convictions; it was more than a cowhand could earn in three years. The charge against George Gordon and George Peterson was for stealing one cow owned by the Powder River Cattle Company (Fred Hesse is listed as a witness). The charge against Joseph Coslett was for stealing one cow owned by Stoddard and Howard Live Stock Company, and Henry P. Rothwell was charged with stealing one of the cows of the Murphy Cattle Company.[37] Two other charges did not involve any of the outfits providing a reward—those against William H. Carroll for stealing three horses and against James Huff and William Nutcher, for stealing six head of cattle (allegedly worth $5 each) owned by an unknown person.[38]

Each of these cases was tried before a jury in June and July of 1889, and each resulted in an acquittal.[39] The big cattlemen were shocked and furious. Here was full and final proof of what they had so ardently believed for so many years, that no matter how strong the evidence, a conviction could never be had for cattle theft. The consequences flowing from these five acquittals were profound, so these cases and their aftermath should be examined in detail.

After the trials, five or six cattlemen, including Fred Hesse, approached Judge Micah Saufley, the district judge presiding over the five cases. This group was probably angry and confrontational, demanding to know how such results could have happened in his courtroom.[40] Judge Saufley would have been less than human had he not sought to deflect responsibility, and the easiest group to blame was the jurors. Saufley is supposed to have said that the defendants "were as guilty as any men he ever tried and the jury turned them loose."[41] It appears that someone in the crowd then demanded of the judge "what we would do to stop the stealing," and the judge said he did not know.[42]

Unfortunately, the only version we have of Judge Saufley's statement is from Fred Hesse. Saufley served as a Wyoming judge only until October 11, 1890; he returned to Kentucky after losing an election to John W. Blake of Laramie. (Blake ran as a Republican and Saufley as a Democrat—significant because of the political overtones that later arose out of the conflict between big and little cattlemen.) Saufley made no public statement about this soon-to-be famous remark.[43] The problem with Saufley's alleged comments is that even if they were reported accurately by Hesse—and, regarding cattle theft, Hesse was certainly a die-hard partisan in 1889 with an emotional commitment to his own version of facts—they are inconsistent with other, more objective evidence about the five cases.

Charges brought by criminal authorities are normally assumed to be valid, but this assumption was not necessarily appropriate in Johnson County in 1889. One of the principal tactics used by big cattlemen in the 1880s and 1890s was to push theft charges, believing that if they could not get convictions, they would at least levy huge fines, primarily in the form of the fees for the attorney of a person charged. As John Burroughs wrote: "There was more than a modicum of truth in the range country adage that: 'Maybe you can't convict a cattle thief, but you can always break him' and indeed it was a fact that many a young would-be cattle rustler not only left his bankroll in the hands of the attorney who defended him, but horse, saddle and sugan as well."[44]

This tactic, vigorously pursued by big cattlemen, was deeply unfair, because it punished the guilty and the not guilty alike, including those who were guilty only of settling in the "wrong" place. In 1889 (as today) no responsible prosecuting attorney should have allowed his office to be used in this manner; his clear public responsibility was to winnow out cases brought for ulterior purposes. With H. S. Elliott, however, the big cattle owners had a county attorney who was susceptible to pressure.

H. S. Elliott was close to Charles Burritt, who had deep ties to big cattle. Elliott and Burritt were law partners for almost three years and, during that time, built a brick building, which they owned jointly. When they split as partners in 1888, it was apparently for economic reasons, because Elliott had become county attorney and a continued partnership would have disallowed Burritt from handling criminal cases. They remained friends and continued joint ownership of their building.[45] We do not know whether it was necessary, but in Burritt the large cattle interests had a real ally to forward their contentions to the county attorney.

The Buffalo papers rarely commented upon criminal cases, but one of the cases resulting in acquittal was addressed by H. R. Mann. In a withering editorial, Mann resoundingly criticized the decision to bring charges against Henry Rothwell. He agreed that cattle rustling "should be prosecuted with vigor," but asserted that the stock interest gained no advantage when cases such as the one against Rothwell were "dragged into court, apparently for the purpose of doing someone up."[46]

Mann wrote that he had carefully read the evidence in the case and had concluded that it was so thin that the motives of the complaining party were called into question. In his closing comments, Mann made sure there was no question about the message of his editorial:

> It is just such cases as this that brings prosecutions under the stock laws into disrepute. Mr. Rothwell stands well in this community as an honest and upright man. If the rule is to be established that the owner of the herd is to be arrested every time a calf is branded by mistake, we have no objections to it, but if established let it be general, and not to suit the convenience of the larger herd owners.[47]

H. R. Mann knew Rothwell; both were delegates to the Republican county convention in 1888. Mann's statement about Rothwell's high standing in Johnson County was certainly manifest after 1889, Through the next fifty-two years, Rothwell was a pillar of the community, successful and respected in every one of his extensive endeavors, which included ownership of a large ranch near Thermopolis, Wyoming; ownership of the Buffalo flour mill and the town's electrical plant; and interests in the First National Bank in both Buffalo and Thermopolis (serving as president for each of them); ownership of the light and power company in Thermopolis; and natural gas interests. At his death in Buffalo in 1940, he was apparently worth more than a million dollars.[48]

It was not only the Rothwell charges that were suspect but also the charges against Gordon and Peterson. The *Buffalo Bulletin* in April 1892 commented about Fred Hesse's role in this case. Although Hesse had claimed he owned the cow allegedly stolen, the *Bulletin* reported, "It was shown that the cow in question belonged to an owner living in the Big Horn Basin, and that Hesse had by right of possession appropriated the offspring for several years prior to this trial. . . . No wonder juries don't convict on such evidence as this."[49]

The charges against James Huff and William Nutcher for stealing six head of cattle each valued at $5 were also questionable. The indictment openly stated that these six head were owned by "unknown persons."[50] In other words, the prosecution began the case not being able to establish that a defendant stole property owned by another person, an essential element for a successful charge of larceny. More than that, the value given to the cattle raises large questions. When the going price was $15 to $20, what kind of cattle were only worth $5 a head? They were apparently not unbranded calves, because otherwise, violations of the Maverick Law would have been charged, rather than the felony grand larceny.

Since the cattle allegedly stolen were mature, the $5 value was truly strange. They may have been wild cattle that had never been branded and were scruffy, impaired animals. Or they may have been cattle with obscured brands, marginal animals, perhaps sick, perhaps malnourished, so much so that they could not breed. The people of Johnson County could legitimately ask why the Johnson County attorney was trying to put two men in the penitentiary in these circumstances. Who had demanded this action?

The details of the remaining two acquittals are not known, but based on what is known (including the fact of the acquittals), it is not an unreasonable inference that none of the cattle charges filed in Johnson County in 1889 were being put forward upon solid evidence and that the charges were instead based upon suspicion and were influenced by pressure from big cattlemen and a sizeable award.[51]

The big cattlemen, though, notwithstanding the weakness of the charges, never doubted they were victims of a terrible injustice, and the five acquittals became a rallying cry. The county attorney's subsequent actions sharpened their sense of grievance. In December, Elliott dismissed all of the charges against Flagg and his associates in the Hat brand.[52]

Fred Hesse later gave his twist to these dismissals, saying that the prosecuting attorney and the judge had concluded that trials would have been a "useless expenditure," because it was impossible to bring stronger evidence than had been presented in the earlier cases.[53] This seems unlikely. Hesse's interpretation was forwarded by a zealous man who had been embarrassed in court and had lost objectivity. The actions of H. S. Elliott in dismissing a series of cattle theft cases are more readily explained by other reasons. Losing five jury trials in a row is a crushing rebuke to a prosecuting attorney, but when those losses are followed by a scathing editorial criticizing the decision to bring a case against one of Johnson County's best citizens, the repudiation is complete. The population of Buffalo was only about a thousand people in 1889; every adult knew every other adult and knew them well. A community of that size can bring to bear a crushing social stigma. By various means the people of the community probably made known to Elliott that they believed he had unfairly prosecuted Johnson County citizens to meet the shrill demands of men such as Hesse and Canton. The more likely reason that H. S. Elliott retreated was that he did not want to be perceived as having been a toady for powerful interests oppressing Johnson County citizens.

CHAPTER SIX

"Cattle Kate"

Johnson County was not the only place in Wyoming to suffer conflict because of competition over the open range. In the summer of 1889, big cattlemen clashed with two people who had homesteaded on the Sweetwater River in central Wyoming. During the hot afternoon of July 21, 1889, six cattlemen lynched Ellen Watson and James Averell.

The people of Johnson County did not learn about this deeply disturbing event until several days later in July (the same month in which the last cases of the 1889 spring term cases were tried). The July 27 issue of the *Sentinel* reported the dual lynching of Watson (referred to as "Kate Maxwell" in the local news reports) and Averell in breathlessly dramatic prose. Although telegraphed from Cheyenne, the article was attributed to the *Nebraska State Journal*. It stated that a "reckless prairie virago of loose morals" had traded her favors for stolen cattle, and local cattlemen had no choice but to kill her. Reference was made to a "notorious cattle queen," the "lawless but justifiable deed," and the "rustler" and the "range queen," and it was said: "Stockmen of the Sweetwater region have been the victims of cattle thieves for years. On account of prejudice against the large outfits, it has become almost impossible to convict on this charge, and the rustlers have become very bold." Averell was said to have whined, but Kate cursed, "challenging the Deity to harm her if He possessed the power. He possessed the power." The article closed with these statements: "It is doubtful if any inquest will be held, and the executioners have no fear of being punished. The cattlemen have been forced to this and more hangings will follow unless there is less thieving."[1]

A week later, another article appeared in the *Sentinel*, much more balanced than the first, setting out a factual recitation of the event and referring to the earlier version as "dime novel literature," which was "the veriest bosh."[2] But the Buffalo people reading the *Sentinel* were never informed of the source of the articles and who was behind them, and they must have wondered why such contrasting articles were being presented.

The source of both articles, who was behind them, and the reasons for the disparate accounts have now been clearly and convincingly established.[3] The same day as the lynching, July 21, 1889, a ten-word telegram was sent from Rawlins, Wyoming, to George Henderson in Cheyenne, Wyoming. Henderson was a cattle detective for John Clay. Henderson had just been working in the Rawlins area, and when he received the telegram, he went immediately to Ed Towse at the *Cheyenne Daily Leader*. In 1889 the *Daily Leader* and every other Cheyenne newspaper were controlled by members of the Wyoming Stock Growers Association (a "kept press," if there ever was one). Ed Towse had no independent knowledge of the lynchings or the people involved; his only source of information was Henderson.[4]

Towse constructed a long newspaper article whose effect was to smear the victims and provide justification for the killings. After completing his article of about 1,300 words, he sent it out by telegraph to area newspapers. The version that ended up in Buffalo came from the *Nebraska State Journal* but was just a limited rewrite of the Towse article. The second article found in the *Sentinel*, the one referring to Towse's article as "dime novel literature," was written by Edward A. Slack, editor of the *Cheyenne Daily Sun*, and first published on July 25. Ironically, Slack had at first written an article as sensational as Towse's but evidently decided he had been misled and then wrote the July 25 article. Then Slack, on July 26, apparently having been reminded who his employers were, did a complete switch and wrote the most fantastic article in this series, one asserting that Watson and Averell had threatened the lives of area ranchers, that they "completely controlled and terrorized the whole region," and that the issue was "a question of life and death between honest men and cut-throat thieves."[5]

These newspaper articles successfully clouded culpability for one of the ugliest crimes in Wyoming's history. The people of Wyoming had limited information about the event, so the version out of Cheyenne was generally accepted, although with skepticism. People were right to be skeptical; a fair view of the facts tells quite a different story from the one out of Cheyenne.

Ellen L. Watson, the woman lynched, was twenty-eight when she died. She was the eldest daughter of a Scottish farm family (she always spoke with a thick Scottish accent) that had settled in north-central Kansas. At age eighteen, she married a man named Pickell, but this marriage was short and unhappy.[6] When the marriage failed, Watson moved farther west, first to Denver, then to Cheyenne, Wyoming, and westward 150 miles down the track of the Union Pacific Railway to Rawlins, Wyoming. Throughout her brief life, she worked as a cook and a housekeeper. She was never a prostitute and was never known in life as "Cattle Kate" or "Kate Maxwell."[7] Unfortunately, there were at least two women in Wyoming with names similar to Ellen Watson who were prostitutes, making it easier for Towse and Slack to confuse her with these women.[8]

Watson was said to be extremely bright and was described as being five feet, eight inches tall and weighing 165 pounds, with brown hair and blue eyes. Those who knew her after she moved to the Sweetwater River north of Rawlins said that she was well-liked, probably because she was uncommonly kind to her neighbors. Ellen was good-hearted, and when she heard people were in trouble, she sought to help.[9]

In 1886 Ellen met James Averell when he traveled to Rawlins. Averell—always referred to as "Jimmy," even as an adult—was ten years older than Ellen, but was smaller than her, less than five feet, seven inches tall and 135 pounds.[10] Jimmy Averell's pathway to Wyoming was considerably different from Ellen Watson's. He joined the United States Army in 1871 and was stationed in several posts in the western United States. While at Fort McKinney, Wyoming Territory, in 1880, he was charged with shooting and killing one Charlie Johnson, a big, aggressive man with a history of brawls, who had threatened on several occasions to kill Averell.[11] Fort McKinney was then part of Carbon County, and Averell was charged in the Wyoming territorial courts and transported to Rawlins, the county seat of Carbon County. He was held in the Carbon County jail when the jail also held "Big Nose" George Parrott—at least until a mob pulled Parrott out of the jail and lynched him.[12] The case against Averell was ultimately dismissed, the state courts deciding it should be handled by military courts, and the military declining to press charges. Averell was honorably discharged from the army on June 19, 1881.[13]

After his discharge, Averell worked in the Rawlins area to gain money for a homestead application (a costly undertaking, usually requiring horses, wagons, fencing materials, and machinery). In a few months he staked a claim on some land in the Sweetwater River valley, near Ferris Mountain, about fifty miles north of Rawlins.[14] The Sweetwater River runs east and west through central Wyoming and provides a direct avenue from the Platte River on the east, to South Pass, on the west; the Oregon Trail followed the Sweetwater River valley for about one hundred miles, virtually the entire length of the valley. The stream is steady, though not large, and is bordered by natural grassy pastures.[15]

Shortly after staking his claim, Averell went back east, to the home of his brother and sister-in-law in Winnebago County, Wisconsin. There he met Sophia Jaeger, whom he courted, married, and brought back to Wyoming. He built a one-room house with a covered front porch and filled it with comfortable furnishings.[16] By all indications, the couple were very happy, and their happiness increased when Sophia became pregnant. But the child was born prematurely and died a few hours after its birth. A few days later the mother succumbed to "childbirth fever."[17] Averell brought the bodies of his wife and baby back to his in-laws' home in Wisconsin. After the funeral, he returned to Wyoming, but the ambitious and hardworking Jimmy Averell passed from sight for more than two years, apparently defeated by grief and depression.[18]

In July 1885, Averell filed a new claim about fifteen miles north of his first one, a particularly attractive site surrounded by the Seminoe and Ferris mountains on the south, the Deer Creek Range on the northeast, and the Rattlesnake Range on the northwest. He built two log buildings, each one story, next to the Rawlins–Fort McKinney military road. His plan was to establish a road ranch, providing meals and a small general store with a bar, supplemented by fresh vegetables he grew.[19]

Averell was in the middle of all these preparations when he met Ellen Watson. The two went to Lander, Wyoming, where they applied for a marriage license on May 11, 1886, which was issued six days later. They never completed the process; there is no indication in any public record that a marriage ceremony was performed.[20] A clue as to why they did not follow through on the marriage may be found in the papers actually filed; in them, Ellen Liddy Watson gave her name as Ellen Liddy Andrews, apparently wanting to conceal her true name. The drawback to marriage for Ellen was that she could not, as a married woman, file a claim to

Albert John Bothwell *(front row, left)* with his family. Photograph by George Fiske. David Historical Collection. Casper College Western History Center.

land under the Homestead Act (as she did later). She may have intended at first to marry under a false name to preserve the Homestead Act right, but then chose to wait until her homestead application was completed.[21]

Whatever their reasoning in Lander, Jimmy and Ellen moved to Jimmy's ranch on the Sweetwater. Ellen did the cooking and otherwise helped at the store and bar. Each made two land claims, so that their lands totaled a complete section, 640 acres; Ellen had a small log cabin built on one of her claims. The two seemed to be well on their way to success. They could not have known that their land claims, while legally valid, would soon conflict with the ambition of Albert John Bothwell, a man who was about to make a big move into the Sweetwater Valley.[22]

In August 1888, Albert John Bothwell brought 1,500 head of cattle to the Sweetwater. He ran them on a huge swath of land, which he claimed as his range. Bothwell's ranch was centered around Horse Creek—where Jimmy and Ellen made their claims—and extended several miles northeast, several miles northwest, and some twenty miles to the south.[23] No legitimate claim could have been made to all this land by Bothwell, but he fenced much of it and insisted it was his. He was referred to as a man who was a "never surrender" defender of his fence system; as late as 1917 he was sued by the United States for illegal enclosure of federal lands. The suit demanded over $40,000 in damages and an injunction for the removal of fences (the injunction was denied, at least in part because Stewart Sanford, to whom Bothwell had sold in 1917, promptly made openings in fences to provide access to others).[24]

A photograph taken of Bothwell in his prime shows him to be a long, raw-boned man with an air of command. He was well read and well educated, especially influenced by the theories of Herbert Spencer espousing social Darwinism. Bothwell was proud and willful, and he continually looked for ways to augment his wealth. He could fairly be termed a "promoter"; in late August of 1888, about the same time he moved cattle into the Sweetwater country, he and associates made extensive claims on seven sections of land just west of the claims of Averell and Watson. Bothwell started lobbying for the development of the area and even established a town named "Bothwell."[25] Of his projects, only his cattle operation came to much. A contemplated railroad never got off the ground, an oil well struck nothing, and the town of Bothwell never had more than a few residents, most of whom were apparently brought in by Bothwell himself. But Bothwell took all his schemes seriously, and he was not happy with Watson and Averell's presence. On more than one occasion, he tried to purchase Ellen's land rights, but she refused to sell to him.[26] He was also unhappy with Jimmy Averell, who, in February 1889, wrote an intelligent, well-presented letter to a Casper, Wyoming, newspaper (also printed in Rawlins) that demolished Bothwell's pretensions about his town and was generally critical of "the land grabber," by which Averell must have been referring to Bothwell.[27]

When Ellen and Jimmy were living on their Sweetwater claims, some people still came west along the Oregon Trail; not everyone could afford to make the westward trip by rail. In October 1888 an immigrant from Nebraska named Engerman sold Ellen Watson twenty-eight head of cattle. They were "foot sore," and she paid $1 a head.[28] She placed the cattle in her fenced sixty-acre pasture but did not brand them. Neither Ellen nor Jimmy Averell had a brand, although they had been trying hard to establish one. They made five separate applications over three years, but the Carbon County brand committee refused to accept any of them. Finally, in March 1889, Ellen purchased the "L. U." brand from John M. Crowder.[29] Most of the cattle Ellen had purchased were heifers and cows, many of which were pregnant, and in the spring some of them gave birth, so that by July 1889, she held some forty-one animals, and in that month she chose to brand the calves.[30] There should have been no problem with this branding, but under the peculiar circumstances of that moment in July, Ellen Watson's decision was a fatal one.

In the middle of July 1889 local cattlemen were just completing the spring roundup.[31] A stock detective, George Henderson, was in the area, perhaps as part of the roundup activities, and he spotted Ellen Watson's cattle and newly branded calves. Henderson reported his finding to Bothwell but then proceeded south to Rawlins, where he caught a train to Cheyenne.[32] Bothwell immediately summoned his neighbors, and four men, M. Ernest McLean, Robert M. Galbreath, John Henry Durbin, and Tom Sun, soon met at Bothwell's ranch, less than a mile south of Ellen Watson's land. Robert Conner joined them later.[33] All of these men, except McLean, were big operators, and one would expect them to have shared Bothwell's perspective about Watson and Averell. Bothwell apparently announced that he had caught a thief red-handed, but surprisingly, Tom Sun and another of the men did not accept Bothwell's view, at least initially, and there were heated discussions.[34] Nevertheless, the men decided to go to Ellen Watson's place.

Most of the men heading to Ellen Watson's land that early afternoon of July 21, 1889, were very angry, one might say steeped in outraged indignation. Too, just before making their short trip, the six men had fortified themselves with alcohol.[35] They charged over to Watson's and found the small herd and the newly branded calves. This possession, standing alone, was embraced as complete proof of guilt, evidently on the grounds that Ellen was a woman of limited means who could not possibly have owned them legitimately.

When the men arrived, Ellen was not home, having visited a Shoshone encampment along the Sweetwater, just north of her cabin. She bought an attractive pair of beaded moccasins, a fine example of Native craftsmanship, and then started walking home. Accompanied her was John L. DeCorey, who was fourteen years old and worked for her; he has been referred to as her ward.[36] She was wearing the moccasins, delighted at her charming acquisition, when she saw cattlemen swarming about her place. John Durbin was furiously tearing down her fence, and the other men were around her house. Her happy mood immediately changed to alarm, and she ran toward her home.[37]

The cattlemen surrounded Ellen, screaming at her that they had found the stolen livestock. She tried to explain that the cattle had been purchased almost a year earlier and that she had a bill of sale, but it was in a bank in Rawlins. Her accusers' blood was up, though, and they contemptuously dismissed her statements. Ellen's frantic protests only gave them further cause to vent their outrage at this woman who had so richly earned their censure. (Bothwell, as Ellen Watson's close neighbor, must have known that the cattle had been on her property since October, but all the evidence is that he suppressed this information.) Bothwell pushed Ellen into the back of Sun's buggy, telling her that if she didn't stay in the wagon, he would rope her and drag her to death.[38]

During these events, Gene Crowder suddenly burst out of the house and ran to his pony. Crowder was an eleven-year-old boy who had trouble with his family, and Ellen had taken him in, acting as his surrogate mother. Crowder jumped on his horse and started riding it toward Jim Averell's establishment. Bothwell stopped him, grabbing the horse's halter, knocking Crowder off the horse, and ordering him to go help John Durbin move the calves.[39]

Tom Sun drove the buggy holding Ellen Watson, and the other men rode horses, as they all set out south to Jim Averell's place. The cattlemen found Averell preparing to leave for Casper for supplies, stopped him at gunpoint, and forced him into the buggy with Ellen. Then the group headed north with their terrified captives. Crowder and DeCorey tried to follow, but Bothwell threatened them, and so the two boys turned around and returned to Jim Averell's store, where they found Frank Buchanan, a man in his early twenties who was a friend of Averell's, and Ralph Cole, Averell's teen-aged nephew. Buchanan immediately grabbed a pistol and a horse and chased after the big cattlemen.[40]

The whole procession first drove south and then north on that hot July afternoon and then stopped for what has been referred to as "a long, loud argument," taking perhaps two hours in all. It must have been a hideous ordeal for Jimmy and Ellen, not knowing what was intended for them but overwhelmed by conflicting feelings, ranging from deep anger to disbelief to extreme fear. The big cattlemen drove near the river, where they apparently threatened to drown their two captives.[41] All this looks like aimless meandering, and there must have been times during the afternoon when Jimmy and Ellen had hope that the farce would lose momentum entirely, and they would be turned loose. It is not known exactly why (one theory is that Ellen got "mouthy"), but the procession suddenly veered up into some rocks and pitch pine trees, south of the Sweetwater River.[42]

Jim and Ellen were pulled over near one of the tall pines, and a rope was thrown over a branch. Ernie McLean finally managed to get a noose around Ellen's neck, despite her continuous resistance, and another cattlemen put a noose over Jim Averell's head. Frank Buchanan arrived upon this scene and was able to move behind some rocks about fifty yards away. (Buchanan later made statements about these events while in Rawlins awaiting the convening of a grand jury.) When he saw the alarming predicament of his friends, he started to fire his pistol at the cattlemen. A pistol in 1889 was an extremely short-range weapon, although Buchanan did manage to hit John Durbin in the hip. But the cattlemen returned fire with their rifles, and soon Buchanan ran out of bullets.[43]

Sometime in the middle of all this, perhaps because of Buchanan's forceful interruption, Ellen Watson and Jim Averell were peremptorily shoved off a rock and began a desperate fight for life. Their hands and feet were unbound, and they struggled frantically against their ropes, flailing about to somehow prevent the grip of the choking rope.[44] During her convulsive struggles, Ellen kicked off her new moccasins and they dropped to the ground just inches from her feet.[45] These hangings were not clean executions by a skilled hangman, ones that would have resulted in quick deaths from a broken neck, but stranglings in which the victims became exhausted and slowly asphyxiated. Eventually, inevitably, Ellen and Jim lost their fight with the ropes.

All the parties scattered after it was clear that Watson and Averell were dead, but it was more than two days before a posse from Casper arrived at the scene of the lynching and cut the victims' bodies down.[46] Several days after that Mr. and Mrs. Frank Jameson came to the scene and found Ellen's moccasins.[47]

Action was immediately taken on behalf of the big cattlemen. It is not clear who traveled to Rawlins, but the same day of the lynchings, George Henderson received that ten-word telegraph that led directly to the articles of Ed Towse and Edward Slack, which have ever after framed the debate over the lynchings. Most significantly, these articles established a precedent, a prototypical method by which big cattlemen used the press to manage their violent actions.[48] When the need again arose in late 1891 and 1892, the method was resurrected and extensively employed.

The sensational news stories were apparently effective, especially when coupled with the mysterious disappearances of Frank Buchanan and Gene Crowder (possibly involving foul play) and the suspicious death of Ralph Cole (poisoning was charged), as well as a bevy of the most expensive defense lawyers in the Territory of Wyoming.[49] Some Carbon County authorities worked hard to bring murder charges against the six cattlemen, but in the end, Albert J. Bothwell, Ernest McLean, Robert Conner, Tom Sun, Robert M. Galbreath, and John Henry Durbin were not even indicted. These six men, clearly guilty of atrocious murders, walked free.[50]

The lynchings of Ellen Watson and Jimmy Averell were not official actions of the Wyoming Stock Growers Association, although all but one of the mob was a member of the association. That year, 1889, both Albert Bothwell and Tom Sun were made members of the association's executive committee.[51]

The people of Wyoming may not have been provided the truth about Ellen Watson and Jimmy Averell, but they were certainly dubious about the published versions, and there was a great deal of discussion about the lynchings. H. R. Mann followed the debate and favorably commented upon an article from a Helena, Montana, newspaper that stated that the lynchings were a disgrace to Wyoming. He contrasted this Montana editorial with a pro-lynching article by Asa S. Mercer, editor of the *Northwestern Live Stock Journal*, a newspaper dedicated to the viewpoint of the large cattle interests. Mann deplored Mercer's position and observed that Mercer probably agreed with a recent comment by a prominent cattlemen, "who, at a public meeting last spring stated that if his interests were not afforded better protection, that it would be necessary to hang men even upon suspicion."[52]

Only two or three weeks later Mercer wrote another article about "the late Sweetwater hanging," which Mann found even more offensive. Mercer asserted that hangings would have to be repeated because of the atrocious actions of rustlers in Wyoming. Mercer editorialized:

> There is but one remedy and that is a freer use of the hanging noose. Cattle owners should organize and not disband until a hundred rustlers were left ornamenting the trees or telegraph poles of the territory. The hanging of two culprits merely acts as a stimulus to the thieves. Hang a hundred and the balance will reform or quit the country. Let the good work go on, and lose no time about it.[53]

Mann was understandably shocked by this ugly comment and stated that Mercer had descended to a criminal level and as "doing more to bring the livestock industry of this territory in disrepute than one could suppose a single paper could accomplish." Mann added, "If cattle men have any desire to protect their reputations and hanging is their panacea for all ills, a mild dose administered to the editor of that sheet, might have a tendency to jerk some sense into it, but of this there is no certainty."[54]

It seemed, though, that this shot across the bow of such powerful interests unsettled Mann. He was obviously being pressured by those on both sides of the issue and was trying to tread a careful middle ground, and in a second, subsequent editorial he first made the obligatory condemnation of cattle rustling, emphasized the importance of vigorous prosecution, and then wrote: "If the crime is growing more prevalent, as it is claimed it is, the increase of the crime must be ascribed to the neglect and careless-ness of the police officers of the territory. . . . *The trouble first originates with the people themselves in their neglect and indifference at election time, in not giving some of their attention to the selection of capable officers*" (emphasis added).[55]

This editorial by a committed Republican was an obvious shot at the Democratic sheriff, Red Angus, and neatly served Mann's intent to follow a middle line. It probably never occurred to Mann, who was simply making a tactical political point, that his editorial presented a rationale for harsh punishment of all the citizens of Johnson County for their failure to elect Frank Canton. He certainly had no idea that within three years the big cattlemen would try to do just that.

Commanding even more attention than lynchings and cattlemen's threats, despite their gravity, was the biggest event in the Territory of Wyoming in 1889—the move to statehood. Governor Francis Warren declared that a constitutional convention would convene at Cheyenne in September, and delegates were to be selected in the various counties on July 8.[56] The Johnson County convention was well attended but was probably not representative of the general attitudes within the county. Although a slim majority of the people in Johnson County later voted for statehood, most of those at the convention were unalterably opposed to immediate statehood. The convention resolved that Governor Warren had no authority to call a constitutional convention. It elected delegates only because a state convention was going to be held anyway, and those delegates were instructed to oppose statehood.[57]

H. R. Mann was a proponent of statehood and viewed the selection of delegates to the state constitutional convention, with instructions to oppose statehood, as sheer nonsense. Writing in the *Sentinel*, Mann declared the convention's actions to be "as silly a lot of twaddle as one will often meet with," "farcical," and "debased."[58] Indeed, the Johnson County delegation— H. S. Elliott, Charles H. Burritt, and John M. McCandlish, men who were clearly in favor of statehood and wanted to pitch into the task of writing a good state constitution—found themselves in an awkward position. These three men were appropriate selections as delegates if Johnson County was to be a serious player in the drafting of a constitution, but not necessarily so if the only purpose for their attending the convention was to oppose statehood.[59]

When the constitutional convention met in September, the Johnson County delegates, after an embarrassing interlude in which they half-heartedly opposed statehood, participated actively, especially Burritt.[60] Indeed, the Wyoming Constitutional Convention was probably the shining moment in Burritt's life. His special focus was Article 8, Irrigation and Water Rights, and he played a significant role, along with J. A. Johnston and Elwood Mead, in the creation and passage of five short sections within that article. These sections, which established an administrative law arrangement to enforce the doctrine of prior appropriation, represent the most significant legislative contribution to American law forwarded by Wyoming.[61]

The Wyoming Constitution included another notable provision, one addressing private armies, and that was Section 6 of Article 19: "No armed police force, or detective agency, or armed body, or unarmed body of men, shall ever be brought into this state, for the suppression of domestic violence, except upon the application of the legislature, or executive, when the legislature cannot be convened."[62]

All the provisions of the Wyoming Constitution, including the above section, were adopted by a 37–0 vote and signed by all the delegates present.[63] Among the delegates were George W. Baxter, Cheyenne cattleman and former territorial governor; William C. Irvine, Converse County cattleman; and Hubert E. Teschemacher, Laramie County cattleman. In just three years each of these men would flagrantly violate the constitutional prohibition against the use of private armies.

The Congress accepted the Wyoming Constitution and on July 10, 1890, President Benjamin Harrison signed the Wyoming statehood bill.[64]

CHAPTER SEVEN

Storm Clouds Build

After 1889 there was a lull in the struggle between small cattlemen and big cattlemen, at least partly caused by the financial difficulties of the Wyoming Stock Growers Association; it was certainly not caused by any change in the attitudes of the members of the association. No complaints of cattle depredations were presented to Johnson County authorities by big cattlemen in 1890, but that was because these cattlemen, led by Fred Hesse, had bitterly rejected the idea that better-supported criminal charges would result in convictions for cattle theft.[1] Despite money limitations, some members of the association still actively pursued its goals—for example, by supporting and encouraging the investigations of the association's Detective Bureau. Fatefully, the most active members were two deeply flawed but unusually forceful and determined men: Frank E. Wolcott (usually referred to as "Major" Wolcott, from his rank during the Civil War) and William C. Irvine. Both were big ranchers from Converse County, and these two willful men shaped all the events leading to the 1892 invasion.[2]

By 1891 Wolcott and Irvine decided that strong action against rustlers should be taken. John Clay was the president of the Wyoming Stock Growers Association in 1891, and during the summer of that year he met with Major Wolcott at Wolcott's ranch near Glenrock, Wyoming. Clay later wrote about this event and presented the moment so lyrically that at first the topic of his conversation with Wolcott seems to be life, not death:

Major Frank E. Wolcott. Courtesy
of Johnson County Jim Gatchell
Memorial Museum.

William C. "Billy" Irvine. Courtesy of
Johnson County Jim Gatchell Memorial
Museum.

Major Wolcott and I were walking across a beautiful alfalfa meadow on Deer Creek, a short distance from his house. The great waves of thick hay lay bristling in the sun and, holiday [Fourth of July] as it was, there was no cessation of work. The rakes and the wagons were gathering the green alfalfa into stacks. The hay lifters elevated load after load and winter feed was rapidly accumulating. The subject of stealing on the range came up, and after a good deal of discussion the gallant major said there was urgent necessity for a lynching bee, especially in the northern part of the state, and he developed a plan he had in his mind.[3]

Clay insists that he vigorously sought to discourage Wolcott, but Clay's recollections, written thirty-three years after July 4, 1891, are highly suspect.[4] Less than two months after his meeting with Wolcott, Clay contributed an article to the *Miles City (Mont.) Stock Growers Journal*, in which he referred to thievery on the range and wrote, "Montana, a sister State, grappled with the above difficulty in a masterly fashion. The law refused protection, the cattlemen made a law unto themselves and the fiery cross of Judge Lynch swept across valley and divide. If the sense of the people of Wyoming will not rise to the situation the cattle owners of that State must take a lesson from their neighbors."[5] Clay was referring to the "stranglers" led by Granville Stuart, who were much admired by Wyoming big cattlemen; in the summer of 1884, Stuart's men hanged at least fifteen alleged horse thieves in eastern Montana. L. Milton Woods wrote that "while the vigilantes were charged with terrorizing of innocent settlers, there is no question but that cattle stealing subsided."[6] But the Wyoming cattlemen saw the actions of the Montana stranglers as a positive example. The strength of that example was "underestimated consistently," according to John Burroughs, author of an official history of the Wyoming Stock Growers Association.[7]

Clay's article is hardly a discouragement from a "lynching bee" but rather a *recommendation* of lynching, tempered only by the possibility that the people of Wyoming would "rise to the situation." Clay did not provide details regarding Wolcott's plan, and the assumption has been that Wolcott discussed arrangements leading to the 1892 invasion. Based on Clay's remark about Wyoming people rising to the situation and a new program, however, it strongly appears that Wolcott discussed with Clay a different kind of "lynching bee." Wolcott probably told Clay that he (Wolcott),

William C. "Billy" Irvine, and Hiram B. Ijams had assembled a squad of employees of the stock growers association for the purpose of killing selected individuals. Their idea was that "if they had some of the thieves killed off it would terrorize the balance in such a manner that the most of them would leave the country."[8] That is exactly what was reported by George Dunning and endorsed by Dr. Charles Penrose—both of whom were privy to the inside secrets of the big cattlemen—and it is a statement that fits the events of the next few months. Wolcott and Clay probably also agreed that if this assassination group did not produce the suppression of theft—that is, if Wyoming citizens did not "rise to the situation"—a more ambitious project might be undertaken.

Wolcott, Irvine, and Ijams were to work as a team through the next year and a half. They were deeply and inextricably involved in the sordid events of that period. Indeed, these three men—especially Wolcott and Irvine—were central figures in the invasion plan. There are a great many writings relating to Wolcott and Irvine but fewer for Ijams.

The descriptions of Wolcott are, by and large, consistent, except that his few friends were willing to overlook his deficiencies and the legion of his enemies refused to do so. He must have had some personal charm, given the handful of people—almost all highly useful, powerful men, such as John Clay—who later reported positively about him. Clay wrote a passage about Wolcott that has been frequently quoted, perhaps because it demonstrates such insight: "He was a fire-eater, honest, clean, a rabid Republican with a complete absence of tact, very well educated, and when you knew him, a most delightful companion. Most people hated him, many feared him, a few loved him." This was one of the most favorable statements written about Wolcott. Clay, on another occasion, referred to Wolcott as "inclined to be erratic and vindictive."[9] Burroughs, in *Guardian of the Grasslands*, refers to Wolcott as "one of the most controversial and colorful men who ever lived in the State" and also quotes E. T. David, who stated that Wolcott "had the reputation of having a chip on his shoulder."[10] David was the longtime manager of Joseph M. Carey's ranch properties in central Wyoming (and was Carey's wife's cousin). David's son, Robert, in his book *Malcolm Campbell, Sheriff*, wrote about Wolcott:

He was a polished gentleman. His attitude was confident almost to the point of being cocky, in fact he was somewhat of a bantam rooster. His build was short and beginning to show the signs of fat at the beltline, yet he had the springiness of a cat. . . . He had a strong, well-shaped jaw that closed with a snap after every sentence that he uttered. Wolcott was a man of very positive convictions, and his experience with small ranchmen around his "VR" ranch had often been of a violent nature.[11]

The comments of Wolcott's friends certainly raise questions, and, indeed, people not bound by friendship had quite a different perspective about this short, truculent man from Kentucky.

Wolcott joined a Kentucky regiment at the beginning of the Civil War. He achieved the rank of major, but there were allegations that he left the army under a cloud.[12] Major Wolcott, as he insisted on being called after the war, arrived in Wyoming in 1872 and quickly became as "thick as fleas" with the territorial governor, John A. Campbell, and the new district attorney, Joseph M. Carey. Only a couple of months after Wolcott arrived in Wyoming, he was appointed U.S. marshal.[13] In 1875, though, a new governor, John M. Thayer, was appointed, and Wolcott was quickly removed from office; Thayer wrote that Wolcott was "offensive to almost the whole people."[14] There were allegations that Wolcott was "obnoxious, hateful, overbearing, abusive, insolent and dishonest," and, worse, that he conducted his office corruptly, taking bribes and money rightfully due his deputies.[15]

After his removal as U.S. marshal, Wolcott began a ranch on Deer Creek, south of what is now the town of Glenrock, and, according to John Clay, "with his own savings and the assistance of a friend, he became a cattle owner and prospered."[16] In 1879 Wolcott was elected a member of the Wyoming Stock Growers Association, a year after the election of Irvine.[17] Wolcott's move to the cattle business was also accompanied by controversy, as he located a ranch on land that included the Deer Creek government hay reserve, which was important to nearby Fort Fetterman. It was asserted that the U.S. government repeatedly ordered him from the reserve, but he ignored these orders and took advantage of choice, natural pastures.[18]

It was in his dealings with other settlers that Wolcott's behavior became truly troubling, and it was because of them that he attracted an army of enemies. Detailed information is available about those dealings, but much of it is not completely reliable, as the most thorough (and damaging) allegations come from an anonymous and vituperative pamphlet published in 1886. This pamphlet—*Alias, the Jack of Spades*—carries some authority, however, because it is cogently written, contains much persuasive detail, and a great deal of it is supported by other, more reliable sources. The pamphlet may have been written by E. H. Kimball, editor and publisher of a newspaper at Fort Fetterman. Whoever the author, *Jack of Spades* is a well-constructed writing that certainly seems to have been penned by an experienced and competent writer.[19]

When Wolcott established his ranch, he claimed a huge swath of land on Big Deer Creek and Little Deer Creek, some twelve by eight miles, containing the valleys of these two streams. He fenced off all of this land and was quoted as stating: "The two Deer creeks from their mouths to their mountains belong, sir, to me."[20] His declaration had not a semblance of legitimacy, but that did not keep him from vigorously defending his asserted ownership against all comers. He resisted, apparently successfully, government demands that he take down his fences. There were allegations that he made a series of fraudulent claims under the Desert Land Entry Act.[21]

When settlers came upon the Deer Creek lands and made claims, Wolcott fought them with every means available. The author of the *Jack of Spades* wrote about a man (identified only as "a certain poor man") who came to Deer Creek, built a cabin and a fence across a pasture, raised a crop of hay, and cut it. He then left his claim temporarily, taking a job for wages. Wolcott saw his opportunity: "In this poor settler's absence, his fence was cut all to pieces; his cabin and hay and wagon and machine were burned up. When the settler returned, he found only the ashes of his home." The "disheartened" settler left, never again to return.[22]

Two other men, however—Sumner Beach and Tom Brannan, former employees of Wolcott's—refused to be intimidated by him.[23] They were soon visited by a series of calamities that read like biblical plagues. Wolcott sent emissaries to threaten false charges of rustling and physical harm, made competing claims on the land claimed by Brannan and Beach, bribed officials to enter an earlier date of claim, and filed false civil lawsuits against his former employees. When Brannan cut logs for a house, Wolcott's men threw them all in Deer Creek. Wolcott threatened to kill Beach, and finally, when all his other tactics failed to force Beach out, Wolcott sent a man to kill him. Beach got the drop on the assassin, though, and shot him to death. Wolcott then railroaded Beach, using his office of justice of the peace—in a flagrant violation of his authority—to force a murder indictment against his hated adversary. That indictment was issued by a grand jury whose foreman was Robert M. Galbreath, one of Wolcott's fellow members in the Wyoming Stock Growers Association and one of the six men who later lynched Ella Watson and Jim Averell.[24]

Jack of Spades was issued just before the murder trial of Beach, and its purpose was to present a case against Wolcott, apparently to help Beach. It was most probably unnecessary, however. In tiny communities, such as the area around Deer Creek and the Platte River, a person's reputation is invariably well known. Indeed, it would have been impossible to obtain a jury that did not know all about Major Frank Wolcott. Pat Hall writes that it took the jury "only minutes" to acquit Sumner Beach, giving another big cattleman a reason to curse Wyoming juries.[25]

Jack of Spades made a series of other allegations against Wolcott, stating that he would not pay his bills, including the wage claims of his employees; that he was a "defaulter" and a "cheat"; that the land commissioner, Slaymaker, was a "tool" of Wolcott's; that Wolcott suffered a $27,000 verdict for having appropriated another man's cattle; that he embezzled about $100,000 when he was a U.S. marshal; that he was almost beaten to death by a former employee to whom he refused a team for the burial of his young daughter (and then was chased off his ranch); that surveyors were bribed; that all his neighbors disliked him; and that the English cattle company that Wolcott represented had a scheme for effecting the "larceny" of land.[26]

It would be a mistake to credit all of the emotional claims in the *Jack of Spades* pamphlet, but so much of it is consistent with information from other sources that it would also be a mistake to discard it. Most telling, all of it fits with Wolcott's proven character. Wolcott, though unusual for his extremity, was a classic type, a man who credited only what he wanted, what he desired. He had little sense of fairness, and almost no empathy—except for those in a like situation to his (and not in competition with him). He seemed unable to relate to how others felt and had a complete incapacity to feel the lash on another man's back (to use Lincoln's example), but was extremely sensitive about his own problems.

One big problem for Wolcott in 1891 was that he was going broke. John Clay had loaned him about $80,000 in 1885, but the winter of 1886–87 almost drove Wolcott out of the cattle business. He struggled on for a few years, desperately trying to preserve his little empire, his ranch of "supreme beauty," but finally, soon after 1892, he had to turn over his property to his mortgagees.[27] At least part of the explanation for his frantically angry behavior was that he was losing all that he had so proudly built and, at age fifty, was faced with complete desolation.

One wonders how a man such as Wolcott would ever form lasting friendships, but he had some. Besides some friends from when he first arrived in Cheyenne, John Clay obviously liked Wolcott, and there was another important man to whom Wolcott was quite close, William C. Irvine, who owned a ranch only a few miles south of Wolcott's.[28] It is understandable why Irvine and Wolcott would become good friends, as their circumstances in life were similar and their personalities were very much alike.

Billy Irvine was from a well-to-do Pennsylvania family, was well educated for the time, and first arrived in Wyoming in 1870, when he was eighteen years old. Like Wolcott, he was short; indeed, in one famous photograph, he appears to be distinctly smaller than Wolcott.[29] He worked as a foreman for the Bosler brothers from 1873 to 1876 and was a good employee, except that he quickly developed a reputation as a "fighter and hothead." In 1876 he purchased 4,000 head of Texas longhorns, and set up his own ranch between Douglas and Glenrock. It was said that "with good management" he doubled the size of his herd by 1878.[30]

Irvine became active in politics much later in life, and one commentator noted that his participation, "as in everything else he undertook, was direct and personal." The same commentator tells of when Irvine was the Wyoming state treasurer and was having disputes with the sitting governor, B. B. Brooks. Irvine barged into the governor's office, brushing aside a series of assistants. He locked all the doors and marched up to the governor, stating: "Now, you son-of-a-bitch, you and I are going to have it out."[31] This was only one of myriad examples in which Irvine's belligerent and confrontational methods were on display. Irvine was like a zealous football player who is a delight to his own team but hated by opponents. His "team" was the Wyoming Stock Growers Association, and the members relished his uncompromising defense of even their most outrageous actions.[32]

Wolcott and Irvine shared some of the same friends, such as Joseph M. Carey, and both were devoted to their wives and their children. Unlike Wolcott, however, Irvine usually avoided confrontation with those on his side (though certainly not always).[33] Still, these two men were close enough in personality that when they embraced the same cause, each fed off the other.

Hiram B. Ijams, on the other hand, was not at all like either Irvine or Wolcott. Rather than being a firebrand, he was an accommodator. Ijams first appeared in the Johnson County area in the late 1880s, when he visited Buffalo and Sheridan while working to establish Grand Army of the Republic posts (for Union veterans of the Civil War) in the two towns.[34] He had a connection to the county: he had obtained 120 acres by purchase and sale along the Powder River, about twenty miles northeast of Kaycee; the patent to his land was issued on May 2, 1891.[35]

Ijams did not run a big spread, and it is puzzling why he became connected to the Wyoming Stock Growers Association (and was not identified as one of the small cattlemen in opposition to the big operators). Nevertheless, by 1891 he was the secretary of the association and would remain so until his death in 1896.[36] John Burroughs, probably faithfully reflecting the opinion of other Wyoming Stock Growers Association members, noted that not much was known about Ijams, but said of him, "He was a little man whose head had been turned by responsibilities beyond his capacity. One thing is certain: *he was a talker*" (emphasis in original).[37] Ijams succeeded in his position because he made himself agreeable to the leaders of the association and was ready and willing to do their bidding. Their bidding included matters relating to the assassination squad, the planting of false newspaper stories, and the Wyoming Live Stock Commission. All of this kept Ijams very busy in 1891.

The Wyoming Live Stock Commission was a subject Ijams probably addressed the first day he assumed the secretary's office. When he replaced Thomas B. Adams as secretary of the Wyoming Stock Growers Association in 1891, a new state law had just changed the role of the association in the regulation of the cattle business.[38] There had been much criticism of the stock growers association as a private organization carrying out what should have been governmental functions. The Wyoming legislature, therefore, passed a law creating a new governmental body—the Wyoming Live Stock Commission—to carry out some of the regulatory actions the association had assumed. At first, many big cattlemen were wary of the idea of a livestock commission, believing that the legislature treated them unfairly (contrary to the overwhelming perception of most Wyomingites). John Clay, when writing about the cattle business, stated that "the great industry of the state got scant justice."[39] But several of the 1890 legislators were cattlemen (five in one chamber and nine in the other) and surely had carefully considered the consequences of the legislation. Clay need not have worried. The Wyoming Stock Growers Association quickly hijacked the Wyoming Live Stock Commission. As Burroughs put it, "The following year [1890] the Association's own men took office as Commissioners" (and its secretary, Ijams, took over as secretary of the Commission).[40] Governor Warren appointed James W. Hammond, Charles Hecht, and Billy Irvine as the three commissioners, all of whom were prominent in the Wyoming Stock Growers Association.[41] The appointment of Irvine was especially significant, because it ensured that the commission would include a man with not only an unshakable allegiance to the cause of the big cattlemen of Wyoming but the iron will to forward that cause.

The legislation creating the Wyoming Live Stock Commission seemed benign enough. The act addressed roundups, the appointment of stock inspectors, and the keeping of brand records. It further required that a record be kept of all "estrays" (more commonly known as strays) and that a receipt be given to a shipper for strays, or, in the alternative, that shippers be required to remit to the livestock commission the proceeds of sales of strays. In the latter case, the commission was to retain the money until proof of ownership was established, by affidavit, with one credible corroborating witness.[42] A provision for dealing with strays was quite appropriate, because in a shipment of cattle, especially a large shipment that commonly included a few unbranded animals, a procedure to address the ownership of such animals was needed.

Section 13, the heart of the act stated: "The board of live stock commissioners shall exercise a general supervision over, and so far as may be, protect the live stock interests of the state from theft and disease."[43] This provision was somewhat broad but should have posed no problem had it been interpreted in good faith. Unfortunately, it was not interpreted in good faith, but by W. C. Irvine, a man with malice in his heart toward Johnson County small cattlemen who shipped cattle in the fall of 1891.

Mr. Irvine and his cohorts on the live stock commission decided to interpret "estrays"—by definition, cattle who were wandering at large or who were lost—in a very broad and creative manner and to thereby afflict enemies of the Wyoming Stock Growers Association. When John R. Smith, Lew Webb, Tom Gardner, Jack Flagg, and Robert Foote (and others from Johnson County) shipped their cattle to market in the fall of 1891, the entire shipments, hundreds of cattle, were declared to be "estrays" and seized, and all proceeds of sale were held up.[44] In other words, what was probably the entire yearly income for several Johnson County ranchmen was confiscated. Such cattle would not seem to qualify as strays, because they were all clearly branded. The Live Stock Commission justified these drastic actions, however, by stating that the cattle taken were strays because they were claimed by men "known to be rustlers," and therefore those who asserted ownership of seized cattle had to come to Cheyenne and prove their ownership. The source for the claim of being "known rustlers" was a "northern protective association," which was an organization created in Johnson County in May 1891.[45]

The Northern Wyoming Protective Association was headed by Fred G. S. Hesse and its board of trustees consisted of Hesse, Frank Canton, Frank H. Laberteaux, Fayette Parker, and H. R. Mann.[46] This new organization, working with the Wyoming Live Stock Commission, finally enabled Hesse to strike a blow at his hated adversaries, the small cattlemen who were competing with him for rangeland. He was given the unchallenged power to condemn them as "rustlers" and, by such self-serving declarations, to shatter the economics of their cattle operations. One historian used a baseball metaphor and aptly observed: "It was the perfect triple play—Hesse to the commission to the market, and the rustler was out."[47]

Oddly, at first the commission's actions created little stir. The Wyoming Live Stock Commission certainly played down the new arrangements. In October the *Buffalo Bulletin* ran a short article from the *Cheyenne Sun*, headlined "Effective Work," which referred to the "policy lately adopted to stop cattle thievery." It quoted H. B. Ijams, who blandly (and cynically) remarked that the new policy was "the most effective yet undertaken and is easily spotted, and all animals of questionable title are seized as estrays, no matter by whom sent to market."[48] One reason for the lack of an outcry at first could be that the proofs of ownership had not yet been presented to the livestock commission, and it was not known how the process would eventually play out; it was possible that the seizures would involve only brief delays, that after presentation of evidence of ownership all the money from the shipped livestock would be turned over to the small cattlemen.

The consequences of control of the Live Stock Commission would become all too apparent later in 1891 and in 1892, but in August 1891, shortly after the fateful conference of Clay and Wolcott, the events that people in Johnson County most noticed were unfavorable newspaper stories.

Buffalo had enjoyed the praise of outside newspapers for so long that it was a bit of a shock when, in August, harsh comments about the area started to appear. An eastern newspaper (it was identified only as "Eastern," which could have meant any large town from Omaha eastward) wrote about Johnson County and presented the "wildest and bloodiest tale of savage outlawry." The *Big Horn Sentinel* had gone out of business in October 1889, and in November 1890 a new newspaper, the *Buffalo Bulletin*, was established, with Joe DeBarthe as editor.[49] DeBarthe, thirty-six years old in 1890, had already owned and edited newspapers in Lander and Bonanza, Wyoming, and he was not afraid to express his opinion.[50] He was obviously taken aback by the eastern newspaper's comments, and, writing in the *Bulletin*, he pointed out that property was relatively safe in Johnson County and asked the rhetorical question: "In what eastern state would the owner place his property where he would not see it for six months and come back and have any expectation of finding it at all?"[51]

Just a week later, the *Bulletin* noted attacks from Cheyenne newspapers, saying, "The state press has taken up the subject of thievery on the cattle ranges and the *Cheyenne Daily Leader* is leading the war on the 'rustlers.'" The *Bulletin* did not tie the recent negative stories to big cattlemen, however, and in fact was conciliatory, agreeing that the problem was bad but asserting that it was "not a whit" worse in Johnson County than in any other place in Wyoming.[52] The *Cheyenne Daily Leader* approved of the *Bulletin*'s response and reprinted the *Bulletin* article, accompanied by "commendatory comments."[53]

DeBarthe was aware of small-scale rustling in Johnson County, disapproved of it, and apparently assumed that he and the Cheyenne newspapers were talking about the same thing. But DeBarthe did not realize that the opinions of Cheyenne newspapers were colored by the perspectives of big cattlemen, who saw "rustling" in quite a different light, believing, as they had since at least 1883, that the great majority of northern Wyoming small cattlemen were thieves. By September 1891, however, DeBarthe began to grow weary of the incessant negative comments from Cheyenne. In the September 10 edition of the *Bulletin*, he wrote a strong editorial, telling the *Cheyenne Daily Sun*, in effect, to back up its contentions or shut up. The *Sun* had asserted that there had been wholesale sales of stolen cattle to railroad crews, but the *Bulletin* challenged the *Sun* to furnish the proper officers with facts (apparently never done).[54] In its September 17 edition the *Bulletin* agreed with the *Bonanza Rustler* that "the people of this state are not the thieving lot that a few thoughtless scribers are trying to make the world believe."[55]

In October the *Cheyenne Industrial Record* published an article saying that the "latest class of crime in the Big Horn Basin is the plundering of range storehouses," that cattle and horses were being stolen left and right, and that "somebody will have to be killed." DeBarthe followed up on these charges and interviewed John Donahue, the deputy sheriff from the Big Horn Basin. DeBarthe was told that no cases of warehouse theft in the Basin had been reported and that Donahue had contacted every horse and cow outfit in western Johnson County to see if anyone had lost stock. Donahue reported that he could not find a single individual who knew of a case of horse or cattle stealing during 1891. Upon being pressed, the Cheyenne newspaper finally cited one example of theft at a storehouse in the Big Horn Basin.[56]

These negative articles from Cheyenne were obviously unsettling to Buffalo people, but the great majority of 1891 articles about Buffalo in other newspapers were still quite positive; indeed, it could be said that in 1891 they rose to a crescendo. In January 1891 some good news about a railroad inspired predictions in the *Bulletin* about Buffalo. It was confirmed that the Burlington railroad was to build to the Powder River in the fall, and this news, together with the "glorious tidings" about an increase of troops at Fort McKinney, led the *Bulletin* to declare, "You have the elements of the grandest upbuilding of our progressive little metropolis that could possibly be furnished. . . . Let nothing come between us and the bright sunshine of prosperity, and within five years Buffalo will have become the best city in the west."[57] Just a week after this article, the *Wyoming Commonwealth* seemed to shout back affirmation, saying, "All honor to the enterprising men of Buffalo, who in the short space of eight years have built out of nothing, at a distance of one hundred and sixty miles from a railroad, such a thriving city."[58]

Thereafter, throughout 1891, as in previous years, one favorable article after another appeared in newspapers around the region. In late February the *Bulletin* published a long story from the *Sioux City Journal*, which described all of Buffalo's progressive features, and in August the paper published an article from the *Omaha Bee* that profusely praised the Buffalo area. On October 1 the *Bulletin* published more laudatory outside articles about Johnson County.[59]

Favorable comments from within Wyoming were also reprinted in the *Bulletin*. When U.S. marshal Joe P. Rankin visited Buffalo, he was interviewed by the *Bulletin* and said, "I did not suppose that your city was anywhere near as large or represented so much in capital and advancement as it does."[60] The paper also quoted the views of Henry D. Merritt, who represented the State Board of Mines: "I was led by my experience in other western frontier towns not wholly in Wyoming to expect a very different and less desirable state of facts in this regard, and I am sure that your city, with its well supported churches, the thorough and efficient municipal officers and its quiet, law-abiding citizens is the peer of any city or town in the west as a desirable place of residence."[61] The *Bulletin* quoted an article in the *Lander Clipper*, in which Buffalo was held up to the citizens of Lander as "that model town in Johnson county, Buffalo, which all persons who have ever been there seem to swear by."[62]

Of course, the *Bulletin* reveled in all this praise for its town and county. It responded to Marshal Rankin's observations by saying that "Mr. Rankin's happy disappointment is shared by every stranger who passes through the city."[63] When it learned that the 1890 census showed that, even after Sheridan County split off, Johnson County was the fastest-growing county in Wyoming, the *Bulletin* boasted, "All of this goes to prove what THE BULLETIN has always maintained, that Buffalo has more natural advantages, is better built, better equipped, and on a better financial basis than any city three times its population in the west."[64]

It is understandable that, despite the negative articles that began appearing, the people of Johnson County chose to embrace the view that the county and its county seat were almost universally admired. Yet, in retrospect, they were naive, unwilling to credit a different viewpoint so alien to their usual perspective, and they certainly did not recognize the great danger for the people of the area. The people of Johnson County had only the dimmest notion that there were grim, angry men who saw their county in a completely different light, men who were still furious at the county whose juries, back in 1889, had issued five consecutive acquittals in favor of criminal defendants charged with cattle theft. Indeed, many big cattlemen in Wyoming already saw Buffalo as a center that sheltered and encouraged "rustlers."

Ugly events in the fall of 1891 would show the people of Johnson County that their world was not as they imagined it, but that a new and frightening reality had arrived.

CHAPTER EIGHT

The Killings Begin

Whatever the faults of Frank Wolcott and Billy Irvine, timidity was not one of them. When they decided to act, they followed through. Indeed, they were most probably responsible for a lynching prior to Wolcott's July 4, 1891, visit with John Clay, and in the following months they ordered the killings of several more men in northern Wyoming.

Wolcott and Irvine led the effort to assassinate men they deemed rustlers, but there is persuasive evidence that the two men had the strong support and direction of the leadership of the Wyoming Stock Growers Association. In 1913 Billy Irvine wrote about the association's process of selecting men who were to be killed. Irvine described what he called "evidence," although his example of such evidence—"Nebraska sources" of information against one man "long after the transaction"—seems little more than rumor. Irvine explained that the so-called evidence was directed to Hiram B. Ijams, who would accumulate it. Irvine said that the evidence "was from time to time submitted to the Executive Committee . . . which was composed of two members from each county of the state." The Executive Committee then selected men "they thought should die for the good of the country."[1]

In his 1913 correspondence, Irvine presented the Executive Committee's deliberations as immaculately fair, neglecting to note the absence of protections such as the right of an accused to present a defense. No such thing was allowed, because the committee permitted statements only from those "who we were not suspicious of." Irvine also tried to present the proceedings as relating only to the 1892 invasion, but what he described was a procedure that had been in operation for some time and had applied to earlier assassinations as much as to the efforts at wholesale killing during the invasion.[2]

The instrument used by Wolcott and Irvine to carry out death warrants was the assassination squad they had formed. The members of the group were Frank Canton, Fred Coates, W. C. "Billy" Lykins, Joe Elliott, and, on at least one occasion, Mike Shonsey.[3] The number of men involved in different events varied, evidently depending upon the number of targets and how they were to be killed.

All of these men except Shonsey were probably employees of the Wyoming Stock Growers Association. Canton certainly was. Since March 1888 he had acted as a stock inspector for the association and still lived south of Buffalo.[4] So, too, with Joe Elliott, who had been employed as a stock detective by the association since 1887. Elliott and Coates were both from Weston County, Coates from Newcastle and Elliott from Upton, about thirty miles northwest of Newcastle. In newspaper reports Coates is referred to as a businessman from Newcastle; Elliott knew him well and referred to him as a friend.[5] Elliott also knew Billy Lykins well and worked with him; he spoke of Lykins as a shadowy character who "did the rustlers more harm than anyone else in the country." Of these men, the Wyoming Stock Growers Association admitted to employing only Lykins from 1877 to 1880, but Elliott's statements indicate that he was working for the association after 1887.[6]

The assassination squad carried out its first lynching in June 1891, against Tom Waggoner. Originally from Germany, Waggoner lived in Weston County, near Newcastle, and dealt in horses; at his death it was estimated that he held more than a thousand horses.[7] The *Newcastle Journal* described him in detail: "Tom was about 35 years old, a hearty, strong looking man of medium height, swarthly complexioned, with a small piercing eye, black hair. He was not regarded as a very 'bad' man, but was shrewd enough to never let the chance of turning over a dollar go unimproved. He was quiet, avoiding every show of hospitality or good fellowship, and was penurious to the extreme."[8]

Three men went to Waggoner's house on June 4, saying they were deputies come to arrest him for horse theft, supposedly to take him to jail in Newcastle.[9] About a year later, Jack Flagg described the events for the *Buffalo Bulletin*. It is not clear where Flagg obtained his information, perhaps only from talk among cowboys on the range, but he wrote as if he had special knowledge of the hanging. Flagg described the anguish suffered by Waggoner's wife after her husband was taken away: "The wife of Thomas Waggoner anxiously awaited the return of her husband after leaving with the three men. The hours grew into days, and days into weeks and still he came not. The poor woman grew frantic." A search was undertaken, and soon the man's body was discovered; "The twelfth day after he left home his body was found hanging to the limb of a tree in an out-of-the-way gully. It presented a horrible appearance; the face was black and swollen beyond all recognition and the rope had cut deep into the mortified flesh of the neck." In a powerful passage, Flagg excoriated the men who would do such a thing and those who would order it, writing of how Waggoner "was left to slowly strangle to death while his tormentors stood around and gloated over their devilish work." Flagg asked rhetorically whether "any devil in hell could perpetrate a more heartless and diabolical cruelty."[10] (Flagg's writing demonstrated one reason why Hesse and his confederates hated Flagg so much; not only was he an enemy, but he was an articulate enemy.)

Still, the assassins had chosen their victim well. Waggoner was not well liked, and he could be accused of moral laxity—he had been indicted in Weston County for living with a woman without being married to her, a woman with whom he had a child.[11] Waggoner had quickly remedied this problem by marrying the woman, and the couple had another child, but they still lived an odd existence. At his death Waggoner's valuable estate included substantial property, chiefly horses, but he and his wife lived in squalor, dwelling in a two-room log cabin that contained no beds or chairs, only a bench and boxes.[12]

A probate was established in Weston County, and, remarkably, the administrator named was Fred Coates, a man believed to be one of the three men who took Waggoner away to his execution.[13] Coates's friend Joe Elliott was also accused of being one of those three, although he insisted he had nothing to do with the killing. Elliott did admit, however, that he had once threatened to get Waggoner, and he was the one who found Waggoner's body during the search. Elliott had assisted with putting Waggoner's body in a box and burying him and had also helped with the disposal of Waggoner's horses. Although the three men who took Waggoner from his home were probably Elliott, Coates and Lykins, no solid evidence was developed against any person, and no one was ever arrested for the killing.[14] The public was provided with little information as to who might have been behind Waggoner's hanging or why, which is the probable reason that no strong objection was registered about such anomalies as Coates's appointment as executor. Accusations were thrown around. The big cattlemen accused rustlers of doing it, and those identified as rustlers accused the big cattlemen of being behind it.

The idea that rustlers lynched Tom Waggoner is absurd. The big cattlemen were the only ones with any motive to kill him, and the only ones who premeditatedly killed their adversaries, at least until May 1892. One need only read later statements by Billy Irvine and Joe Elliott to know what the big cattlemen thought of Waggoner. Many years after Waggoner's death, Irvine referred to Waggoner as "one of the most successful thieves that the country ever knew," and Joe Elliot said Waggoner was "one of the worst thieves I ever knew of." Waggoner was never charged with any crimes, although Elliott asserted evidence of the theft of at least two horses. Waggoner was a sharp dealer, but Joe Elliott admitted before a half dozen Buffalo residents that "he had tallied out 1100 animals and had not found a crooked animal in the lot."[15]

Hiram Ijams also made admissions about Waggoner's killing. In February 1892, Ijams told George Dunning about the methods of the Wyoming Stock Growers Association, saying that it "made a contract with certain parties to kill off 15 men who were considered by the stock association to be the leaders among the thieves in Johnson co." Ijams mentioned several examples, including "the hanging of a man by the name of Wagoner."[16] Jack Flagg asserted that Ijams gloated after Waggoner was hanged, saying, "We hung one of the sons of b——s and we will get some more of them, and their families won't save them."[17] This statement is not independently substantiated but is consistent with Ijams's reported penchant for talk.

After Waggoner's lynching, the assassination squad turned to new victims. A logical next choice was the men of the Hat brand, Fred Hesse's bane. Hesse was so obsessed with pinning something on these men that in late 1889 he hired a spy who pretended to be an itinerant cowboy in need of work and got on at the Hat Brand Ranch. But Hesse's spy apparently never uncovered wrongdoing, for nothing ever came of this scheme.[18] By 1890, however, the Hat brand had broken up, and three of the members had taken up other ranches. These operations were still within Johnson County, but good distances away from the Hat brand headquarters on

Nate Champion. Courtesy of Johnson County Jim Gatchell Memorial
Museum.

the Red Fork of the Powder River. Tom Gardner removed to Lower
Crazy Woman Creek, which was the next drainage north of the Powder
River, and Lew Webb and Billy Hill moved downstream from the Red
Fork, east to the Middle Fork of the Powder River. Flagg and Al Allison
stayed on the Red Fork, where Allison was joined in 1889 by his half-
brother John A. Tisdale. (Allison used a different last name because of
trouble back in Texas; his true name was Martin Allison Tisdale.)[19]

The men of the Hat brand had distributed their cattle so that each got
"35 two-year-old steers, 30 cows, eleven yearlings, 4 two-year-old steers."
In general, this arrangement would indicate that the five men divided a
herd that had naturally increased from an original herd of about 150 cows
and calves in 1888 and probably also included at least a few mavericks and
some animals acquired through small trades.[20] The big cattlemen attributed
this increase not to "good management," as was done in the similar case
of Billy Irvine, but to rustling.[21] By 1891 big cattlemen apparently viewed
other small cattlemen as more of a threat—most notably, Nate Champion.

Nate Champion was admired and respected by most of the people in
Johnson County. He was small and quiet but had a well-earned reputation

as a tough man. The *Bulletin* wrote of him in early 1892: "No man who knows him would not swear by him. His reputation among men has always been the best. He was formerly one of the most trusted of Wyoming cowboys, but when he bought cattle for himself, he was put upon the black list, and has never complained."[22]

Champion was born in September 1857 in Williamson County, Texas (just north of Austin), and he went to Wyoming in the early 1880s. He was a boyhood friend of Al Allison and John Tisdale, as well as Tom Gardner and Billy Hill.[23] Champion was a valued hand on the EK Ranch of Horace Plunkett when Ed Spaugh was the EK's foreman. When the EK's herds were purchased by the American Cattle Trust, Champion followed Spaugh to a new employer. But then Spaugh was fired in late 1888 (apparently because he was too accommodating to small cattlemen). Champion was let go at the same time and shortly thereafter obtained his own brand.[24]

Champion was later referred to as "King of the Rustlers" by big cattlemen, but this nickname was an outrageous lie, a convenient slogan without support. There is no record in Johnson County of any charges having been pressed against Nate Champion. Most significantly, Willis Van Devanter, the chief attorney and ally of the big cattlemen in Wyoming, made an important admission regarding Champion. In June 1892, when Van Devanter would have given almost anything to prove that Nate Champion was a prolific cattle thief, he had to admit to Senator Joseph M. Carey that "there is absolutely no proof of any kind against him [Champion],— not even that he stole a calf."[25]

Two 1891 incidents demonized Champion in the minds of big cattlemen. One occurred in the early part of the 1891 season, when four or five of Champion's cows became mixed with herds belonging to other ranches (EK, NH, Bar C) of which Mike Shonsey was the foreman.[26] Champion went to Shonsey and asked him to separate his (Champion's) animals from those of the big cattle outfits for whom Shonsey was working. Shonsey agreed to do so, but when it was done, Shonsey just scattered Champion's cattle. In the West, known for its hospitality, such a gratuitously rude action would have been considered particularly offensive. Champion let Shonsey know that he did not appreciate his actions, and it created lasting hard feelings between the two men.

The second incident was more significant and involved Robert Tisdale (brother of John N. Tisdale, no relation to John A. Tisdale), who ran a big operation in far southern Johnson County. It is hard to know exactly what happened, because the accounts of this incident are muddled and, in the case of Robert David's version, deliberately distorted, but the general outlines are clear enough.[27] Tisdale moved 2,000 cattle into a huge pasture—100,000 acres has been given as the estimated size—lying generally in the southern part of the Hole in the Wall country (about forty miles south of Buffalo and west of Kaycee). Thereafter Champion, reasoning that there was room for his small herd of 200 animals, also brought his cattle to this pasture. Tisdale apparently took offense at this and pulled his cattle out of the area, but in so doing, he also pulled out some of Champion's cattle. Champion and some of his friends pursued the Tisdale herd and proceeded to reclaim Champion's cattle, including the associated calves. Champion and his group were well armed and acted aggressively in seizing the cattle. Fred Hesse was later to present this episode as an example of brazen cattle theft. He asserted that Champion and the men with him had worked openly, while brandishing Winchesters and revolvers, and had intimidated owners and foremen and branded "anything they chose." Hesse declared that, "the law being inoperative," the foremen of several outfits acted so as not to endanger their lives.[28]

This seems to be one more example of overstatement by Hesse, although it certainly shows how big cattlemen regarded Champion. After April 1892 both Hesse and John N. Tisdale were represented by Willis Van Devanter and had full opportunity and incentive to persuade their lawyer that Champion was guilty of crimes. Obviously, based upon Van Devanter's comments set out above, they were unable to do so. What is most important about Champion's disputes with Shonsey and Tisdale, however, is that they were the source of deep anger against Champion by big cattlemen. From the viewpoint of the big cattlemen, Nate Champion, by vigorously standing up for his rights to the grass on the public domain, was a bad example, an example made all the worse because Johnson County citizens looked up to him.

Champion ran his cattle in the Hole in the Wall country, a large valley in southern Johnson County. Jack Flagg provided a good description of this area, observing that it consisted of "a strip of land thirty miles in length, bounded on the west by the Big Horn Mountains, and on the east by a natural wall of rocks, [such] that the whole distance of thirty miles only had four openings through which stock could go, and as none of the openings were over a quarter mile wide, it was a very small matter to keep them fenced."[29] What Flagg did not say is what beautiful country it is. The topography—the up and down of the place—is dramatic, as the area sits between the east wall and the east slope of the Big Horn Mountains. The east wall consists of striated formations of deep, dusty red sandstone, and that red wall seems to go on forever, stretching across the length of the horizon. The colors of the place are striking too, not just the red and white of the rock formations but, especially in the spring, the many subtle shades of green, from bright green grass to the timber's deep forest hues and the silver-green leaves of the sagebrush.

The whole valley opens up when a traveler climbs a rise, such as the high bluffs above the emergence of the Middle Fork from its canyon. The stream flows from the mountain into a small alluvial plain, and since the 1880s this plain has been irrigated for grass. From that high bluff the narrow floor of the canyon can be seen, including the water in the creek and, not thirty yards from the creek, the foundation of an old cabin probably built sometime in the 1880s. On the morning of November 1, 1891, that cabin was occupied by Ross Gilbertson and Nate Champion.

The cabin was "unbelievably small," just large enough to hold a stove and a bunk bed (the bed kept the door from swinging all the way open), and the roof was so low that an average man had to stoop to get in.[30] The season must have been warm before November, because Champion reported it was the first time that the cabin door had been closed since spring.[31] He also remembered that he had awakened early, had petted the cat, and then had gone to sleep again. Perhaps the cat's gentle purring soothed him and helped him drift back to sleep. But as Champion dozed, four men crept toward the cabin.

Frank Canton, Fred Coates, Joe Elliott, and Billy Lykins stealthily worked their way through the brush, quietly approaching the cabin with guns drawn. Seventy-five yards behind them, Mike Shonsey was holding their horses.[32] The five men had apparently decided that the best way to kill Nate Champion was to ambush him early in the morning while he was still asleep in the cabin. This tiny structure was tucked into the canyon and could be approached safely, because it was fronted by trees, bushes, and undergrowth.

Champion said later that he was suddenly jolted awake when two men burst in the front door and stood with guns drawn at the foot of his bed. A third man stood just outside the door. Nate could see the bright light from the open door but could not identify any of the men.[33]

Nate heard a voice say, "Give up, boys, give up."[34]

"Who are you and what do you want?" Nate asked. As he spoke, he stretched as if in a yawn, but was actually reaching for his gun under a pillow. The strangers in the cabin apparently saw Champion pull the gun out of its holster, because two shots were immediately fired at him, one so close that it barely missed his head and left powder burns on his face.

In those small confines, the shots must have sounded like cannons firing, a sound that would panic almost any man but Nate Champion. His return fire, on the other hand, did cause panic, as the intruders piled out of the cabin. Champion fired another shot at the fleeing men through the door space, aiming about middle level. When he looked out of the window, he saw a man running away, holding his stomach.

The man running away was Billy Lykins, and Champion had wounded him mortally. It took more than a month for Billy to die, though, and his death came not in Wyoming but in Missouri, where Lykins was taken.[35]

Champion spotted a rifle outside the cabin, and, thinking it would be handy in a gunfight, went outside to get it. Just at that moment a man emerged from behind the side of the cabin and leveled down on Nate. Nate jumped back into the cabin, and the man did not fire but ran back into the brush, away from the cabin. Nate did not recognize this man, but he did get a good look at him.[36]

In a short while, Champion and Gilbertson, who was showing a distinct lack of stomach for the whole business (throughout the ordeal it seems he just sank into a corner while Champion fought for their lives.), set out after the attackers. About seventy-five yards from the cabin they found four overcoats as well as tracks indicating that four men had approached the cabin.[37] Two or three days later, Champion heard that he might find some evidence in Beaver Creek Canyon and went there with John A. Tisdale and another man. Champion found six branded horses (including one owned by Joe Elliott), as well as gear, including a bloody tarpaulin.[38]

After the attack, Champion had gone up the Red Fork of the Powder River, a stream that flows within the Hole in the Wall and extends northwest from its juncture with the Middle Fork of the Powder River. His purpose was to visit Tisdale, whose homestead was the farthest upstream of several on the Red Fork. Flagg, Orley E. "Ranger" Jones, and Johnny Jones, Ranger's brother, also lived on the Red Fork, but downstream from Tisdale. When riding to Tisdale's home, Champion probably went past Jones's homestead.[39]

John A. Tisdale, born in Texas in 1855 of a prosperous and well-respected family, was unusually well educated for a nineteenth-century man, having graduated from St. John's College in Texas. Tisdale went north in 1883 and then worked as a foreman for Theodore Roosevelt in North Dakota and Montana. A family friend, Roosevelt presented a high chair to Tisdale and his wife, Kate, upon the birth of their oldest son, Martin, in 1887. (By 1891 the couple had two more children, with another on the way.) In 1889 Tisdale inherited some money and used it to stake a homestead on the Red Fork. Al Allison, his half-brother, was already there, and Tisdale joined him. The two men were apparently compatible but were dissimilar in many ways. Allison was not well educated and had a reputation as a black sheep in the family because of his past criminal trouble; he did not have Tisdale's high standards and character. Allison, as part of the Hat brand, had been blacklisted, but Tisdale never was. During Tisdale's lifetime, there was never an accusation that he was a rustler, although his relationship to Allison probably did him no good in the eyes of big cattlemen.[40]

Champion went to Tisdale because he wanted to enlist the help of a well-regarded and capable citizen. Champion told Tisdale that he knew there was going to be a fight, but that while he (Champion) could fight, he felt he couldn't lead a fight (apparently meaning that he was a good soldier but not necessarily a good general).[41] Tisdale agreed to go with him to Beaver Creek Canyon in search of the culprits. At least one other man, whose identity is unclear, accompanied Champion and Tisdale to Beaver Creek Canyon. (T. F. Carr said the other man was Nick Ray, but was possibly Orley E. "Ranger" Jones; both Jones and Ray were small stockmen.)[42]

When Champion and his companions arrived at Beaver Creek Canyon, Champion saw Mike Shonsey, whom he suspected as one of the attackers.[43] Seeing Shonsey not far from where the incident had occurred at the cabin, Champion was angry. He threatened to kill Shonsey if he did not divulge the names of the men who had attacked him and Gilbertson.[44] Shonsey had surely been told all about the incident at Champion's cabin— and he must have heard the shots and seen what happened to Lykins. He would have had little doubt that instant death awaited him if he refused

John A. Tisdale and his wife, Kate. Courtesy of Johnson County Jim Gatchell Memorial Museum.

to comply with Champion's demand. Indeed, Martin Tisdale, John A. Tisdale's oldest son, later stated that he believed that the only reason Nate Champion did not kill Shonsey on the spot was that Shonsey told Champion what he wanted to know. In the presence of Champion, John Tisdale, and their companion, Shonsey admitted that the men who had tried to kill Champion and Gilbertson were Joe Elliott, Frank Canton, Bill "Likens" [sic], and Woodbox Jim.[45] By process of elimination, "Woodbox Jim" had to have been Fred Coates. (Significantly, Shonsey later sent Woodbox Jim to Buffalo to tell Canton that he had been forced to admit who was in the attacking party. No doubt Canton was also informed who was present when the admissions were made.[46])

At the moment Shonsey made his admissions, John Tisdale and his companion (that "other man") ceased to be onlookers and became witnesses to the attempted murder of Champion and Gilbertson. They could each testify in a court of law that Shonsey had identified the attackers, because the admissions of one member of a criminal conspiracy are admissible in evidence against all members.[47]

News of the assault on Champion and Gilbertson quickly reached Buffalo, but people in Buffalo did not recognize it as an attack by big cattlemen. The *Bulletin* ran a relatively short article, which did not express great alarm but viewed the event as a puzzling happening out on the range. The article closed with, "The attack on Nate and Ross is shrouded in considerable mystery, for there is not the least known cause for any such attempt at murder."[48]

Those behind the attack, however, had to have seen the event in more dire terms. Wolcott and Irvine were presented with a catastrophe. Not only did the assassination squad fail to kill Nate Champion, not only was one of their employees mortally wounded, but the squad also left two witnesses to a charge of attempted murder, a number that grew to four with Shonsey's confession before Tisdale and the other man. Worse, convictions of the perpetrators could lead back to those who hired them. Irvine, Wolcott, Ijams, and, probably, every member of the Wyoming Stock Growers Association's Executive Committee could be looking at long prison terms.

It would not take long for people in Johnson County to lose their naiveté and see the attack, and subsequent attacks, in exactly the terms feared by big cattlemen—that the killings were part of a conspiracy among big cattlemen. In December the *Bulletin* started running editorials declaring that the authorities should concentrate on bringing charges against the higher-ups, the "stock interests of this state."[49]

Unlike the public at large, Sheriff Red Angus and his deputies took the assault on Champion and Gilbertson seriously from the time they learned of it, undertaking an extensive investigation while preparing a case against the attackers.[50] Contrary to the contentions of Johnson County Republicans, Angus had been diligent about his responsibilities from the day he took office.

Before his first term began in January 1889, Angus sought to learn about his new job, going to work in early December as a deputy for Sheriff E. U. Snider, so that he could "see how it seems" to act as a peace officer.[51] In 1889 Sheriff Angus brought only a few new cases, but in 1890 the sheriff investigated and forwarded about fifteen charges, including four livestock theft charges.[52] Only one of these charges was brought to trial by the Johnson County attorney, however, and not until H. S. Elliott left office. Elliott, still the county attorney in 1890, seems never to have recovered from his disastrous experience in July 1889; he never again brought a criminal case before a Johnson County jury.[53]

The remaining case was *State v. B. Rice McCarthy*, which was brought to trial in November 1891, a year after the charges were first filed and after Elliott had left office.[54] Angus and the Buffalo town marshal had fashioned a good case against McCarthy. They had suspected him of cattle stealing for some time, so they trailed his wagon and discovered the hide of a beef belonging to John Stevenson. Then they searched McCarthy's ranch and found suspicious circumstances indicating that McCarthy might have killed another cow owned by Stevenson.[55] The trial took several days and resulted in a conviction of petit larceny, as the jury determined that the value of the cow that McCarthy had clearly taken and killed was $18.75. Judge John W. Blake, who was tougher on criminals than Judge Micah Saufley had been, gave McCarthy the maximum penalty: six months in jail and a $100 fine.[56]

In 1891 Angus brought several criminal charges, including two for the killing of cattle, as well as other serious charges for burglary and theft.[57] One of the 1891 cattle cases resulted in acquittals, and the other in a conviction (with the help of the testimony of Sheriff Angus), for which a defendant was sentenced to a year in the penitentiary in Laramie. The burglary and theft charges produced a two-year prison sentence and a ten-year sentence, respectively.[58]

Several articles appeared in the *Buffalo Bulletin* about Angus in 1891. They showed that the sheriff was working hard to prevent escapes from his jail; that he could regale a group (by being a "capital story teller"); that he had been diligently working at his job, even when a big chunk of glass embedded in his thumb tried "to become part of his anatomy" (as a local newspaper described a piece of glass that took months to work its way out of Angus's thumb); and that the residents of the new town of Gillette thought enough of the Johnson County sheriff to name a street after him.[59] Men in the Johnson County area liked and identified with Red Angus. Like most of them, the sheriff was a down-to-earth person who was trying to do the best job he could. The big cattlemen, heavily influenced by Frank Canton, condemned Angus as not performing his job as sheriff and presented cattle theft as a problem of major proportions, but the independent evidence is contrary.

The 1890 and 1891 cattle theft prosecutions were like those of the 1880s, in that virtually all of them involved single animals, and there was little evidence of large-scale "depredations" of the big cattle herds owned by Johnson County members of the Wyoming Stock Growers Association. Even into late 1891, the criminal case records in Johnson County support none of the complaints and allegations of the big cattlemen. Rather, they are consistent with the belief of most Johnson County residents that rustling was a minor problem, used as an excuse by the big cattlemen to go after competitors they could not otherwise run off through intimidation. Whatever their true motivations, however, the big cattlemen were determined adversaries, not easily deflected, and their attempts at intimidation had just begun.

CHAPTER NINE

More Killings

The first terrible thunderbolt in what was thought of as the Johnson County War was the assassination of John A. Tisdale on December 1, 1891. Tisdale's murder so shocked the residents of the county that they gave their whole attention to it, and their in-depth newspaper stories, as well as testimony before a coroner's jury and at a preliminary hearing, allow the reconstruction of the Tisdale murder in remarkable detail.

Tisdale had come to Buffalo about November 25, probably for the first time since the attack on Champion and Gilbertson on November 1.[1] While there, he undoubtedly spoke to Sheriff Angus and county attorney Alvin Bennett. Whether because of his conversation with the criminal authorities or other information he received, Tisdale became alarmed for his safety. For three or four days before he left Buffalo, he drank heavily. This behavior was uncharacteristic of him—the *Bulletin* said it was the first time the people of Buffalo had seen Tisdale "in his cups." He told people that he was afraid to set out for his home alone, because he thought someone would try to kill him. There is evidence that he wanted Nate Champion to accompany him home, but despite delaying his departure, he was unable to find his neighbor.[2] On Monday morning, November 30, he finally decided to set out but first purchased a double-barreled shotgun, which he had by his side when he left Buffalo. His wagon was full of provisions, including his children's Christmas gifts, which sat on top of his supplies; John Washbaugh later remembered seeing a toy drum that was intended for Tisdale's oldest son, Martin.[3]

The roads were reported to be heavy with mud, and slow, and Tisdale's team could proceed only at a slow walk. He had traveled about five or six miles when he stopped at sundown at the Cross H Ranch.[4] At the Cross H he again expressed fear for his safety, and asked that the window curtains be pulled down.

The next morning, Tisdale ate breakfast at the Cross H and then set out about 8:00 A.M.[5] His team had made only about three miles when he came to a deep gulch, probably close to 10:00 A.M.[6] There a man lay in ambush, using a "high rising bank" next to the road to conceal himself. The man had arrived at the scene on horseback and had tethered his horse about a hundred yards up the gulch. He had then walked to the spot where the road crossed the gulch. He stayed there for some time and on several occasions walked from the gulch to the brow of the hill, apparently watching for Tisdale. Tisdale drove his team into the gulch, and when the wagon started uphill, the waiting man had an open shot at point-blank range. He fired his rifle twice. The slug from the first shot hit Tisdale's six-shooter and glanced off. Tisdale was trying to turn around and fire his shotgun, when a second shot smashed through the center of his torso, inflicting a mortal wound. The killer then led the wagon about eight to nine hundred yards down the gulch (eastward), where he shot the horses. Tisdale had collapsed with his feet over the dashboard, and the gunmen left him lying in the wagon. Tisdale's dog apparently followed the killer, and the killer shot the dog.[7]

Only a few minutes after 10:00 A.M., Charlie Basch came along the road, proceeding northward toward Buffalo. He saw a man leading horses into the gulch and as he continued on the road, he saw the man four times in and around the gulch and once came within about fifty to sixty yards of the man, who spurred his horse and moved away from Basch. At first, Basch said he had not recognized this man, nor his horse, although the horse the man was riding seemed familiar.[8] Basch was continuing northward when he heard two shots coming from about a mile behind him; they were probably the shots that killed Tisdale's horses. Basch did not go back to the gulch, though, and soon met Elmer Freeman of the Cross H Ranch, who was riding south. Freeman asked Basch if he had seen Tisdale; Bausch told him he had not and relayed what he had seen and heard. All of this seemed highly suspicious to Freeman, who immediately rode back to Buffalo to report to Sheriff Angus, arriving at about 11:35. Undersheriff Howard Roles, Freeman, Deputy John Donahue, and Tom Gardner left Buffalo about noon and arrived at the crime scene at about 12:30. They found a blood trail starting from the road, as well as the unshod tracks of a third horse, probably the killer's horse. The blood trail led down the gulch, directly to Tisdale's body in the wagon. Tisdale had fallen backwards and had bled all over his children's Christmas gifts.[9]

A "special messenger" was assigned the grim task of going to Tisdale's home and giving Kate Tisdale the worst message a loving wife could ever receive. For their part, the people of Buffalo were stunned. They found Tisdale's murder hard to believe. They could assign no reason for, as the *Bulletin* put it, this "dastardly, cold-blooded, deliberate murder," as Tisdale had "borne the name of a straight-forward, honest-dealing man" since coming to the area. "If he had any enemies nobody seemed to know them," the *Bulletin* reported. "He paid his bills regularly, was popular with his neighbors and was getting some little property about him. He had a few head of cattle on the range, but was never known as a rustler. The motive of his murderer is therefore unfathomable."[10]

The people of Buffalo probably had no idea that Tisdale had become an important witness in the case against Nate Champion's attackers. The county attorney and the sheriff would have been reluctant to give that information to the local newspapers. To lament that they had just lost an important witness would have been an invitation for assassins to go after the remaining witnesses. Too, Red Angus and Alvin Bennett may not have realized how uncomfortable their investigation of the assault on Champion and Gilbertson was making some high officials of the Wyoming Stock Growers Association. The big cattlemen were acutely aware of witnesses against their employees, and they emphasized the importance of killing all such witnesses.[11]

Though the people of Johnson County may not have understood why Tisdale was killed, they were certainly aware that his killing was a deliberate act, an execution undertaken for a purpose, and they were irate. The *Bulletin* reported that the feeling about this murder was "pretty high," but cautioned the people of the county to remain calm, saying that the murderer was certain to be discovered and that it was imperative that everyone proceed "with the greatest care and circumspection." The editor of the *Bulletin* observed that the people of Johnson County were a "law-loving and law-abiding class" and that it was more important than ever that they continue that way. But another shocking event would test Johnson County even more. Two days after Tisdale's body was found, authorities discovered another body in a wagon. Orley "Ranger" Jones, like John Tisdale, had been shot to death.[12] (Later investigation would show that Jones had actually been shot before Tisdale.)

Ranger Jones was a young man, only twenty-three. He was engaged to be married and was building a cabin on Red Fork for himself and his wife-to-be. On November 20, 1891, he set out for Buffalo in a wagon. His purpose was to get some flooring lumber for the cabin, and he told his brother that he would be gone for four or five days. When he did not return within that time, Johnny Jones went to Buffalo. The authorities in Buffalo, fearing that Jones may have suffered the same fate as Tisdale, immediately launched a search. Jones had left Buffalo on November 28, and several people reported seeing him heading south. The last sighting had been near Muddy Creek, about fourteen miles south of Buffalo.

On December 3, James Rinker was riding south from Buffalo and was watching for wagon tracks leaving the main road. He noticed some tracks near the Muddy Creek bridge and followed them. Soon Rinker came upon Ranger Jones's buckboard with Jones's body inside; he appeared to be dead. Evidently Rinker did not go up to the wagon but immediately rode back to Buffalo and found the sheriff. A posse followed Rinker to the scene and found that Ranger Jones had been shot and was quite dead.[13]

The evidence at the scene showed that killers had waited under the Muddy Creek bridge and then, when Jones drove over it, had come out and shot him in the back. Three shots had been fired. As with Tisdale (shot two days later), the first bullet did no damage but the following shot was fatal. In fact, there were two following shots at Jones. One went through his side and the other through his chest, and either would have been fatal. There was another way in which the two killings were different. According to both Jack Flagg and John Washbaugh, there were at least two perpetrators of the Jones killing, and perhaps three.[14]

The headline in the *Buffalo Bulletin* that announced the killing of Ranger Jones ("HORRORS ACCUMULATE") shows the reaction of the community to this second event.[15] Jones was well liked and was admired for his athletic prowess in breaking horses. Noting that Jones was a "splendid rider," Flagg wrote, "It was really wonderful to see him ride; he had such a grip in his knees that he could fairly make a horse groan, and a horse could only pitch a short while until he would have to stop to get his breath."[16]

The Jones murder caused the community to be "terribly worked up," said the *Bulletin*, and the newspaper said that trouble was expected. Every man started carrying a Winchester rifle to protect himself. The remarkable thing is that no trouble arose, not even for Frank Canton, almost universally believed one of the killers. The reason for the calm, stated the *Bulletin*, was Red Angus. In an editorial, the paper congratulated the people of Buffalo for having a sheriff "who has proved himself worthy of the great trust imposed in him." The newspaper wrote of how Angus gently but firmly dealt with a "sea of angry men who came here crying for vengeance" but who were "lulled and quieted . . . by the earnest appeal of this man to a justly indignant people."[17]

The threat of vigilante action was real. Even some of the soldiers at Fort McKinney recommended it. Fort McKinney's troops took a surprisingly active interest in Johnson County events and had strong views. They contributed a column to the *Bulletin* each week, and in the December 10, 1891, column, the writer recommended a lynching if justice could not be obtained against the men who killed Tisdale and Jones.[18]

That same issue of the *Bulletin* told of recent reports from Cheyenne to the effect that Angus was in league with rustlers. Asserting that these statements were a "vile slander" and "a lie, pure and simple," the paper observed that Angus had even been considerate to Frank Canton, that his treatment of Canton had "called forth merited commendation," and that publishing that fact had been done "at Mr. Canton's personal request."[19]

Frank Canton had occasion to praise Red Angus because he spent a few days in Angus's jail. Canton had asked to be there. So much talk was sweeping Buffalo about Charlie Basch's having seen Frank Canton's horse Fred at the scene of the Tisdale murder that Canton demanded to clear his name, insisting upon his own arrest and examination for the murder of John Tisdale.[20] Given the excited state of the community, it was a bold move, even for Frank Canton, but as a result, on Tuesday, December 8, 1891, a strange and remarkable procedure began, wherein the accused took charge of his fate, challenging his accusers to produce the evidence they had against him.

Canton was predictably represented by Mayor Charles Burritt, and the state by Alvin Bennett, the county attorney. The case was heard by Justice of the Peace C. H. Parmelee. Testimony was heard from twenty-eight witnesses, and it continued until 10:00 P.M. in the evening. [21] In the end, the decision was not a difficult one. Mr. Bennett had the burden of establishing probable cause to believe that Frank Canton had shot and killed John A. Tisdale at about 10:00 A.M. on December 1. All the attorney was able to show is that the killer appeared to be riding Frank Canton's horse Fred, that the killer wore clothes similar to those Canton sometimes wore, and that Canton's horse had been newly shod on the afternoon of December 1. Against this evidence—which proved no more than a suspicion—Canton presented ten witnesses, who, taken together, established a solid alibi for him, showing him to have been in Buffalo the entire morning of Tisdale's killing.

Charles Basch was the main witness for the prosecution, and his testimony was not strong. He testified that he was riding north toward Buffalo the morning of December 1, and when he reached a gulch about eight miles south of the town, he saw a man riding a horse. Basch confirmed his observations of this man. When Basch had testified earlier before the coroner's jury, he was unwilling to swear that the horse was Canton's horse Fred, though he knew the horse well and had once ridden him for twelve miles. Now, however, Basch said that he was willing to swear that the horse he saw was Fred.

Basch also knew Canton well, had known him for over nine years (during seven of which Basch lived on his ranch near Canton's homestead south of Buffalo), but he did not recognize the man he saw in the gulch and could not say that he had seen that man since. He testified that he had seen Canton wear an overcoat and hat similar to the ones worn by the man in the gulch, but he did not know if Canton had worn these recently.

The problem with Basch's testimony is that it did not establish the probability that Canton had been the man Basch saw the morning of December 1—and Basch was the prosecution's strongest witness. Other witnesses, including Thomas Gardner and Lew Webb, testified only that Canton had admitted having Fred shoed on the afternoon of December 1, but this did not go very far toward meeting the prosecution's burden.

In contrast to the prosecution's witnesses, the defense witnesses testified directly to a crucial point—where Frank Canton was the morning of December 1. His lawyer called Dr. John Lott, a physician; George W. Munkres, a hardware store owner; Frank H. Eggleston, a drugstore owner; Dr. Park Holland, another physician; and H. W. Devoe, a local ranchman and apparently the brother of a Johnson County commissioner; as well as James T. Craig, an area cattleman, Buffalo residents I. N. Pearson and Robert Dunn, and Canton himself. Every one of these witnesses put Canton in Buffalo at times between 9:00 and 11:00 A.M. on the morning of December 1, which was the probable time the killer was abroad.[22] As is always true in such situations, the times remembered were not exact, but Canton could put forward at least four credible witnesses covering each half hour interval between 9:00 and 10:00 A.M., and four more who would show him in Buffalo at 11:00 A.M.[23] It was a compelling case, showing that Canton could not have been the man who killed Tisdale. The prosecution offered nothing to rebut the testimony of any of these witnesses.

C. H. Parmelee was a conscientious lawyer and, though a political partisan, was a man of integrity.[24] No lawyer could fairly look at the case presented and believe that probable cause had been shown, and Parmelee had little choice but to rule that probable cause had not been established. Parmelee was particularly skeptical about the identification of Fred, citing several instances of mistaken identifications of horses, but he also ruled that the evidence thoroughly satisfied him, as it should have satisfied every person who heard it, that "the defendant was not present at the time and place that the deed was committed."[25]

The decision upset Tisdale's family and friends, as well as the criminal authorities, but it is important to note what the decision did not do. It did not acquit Canton. It simply found that the prosecution had not then shown probable cause. Should additional evidence come to light, the charges could be refiled. Too, although the evidence Canton forwarded was persuasive, it showed only that he was probably not the one who pulled the trigger. It did not establish that Canton was not part of a conspiracy to kill Tisdale. Indeed, one of the reasons Canton was confident that he could show he did not shoot Tisdale was that he most probably knew who did. He was one of the members of the assassination squad responsible for the killings of both Tisdale and Jones, probably knew all about the activities of the group, probably helped plan them, and may have taken action in furtherance of those plans, although he likely did not pull the trigger of the gun that killed John Tisdale.[26]

Knowing that Canton was probably not the man who shot Tisdale helps to determine who might have. Billy Lykins was dead or dying, and if Canton should be ruled out, there were only two other possibilities:

Joe Elliott and Fred Coates. Developments after the arrest of Joe Elliott in February indicate that he was Tisdale's killer. Canton may have been more directly involved in the killing of Ranger Jones, however. There have also been persistent rumors that Fred G. S. Hesse was the man who shot Jones, supposedly because of personal animosity between the two.[27]

The truth is that no one knows why Jones was killed. He had no particular reputation as a rustler, except that he was a small cattleman in Johnson County, which in late 1891 meant that he was considered a rustler by the big cattlemen. The most plausible reason is that he somehow became involved with Champion's investigation after the assault, whether because he was that "other man" present when Shonsey confessed or because he was otherwise involved.[28] Jones lived on the Red Fork of the Powder River, as did John A. Tisdale, and he was probably a friend of both Tisdale and Champion. Still, this is speculation. The reason for Jones's assassination remains unclear.

Every issue of the *Buffalo Bulletin* in December 1891 showed Johnson County's preoccupation with the Tisdale and Jones killings. The December issues were filled with items about the two victims, including editorials, news stories, letters, probate notices to creditors (a brother of the deceased was named as the administrator of each estate), and notices of rewards (a total of $5,000 from the Johnson County commissioners and $600 from the acting Wyoming governor Dr. Amos Barber). The *Bulletin's* editorial position condemning the assassinations remained unequivocal, and the paper seems to have reflected the general opinion in the county.[29]

On December 17, 1891, editor Joe DeBarthe wrote a long, emotional editorial. He had lost all illusions about the special status of Buffalo and Johnson County (it was just the beginning of his education). He cited a recent article from the *Omaha Bee*, one full of "the most villainous abuse of northern Wyoming it could possibly put in print."[30] DeBarthe seemed shocked that the *Bee* had tried "to justify the horrible assassinations which recently took place near Buffalo," and he was greatly offended by the attempt to prove "that Johnson county is a nest of thieves—a refuge for the scum of the rest of the states, and the El Dorado of the lawless."[31] DeBarthe found this article particularly vexing because not four months earlier the *Bee* had run an article full of praise for Buffalo and Johnson County.[32] Even during these deeply trying times, though, DeBarthe insisted upon fairness to all sides, declaring, "We enter our most solemn and emphatic condemnation of all thievery, and also protest against the arbitrary power of any class who arrogate unto themselves the right to sacrifice human life upon the altar of greed." DeBarthe admitted that cattle thieves existed in northern Wyoming, but he stated that they were very few in number and could be reached by the long arm of the law.[33]

The *Omaha Bee* article also singled out John R. Smith as the "King of the Rustlers" (big cattlemen tried to fit this title to more than one man; it was soon applied to Nate Champion). Joe DeBarthe could hardly believe this charge. He cogently observed that Smith had driven two hundred cattle into the area in 1875, and now he had only 150. Within Johnson County, where the people knew Smith well and admired him, the designation of Smith as a thieving "king" was perceived as utter nonsense, a statement disassociated from reality. Smith's real sins were that he was active in a local small cattlemen's association and that he had supported two men charged with cattle theft in 1889, signing as a bondsman for George Gordon and George Peterson.[34]

The sources for the *Omaha Bee* article were supposed to be an old-timer from the Black Hills and "extracts from untrustworthy dispatches sent out from this state." DeBarthe assumed that the article had originated in Omaha, but in fact it resembled the "Cattle Kate" articles, contrived and dispersed by Cheyenne editors on behalf of big cattlemen to cover an earlier set of murders.

The *Bulletin* revisited the attack on Champion and Gilbertson, observing that at first people were inclined not to take the event seriously. Now, however, it was clear that only the quick actions of Champion saved him and Gilbertson from the fate of Waggoner, Tisdale, and Jones.[35]

Interest in the assassinations of Tisdale and Jones was not confined to Johnson County. Every newspaper in Wyoming seems to have written at least one editorial about the events. Their positions varied, depending on whether they were friends of the Wyoming Stock Growers Association or foes, and the debate illustrated the depth of conflict within Wyoming.

Those on the side of the Wyoming Stock Growers Association were not particularly bothered by the killings, saying that the reason for the problem was cattle stealing and that it was time to take it seriously. They readily adopted the line of the big cattlemen that Jones and Tisdale were killed because they were rustlers.[36] Those on the other side deplored the killings and recalled similar events. The ugliest comment made about the assassinations came from John Durbin, one of the lynchers of Ella Watson and James Averell: "If there is anything that ever did a stockmen's heart good it was to read in the morning *Bee* the news that a cattle thief had been shot." The *Laramie Republican* criticized the remark, saying it hurt the interests of the state. The *Carbon County Journal* was more pointed, inviting Durbin to provide all the details about the crimes and, while he was at it, to tell all about the "cowardly lynching of Averell and Watson."[37]

People throughout Wyoming reacted emotionally to the killings. The *Laramie Boomerang* opined that the people most fundamentally responsible for the tragedies were the editors of the Cheyenne newspapers. The *Boomerang* published an impassioned declaration of conscience, a criticism as harsh as one is ever likely to find by one member of the fourth estate toward another:

> The agitation stirred up by reckless and incendiary editorials in Cheyenne and other papers encourage[s] men to resort to the rope and the Winchester instead of the courts. This is the real cause of the cold blooded murders perpetrated in Johnson county. The editors who have been defending lynch law should sleep sweetly, now that their work has borne fruit. When they think of Tisdale's wife and children, of the Christmas gifts he had purchased for them that were drenched with his blood and of the fact that the murderers they manufactured are now skulking away with terror in their hearts at the crimes they committed, they should have an excellent appetite for their Christmas dinner, a joyous heart at their own children's pleasure around the Christmas tree and souls full of gratitude to their creator for sparing their wretched lives.[38]

The most significant development in the *Bulletin* editorials was the newspaper's position regarding prosecution of the assassinations, which, in turn, reflected a full awakening in Johnson County to a conspiracy against the county by big cattlemen. In its December 24, 1891, issue, the *Bulletin* declared,

> We verily believe and sincerely hope that the plotters as well as the assassins will be discovered. If, as is generally believed in this country, the stock interests of this state are at the bottom of these murders, there is no use of whining around about punishing the wretch or wretches who did the awful deed. Money will purchase

life and liberty for him or them, and the affair will go into history as mysterious murder.[39]

A week later, the *Bulletin* stated, "The murders of Tisdale and Jones have been instigated and perpetrated by men interested in the stock business, and time will prove it." A week after that, the paper predicted, "The entire conspiracy will be laid bare and the responsibility placed where it belongs."[40]

The editor of the *Bulletin* was obviously talking with the Johnson County criminal authorities—in a county seat of 1,000 people, it would be surprising if he did not—and their intentions were clear: Angus and Bennett were going after the big cattlemen, the men behind the killings. It was a message that the men behind the killings—Irvine, Wolcott, Ijams, Hesse, and others—heard loud and clear.[41]

CHAPTER TEN

A New Plan

Early 1892 was a bewildering time for the people of Johnson County. Their model community became the principal target of big cattlemen and their kept journalists, who hurled accusations that seemed to turn the notion of right and wrong on its head. The Johnson County criminal authorities were determined to pursue a criminal conspiracy by big cattlemen but needed more evidence. Their persistence infuriated the cattlemen, angry because the people of Johnson County refused to quietly accede to the aggressive attempts to force small cattlemen off the range in southern Johnson County. Even in January 1892, however, although angry anti–Johnson County newspaper stories did continue to appear (undoubtedly sponsored by Wyoming big cattle interests), the big cattlemen had not yet decided how they would strike back at this defiant county. Indeed, a final decision on a plan was not made for two months.[1]

The Johnson County authorities had filed new charges against Canton in December 1891 (apparently Charlie Basch was now willing to say that it was Canton he saw on December 1), and they tried to arrest Canton before he left Buffalo. Canton wasted no time getting out of the area, though, and he and Hesse rode hard to catch a train in Gillette.[2] Hesse soon declared (to the *Omaha Bee*) that he and Canton had been threatened with death from "rustlers" but had just managed to elude them. In fact, the only "rustlers" after Hesse and Canton were Johnson County deputy sheriffs trying to serve a warrant on Canton.[3]

Canton traveled to Chicago in January, where his wife and two little daughters had gone in November. In Chicago, Canton suffered a calamity so wrenching that even the people of Buffalo sympathized with him. Canton's wife and daughters contracted diphtheria. One of the daughters died, and it was thought that Mrs. Canton and the other daughter would also succumb. But then the two surviving members of Canton's family slowly recovered.[4]

The first big news article attacking Johnson County in 1892 was published in the *Washington Star*. Wyoming has always been a tiny, rural state, and it has always been remarkable when a big-city news organ notices anything about Wyoming. In this case, however, the attention given by a big newspaper in the nation's capitol was not welcome. The article was republished in its entirety by Joe DeBarthe in the January 14, 1892, *Bulletin*. He was so taken aback by the enormity of the distortions within the *Star*'s article that he simply offered the piece to his readers and said: "Read it, and then ask yourself if this city ever presented the lamentable picture presented by the Star."[5]

The *Washington Star* wrote about Buffalo, "They call it a city because it has a thousand inhabitants. These are nearly all bullwhackers, cow punchers and freighters. It is the last and strongest purely cowboy outfit in the west." The article commented about huge losses to the owners of the big cow companies and their determination to protect themselves, explaining that the first bloodshed "is naturally set down to the credit of the cowmen, because the victims have all been rustlers." The first person to die was "Cattle Kate," stated the *Star*, who was a rich woman because of her cattle acquisitions. The article declared,

> Rustlers own the place and the organization of Johnson county.
> . . . The best lawyers are in their pay, the city is under their
> thumb and they neither skulk nor try to keep any secrets about
> what they are doing. They have begun the naming of cowmen
> who are to be put to death, and both sides are so angry and com-
> posed of fearless men that nothing short of a petty yet horrible
> war is looked for.[6]

DeBarthe's perplexity is understandable. How could he respond to a writing so wrongheaded, so deceptive? The bigger question, which DeBarthe just touched upon, was the source of the article.[7] It could only have come from the big cattle interests in Wyoming, and in fact this article, like several similar ones in 1892, was datelined Cheyenne.[8] It bore all the hallmarks of the Cattle Kate articles produced by Ed Towse—the same writing style, and full of brazen and convenient lies.

Amity between the big cattlemen and the rest of Johnson County broke down entirely. The *Bulletin* ran a story about intimidation by North Dakota cattlemen against settlers and followed it with a sarcastic comment:

> Must be a mistake here somewhere. It is not possible that cattle-men would try to intimidate legitimate settlers! Haven't they denied it in the public prints and shown to what extent they have gone to induce settlers to come in and partake of the blessings of free land and free water so generously offered by the government? Some unscrupulous rustler most probably instigated this dispatch in order to create a prejudice against the North Dakota stockmen.[9]

The hard feelings worsened in February 1892, when disputes involving the Wyoming Live Stock Commission exploded into the news. By then it had become clear that it was impossible to present evidence of owner-ship that would satisfy Billy Irvine and the other members of the com-mission. None of the hundreds of Johnson County cattle seized by the commission had been released to their rightful owners, and this experience was not unique to Johnson County.[10] Joe DeBarthe bravely attacked the issue, but his bitter articles revealed such anger and frustration that his readers must have wondered about his emotional endurance. DeBarthe wrote:

> Of all the contemptible, unauthorized, bold-faced schemes to commit robbery, under the guise of law that has emanated from western legislative halls in a decade, commend us to the Wyo-ming stock commission. . . . Say, under what name Mr. Stock Commissioner did you take up the cattle of Lew Webb and John R. Smith and Tom Gardner and Jack Flagg and Robert Foote and others of Johnson county? Like a leather-lunged Lucullus you have been yelling "thief" and pointing to Johnson county. You have attracted the eyes and attention of the entire country to our county: you have libeled us shamefully.[11]

A week after this article, the *Bulletin* ran a story telling about a petition being circulated in Johnson County directed to the livestock commissioners

and declaring that the owners of the seized cattle "are good and reputable citizens of said county" and that "the proceeds arising from the sale
of their said stock rightfully and justly belongs to them." The *Bulletin*
predicted that every official of the county would sign this petition,
whereby the livestock commission would realize the strength of Johnson
County's feelings about "the high-handed outrage" perpetrated by the
commission.[12] The *Bulletin's* editor, still not fully realizing how Johnson
County people were viewed by the big cattlemen of the state, was
being naive. The big stockmen's view soon became very clear, when a
spokesman for the livestock commission responded to the petition. The
Cheyenne Daily Leader took the petition to a man identified only as a
"prominent member of the Wyoming Live Stock Commission" (probably
Ijams or Irvine), and his unequivocal response was printed in the *Leader*:
"The rustlers in Johnson county have just about reached a stage where
they control everything, officially, socially and commercially."[13] The "prominent member" declared that the rustlers coerced everyone in the county
and so, when asked if the commission would pay any attention to the
petition, replied: "None whatsoever. We know that in every case where
it is signed by a reputable man it has been done through fear of antago-
nizing the rustling element. Therefore, it doesn't represent the honest
views of even Johnson county, and is for that reason unworthy of our
consideration."[14]

This response must have been maddening to people in Johnson County.
Instead of fairly addressing the issue, the commission just packaged
together all the people who disagreed with it as "the rustling element"
and called all of them a pack of thieves. It is an old device (lawyers refer
to it as ad hominem argument) and was used frequently by the cattle
interests. Whenever anyone disagreed with the cattle barons, he was accused
of being a thief or on the side of thieves, and no further response was
deemed necessary. DeBarthe tried to reply to the livestock commission's
statement, pointing out that only a small percentage of Johnson County
people were stockmen, but he realized that anything he said was futile.[15]

It was not just the *Bulletin* that was offended by the actions of the
Wyoming Live Stock Commission. The *Lusk Herald* lambasted the
commission, saying that the people of Lusk had never thought that
when Ijams and Irvine were put on the commission, they would attempt
to supplant and supersede the courts and statutes.[16] The *Douglas Graphic*

was harsher, saying that the voters must knock "that infamous, damnable, hellish stock law from our statute books."[17]

The biggest surprise came when the *Cheyenne Daily Leader* announced its opposition to the actions of the Wyoming Live Stock Commission. Cattlemen no longer controlled the *Leader*; in 1892 the principal owners were John F. Carroll and Joseph A. Breckons, and Ed Towse had moved on to the *Cheyenne Daily Sun*.[18] As well, the *Cheyenne Daily Leader* was a Democratic newspaper, never wholly comfortable with the rich men who made up the Wyoming Stock Growers Association. Still, it was a shock to the big cattlemen when Carroll, previously supportive of the positions of the large livestock holders, excoriated the actions of the Wyoming Live Stock Commission. He railed against its usurpation of power, stating that the commission seized property "until proof of ownership is established," and added, "This it is usually, if not always, impossible to do to the satisfaction of the board in the cases of brands which are alleged to belong to rustlers. There is therefore no recourse open to the man whose money is thus held, whether he be honest or dishonest, except through litigation in the courts, a heavy contract for any ordinary poor ranchman to undertake."[19]

John Carroll's editorial made him very popular in Buffalo, where the people were feeling besieged. Joe DeBarthe told how forty men waited for the latest edition of the *Leader*: "So eager were these people to hear what the paper had to say that one of the party read while the others listened, shouts of joy and ringing cheers greeting every sentence of the *Leader* Editor's eloquence."[20] DeBarthe suggested that the *Leader* send a reporter to Buffalo: "Let him go about the country and interview all classes, and find out for himself who are the men who have been hiding facts, writing lies and aiding and abetting assassination. . . . Let him acquaint himself with the owners and representatives of Johnson County's great cattle herds (great on paper and small on the range) and with the owners of the small outfits. Then let him write the entire matter up, just as he found it."[21]

February 1892 was also the month in which Joe Elliott's preliminary hearing was held for the attempted murder of Nate Champion. Elliott had been arrested in Newcastle and brought to Buffalo, and on February 8 a hearing was convened before Justice Joseph Reimann. The morning was primarily taken up by long legal arguments made by Charles Burritt, who represented Elliott, but then the prosecution was allowed to proceed and the first witness called was Nate Champion.[22] Joe DeBarthe's description of Champion's testimony is a classic of frontier journalism and should be read and savored in its original form:

> Every ear was strained to catch the words that came so low and slow from his lips. Not a muscle in his face moved. His piercing, steel-grey eyes were riveted on Elliott's face. He was not looking at, but through him.
>
> Elliott sat four feet away and busied himself knocking the ashes off the end of a half-smoked cigar. When the county attorney asked the witness if he recognized any of the men making the attack, Champion slowly inclined his head toward the prisoner and said:
>
> "Yes, that man."
>
> There was no change in his voice. His demeanor was the most commonplace. As he spoke the words "that man," Elliott looked him straight in the eye. For ten seconds, while these two men looked into each other's faces, there was a sickening silence.
>
> Then someone coughed and the spell was broken. Elliot's face had not paled, but a sallow color had crept over it.[23]

Elliott was kept in the Johnson County jail after the preliminary hearing (Justice Reimann bound him over to the district court for trial), and he was having trouble. He complained that he wasn't safe in Johnson County, and it was reported that he "has broken down entirely": "He is said to cry like a child almost constantly, and is afraid that he has been brought up to Buffalo to be killed."[24] Wolcott and Irvine were probably aware of this report (Charles Burritt, Elliott's lawyer, kept the big cattlemen well informed), and it must have alarmed them. If Elliott had broken down entirely and admitted the identity of his employers, Wolcott, Irvine, and other big cattlemen would have been charged with attempted murder, and a Johnson County court would have undoubtedly sent them to the penitentiary for a long time. (Another possible explanation for Elliott's behavior is that he may have feared the reaction of his employers if their involvement came out.) After a while, though, Elliott stabilized and even made jokes about his fears.[25]

Elliott's behavior raises a question: why would he respond this way, seemingly with irrational fear? After all, the people of Johnson County were unlikely to lynch a man for an attempted murder. One plausible answer is that his fears were not irrational. He may not have been threatened with lynching for the attack on Champion, but the killings of Jones and Tisdale were another matter. He and Fred Coates were the most likely suspects for Tisdale's assassination, and Elliott was also likely one of the two or three men involved in the Jones killing. Years later, Elliott seemed to clear Fred Coates of the killings when he said that Coates never carried a gun "and never lifted a hand against those fellows."[26]

If, in fact, Elliott was the gunman in one or both of these assassinations, he would deeply fear that he would be discovered and that the enraged people of Johnson County would lynch him. He was present in Buffalo when the body of John Tisdale was brought in, and probably two days later when the body of Ranger Jones was found, and he saw firsthand the fierce anger of Johnson County men.[27] Regardless of the appropriateness of Elliott's fears, however, his employers, Wolcott and Irvine (and, probably, the members of the Executive Committee of the Wyoming Stock Growers Association), must have dreaded the consequences of a conviction of attempted murder. Johnson County had Elliott in its sights: by the testimony of Sheriff Angus and the identification of his gear, they could put Elliott in Johnson County at the time of the attack on Champion, and Champion would have been a devastating witness against Elliott.[28] Would Elliott break down again following a conviction? How would he respond if he were offered a reduction of a long prison term for the answer to a simple question: who were your employers when you attacked Champion and Gilbertson? Indeed, the situation might become more dramatic than this. Johnson County might develop a case against Elliott for the killing of Tisdale. And then Elliott might be offered a reprieve from a death sentence. Again, the only condition would be the answer to a simple question: who were your employers when you killed John Tisdale? His answer could have put nooses around the necks of Wolcott, Irvine, and probably others, and if Johnson County officials could have, they would have done so in a heartbeat.[29]

Remarkably, Joe Elliott came away from his stay with Sheriff Angus with high praise for Angus's treatment of him. Almost fifty years later, Elliott said, "I wish I could do something to square the feeling against Red Angus. He did me favors, treated me square all the way." Elliott also indicated that Frank Canton's negative opinion of Angus had carried the day (Canton's appreciation for Angus's kindness was very brief).[30]

Another item of note is that Ross Gilbertson was not mentioned in the stories about Elliott's preliminary hearing. He was apparently not then in the Buffalo area, although he was there in 1894.[31]

Throughout the early months of 1892, Joe DeBarthe time and again found himself standing up for the people of Johnson County. He obviously felt a responsibility as the spokesman for an entire, frightened community of people who knew exactly what was at stake. The fear of Johnson County residents was well shown by a correspondent named "Boz," who was from a small ranching area near Buffalo. He wrote the *Bulletin* and stated that there had been very little in the way of social gatherings during the winter because of an overriding insecurity:

> The assertion of a prominent stockman that all settlers were to be classed as rustlers, their stock confiscated and themselves and their families run out of the country has not had a tendency to allay their apprehensions of coming trouble. Must we, who have committed no crime but that of taking up 160 acres of government land and are struggling to make a home for our wives and little ones, submit to be robbed by men who for years have had the benefit of the entire range?[32]

The anti–Johnson County stories continued, not simply in newspapers but by any means the big cattlemen could forward their position. They were being disseminated because they were effective, as demonstrated by a March 1892 letter written by Judge John W. Blake, who was Judge Jacob Blair's successor as the district judge of Wyoming's Second Judicial District, which included Johnson County. Blake's letter, which was published in the local newspapers, was directed to the Johnson County attorney, Alvin Bennett, on the eve of the upcoming spring term of court. In his letter Judge Blake wrote, "I hear a great many things." The judge referred to "things" such as allegations that the small stockmen were threatening and driving out the larger ones, that cattlemen would not be allowed to round up their herds, and that reputable businessmen were being threatened and terrorized. Blake described what his response was to be if he found that even one-quarter of these things were true: "I cannot do justice to all parties as an impartial judge of a court without letting my hand fall very heavily upon the members of such organizations and upon the county officials who may aid and encourage this sort of method."[33]

The big cattlemen were scoring a big success here. Judge Blake did what most people do in such situations; he discounted all the wild claims he had been told, but still gave the stories some credence. Based solely upon the big cattlemen's claims, Judge Blake had already formed a negative opinion against the people of Johnson County, and soon he would be making important decisions fateful to the county.

In a letter that was also published, Alvin Bennett dutifully replied to the judge. He referred to the stories the judge had mentioned and stated that that was the first time he had heard of them and that he was not aware of any secret societies. Declaring that nine-tenths of the reports were untrue and that there were two factions in Johnson County, he observed, "The waves of public opinion are strong and at times run wild. I do not belong to nor favor either of these parties." After noting that he understood that someone from Johnson County had written the judge (who was apparently in Laramie during all this), Bennett added, "If this is a portion of the reports referred to, I know them to be false, and that the citizens here should be thankful that we had as good peace officers as we had the first of December last, when to my certain knowledge they stayed up nights and had deputies out to prevent the commission of crimes, which were likely to have taken place, and which would have eclipsed the crimes already committed."[34]

The impression from Bennett's letter is that he was an earnest and sincere young man but lacked fire. One wonders, where was his indignation? Where was the fiery anger at these slanders, these calumnies that were tarring his constituents and, apparently, setting them up?

Other allegations were being thrown about in March of 1892. One was that large numbers of cattle on the range were being shot. An alleged example was the gunning down of some dozen cattle near Nine Mile Creek, south of Buffalo. A delegation of officials and interested parties went to the area to investigate. Upon completing their investigation, the men filed a report saying that they had found the carcasses of thirteen head of cattle piled up, but only one was "green" (taken maybe two months earlier). The men declared that there was nothing to indicate killings had taken place there and that the tale was "unequivocally false." The report was signed by Deputy Sheriff Howard Roles, the three Johnson County commissioners, and John R. Smith, Nathan Champion, and Lew Webb.[35] Within Johnson County, the statements of these men carried weight, for the people in the tiny county had dealt with all of them and

knew them to be reliable men. But outside Johnson County an entirely
different view predominated.

The next installment of sensationally slanted news stories appeared in
the *Chicago Saturday Blade* on March 22, 1892 (by way of Cheyenne).[36]
It was unsubtle (the headline was "Four Bad Men") and referred to four
"unhung scoundrels"—namely, Nate Champion, Lee West, Al Allison,
and Jack Flagg. The *Blade* wrote about "the big and bold bandit gang
which infests Wyoming" and said that Nate Champion was the "captain-
in-chief." The paper stated that Nate Champion's true name was unknown
(the truth is that the Champion family in Texas was large and well
known; Nate Champion never used an alias) and that although he was
a good hand, he "was troubled with a natural inability to distinguish the
rights of stock ownership."[37] The *Blade* stated further that Jack Flagg
had been "longer notorious as a stock thief than perhaps any other
member of the present great Wyoming rustler organization," and added
that he was part of "the Avery gang of rustlers from Sweetwater valley."
(Apparently this was a reference to James Averell, who never had a "gang.")
Oddly, the *Blade* article went easy on Al Allison. It said that he was a
Missourian and the brother of John Tisdale, "one of the rustlers shot
and killed, presumably by cattlemen, last fall."[38] Of the four men listed,
Allison was the only one using an alias and the only one who had defi-
nitely committed crimes.

Chicago seemed to be a favorite outlet for the Cheyenne writers,
perhaps because Chicago was the home of John Clay, a man with many
connections. About the same time that the *Chicago Blade* article was
printed, an article appeared in the *Chicago Herald*. The *Buffalo Bulletin*
reprinted the article, saying it had been "sent from Cheyenne to the
Chicago Herald" and lamenting the damage such writings were doing
to the image of the Johnson County area.[39] Even at this late date, the
people of Johnson County were worried about the effect of all this bad
press on their hopes for growth and prosperity. This *Chicago Herald* article
was one of the worst of the pieces attacking Johnson County. It referred
to "newer and bolder outrages by range rustlers" and to the shooting
down of horses and cattle, resulting in "scores of carcasses" lying on the
range. It alleged that the "prairie pirates" selected the animals of large
owners, ones who had been vigorously trying to stop the stealing. The
article declared that the thieves were running Johnson, Natrona, and
Converse counties, that they had claimed ownership of every cow in

the state, and that nearly every prominent range owner had been threatened with death.[40]

The frequent allegations of threats to the lives of big cattlemen is remarkable. Other than the statements of big cattlemen and their supporters, there is no evidence substantiating these charges. It seems to be a case of projection; by March 1892, five "rustlers" had been killed by big cattlemen or their employees, but the only person slain who was associated with the big cattlemen was Billy Lykins, when he tried to kill Nate Champion.

A consistent theme within all of the sensational stories was the underlying threat of future violence. The *Big Horn County Rustler*—which was printed in Bonanza, in the eastern half of the Big Horn Basin, within Johnson County—had noted this. The newspaper stated that there were vague hints in Wyoming newspapers of the intention of the big cattlemen "to begin a war of extermination in the spring against the so-called rustlers in the state," and that "a few of these sanguinary hints bear the mark of having been inspired by certain knowledge based upon authentic information." The *Rustler* hoped that such hints might be "wholly imaginary," but noting that "recent events refute that belief," the paper lamented, "It has reached a deplorable stage in our civilization if certain men, strong only in the possession of wealth as represented in large herds of cattle can with impunity arrogate to themselves the right to judge, convict and execute punishment upon those whom they may regard as in the way of their money-making schemes."[41]

The *Rustler* editor did not know it, but the decision to launch an expedition and carry out a war of extermination had already been made in early March—it followed the preliminary hearing of Joe Elliott, at which Nate Champion had testified, by about three weeks.[42] Agents had been sent out from Cheyenne to carry out the plans of the expedition. Among them was H. B. Ijams, who had gone to Nampa, Idaho, in early March 1892 and there spoken to George Dunning, a man Ijams wanted to recruit for the expedition. Seven months later, Dunning would set out in exhaustive detail the entire exchange with Ijams.[43] Dunning remembered the event distinctly, as it was surely the most astounding conversation he had ever been a part of. Afterwards, an incredulous Dunning remarked that Mr. Ijams had not seemed mad or excited but had made startling pronouncements about the mass murder of men "in much the same manner that many people would talk about taking a picnic excursion."[44]

In his conversation with Dunning, Ijams "complained very bitterly" about depredations against livestock he said were committed by rustlers in Wyoming, especially Johnson County. He told Dunning all about an expensive program for hiring men to kill thieves. Ijams said that the Wyoming Live Stock Association had felt that killing a few men would terrorize the remainder of the rustlers and they would leave the region. Ijams admitted, however, that the stock association had been mistaken with regard to the effect of killing a few thieves, for "instead of terrorizing the rascals . . . the thieves were becoming more bold in committing their depredations upon live stock" and "were getting more on the warpath every day of their rascally lives." Ijams explained to Dunning that the stock association "had not gone about the killing off of thieves in the right manner" and that "since the assault on Champion and his partner and the killing of Tisdale and Jones, on Powder River, . . . the stock association had another scheme for doing up the thieves."

Ijams explained that this new scheme should meet the approval of many law-abiding people of Johnson County because it would be so straightforward, publicly wiping the thieves out, as had been done in Montana a few years previous. Ijams told Dunning about arrangements for hiring a number of men from Texas and giving them good pay and a bonus for every man killed; he thought the work would take about a month and that the men, broken up into five-man squads, would kill thieves wherever they could find them. Mr. Ijams felt that only about thirty men would be killed in Johnson County, because so many others would leave the county, but then the squads would fan out to other parts of the area and eventually, after three or four months, cover all of Wyoming. After that, they would move on to other parts of the region. It was not just those labeled as rustlers who would be killed, either, but also those who might bear witness against the assassination squad that had attacked Waggoner, Champion, Tisdale, and Jones, and men such as Sheriff Angus and his deputies, who were trying to obtain convictions against the assassination squad and those who directed them.

Joe DeBarthe, in Buffalo, had no idea of the actions of H. B. Ijams and other agents of Wyoming's big cattlemen, but their deeds would not have surprised him. By the end of March, DeBarthe did not need to be convinced of the accuracy of the *Big Horn County Rustler's* comments. He knew by then that the sensational stories being printed around the United States were plants out of Cheyenne and that his county was immediately and directly threatened by violence.[45] DeBarthe did not relish ugly wars of words—he did not seem to have the feisty character of some editors, such as Becker—but so long as he remained editor of the *Bulletin*, he was going to do his job. In early April 1892, DeBarthe wrote a defiant editorial in the *Bulletin*, demonstrating the posture of the people of Johnson County. After excoriating "paid lickspittles" from Johnson County who had been writing lies to the outside world, DeBarthe said, "No man who has not sanctioned murder has escaped the calumnies of these vipers." He asserted that these men prattled about a "reign of terror," but that the only such reign "raged in their own breasts": "The only thing they had to fear were the ghosts of the men who had been murdered. And this fear grew to such proportions that they imagined they saw daggers in the eyes of every man who was not numbered in their coterie, and they have left the country."[46]

DeBarthe closed his editorial with a fire-breathing declaration:

> If they imagine they can creep back and shoot some more men in the back without leaving their [own] bodies to pay the forfeit, they are awfully mistaken. There are times in the history of every people when patience ceases to be a virtue, and we wish to be understood as saying no gang of assassins can come into this portion of Wyoming without meeting the muzzle of a Winchester at every turn. . . . Our people are not tenderfeet. The majority of them have faced all the dangers of frontier life in securing their homes and what little they have in them, and these treasures, as well as their lives, they will guard and defend against the world.[47]

CHAPTER ELEVEN

The Calm before the Storm

Charles Bingham Penrose was born into the family of a distinguished Philadelphia physician. Like his father, he became a physician, receiving his medical degree from the University of Pennsylvania Medical School in 1884; he was also awarded a Ph.D. in physics from Harvard at the same time.[1] One of his friends in medical school was Amos Barber, from Doylestown, Pennsylvania, who graduated one year before Penrose.

Until about 1891, Dr. Penrose practiced medicine in Philadelphia, but then he became ill with tuberculosis. He was determined to regain his health, and this led him to the western United States and Cheyenne, Wyoming. He arrived there in December 1891, apparently at the urging of his friend Dr. Barber, then the acting governor of Wyoming. Barber had practiced medicine in Douglas, Wyoming, had been elected the Wyoming secretary of state in 1890, and became governor when the elected governor, Francis E. Warren, was sent to the U.S. Senate. Barber put Penrose up at the Cheyenne Club, an exclusive social club that catered primarily to members of the Wyoming Stock Growers Association. Barber had been close to big cattlemen since he was first brought to Wyoming by the Fetterman Hospital Association, a health care cooperative organized by cattlemen and cowboys.[2] Indeed, Penrose's writings show that Barber was part of the stock growers' social circle. It appears this small-town physician was flattered by attention to him as the governor of Wyoming, saw big cattlemen as his friends, and wholly sympathized with their views.

To address his illness, Dr. Penrose undertook a rigorous program of physical exercise that included digging with a pick and shovel during the morning and riding horseback all afternoon. It seemed to work. He reported that by March of 1892 he felt well again and had gained twenty pounds.

In the Cheyenne Club, Penrose became aware of plans for an expedition into northern Wyoming. He was asked to join the expedition as a surgeon, and he agreed, "because the men who asked me were my friends, and I was glad for the opportunity to take part in an adventure of this kind," and also because Governor Barber recommended that he join the group.[3]

Penrose is a particularly significant figure because he was on the inside of the planning for the invasion of Johnson County and he wrote an extensive memoir about it, which he called *The Rustler Business.* Much of this document parrots the big cattlemen's line, as Penrose faithfully repeated stories about Cattle Kate (a "cowboy's harlot" who "had to be killed for the good of the country"), about the complete inability to obtain a conviction for cattle theft no matter how strong the case, and about the "complete control" of Johnson County by the rustlers. He had never been to Johnson County, but he dutifully wrote that these rustlers "terrorized the country" and "drove out by threats and assassination the agents of the cattlemen."[4]

More importantly, however, Penrose also made some startling admissions that did not follow the line at all—probably because he was not that familiar with all aspects of the official line and so told the simple truth. Given the program of obfuscation, half-truths, and complete untruths that so polluted the public record before and after the invasion, Penrose's admissions are invaluable to get to the heart of what really happened in Wyoming in April 1892. In addition to his writings, there are writings from other men and further evidence that point to the inside truth, information that confirms and supplements what Penrose admitted. It includes the letters of Billy Irvine to Penrose, the admissions of Robert David (relying upon David's father, who was actively involved in the invasion, and two other members of the invading force) in his book *Malcolm Campbell, Sheriff,* and the chats of H. B. Ijams with George Dunning.[5]

Taken together, this valuable evidence allows for a dependable reconstruction of the true story of the last weeks and days before the invasion of Johnson County.

Penrose said that in early 1892 there had been much general talk among big cattlemen about an expedition to Johnson County. It was not until the first few days of March 1892, however, that a plan was settled upon, when big cattlemen met in Cheyenne.[6] The men then heard the statements of their range detectives about rustlers and from those statements produced a list of men from Johnson, Natrona, and Converse counties about whom there was supposedly no doubt of guilt. It was resolved that seventy men would be "exterminated," either by shooting or hanging. These included Sheriff Angus as well as the three Johnson County commissioners, so that "a proper set of officials could be put in their places." It also included Joe DeBarthe, the editor of the *Buffalo Bulletin*, and Robert Foote, a Buffalo merchant.[7] Nate Champion was a specific target of the expedition.[8]

Wolcott and Irvine were the ones who had formulated the plan, and they probably presented it to their fellow big cattlemen. They no doubt continued the rationalization that all this was undertaken to stop rustling. Wolcott and Irvine each had a conflict of interest, though. The truth was that those two men were in trouble and desperately needed something to change the situation in Johnson County; otherwise, the prosecution of Joe Elliott and Fred Coates would continue, step by inexorable step, and things could end very badly for the two big cattlemen. Stopping thievery was the battle cry, however, not the dire necessity to kill witnesses, although witness killing was discussed among the cattlemen.[9] Then again, the rationale for the invasion was hardly subjected to critical scrutiny. Wolcott and Irvine did not bear a heavy burden of persuasion since so many of the members of the Wyoming Stock Growers Association, fed by their implacable hatred of settlers, were eager for a punitive expedition against northern Wyoming. More than that, at least some of the leaders of the association, the members of the Executive Committee, must have feared criminal prosecution if witnesses were not killed.

David, Penrose, and Dunning wrote that the cattlemen recognized there were special problems. One was that the local militia might interfere with the raiding force. Also, men had to be hired and horses had to be purchased in such a way that the plan would not be revealed. The first problem was readily dealt with through the assistance of Acting Governor

Barber. Barber was completely informed about the plan and rendered assistance from the beginning, not least by neutralizing the militia.[10] On March 23, 1892, a telegram was sent out of Cheyenne "by Order of the Governor and Commander-in-chief." This telegram, which by April 2 found its way to the commander of every Wyoming National Guard company, ordered each commander to follow the directions of only the governor and *not* any local sheriff.[11]

The logistical problems were also readily addressed—in the case of horses, by sending R. S. Van Tassell into Colorado to buy fifty-two of them, and in the case of hiring men, by sending Tom Smith, a Texan who had been a deputy marshal for some years, to Texas.[12] H. B. Ijams also tried to recruit men, traveling to Idaho in March, where he spoke to George Dunning. Ammunition was found in Colorado, "enough ammunition to kill all the people in the state of Wyoming." Studebaker wagons were ordered, as well as provisions and bedding.[13] All of these acquisitions were costly, but, as David wrote, the expedition was well funded from the contributions of big cattlemen, which amounted to more than $100,000, a staggering sum in 1892.[14]

Special attention was given to telegraph wires because the telegraph might be used as a means of warning, and E. T. David, the manager of the C. Y. Ranch, was designated to cut the line at points north of Douglas, Wyoming.[15] David was considered of great value because his employer, the owner of the C. Y. Ranch, was U.S. senator Joseph Carey, and the big cattlemen wanted Carey fully committed to the expedition.[16]

The expedition was set to commence immediately after the April 5 meeting of the Wyoming Stock Growers Association, at which the plan would be endorsed.[17] Billy Irvine acknowledged that at first, the idea was that only hired men would go to Johnson County, but at one early meeting, John Winterling moved that all owners and managers who could possibly go should go. Winterling explained that the presence of the owners and managers would show the Texans the way, would give the expedition prestige and would prevent mistakes. After some discussion the motion passed.[18] Following this motion, Irvine immediately challenged each man in the room, asking who would go. All present said they would, except a Colonel Pratt (referred to by Irvine as "old Colonel Pratt") and George W. Baxter. Baxter was extensively involved in the planning, however.[19]

It was not long before the plan started coming together. Irvine said that he, Van Tassell, Tom Smith, and Ijams fanned out from Cheyenne, and all were quickly able to accomplish their objectives. Governor Barber was kept abreast of the expedition—Penrose recalled a meeting of himself, Willis Van Devanter, and Governor Barber at which either Van Devanter or Barber gave him a telegraph code "by which to communicate with them if I found it advisable to do so on the trip."[20]

Penrose reported that Barber assisted the big cattlemen "as much as he could" and, throughout the event and its aftermath, acted "with unwavering loyalty."[21] The big cattlemen were also confident of the assistance of Wyoming's U.S. senators, although Carey was certainly more involved in the enterprise than Warren.[22] As well, they considered Buffalo's mayor, Charles Burritt, to be the leader of the big cattlemen's supporters in Johnson County. (A small group consistently overestimated by the cattlemen, those supporters were mostly Buffalo businessmen who were allies of Frank Canton.) According to Dunning, H. B. Ijams asserted that Judge Blake, the sitting district judge in Johnson County, and the U.S. marshal were also on their side. Given Ijams's penchant for talk, however, his statements have to be treated skeptically—the U.S. marshal proved not to be a supporter of the big cattlemen.[23]

After H. B. Ijams left Idaho, he sent two letters to Dunning on Wyoming Board of Live Stock Commissioners stationery.[24] In the letter dated March 16, 1892, Ijams told Dunning about the pay and supply arrangements. On March 17, Ijams instructed Dunning to leave for Cheyenne on March 31 or April 1, threw in an extra $50, and assured him that funds were available to cover the expenses of five men from Idaho. Ijams had pushed Dunning to recruit more men, but Dunning was never able to do so.[25]

At first, Dunning could not bring himself to believe that Ijams was really serious, but after receiving the letters, he decided to go along with the proposal, although professing disapproval.[26] Dunning got his pistol out of hock, boarded a train in Idaho, and arrived in Cheyenne on April 2, 1892. He met Ijams in Cheyenne, and Ijams confirmed the pay arrangements—wages of $5 per day (the usual cowboy's wages were about $1.50 per day) and $50 to each hired man for every "rustler" who was killed.[27]

The big cattlemen had set up charge accounts in Cheyenne stores, and Dunning received a new .45-90 Winchester, then the state of the art in rifles.[28] When Dunning first arrived, he met two employees of the Wyoming Stock Growers Association, Morrison and Tabor, and of

March 1892 letters from H. B. Ijams to George Dunning. Courtesy of Johnson County Jim Gatchell Memorial Museum.

course all the talk was about the coming expedition.[29] Dunning was told that the stockmen expected to kill about thirty men in Johnson County, which would terrorize settlers so much that three hundred to four hundred of them who supported the men killed would leave the country; the stock association would then appropriate all their livestock.[30] Morrison and Tabor were confident but expected a good deal of fighting in Johnson County. They did not expect any organized opposition in other counties (Natrona, Sheridan, and Converse) after they were done with Johnson County, however, so that "all the mob would have to do would be to hang them up as they come to them."[31] The next day, Dunning spoke to more of the invaders (Joe Elliott, H. W. Davis, John N. Tisdale, D. R. Tisdale, R. S. Van Tassell, Ewing, Arthur B. Clarke, among others). Later, Dunning said of the occasion, "There was a good deal of talk about the necessity of killing off all men who were witnesses against Elliott, Canton, Tom Smith, and Coats [sic]. These were the four men that it was claimed were in the employ of the Wyoming Stock Association for the purpose of killing off the rustlers last fall."[32]

During these first few days in April, twenty-five Texans, recruited by Tom Smith, waited in Denver for the Wyoming Stock Growers Association's final approval of the plan.[33] Most of the Wyoming men who were going on the expedition were already in Cheyenne.

Major Frank Wolcott was selected to lead the expedition, and W. C. Irvine served as his number two man.[34] Besides Wolcott and Irvine, there were twelve other Wyoming owners of large ranches: Fred Hesse, John N. Tisdale, H. W. "Hard Winter" Davis, D. R. Tisdale, William E. Guthrie, W. J. Clarke, A. B. Clarke, H. E. Teschemacher, A. R. Powers, Frederick O. de Billier, E. W. Whitcomb, and C. A. Campbell.[35] Of these, Hesse, the two Tisdales, Davis, and Clarke were from Johnson County.

The men about to engage in the invasion of Johnson County had different motivations. About half of the Wyoming men were from Johnson County, and they had personal reasons for wanting to participate in this punitive raid—anger because of perceived slights such as being voted out of office or being disrespected by the populace, or the inevitable anger that arose because of conflicts over the competition for the grass on the range. Hesse and Canton were the central figures among the Johnson County group, forceful men with grudges, and they influenced other Johnson County men. W. J. Clarke was one example, a man whom Hesse admired and had supported, although Clarke's involvement was still a surprise.

Clarke had never been a controversial figure in Johnson County. In January 1891 he was appointed water commissioner and for the next fifteen months was very active in this position, hearing the disputes of his fellow citizens and seeming to do his best to resolve their differences "with but little litigation and small expense."[36] At the time of his appointment, the *Buffalo Bulletin* commented that it was an "eminently satisfactory one," since Clarke was "a man of intelligence," a man who "enjoys the respect and esteem of the people of this county."[37] But Clarke had remained active in the Johnson County and Wyoming stock growers associations, and his appointment as water commissioner was helped by the support of Fred Hesse, who declared that Clarke was a "clear-headed, fair-minded man."[38] Hesse's friendship must have overridden any commitment Clarke had made to the citizens of Johnson County. It is nevertheless a puzzle why an apparently decent man—who had once professed his deep appreciation to the people of Buffalo for their kindness to his family, as well as a commitment to "return some aid to them . . . in their time of trial"—would participate in an expedition to lynch and terrorize Johnson County people.[39]

The cattlemen from outside Johnson County included, of course, Frank Wolcott and Billy Irvine. They were angry and excitable men and, when excited, completely lost good judgment; at times, the depth of their folly was exceeded only by the strength of their wills. Worse, Wolcott and Irvine were in positions to maximize their influence. The Johnson County invasion would probably not have occurred but for the presence of these two deeply unsound men.

The remaining big cattlemen were all active in the Wyoming Stock Growers Association and frequently formed close friendships with other Wyoming big cattlemen. These bonds were enforced by social interaction, such as membership in the exclusive Cheyenne Club, which was founded by one of stalwart members of the Wyoming Stock Growers Association, Hubert E. Teschemacher.[40] As a member of the association's Executive Committee from 1883 to 1892, Teschemacher almost certainly pronounced death sentences upon Johnson County men. Irvine had also been appointed to the committee as well in 1883, and Teschemacher had also served with William E. Guthrie in 1887, as well as with John Clay and George Baxter.[41] Ties of friendship and peer group pressure no doubt influenced those who became invaders. For example, though Frederick de Billier was never part of the leadership of the Wyoming Stock Growers Association, he was Teschemacher's partner. All of these men except Clay and Baxter participated in the invasion.

Several trusted employees of the big ranches and the Wyoming Stock Growers Association joined the group. These included range detectives Frank Canton, Scott Davis, Phil DuFran, Joe Elliott, Ben Morrison, Mike Shonsey, and W. H. Tabor, and the managers and foremen included men such as Charles Ford, manager of the T. A. Ranch south of Buffalo; Richard M. Allen, assistant manager of the Standard Cattle Company out of Cheyenne; and Lafayette H. Parker, manager of the Murphy Cattle Company of Piney Creek, north of Buffalo.[42] Many of these men were deeply loyal to their employers, but not all of them were.

The big cattlemen in the invasion, as a group, were remarkably well educated and remarkably well-to-do. Teschemacher and de Billier were Harvard men, and the total holdings in Johnson County of the invaders were estimated to be 116,905 head of cattle, 4,657 horses, 86,020 acres of land, and $506,000 in improvements. Their education and wealth were repeatedly trumpeted by the newspapermen who supported them, especially after the invasion, as if such status conferred a special privilege to kill other human beings.[43]

During their final preparations for the invasion, the big cattlemen received a windfall when the Northern Wyoming Farmers' and Stockgrowers'

Association meeting declared its own roundup. The northern Wyoming association had nothing to do with the Wyoming Stock Growers Association but instead was composed of most of the small cattlemen of the Johnson County area. Its president was John R. Smith, and Joe DeBarthe was its secretary.[44] The group was first formed in the fall of 1891, had solicited the involvement of women, and had conducted all of its meetings in the open. That did not prevent the big cattle interests, however, from painting it in the most sinister terms as a secret organization that was plotting the assassination of Ijams, Irvine, Hesse, and Wolcott. As one historian observed, this declaration was "a textbook case of paranoid projection."[45] On March 26, 1892, the small cattlemen's association appointed roundup foremen, including Nate Champion, and announced that they would hold a roundup beginning on May 1, about one month before dates set by the Wyoming Live Stock Commission. This announcement was released to the public but was not printed in the *Buffalo Bulletin* until March 31, and apparently did not reach Cheyenne until two or three days later. Still, the big cattlemen pounced upon the roundup announcement, declaring that it was "the last straw" and that it was impossible to allow this "aggressive action to proceed unchecked."[46]

The small cattlemen felt that it was appropriate to band together and set an early roundup because of some common problems. One long-standing complaint was that the big outfits moved large herds through settlers' small farms, knocking down fences, destroying gardens, and pulling the settlers' cattle along with the main herd.[47] Lewis Gould wrote that one of the concerns of the small cattlemen was that the Wyoming Live Stock Commission would attempt a "wholesale confiscation" of their stock at the 1892 roundup.[48] Still, unfair though it may have been, state law supported the big cattlemen here; the Wyoming Live Stock Commission was given the authority to establish and conduct roundups.

The big cattlemen deliberately overreacted. They painted the actions of the small cattlemen in the worst possible terms, declaring that their roundup was set early so that all the mavericks on the range could be stolen before the regular roundup began—again assuming that only large cattlemen were legitimate and would act honorably, and that all small cattlemen were thieves. Because state law supported the big cattlemen, though, they had a clear legal remedy, and they had a highly competent instrument—Willis Van Devanter—to enforce it, a man whose acumen as a lawyer was so strong that he ended his career as a member of the

U.S. Supreme Court. And turning to their legal remedy is exactly what the big cattlemen did in early May, when Van Devanter obtained an injunction against the roundup of the Northern Wyoming Farmers' and Stockgrowers' Association. The attorney's task was made easier by the lack of resistance by the small cattlemen, who conceded a later setting of the roundup by the Wyoming Live Stock Commission.[49]

The setting of an early roundup by the small cattlemen of Johnson County became an excuse but was never a reason for the invasion of Johnson County. When, in early April 1892, the big cattlemen in Cheyenne first heard about the small cattlemen's roundup, they had already hired bands of killers, armed them, and supplied them. The planning for the northern expedition was then complete and needed only to be finally set into motion. On April 5, 1892, the big cattlemen of Wyoming did just that.

CHAPTER TWELVE

The Invasion Begins

The invading force left Cheyenne about 6:00 P.M. Tuesday, April 5, 1892. They had one overriding imperative—to get to Buffalo as rapidly as possible, there to kill Sheriff Red Angus and his deputies and to kill all the Johnson County commissioners. Having destroyed the leadership of the county, they could then kill Johnson County men at their leisure. The invaders had to undertake "a quick invasion, conducted with all secrecy."[1] It was an article of faith that unless they were able to strike and destroy Johnson County officials before resistance could be formed, the rustlers of Johnson County would band together and rise up.[2]

Immediately after the adjournment of the annual meeting of the Wyoming Stock Growers Association, word was spread to "the faithful" that they should go to the stockyards, walking in twos and threes "so as not to excite attention."[3] These men promptly arrived and were placed in a horse stable, and then when Wolcott's train from Denver pulled in, they quickly boarded. Wolcott had gone to Denver to bring the Texans up to Cheyenne, and when his train arrived "with the sun blinds pulled down," it was backed into the stockyards, and the stock cars and baggage cars were quickly attached. Some seventy-five horses and three wagons were thus added and with the men from Cheyenne, the total number of men reached fifty-two. Irvine thought the whole operation "beautifully done," that the men in the cars were not noticed at all, and that no one was "the wiser to what was going on."[4]

The train soon pulled out and proceeded north toward Casper, traveling through the night.[5] Eleven men on the train were headed back to their home county—Johnson County.[6] Of the officers and board members of the Northern Wyoming Protective Association, the group that was so helpful to the Wyoming Live Stock Commission in identifying "rustlers" in Johnson County, only H. R. Mann was not part of the invading army.[7] Frank Wolcott, Billy Irvine, and C. A. Campbell were from Converse County, and Hubert E. Teschemacher, Frederick de Billier, W. E. Guthrie, A. B. Clarke, and E. A. Whitcomb were from Cheyenne.[8] These men, with their out-of-state hirelings, were a private army, an armed body of men specifically brought into Wyoming for the "suppression" of domestic violence. Teschemacher and Irvine had been delegates to the Wyoming Constitutional Convention and, less than two years earlier, had signed their names to the new Wyoming Constitution, which so clearly and specifically forbade such private armies.

Most of the remaining invaders were hired men from Texas, but, as well, there was a surgeon (Dr. Penrose), two journalists, and three teamsters.[9] One of the journalists was Ed Towse. The big cattlemen had appreciated his journalistic work in the Cattle Kate affair so much they brought him along, apparently for a repeat effort. The other journalist was Sam T. Clover, of the *Chicago Herald*, a brash young man who had talked his way into the expedition by persuading Wolcott and Irvine that he would get their side of the story out, and whose writings about the invasion would catch the attention of the nation.[10]

There was considerable excitement aboard the train as it traveled away from Cheyenne. Some of the expedition leaders thought that Angus and his deputies might have heard about the invasion plot and decided to make an investigative trip to Cheyenne. Angus would have gone by way of train from Casper, and if Johnson County law enforcement officials were on that train, the plan was to stop it and hang the sheriff and his deputies. Orders were given for every man to "get a rope and have his guns ready."[11] It was not clear how, but the leaders learned that Angus was not on the train from Casper, and things aboard the invasion train settled down as men tried to get what rest they could.[12]

As the invaders' train lurched and swayed through the dark, other men were helping the expedition. E. T. David, following Wolcott and Irvine's instructions, had started cutting telegraph wires and continued doing so through the next day, Wednesday, April 6.[13] The northbound train stopped at Orin Junction, about sixty miles east of Casper, so that Wolcott could test whether David had performed his assignment. Wolcott found just what he had hoped: no message could be sent to Buffalo because the lines were down.[14] When the train stopped at Fetterman (near Douglas), however, Irvine and Wolcott were disappointed to learn that David did not want to join them in the ride to Buffalo. David "could not square himself with his wife," Irvine wrote later. Irvine had angrily responded, "It is a damn poor man who gets behind his wife."[15] When the train resumed its journey to Casper, Senator Carey's foreman was not on it.[16]

One incident on the trip to Casper would have serious consequences. Major Wolcott had ordered everyone out of a baggage car so that he could prepare the baggage for a quick exit when the train stopped in Casper. Frank Canton came onto this car, apparently not knowing of Wolcott's order, and Wolcott brusquely ordered him off, an action that created "bitter feelings" between Wolcott and the thin-skinned Canton.[17]

When the train arrived in Casper about 4:00 A.M., April 6, 1892, its passengers intended to march briskly to Buffalo, hoping to reach southern Johnson County that evening. At first, they had little trouble. They promptly disembarked and traveled a few miles north of Casper, successfully negotiating this short trip before the people of Casper awoke. The wagon and the men on horseback assembled about 9:00 A.M. at a spot on Casper Creek.[18] Then the invaders began to encounter frustrating delays, after fifteen horses broke away and stampeded. It took hours to round them up, and some never were found. The wagons carrying some of the men who had lost their horses tried to proceed, but the horses drawing the wagons over ground saturated with snowmelt slipped and slid and became mired in gumbo, and one wagon crashed through a bridge. The column made only twenty miles that day.[19]

The morning of April 7 began with another delay. The "bitter feelings" between Wolcott and Canton had festered, and early Thursday morning Wolcott made a "manly" speech, resigning command for the "sake of peace and harmony" and ceding control of the Texans to Tom Smith and the rest of the expedition to Frank Canton.[20] Smith and Canton were not heirs to an easy task. A vigorous snowstorm moved in that day, and the expedition had to forge through it. Their destination was the John N. and David R. Tisdale Ranch on the South Fork of the Powder River. The invaders took two long, miserable days to reach the ranch, proceeding "in the teeth of a blizzard that coated every horseman with a white rime of frost from head to foot."[21] The men broke into separate groups to slog through this spring snowstorm, and some did not arrive until the afternoon of Friday, April 8. Wolcott got lost and had to spend the night of April 7 in a haystack, and Ed Towse had a nightmare journey because he was suffering so acutely from "piles" (hemorrhoids).[22]

Late in the afternoon of April 8, Mike Shonsey made a fateful ride south to the Tisdale Ranch.[23] Shonsey brought the news that rustlers (Shonsey said there were fourteen or fifteen), including Nate Champion and Nick Ray, were at the KC Ranch, just fourteen miles north on the Middle Fork of the Powder River. Shonsey recommended that Champion and Ray be attacked immediately. That Irvine and Wolcott readily agreed was no surprise; they had their own special reason to want Nate Champion dead.[24] Champion was the primary threat against Joe Elliott, member of the stockmen's assassination squad, and a conviction of Elliott would put Irvine and Wolcott in great peril. However, though killing Champion would be a very good thing for Elliott, Irvine, and Wolcott, the move made little tactical sense for the expedition. Supported by Canton, Charles Ford, and Campbell, Hesse pointed out that it was crucial to get to Buffalo to attack "the fountainhead." If just one man got away to warn Angus of their presence, the expedition could be "doomed to extinction."[25]

The need to get to Buffalo was more urgent than even Hesse knew. Although Irvine was confident that the expedition had gotten out of Cheyenne without being noticed, that much activity was difficult to keep secret in a town of fewer than twelve thousand people. In fact, many people were aware of their actions.[26] A letter had even been sent to Sheriff Angus, telling of a mystery train passing through Douglas.[27] And newspapermen were beginning to ferret out what was happening. On April 8, the day of Shonsey's fateful ride to the Tisdale Ranch, the *Cheyenne Daily Leader* told a great deal about the expedition. The *Leader* put a good investigative reporter on the story (adding to the anger of big cattlemen toward the owners of the *Leader*), and the reporter wrote of a special train "headed to the northern country to there begin the work of exterminating the rustlers." His article contained extensive detail about the people and cargo on the train and told of a train passing through Douglas and Casper and heading for "a certain Powder River Ranch in the first day out."[28] In addition to the *Leader* story, carefully presented information appeared in friendly Denver newspapers on April 8, articles providing justifications for the invasion. H. B. Ijams and other agents of the big cattlemen were behind these stories, apparently assuming that the invading force would already be in Buffalo by April 8 and that the stories would not tip off authorities in Johnson County.[29]

The dispute at the Tisdale Ranch aggravated the bad feelings between Canton and Wolcott. The Texans, who sided with Frank Canton, demanded that Wolcott produce the warrants he told them he had for the arrest of the rustlers, but he had nothing to produce.[30] When the men started drinking, the debate turned ugly. Irvine, soon "well liquored up," was "quite loud, belligerent and profane." This was not surprising to Sam Clover, who wrote that, when drinking, Irvine became "irritable, quarrelsome, and thoroughly unreasonable." Irvine demanded that the men immediately saddle up and travel to the KC.[31]

Wolcott, knowing what the result would be, slyly resolved the argument by taking a poll of the Wyoming cattlemen. A majority sided with him and Irvine and elected to head to the KC Ranch. By midnight of April 8, the invaders who had horses had departed the Tisdale Ranch.[32]

Despite all the fumbling and delays, which cost the invaders two full days, they still had a little time on their side. Although Johnson County authorities had heard rumors of a killing expedition for months, they did not know that a lynching party was advancing in their direction, nor that the sheriff, his deputies, and the county commissioners were targeted victims. The information received by Sheriff Angus was never sufficiently definite to act upon, and the mail, which was still running to Buffalo, took two or three days to arrive.[33] So those April 8 articles in Cheyenne and Denver newspapers, and possibly other letters telling of the invasion train, would not arrive in Buffalo for two or three days. If the invaders had gone directly to Buffalo on April 9, rather than to the KC Ranch, they probably would have surprised the Johnson County authorities and killed every man in Buffalo on their death list. Still, if the side venture to the KC Ranch did not unduly delay the invaders and give away their presence, they might yet accomplish their purpose. The fate of the invasion depended upon what would happen at the KC Ranch.

It was not an easy trip from the Tisdale Ranch to the KC Ranch. The weather was even worse than the previous night's. Accounts of the ride to the KC describe gruesome conditions: gale-force winds and snow so thick that it made the beards and mustaches of the men "solid with icicles." For four or five hours, what must have seemed an eternity, the column miserably plodded forward into the teeth of the storm.[34] Finally, at around 4:00 A.M. the invaders descended into a gully about four miles south of the KC. There they used sagebrush to fuel deeply appreciated "hot, pungent fires." The snowstorm stopped, and Shonsey, having been sent ahead to scout the KC Ranch, had rejoined the members of the invading group in the gully.[35] Shonsey reported that "the parties were not expecting anything and that they were playing the fiddle and having a good time generally."[36]

After about an hour's rest, the invaders mounted up and proceeded north. Joe Elliott, then out on bail for the attempted murder of Nate Champion, tied about ten pounds of dynamite, what he called giant powder, behind his saddle. The intent was to blow up the KC Ranch house and then shoot any men who appeared after the explosion. It was almost daylight when the mob arrived at the ranch, however, and the leaders decided that it was too late to use the dynamite.[37]

The Middle Fork of the Powder River runs generally eastward from its headwaters high in the southern Big Horn Mountains to a point about twenty miles east of Kaycee, Wyoming, where the Powder River turns due north. In 1892 the KC Ranch was located near the Powder River, at the future site of the town of Kaycee. The Middle Fork of the Powder River is not a large stream, except, perhaps, by Wyoming standards, but it has a dependable flow. Near Kaycee, it is about thirty feet wide, and its valley is substantial, which, in northern Wyoming, means a relatively narrow alluvial area full of large cottonwood trees. A low east-west ridge runs a few hundred yards southwest of the ranch buildings, coming much closer to those structures where the ridge dips southward. This ridge provided a convenient stopping point for the invaders to make final plans. Looking down from the ridge, the men could see the Middle Fork flowing from the northwest until it turned almost exactly east for about two hundred yards. They could also see the road to Buffalo; it came from the southwest to a bridge crossing the stream, after which it proceeded at an angle perpendicular to the Middle Fork, heading due north. The KC ranchstead sat in the valley floor south of the stream and southeast of the road, and it included a barn and a small house the invaders frequently referred to as a cabin. The two structures were approximately comparable in size. The barn was farthest north, about fifty yards from the Middle Fork. The house was about seventy-five yards southwest of the barn.[38]

The KC Ranch barn. Courtesy of Johnson County Jim Gatchell Memorial Museum.

"The orders are simple," Major Wolcott is said to have told the men. "Shoot down every man in that cabin when he comes out, and be careful how you place your shots."[39] Wolcott, Canton, and Tom Smith deployed the men around the KC Ranch, circling the ranch house, where Nate Champion lay sleeping. They also put Texans in ravines south of the house, and the "Texas Kid" (C. D. Brooks), Frank Canton, and another Texan, Alex Lowther, in the barn. The rest of the invaders surrounded the house, using natural features, especially the big cottonwoods, for protection.[40] In the course of this deployment, however, Wolcott discovered some freight wagons near the barn. They should not have been present, and he hesitated, apparently because these freight wagons might not belong to rustlers. For that matter, it was never firmly established that anyone at the KC the evening of Friday, April 8, besides Ray and Champion, were among those the invaders considered rustlers.[41] George Dunning said that he told John Tisdale he did not want to just gun men down as they came out of the house, and Dunning suggested that someone go to the door. Wolcott indignantly vetoed that idea.[42] Whatever the process, if no one was going to march up to the cabin—and, George Dunning notwithstanding, very few of the men relished the idea of openly approaching a cabin with Nate Champion inside—the mob could do little but wait.

Wait they did, for about two hours.[43] Frank Canton and Fred Hesse must have been beside themselves, as precious minutes ticked by with no progress toward anything, and as they increasingly fretted that the invaders and their expedition would be discovered.

Finally, an old man, Ben Jones—a cowboy who, with Billy Walker (also in the cabin), was getting through the winter by trapping—came out of the cabin.[44] Whether because of orders or because Jones was clearly not an identified rustler, the men held their fire. Jones made his way toward the river with a water bucket in his hand. When he came around the corner of the barn and was out of sight of the house, he was seized at rifle point. About fifteen minutes later, Jones's partner, Billy Walker, came out of the ranch house and sauntered toward the stream. In no hurry, he spent some time whittling and threw a stone at a sage hen. After about half an hour, Walker finally drifted to the back of the barn, where he was grabbed, much as Jones had been. From the two captured men, the invaders learned that only two more men, Champion and Ray, were in the cabin.[45]

After a few minutes more, a large man appeared at the door of the ranch house and then proceeded out of it cautiously. It was Nick Ray, who remained out of the cabin no more than ten minutes. No one shot at Ray, because Wolcott had ordered the Texas Kid, who was a crack shot, to fire first. Wolcott finally told the Kid to fire and when he did, all started a general firing.[46] Nick Ray fell after the Texas Kid shot, but then started crawling on his hands and knees back toward the door. All the while a rifle barrage aimed at Ray continued. Dunning estimated that a hundred shots had been fired when a small man appeared at the doorway and starting rapidly shooting back at the mob. His firing was so accurate that one of his bullets grazed the cheek of the Texas Kid, drawing blood. The small man was Nate Champion, and he put down his pistol, pulled Ray the last few feet into the house, and banged the door shut. Billy Irvine tried to persuade the men to rush the ranch house door while Champion was "disconcerted," but the Texans would have none of it. It was then about 8:00 in the morning on Saturday, April 9, 1892. About fifty miles from Buffalo, the invading army was stalemated.[47]

For the next five to six hours, the invaders tried to dislodge Champion, at first with a barrage, and then with only occasional potshots at the ranch house. Champion maintained an effective counterfire. As Clover wrote, "If a man was exposed for a second a bullet quickly whistled in his direction from the shattered window-frame of the ranch-house."⁴⁸ Champion wounded three men, two seriously. He hit one Texan in the arm and creased another deeply in the thigh. The invaders soon learned to be more cautious. Deciding "that ammunition was being wasted," the men were ordered to cease firing. To burn the ranch house, men were dispatched to a nearby ranch to buy some hay, but they returned in two hours saying that no hay was available.⁴⁹ Crucial time kept slipping by; hours passed, and the mob had not budged Champion. It was almost as if Champion had the invaders under siege.

Then something happened to change everything. The road that ran by the KC Ranch was the principal road from the Hole in the Wall area to Buffalo. Sometime after 2:00 that afternoon, a hay wagon driven by seventeen-year-old Alonzo Taylor, Jack Flagg's stepson, came down that road, heading northeast toward the bridge. The youth was followed by Flagg himself, on horseback. Then thirty-two, Flagg was making the first leg of a journey to Douglas for the Democratic State Convention.⁵⁰ Expecting to spend the night at the KC, Taylor and Flagg had no idea Nate Champion was besieged. There had been no firing recently, and the invaders had even pulled some of their pickets from their stations beside the road above and below the ranch. At first, the invaders did not recognize Flagg or Taylor, and the two rode right into the center of the scene. Something about the situation, though, bothered Taylor, because rather than pull his wagon into the grounds about the house and barn, he passed the ranch buildings and kept driving toward the bridge even though someone hollered for him to stop. Flagg later noted seeing more men than should have been there and said that "they seemed to be watching me." He started to pull in next to the ranch house, when someone leveled a gun on him. At first Flagg thought it was a joke, and said, "Don't shoot boys, I'm all right." Suddenly, both sides recognized each other. Flagg recognized Mike Shonsey's horse and Charley Ford, foreman at the T. A. Ranch. At the same time, someone yelled out something like, "That's Jack Flagg. Shoot him!" Flagg immediately spurred his horse to a gallop and charged after his stepson, who was then at the bridge. Several of the invaders started firing at the horseman and the wagon from the KC, but Flagg and Taylor were quickly across the bridge. Remarkably, neither Flagg nor Taylor were hit, and only one shot hit one of their horses. Brush and timber grew right up to the bridge, so after the two men crossed it, the invaders get a shot at them only by coming up to or past the bridge, but they were inhibited from doing that for fear of exposing themselves to Champion's fire from the ranch house.[51]

Flagg and his stepson rode on for perhaps a half mile, when Flagg stopped the wagon to get his rifle. Flagg grabbed the rifle from the wagon and pointed it back toward pursuers. Flagg said he only had three bullets and did not want to use them, but the men chasing him hesitated, apparently seeing the rifle. Taylor quickly cut the traces on the wagon's horse that had not been hit, and Flagg and Taylor rode hard away, pursued by ten horsemen. The pursuers fired at Flagg and his stepson from as far as one thousand yards, peppering sagebrush around them, but soon gave up the chase. The two men got away cleanly.

It was near 3:00 P.M., and all the invaders knew that Flagg and Taylor were ahead of them and traveling straight to Buffalo to spread the alarm. Robert David wrote that Wolcott said: "That ends our raid. There will be a thousand men here by morning. We had better hurry on to Fort McKinney."[52] The situation was worse than Wolcott knew. Terrence Smith owned a ranch about four miles north of the KC. Early that morning, he was hitching up a horse outside his home when he heard rapid firing in the direction of the KC Ranch.[53] The time was probably about 8:00 A.M., when the mob first blazed away at Nick Ray. Smith had saddled one of his horses and ridden quickly to a ridge about a mile north of the KC. Carefully looking over the ridge, he saw many men coming and going around the KC. He watched for about an hour, long enough to see the men begin to fire again and keep up a rapid fire for a half an hour. "Then they stopped shooting entirely." Smith had seen enough, He got on his horse and rode to Buffalo as fast as he could. When he arrived that evening, he went directly to Sheriff Angus.[54]

The invaders knew nothing of Terrence Smith, but given what they did know, to salvage the expedition they should have left a few men to watch Champion and sent the rest of the men to Buffalo as fast as they could go. They might have beaten Flagg there; if not, they might still have caught the county officials unprepared. As Irvine later wrote, "the Buffalo fellows of our party argued that Flagg would go there, report our being in the country, and that the rustlers would kill their friends in Buffalo, and they would have wanted to strike that minute for Buffalo." Wolcott, however, despite his appreciation for the need to quickly get to Fort McKinney, would have none of it, declaring that "we will do one thing at a time."[55]

This decision revived the dispute that first arose when Shonsey reported rustlers at the KC. Irvine probably understated the situation when he said, "We were all so mad and chagrined at Flagg's escape that we came near to fighting among ourselves." Wolcott adamantly insisted, though, that "we will get these fellows first while we are at it and then we will go to Buffalo as fast as we can."[56] For Wolcott, the killing of Champion was the real prize. If Champion was killed, the expedition would be a success regardless of whether any other "rustlers" were lynched. Whatever Wolcott's motivation, his decision stood, and it meant doom for Nate Champion.

CHAPTER THIRTEEN

The Death of Nate Champion

Disappointed though they were about the escape of Flagg and Taylor, the invaders recognized that Flagg's abandoned wagon presented an opportunity. The men dragged it back to the safe side of the barn, and there they transformed it into a torch.[1] They found a small amount of hay in the barn and split some pitch pine posts found around the hay corral. A layer of hay was first laid down on the back of the wagon. On top of this they put a layer of pitch pine, then alternated hay and pine layers, all "built out wide and high."[2]

The plan was to push this wagon incendiary from the barn to a part of the ranch house that had only one window from which Champion could fire his weapons. This maneuver carried great danger, for six men were needed to propel the wagon. John Tisdale and Frank Wolcott said they would be part of the team, but the Texans balked. Finally, Tom Smith, their leader, stepped forward and announced that he and three of his men would complete the group.[3]

At Wolcott's direction, Irvine had six men train their rifles on that single window facing the barn. Their instructions were to start firing through the window opening and keep up a steady fire. They commenced to fire, and Wolcott, Tisdale, and the Texans immediately seized the wagon and slowly rolled it to the ranch house, a distance of about seventy-five to a hundred yards.[4] Once it was rammed against the house, the contents of the wagon were ignited with "instantly applied" matches. Then the six

153

men ran back to cover, with the men displaying "by far the best sprinting ever seen in Wyoming," according to Sam Clover."[5]

Oddly, no shots were returned from the ranch house, and the invaders even speculated that both of the men inside had been killed. The fire took. At first, only the north wall burned, but then the flames spread rapidly, so that soon "every discernable portion of the house was ablaze."[6] It seemed that no man could survive the heat and smoke of that fire, but suddenly a figure leaped out and ran to the south.

"There he goes" was shouted from the bluffs west of the ranch house. Nate Champion had broken through the flames and was holding a Winchester in his left hand and a "huge pistol" in his right.[7] Champion ran in his stocking feet and seemed to be working his way south within the smoke. As he ran through the smoke, several of the men around the house saw glimpses of his fleeing figure, but though many shot at him, no one hit him.[8] Then Champion broke out of the smoke into a ravine south of the house. He ran directly into two men Tom Smith had stationed there; Smith had correctly deduced that the ravine was a logical escape route.

An instant too late, Champion saw Jim Dudley and Jeff Mynett, two Texans who blocked his escape. Champion snapped off an errant shot, but Dudley fired more accurately, hitting Champion in the left arm and shattering the elbow. Champion moved to use his pistol with his right hand, when a shot from Mynett struck him in the chest. Then he was hit by several other bullets, ten in all. Champion, David wrote, "leaped high into the air and fell prone upon his back."[9]

Nate Champion was dead. The invaders came running and gathered around the body. The men in the invading army never could bring themselves to abandon the lies about Nate Champion, but they could not hide how much they respected him as a fighting man. When Wolcott came huffing up to the group, he was reported to have looked down at Champion and said, "By God, if I had fifty men like you I could whip the whole state of Wyoming."[10] Much later, Frank Canton wrote, "Nate Champion was the only man among the rustlers that I considered a dead-game man. . . . If he had been fighting in a good cause he would have been a hero."[11] Sam Clover, surely the best writer of all those who left an account of the Johnson County War, contributed this memorable passage: "Nate Champion, king of cattle thieves and the bravest man in Johnson County, was dead. Flat on his back, with his teeth clinched and a look of mingled defiance and determination on his face to the last, the intrepid rustler met his fate without a groan and paid the penalty of his crimes with his life."[12]

Clover was not just a passive observer, though later he would so profess. During the siege of the KC cabin, he used a pistol and "banged away" at the ranch house.[13] One of the invaders wrote out "Thieves Beware" on a piece of paper. Irvine stated that Clover then pinned this primitive placard on Champion's chest.[14] In so doing, Clover found a diary in Champion's shirt pocket; a bullet had torn through it. Wolcott read this paper to the gathered group, to their rapt attention. Within two hours Clover had wheedled the diary from Wolcott.[15]

This diary by Champion became famous, at least Sam Clover's version of it, which was first published by the *Chicago Herald* in an April 16, 1892, story written by Clover.[16] But from the beginning there have been questions. Clover told different stories about the Champion diary. In his book, *On Special Assignment*, published in 1903, he said he first worked up a shorthand version of the diary and then at some place south of Buffalo, tore up the diary and threw it away.[17] In a May 15, 1892, letter to Henry Blair, however, Clover thanked Blair for the return of the diary pages and vowed, "I shall keep them as long as I live."[18] When, after the invasion, Billy Irvine asked him for the diary, he swore that he had destroyed it in Buffalo. Irvine later wrote, "I thought then, and still think, he lied."[19] One thing is reasonably certain: the diary never resurfaced. It is strange indeed that Clover, the ultimate ambitious journalist, would destroy or conceal the source of the scoop of a lifetime. These circumstances are made especially troublesome because of Clover's reputation, that of a young man who freely bent the rules when it suited his purposes.[20]

Clover may have embellished the diary in his April 16 story and thus did not want the original diary to see the light of day. An article printed in a Douglas, Wyoming, newspaper, *Bill Barlow's Budget*, on April 13, 1892, three days before Clover's *Chicago Herald* story, shows this is a reasonable explanation.

On his [Champion's] body was found a diary he had kept on his doomsday. In it appeared the following entries, in lead pencil:
"April 9—6 a. m.—House surrounded by armed stockmen, who are firing at us. About daylight Old Man Jones went out after a pail of water, but did not return. About that time another man went out, and did not return. Soon Nick Ray went out to see

what had become of them, and as he stepped out he was shot in the head. He staggered back and fell on the bed, and I closed the door in the face of a storm of bullets. I must go and see how Nick is.

"Just 9 o'clock, and Nick is dead. If I can stand them off until night I will try and make a break for liberty."[21]

This version submitted by the *Budget* is starkly different from the *Chicago Herald* version. (The entire *Chicago Herald* statement is set out in the appendix herein for comparison.) The *Herald* diary is 518 words, whereas the *Budget's* is only 117 words. The *Budget* diary seems to cover the same general subjects as the first quarter of the *Herald* diary, but the wording is distinctly different. The most obvious difference between the two versions is that the *Herald's* version is full of poignant and homey passages—and bad grammar—not found in the *Budget* version. It is too perfect.

There is no question that Nate Champion, in his last hours on earth, wrote a calm narrative about what was happening to him. Several people, including Irvine, Dunning, and David (via Guthrie and Shonsey), verified that Champion wrote a diary. It seems probable, however, that Sam Clover's version is not what Champion wrote.

Champion was killed about 4:00 P.M., and the invaders refocused on Buffalo. They first decided to turn loose the two trappers they had seized at the KC Ranch, Ben Jones and Billy Walker, after paying them money for some of their losses in the cabin fire.[22] Two of the men wounded by Champion had their wounds "roughly cauterized" but could still ride. They were given bandages and ointment and sent back south. The third wounded man, Calhoun, felt he could continue with the expedition.[23]

That afternoon, the supply wagons caught up with the mob, and a long, leisurely hot meal was had. According to one historian, Hesse and Canton resented this further delay. When the wagons arrived, the invaders must have immediately noted that three members of the expedition— Dr. Penrose, Ed Towse, and H. W. Davis—were not with the wagons. They had split off at the Tisdale Ranch and gone to Davis's ranch.[24]

At 9:00 P.M., April 9, 1892, the invaders finally resumed their march north.[25] The invading army had lost almost another full day, and although they had killed two "rustlers," they had given away their presence. At least for a while, however, the invaders seemed determined to smash through regardless of the changed situation. They rode for about five hours through the middle of the night, supposedly at a gallop, covering half the distance to Buffalo, about thirty miles. Their first destination was the Western Union Beef Company Ranch, whose foreman was Mike Shonsey and general manager was George Baxter. There they received some one hundred fresh horses. They took about a half hour to change their saddles and were on their way again.[26]

Other men were up and about in Johnson County during the very early morning hours of April 10, 1892. Jack Flagg had spread the word about the invaders as he and his stepson rode north, arriving at John R. Smith's ranch in the evening of April 9.[27] There Flagg enlisted the aid of four men and started back to the KC Ranch. The men went by way of the Carr Ranch and found twelve men there who were also preparing to ride to the KC. About the time Flagg arrived at the Carr Ranch, somewhere between midnight and 1 A.M., someone in the group spotted the invaders a half mile in the distance and shouted out, "They are out there, 100 strong on the flat." One of the Flagg group accidentally discharged his rifle and immediately alerted the invaders, who were skittish in the deep night, suspecting a trap. Maneuvering westward, away from the Carr place, they cut the Carr fences and then headed north toward Fred Hesse's 28 Ranch. Wolcott assumed command again, supposedly because the men were in an excited state over the encounter near the Carr Ranch.[28]

The Flagg group stayed the night at Carr's and did not learn until the next morning where the invaders had gone. The invaders had stayed at Hesse's ranch for only a couple of hours. At 4:00 A.M. they set out for the T. A. Ranch, fourteen miles south of Buffalo, and arrived there about 6:00 A.M.[29] Shortly thereafter, one of the Texans, Jim Dudley, a large man who had great difficulty finding a horse suitable for his bulk, was thrown from his latest horse and shot in the knee with his own Winchester. The leaders of the invading army were debating what to do with him when a rider charged in from Buffalo. It is not clear whether the rider was James Craig or Phil DuFran, but all reports say he was excited and alarmed.[30] The rider told the invaders that all of Buffalo was up in arms and that they should expect the onslaught of as many as 250 heavily armed men. The invaders were also told that a plan for their supporters in Buffalo to assassinate the sheriff and his deputies the night of April 9 had come to nothing.[31]

The rider's news struck home with the invaders. In truth, most of them were already losing heart, and the rider's declarations finished them off. They faced a grim reality. Their horses were exhausted (they may have expected to get fresh mounts at Hesse's ranch but were frustrated by two of John R. Smith's daughters, who supposedly drove off a herd of horses from one of Hesse's pastures) and they had outpaced their supply wagons, left somewhere far to the south when the men galloped through a long night. The invaders knew they were about to confront a host of rested, well-supplied, well-armed enemies riding fresh horses. The talk turned to going on the defensive and staving off disaster, giving their powerful friends time to call out the troops from Fort McKinney to save them.[32] Some dissented, however.

Canton bitterly opposed the idea and argued that the invaders should ride immediately to Buffalo, where two-thirds of the people supported them and where they could explain their purpose to Johnson County citizens, before Flagg and others stirred the people up with distortions and misrepresentations. Canton later insisted that Fred Hesse, W. J. Clarke, Charley Ford, and others from Johnson County agreed with him.[33] The idea that two-thirds of the people of Johnson County supported the invaders was self-deception, but for other reasons Canton's argument may have had merit. Resistance to the invaders was disorganized in the early morning of April 10, little more than a spontaneous outpouring of emotion, and Sheriff Angus was not ready to battle a group of determined men.

In fact, after 11:00 A.M., Sheriff Angus was not even in Buffalo. When Terrence Smith gave his sensational report to Angus the evening of April 9, Angus immediately approached Captain J. B. Menardi of the local militia for assistance but met with outright refusal.[34] Menardi told Angus he had just received a message from Governor Barber's adjutant general commanding local National Guard units to honor only direct requests from the governor and *not* from local sheriffs. Seeing that he would receive no help from the Wyoming militia, the sheriff, undeterred, mustered a posse of six men to go to the KC Ranch.[35] Leaving Buffalo about 11:00 A.M., they rode to the KC, reaching the ranch at dusk, where they found Champion's body and the charred remains of Nick Ray. This small posse then quickly rode back to Buffalo, arriving at 1:00 A.M., April 11, having made in all a 120-mile journey that Helena Huntington Smith described as "a sensational ride."[36]

If the invaders had ridden directly into Buffalo from the T. A. Ranch, they would have found the county seat without its sheriff and full of angry, disorganized men. Then again, Angus had capable deputies—especially Howard Roles, "a tall fellow with red hair" who was described as "Sheriff Angus's right-hand man"— and some of them had remained in Buffalo.[37] The populace was so aroused that a great deal of leadership may not have been required to mount an adequate defense. Men already in Buffalo and those on their way there were determined to fight the invaders.

The invaders had no idea of the depth of alarm and antagonism most Johnson County citizens held against them. As Frank Canton's remarks show, one bizarre theme of the invaders was that Flagg and others would stir the people up and unfairly misrepresent the invaders' intentions, and then, solely because of this agitation, the people would rise up and resist.[38] The invaders' perceptions were a flight from reality. After tarring the entire population of the county for months, after threatening vicious retaliation against the whole community, after killing men in Johnson County who, the people knew, were not remotely rustlers—men such as Tisdale and Champion, who were among the best citizens of the county— it is astonishing that the invaders were surprised by the hostile response their presence generated. It was hardly necessary for Jack Flagg to "stir the people up." They were already stirred up and spontaneously rose to drive the invaders out.

Among the men who rallied to the defense of their county was George Campbell. Campbell was only eighteen years old at the time, but he firmly believed that big cattlemen were trying to rid the country of the homesteaders and independent cowboys who were staking claims to land and trying to build up small herds of cattle. He also believed that all the accusations of rustling were just an excuse for the big cattlemen. His family and friends thought likewise, and they had no doubt that the big cattlemen were behind the assassinations of Tisdale and Jones and the attempted assassinations of Champion and Gilbertson. When young Campbell heard of the murder of Champion and Ray at the KC Ranch by a large group of armed men, he did not hesitate. He grabbed his rifle, joined with thirty-seven other men, and headed toward the T. A. Ranch.[39]

The invaders would stay at the T. A., using its natural defensive advantages and hoping to hold on until the cavalry rescued them. They were disappointed that Angus had not been assassinated, in part because they believed that killing the Johnson County sheriff would have delayed the organization of a besieging party and given the invaders' friends such as Governor Barber and Senators Carey and Warren, more time to have the

McKinney troops mobilized to rescue them.[40] It was decided to put Jim Dudley in a T. A. wagon and have two of the T. A. cowboys, not part of the invading force, drive him to Buffalo for medical care.[41]

The decision to remain at the T. A. was a momentous one, meaning, as Sam Clover wrote, that the battle "was now irretrievably lost."[42]

CHAPTER FOURTEEN

The Siege

The T. A. Ranch sits a few miles east of the base of the Big Horn Mountains on a wide plain only a bit lower than the surrounding land. In
1892 there were two main buildings at the T. A., a house built of hewed
logs ten to twelve inches thick, and a barn about a hundred yards west
of the house. The North Fork of Crazy Woman Creek looped around
to the east of the buildings. It is a small stream, only a few feet wide,
that sinks into the level grassland. Unlike the Powder River, this stream
has only a few trees along it. All through Sunday, April 10, 1892, the men
of the invading army worked feverishly to construct defensive works,
protection against the onslaught they expected soon.[1] Besides enforcing
the barn, ranch house, and stable, the men dug trenches, fortified an ice-
house, and crafted a structure on a knoll about one hundred yards west
of the barn. One newspaper referred to this construction as a "small
fort," consisting of "hewed logs and earthworks." The invaders found a
log fence surrounding the whole ranch, as well as "a huge pile of thick
timbers," and these were of great assistance in the construction of effective fortifications.[2]

No hostile men from Buffalo topped the short horizon above the T. A.
that day, and the invaders probably continued their preparations quietly
and diligently. Other than their talk, there would have been no sounds
on this grassy prairie south of Buffalo.

The T. A. Ranch barn and house. Courtesy of Johnson County Jim Gatchell Memorial Museum.

Two participants in the invasion, Sam Clover and Richard M. Allen (assistant manager of the Standard Cattle Company of Cheyenne), decided that it would be inadvisable for them to remain at the T. A. As the mob was barricading the ranch house, digging rifle pits, and otherwise preparing their defensive positions, Clover realized he might be caught in

The fortification built by the invaders in front of the T. A. Ranch barn and house. Courtesy of Johnson County Jim Gatchell Memorial Museum.

a siege and that it could be days before he could get to a telegraph and send his sensational story. Clover, an active supporter of the invasion, suddenly remembered Clover the journalist and declared to himself that "it was his duty to get into Buffalo," go to Fort McKinney, and get his story out by military wire.[3] Clover seemed to have particular sway over Wolcott, and when the journalist impressed upon the cattleman the great benefits that would accrue if he were able to get out the invader's version of the events, Wolcott acceded. Clover quickly saddled his horse and started for Buffalo.[4]

Clover took Richard Allen with him. Allen declared that he had big cattle payments due and that he had to get to Buffalo, and then to Cheyenne, for the sake of his credit. No one could talk him out of his announced purpose.[5] After he left the T. A. with Clover, however, a new motivation surfaced. Allen started pitching all his guns and ammunition, and as he threw out the bullets, he accompanied each fling "with a bitter expletive on the fool notion that had led him to embark on such a venture." Clover said that Allen had come on the expedition for adventure but "a man more thoroughly cured of that impulse could hardly be found."[6]

As they rode into Buffalo, Clover saw that the town was in a ferment, and the agitated men cruising throughout Buffalo quickly focused on these two strangers. Soon a small group of armed men surrounded Clover and

Allen. Allen was riding a horse with the Western Union brand, which the men in Buffalo knew was the brand of the replacement horses obtained by the invaders. Allen represented himself as a peaceable traveler, but his story quickly collapsed and he was led away to the jail, to his immense relief—he had feared much worse. The armed men likewise demanded to know what Clover was doing in Buffalo. Ever glib, Clover "nonchalantly" declared he was on his way to see Major Edmond Fechet at Fort McKinney.[7] This threw off the angry men, who had been given instructions by Sheriff Angus to arrest every stranger who came in from the south. Clover had earlier learned that Major Fechet, a man whom he had met when covering another story, was stationed at McKinney. Boldly, Clover asked that Fechet be contacted, saying that the major would vouch for him. When contacted, Fechet quickly came to where Clover was being held and. to Clover's great good luck, declared, "It's all right, Mr. Deputy, he's no more a regulator than I am. Tell Sheriff Angus I'll vouch for him." The soldiers at McKinney were greatly sympathetic to Johnson County citizens, and the people of Johnson County knew it, so Fechet's endorsement was sufficient to protect Clover, who went off with the major to the fort.[8]

Returning to Buffalo about 1:00 A.M., Monday, April 11, Sheriff Angus brought with him the body of Nick Ray—little more than a torso—and the shot-up corpse of Nate Champion. When they were seen the next morning, lying in an undertaker's facility on the Buffalo main street, they "set the town wild," Clover wrote.[9]

Sheriff Angus got a few hours' sleep and then headed south the fourteen miles to the T. A. Ranch. Some men from Buffalo had already traveled to the ranch—Jack Flagg led forty-nine men out of Buffalo during the evening of April 10. These first besiegers arrived about midnight, and other men kept coming to the T. A. throughout the night. Early the next morning, the men felt they needed some leadership, and Arapahoe Brown was elected field commander; E. U. Snider acted as second in command.[10] Angus was constantly on the go in Buffalo and at the T. A., as new recruits kept arriving, not just from Johnson County but also from Sheridan and other counties. Shooting between the two groups soon started. Who fired first was disputed, but it was a moot point. The deeply entrenched invaders were not going to surrender to Johnson County officials, and nothing in subsequent events remotely indicated otherwise.[11]

Something of a troublemaker, Arapahoe Brown was an odd choice for field leader. He ran a lumber mill near Buffalo and was hardly an established leader of the community.[12] The men who rode to the T. A. must have recognized some special quality in Brown, however, and from the beginning, those who besieged the invaders exhibited good discipline and pursued their task intelligently. They recognized they had their quarry in a trap and that they could safely achieve their objective if they remained patient and proceeded cautiously. Brown should be largely credited for this tactic. Even the invaders acknowledged that he "showed remarkable knowledge of military strategy and procedure." There was an active Grand Army of the Republic post in Buffalo, and several Johnson County men, perhaps including Brown, had taken part in sieges during the Civil War. One, John R. Smith, was with Ulysses S. Grant at the long siege of Vicksburg.[13] The advice of these men would have been heeded.

All the men besieging the T. A. knew that they faced a long, hard task in trying to dislodge the invaders. But that Monday morning, the posse scored a major success when John R. Smith and other Johnson County men captured the invaders' supply train.[14] The three teamsters in charge of the supply wagons offered no fight, and the contents of their wagons were a revelation. Among supplies of all kinds, including thousands of rounds of ammunition, Smith and his men found two cases of dynamite. Most shocking to the people of Johnson County was the paper found in Frank Canton's valise, what Robert David acknowledged to be "the official list of seventy names of those to be exterminated." The list included seven townsmen from Buffalo and showed that the invasion was one against the whole community, not just a few rustlers.[15]

Mary Watkins, the sister of a local physician and soon to become the Johnson County superintendent of schools, wrote a letter to the *Laramie Boomerang*, and it demonstrated that despite all the threats in previous months, many of the people of Buffalo were still surprised by the invasion. She exclaimed that "some one must tell the truth," but that none of the newspapers had done so, except for the *Bulletin*. The people of Johnson County were "going about their daily business unsuspicious of any danger," Watkins wrote, when an armed group invaded them: "The Cheyenne band has committed murder, the most outrageous and dastardly that can be imagined, and that, to all outward appearance, with the sanction and help of the acting governor of Wyoming."[16] Another Johnson County resident reacted to word of the invasion by hiding in his attic. Joseph Reimann, the justice of the peace who had bound over Joe Elliott for the attempted murder of Nate Champion, lived in Buffalo, in a small house with an attic accessible only from the outside. When Reimann heard of the invading force headed to Buffalo, he climbed up into his attic and hid for two days.[17]

During Monday, April 11, men continued to pour into the area around the T. A. Ranch. All of them had rifles, including those who may not have begun the day with them. On that same day, perhaps right after the assassination list was made known, an event occurred that has assumed mythological proportions in Johnson County history. To ensure that no men would be kept from the fray because they lacked equipment, the Buffalo merchant Robert Foote threw open all the resources of his store, passing out guns, ammunition, slickers, blankets, and flour to anyone who wanted them. Foote rode up and down the Buffalo main street, "mounted on his celebrated black horse, with his long white beard flowing in the breeze," and shouted: "Come out, you —— ——, and take sides. Now is the time to show your colors."[18]

Show their colors they did, as great numbers of men surged toward the T. A. Ranch. Estimates of the size of the besieging force differed, but on April 11 the group numbered at least two hundred men and was still growing. More than that, in other parts of northern Wyoming, there was a great reserve of men willing to join the battle. They filled the streets of Douglas (the seat of Converse County), talking of nothing but the outrageous actions against the people of Johnson County, and preparing to go to Buffalo to support them against the invaders.[19] A report from Douglas stated, "If Wolcott's party has any sympathizers they are afraid to express themselves so bitter is the feeling." As to the makeup of the posse, a *Cheyenne Daily Leader* correspondent traveled to the T. A. and reported that of his estimate of 175 men then at the site, 125 were ranchmen, 25 were "mechanics and workingmen who each own a piece of land," and the remaining twenty-five were "rustlers, gamblers and men from about town."[20]

All through Monday and into the following evening, Sheriff Angus's posse worked at strengthening its positions around the ranch. There was quite a bit of firing back and forth, but no concentrated barrage, nor, certainly, anything like a charge to the ranch structures. Instead, the men of the posse worked hard on emplacements. By Tuesday morning, the T. A. was completely surrounded, with six breastworks on the far side of the North Fork of Crazy Woman Creek (east), two to the south that were also outside the stream, one to the north of the barn, and one to the northwest. The entire western portion of the siege lines was filled with men.[21] By then the huge posse, swollen to about three hundred men, held complete command of the field.[22] The men inside the T. A. knew they were in deep trouble, and they feared that Governor Barber did not know of their predicament.

When the invaders left Cheyenne, the governor's intention was to provide them an open field, to keep them from being inhibited in their intended killing spree. Knowing the telegraph lines were being taken down, Barber had made sure that the state militias first received orders not to assist the local sheriffs. He assumed that if the public remained unaware of the invaders, they could complete their murderous work. In the end, however, the loss of telegraphic communication worked against the invaders.

For the first few days of the invasion, only the most general of news filtered back from the north. On Saturday, April 9 (the date that Champion and Ray were attacked and killed), the *Daily Leader* interviewed Governor Barber and asked him whether he had taken any action about "the armed body of men which passed through the state on Tuesday evening."[23] "I have not," the governor replied. "The matter has not been brought to my attention officially." The governor then added with a smile: "I only know of the matter through newspaper reports, which, as you know, are somewhat conflicting on the subject."[24] The governor was telling the people of Wyoming an outrageous lie. He knew all about "the matter"; nobody had to inform him about the invasion, officially or otherwise.

On April 10, when the invaders made the decision to hole up at the T. A., the telegraph wire was still down and the *Cheyenne Daily Leader* had nothing to report and said so under the headline "Still No News," but the paper did repeat a rumor that Jack Flagg had been lynched.[25] The *Cheyenne Daily Sun* was in essentially the same predicament but provided more for its readers, presenting the situation as an impending epic struggle between the "rustlers" and the cattlemen's army. The event was described as the "rustler war" or the "war against thieves," but not as an invasion, and the paper wrote about another such struggle soon to arise in Montana, where thieves were indiscriminately killing stock on the range.[26]

The telegraph wires remained down during most of April 11 and 12, but some messages did get through, although not flowing very rapidly. The earliest information to arrive in Cheyenne came through on the April 11: the cattlemen had supposedly met some obstacles and might even be in trouble.[27] The *Cheyenne Daily Sun* reported what it referred to as a "wild rumor" of the "silliest character" that "seventy-five rustlers had the cattlemen surrounded and that a terrible battle would soon be fought."[28]

The shortage of information did not keep the *Cheyenne Sun* from taking some strong editorial positions. Indeed, the *Sun's* impartiality, never more than a thin veneer, seemed to disappear entirely. It ran a front-page article about a Mr. Johnson, who had experience as a small cattleman "up north." Johnson reported, according to the article, that the officers conducting the roundups (usually foremen of big cattle companies) gave him every possible help, but that he was bedeviled by rustlers. The *Sun* declared that Mr. Johnson's experience was the same as for hundreds of others and that "for the good of the state the rustlers must be driven out."[29]

The *Sun* then devoted its entire editorial page to a series of articles that unblushingly favored the positions of big cattlemen. One article stated that it was imperative for the big cattlemen to take a stand, to combat the huge problems with cattle stealing, to smash down once and for all the kingdom of thieves in northern Wyoming—where twenty-two big cattlemen had been put on a death list (no proof of this fantastic charge was provided) and all the cattlemen had been ordered away from their property.[30] Other articles repeated the charges that cattle were being shot down on the range by rustlers, that it was impossible to obtain convictions, and that the rustlers were so boldly threatening that the big cattlemen must protect themselves.[31]

Later on April 11 the telegraph lines to Buffalo were temporarily restored, and Governor Barber received a telegram from C. H. Hogerson, the acting mayor of Buffalo and the chairman of the board of county commissioners. Hogerson said that Johnson County had been invaded by armed men and asked the governor to order the assistance of the militia.[32] The governor then sent out several telegrams, the apparent purpose of which was to create the appearance of acting, while doing nothing. He telegraphed his aide-de-camp, Captain C. H. Parmelee, in Buffalo and directed him to confer with Hogerson and report back. Barber also telegraphed the militia in Douglas and Buffalo to be "in readiness" to move at a moment's notice and to provide authority for them to move upon receiving orders. The governor gave no orders to do anything, however, and urged "extreme caution" in making any move. The telegraph line then went down again.[33]

In sum, until April 12, Governor Barber, apparently assumed that his friends were faring well, and took no action whatsoever. Governor Barber's friends, however, were not faring well at all.

From the beginning of the siege, the weather had been bad. A cold rain began to fall shortly after men from Buffalo first arrived at the T. A., about midnight the evening of April 10, and during that night the rain turned to snow, meaning that the invaders in the cramped quarters of their fort "suffered intensely."[34] The peril of the invaders was obvious, and knowing that the telegraph lines were probably still down, they wanted to get a message to the governor in Cheyenne "stating their predicament and asking for immediate help."[35] A young man named Dowling stepped forward and offered to try to get through the lines around the ranch to Buffalo. His offer was immediately accepted, and H. E. Teschemacher wrote a telegram to Governor Barber, which was signed by Major Wolcott.

It was an especially dark evening, and Dowling had a harrowing adventure, wading through the icy creek and then briefly falling in with some of the besieging men. In the darkness nobody identified him, however, and he managed to split off from them. He was then able to "commandeer a horse" and ride to Buffalo. All of this must have taken him most of the night.

At Buffalo, Dowling presented the telegram to Frank Eggleston, the druggist, and George Munkres, the hardware man and Canton supporter. The telegraph from Buffalo was not operational, however, and so Monday morning two men were directed to ride toward Douglas, more than a hundred miles south of Buffalo, until they found the telegraph lines open, and then to send Wolcott's wire to the governor.[36] These two men rode as far as they could on April 11 and into April 12.

Meanwhile the situation grew progressively worse for the invaders. At first the members of the posse just shot at anything that moved, and their shooting was not particularly accurate. As the day proceeded, though, the besiegers got the range, so that it became dangerous for the invaders to leave cover.[37] At one point during the day, Calhoun, one of the men wounded by Nate Champion, made a dash out of the ranch and escaped to the south. Calhoun's wound was becoming infected, and the apparent reason for his risky action was to get medical help.[38] The posse was determined that no one else would escape, however, and started firing at the invaders' horses. Some twenty of the invaders made an attempt to saddle horses in the corrals, but the posse poured in hot fire, killing several of the exposed horses and driving the men out of the corral.[39]

Throughout the day, the men besieging the invaders pushed their lines forward, energetically employing baled hay to advance a few feet and then dig in. Arapahoe Brown made his presence felt as he moved around in the circle of lines, directing and assisting so that "systematic advances were made with military thoroughness." As they moved forward within a tightening circle, the posse members kept up a steady fire, and "the roar was continuous in the valley."[40]

Remarkably, for a long time no one was hit on either side. But there were several close calls for the invaders. Billy Irvine related that he spied H. E. Teschemacher standing with his back to a window and told him to move; Teschemacher did so, and a moment later a bullet came crashing through the window. Irvine also told of an incident involving a sixteen-year-old boy who was at the T. A. when the invaders arrived. The young man was anxious to get involved and loaded an old shotgun. But then a bullet came through one of the windows and creased the back of the young man's neck, causing a thin flow of blood. This took all of the starch out of the would-be warrior, and he retired to a safer place.[41]

Later in the day, John N. "Jack" Tisdale was struck by a bullet. He was standing in the ranch house when a bullet smashed through two doors and into the room, hitting him in the back. Tisdale staggered and tried to keep his balance, but started sinking to the floor. Someone shouted, "Jack's hit!" When he was examined, though, it was found that the bullet had not penetrated; Tisdale only had "a large, blue bruise."[42]

The night of April 11 was long and uncomfortable for the invaders. It was especially bad for those not in the barn or the house. Those stationed outside, in the fort or the ice house, had little shelter and no source of heat. The invaders' supply of ammunition and food was "entirely inadequate." David wrote: "There was plenty of bullet-riddled beef, and potatoes in the cellar, but flour was scarce, the ranch having held but little in the way of provisions." The members of the posse, on the other hand, had ample supplies of food, and their greater numbers meant that men could rotate from the front lines to tents and the Covington Ranch in the rear.[43]

It had continued to snow throughout the day and night of April 11, and it made for a bright background, even at night. The leaders of the invading force talked about making a break that night and fighting their way back to Casper. The clouds cleared during that evening, however, and any escaping invaders would have been visible and vulnerable, so the attempt to break out was called off.[44]

During the night, more men joined the posse and the besiegers dug more works and pushed their lines closer, so that when the shooting resumed in the morning of April 12, it was by more guns at closer ranges.[45] Some of the posse had gotten the range very well indeed. The invaders identified one man as Old Dan Boone. He fired a heavy rifle to devastating effect, his bullets tearing through thick slabs of wood. Elmer Brock later wrote that "Dan Boone" was Herman Franker, who owned an eighteen-pound Sharps rifle, .45-145.[46]

The barn at the T. A. stands today, and one cannot help but notice perfectly circular holes in the side walls, about half an inch in diameter. Many of the rifles used in the siege, such as the .45-70 or .45-90 Winchesters, fired huge bullets, 400 to 500 grains. By modern standards, they were extremely slow, with a muzzle velocity of about 1,300 feet per second, but they carried frightening momentum and had great penetrating power.[47] Close calls became frequent. The invaders hardly dared walk upright in the ranch house, because bullets broke through the walls and streaked through the rooms. David wrote that a bullet clipped off a piece of Joe Elliott's hat, Tom Smith had his pipe knocked out of his mouth by a bullet, and Scott Davis caught a bullet in his blanket.[48] Billy Irvine suffered more than a close call, when a spent bullet hit him in the foot as he was outside at the east end of the ranch house, on "picket duty," leaning back against a building. In his later writings, he minimized this event, indicating that he barely noticed the bullet. The truth, however, is that he yelled out, "Bill, I'm shot," and the pain "felt as though the whole foot had been torn away." He was later hospitalized for the wound.[49]

The invaders were well entrenched, and the posse was aware that it would be difficult to finally roust them out of their fortifications and arrest them. Foote went so far as to ask for cannon at Fort McKinney, but the commanding officer politely declined.[50] Another idea was forwarded, though, that might allow a closer approach for either a final rush or the use of explosives. The posse took a page out of the invaders book and found a use for captured wagons. With the running gears from the invaders' supply wagons, they constructed a device referred to as an "ark of safety" or a "go-devil." The idea was that when it was pushed forward, close to the invaders' lines, the sheriff would give the invaders a last chance to surrender, and if they refused, their own dynamite would be hurled against them.[51]

A .270 rifle cartridge and a .45-90 rifle cartridge. This .270 shell, which is a twentieth-century cartridge, fires a 150-grain bullet with a muzzle velocity of about three thousand feet per second. The nineteenth-century .45-90 fires a much larger bullet at a much slower velocity. Photograph by the author.

All during April 12 the posse worked on the go-devil in a safe area behind the siege lines. A "movable breastwork" was built upon the running gears. It was made of heavy logs about six feet high, and its purpose was to allow some forty men to advance on the fortifications.[52] The invaders were well aware that the posse was working on a device to be used against them; Irvine recalled hearing a cheer that went up when it was finished.[53] But the go-devil was just one element of the invaders' predicament. Each man in the invading army could see that more and more besiegers were arriving—David estimated that at the end there were 434 men—and their works were coming ever closer, meaning, among other things, that an attempted breakout would have been suicidal.[54] For the invaders it was a dark time. David admitted that "the situation was becoming hourly more desperate," that ammunition and food were almost expended, and that the lack of sleep and proper food were taking their "unerring toll."[55]

For a time the invaders believed they would be rescued, if not by troops, then by reinforcements from other big cattlemen. But a message sent to John Winterling in Sheridan County urgently seeking help (Winterling was the man who made the motion for the big cattlemen to personally participate in the invasion) produced only a deafening silence.[56] David summarized the attitudes of the invaders the evening of April 12, 1892:

The go-devil, or "ark of safety." Courtesy of Johnson County Jim Gatchell Memorial Museum.

"Each man gave up hope in his heart that day. Each knew the impossibility of rescue, and all understood the ruthlessness and vindictiveness of some of the most active of the besiegers. There was absolutely no hope of life beyond the following daybreak."[57]

CHAPTER FIFTEEN

The Siege Ends

Tuesday, April 12, 1892, was the day Governor Barber finally realized his friends were in profound trouble. April 11 telegrams from Parmelee and Hogerson probably caused him concern, with their references to a posse surrounding the invaders at the T. A. Ranch. The next day, however, Barber most probably received the Wolcott telegram (slipped out by Dowling), and this message would have left little doubt of the peril of the invaders.[1] Governor Barber sprang into action. No more would he declare he had not been notified officially or complain about conflicting reports. Instead, he fired off telegrams to President Benjamin Harrison, to General Brooke, Commander of the Army of the Platte in Omaha, and to Hogerson and Parmelee in Buffalo.[2]

The first sentence of the telegram to President Harrison is famously ambiguous. "An insurrection exists in Johnson county, in the State of Wyoming, in the immediate vicinity of Fort McKinney, against the government of said state," the telegram said. The governor did not explain to the president just who was engaged in the "insurrection," and he certainly did not say that the lawfully constituted authorities in the county had lawbreakers under siege and were proceeding to apprehend them. Despite its initial lack of clarity, the telegram's overall thrust was quite clear—the governor wanted the president to order troops at Fort McKinney to the T. A. Ranch immediately, "to suppress the insurrection, restore order and protect both life and property."[3]

At some time during April 12, Barber realized his messages were failing to get through to the President, and he started sending wires to Wyoming's two Senators, Carey and Warren. Barber finally reached them late that evening, and they in turn contacted the Assistant Secretary of War, Lewis A. Grant. Together, Carey, Warren, and Grant went to the White House and got the President out of bed. Carey and President Harrison were said to be old Senate friends, and no one was present at this session to speak for Johnson County. Quickly convinced of the necessity for immediate action, Harrison ordered a telegram send to General John R. Brooke in Omaha shortly after 11:00 P.M.[4] At 11:05 P.M. the president wired Governor Barber that "in compliance with your call for the aid of the United States forces to protect the state of Wyoming against domestic violence," he had ordered the secretary of war to send troops.[5] The president did not have his facts right—the state of Wyoming needed no saving from domestic violence—but Governor Barber made no effort to set the record straight. At 11:37 P.M. General Brooke telegrammed Governor Barber, informing him that the commanding officer at Fort McKinney had been ordered "to prevent violence and preserve peace."[6] This message was received in Buffalo at 12:05 P.M., and within two hours, troops rode out of Fort McKinney under orders from the post's commanding officer, Colonel J. J. Van Horn.[7]

Van Horn issued several official communiqués during the next few days, and these comments by an officer on the ground, standing between warring factions but not personally involved, help pierce the blizzard of emotional charges soon made by people on both sides. Acknowledging the order to proceed to the T. A. Ranch, Van Horn wired back to General Brooke: "Entire county is aroused by the killings at the KC Ranch and some of the best citizens were in the posse."[8] This was quite a different tone from the other messages flying around the country, but then again, Van Horn had been speaking, not to federal politicians in the previous few days, but instead to Johnson County citizens as he watched the invasion unfold.

Colonel Van Horn had a good working relationship with Sheriff Angus, and when Angus returned from the T. A. Ranch the night of August 11, 1892, the two men had a talk. Sheriff Angus "talked very sensibly regarding the situation of Ray and Champion," Van Horn said later in his official report, "and for that purpose has sworn in a large posse to act as deputies." The colonel added, "Should the so-called regulators resist arrest, he cannot be answerable for their lives."[9] (The "regulators" were also referred to by Johnson County people as "white caps," another term for vigilantes.) Van Horn also spent some time with the Johnson County commissioners, who "talked very feelingly," he said. "They resent the many slurs cast upon their county by the cattle barons who are trying to drive the smaller stockmen off the range."[10]

Eleven officers and ninety-six enlisted men rode out of Fort McKinney, accompanied by Sheriff Angus and three civilians (including Sam Clover), as well as C. H. Parmelee. Before troops left McKinney, Governor Barber had telegraphed Colonel Van Horn to request that, as the governor's "aide-de-camp" and representative, Parmelee be included with those riding to the T. A. The governor expressed his concern for the well-being of the invaders, insisting: "It is very important that all hostilities be stopped at once, and that no violence be permitted to any of the persons concerned. Considering the excitement in the vicinity it seems advisable that the people who are now besieged should be given protection at Fort McKinney until time can be had for further action."[11] The request for "protection at Fort McKinney" soon assumed great significance.

It was eighteen miles from Fort McKinney to the T. A. Ranch, and the cavalry detachment rode through the night to get there. But when the sun rose about 6:00 A.M. on April 13, 1892, the troops had not yet reached the T. A.

The weather had been clearing, and neither snow nor rain was falling that morning. The dawn revealed two fortified camps—besieged invaders surrounded by hundreds of men. It was a scene visible to any rider coming over a high point near the T. A. Such a rider could have watched the beginning of a major push to dislodge and capture the invaders. The besiegers' go-devil was in place about three hundred yards west of the invaders' fort. At dawn the go-devil began its ponderous progression toward the invaders' lines. It was manned by fourteen men with rifles and a box of dynamite. The go-devil advanced about one hundred yards, slowly closing the short gap to the invaders' fort. In only a short time, the men in the go-devil would be close enough to hurl dynamite into the fort, which, in turn, would have pushed the invaders into the open and, as Mercer wrote, "the sharpshooters in the rifle pits would have sent them to earth."[12]

The posse never got its chance, however. Suddenly, in the far distance, a bugle was heard, heralding the troops from Fort McKinney. The fighting at the T. A. did not stop immediately, though. Van Horn later reported that both of the hostile parties discovered his presence, and from that time the besiegers "kept up an almost continuous fire upon the buildings." Shortly, the troops pulled up near the ranch, and about 6:45 A.M., Colonel Van Horn asked Sheriff Angus to order the posse to stop firing, which, in Van Horn's words, "was soon effected."[13]

The invaders watched the approach of the troops with intense interest. In a dramatic passage, David wrote that Major Wolcott, seeing the troops, "threw his hand in a gesture of stunned groping to the table and whispered: 'Gentlemen, it is the troops. We are to live.'"[14] Sam Clover interviewed a stockman he called Bertram, who told him, "We were up against it hard, and knew our case was hopeless unless the soldiers were ordered out. When that bugle sounded I could have wept; as it was, I howled for joy."[15] On the other hand, some of the invaders continued to show disdain for the sheriff's posse, refusing to admit that they were ever in peril. Frank Canton wrote much later that the invaders could have broken out any-time they wanted. They only bothered to stay, Canton said, because they had gone to the trouble of making fortifications.[16] Canton's bravado not-withstanding, most of the invaders were deeply relieved. Surrounded and outnumbered almost ten to one, they faced determined men with ample ammunition and food. The four hundred besiegers, according to a *Cheyenne Daily Leader* correspondent on the scene, "were invariably small ranchmen, distinct from the rustlers, who believed that their lives and homes were in danger from the invasion."[17] Clover described the invaders, on the other hand, as presenting a "desperate appearance . . . hollow-eyed, begrimed and half-frozen."[18]

Still, they made a final show of defiance. When Van Horn interviewed Wolcott, he demanded that Wolcott and his followers surrender to the federal troops. Wolcott said he would do so, if the invaders were taken to Fort McKinney and protected by the military. Wolcott declared, however, that, "he and his party would die rather than surrender to Sheriff Angus," adding that Angus "has the best of us now because our plans miscarried, but it will be different yet."[19] Many of the men in the posse probably would have wanted the sheriff to refuse Wolcott's demand and then granted Wolcott his wish to die. For Angus and Arapahoe Brown, though, the only condition was that if the stockmen surrendered, they would be turned over to civil authorities. Viewing confinement at Fort McKinney as just the first step in that process, they readily agreed to the proposed arrangements, little realizing the consequence of accepting these conditions.²⁰ Actually, they had little choice. Unless the posse was to fight the troops (an absurd possibility having life only in the twisted speculations of some supporters of the big cattlemen), the McKinney soldiers were going to become the custodians of the invaders.²¹

Wolcott surrendered forty-five men, fifty revolvers, five thousand rounds of ammunition, and all the horses of his expedition.²² One man was discovered who was seriously wounded—Alex Lowther, one of the Texans. The cattlemen said that Lowther accidentally shot himself, but the claim is dubious, considering their deep desire to minimize their humiliation, as well as the comments of several writers. Lowther was said to have been shot in the belly or his side, an odd place for an accidental wound. He died at Fort McKinney almost one month later, on May 12.²³ Not a single member of the posse was hurt.²⁴ Some of the invaders bitterly objected to the besiegers' tactics, complaining that the posse members had not mounted a charge against the T. A. fortifications.²⁵

Colonel Van Horn reported that during the surrender proceedings "the besiegers collected in a large party of about 200 horsemen and observed the proceedings very attentively, coming as close as the cordon of troops would permit."²⁶ Van Horn stated, though, that when the return march formed up, the posse members, while arraying along a hill beside the road, did so "without any attempt at disturbing or molesting the movements." Van Horn went further and said that their conduct was "extremely moderate and creditable to themselves."²⁷ The colonel may have been overly generous to the posse members. Another reliable report tells of somewhat greater agitation between the invaders and the besiegers than Van Horn described.

The *Buffalo Bulletin* had suggested on March 31 that the *Cheyenne Daily Leader* send a reporter to Johnson County to undertake a thorough inquiry of the situation there and then "let him write the entire matter up, just as he found it." Something very close to that suggestion came to pass at the time of the invasion.²⁸ The *Leader* employed a talented journalist in 1892, one Edgar T. Payton, and Payton was in Newcastle in early April of that year. He became ill, but when he heard of "Pinkertons" invading northern Wyoming, he summoned the strength to reach Buffalo by April 12.²⁹ Once there, he went directly to the T. A. Ranch. For the next several days, writing as a special correspondent for the *Leader*, he provided detailed and objective reports, relaying reliable information to his editors, a tiny but important group of men in Cheyenne who were willing to listen to a version of facts not endorsed by the big cattlemen. Payton's reporting seems to have influenced the editorial positions of the *Cheyenne Daily Leader*. He contributed an excellent story about the march of the cattlemen from the T. A. Ranch to Fort McKinney, seeming to catch the nuances of an unusually complex situation. He wrote of the posse's "extreme curiosity" as they crowded along the exit route. "Expressions from the younger men particularly were very far from friendly," Payton observed, "but the general feeling seemed to be one of intense satisfaction." As the cattlemen passed by, several of them were pointed out to friends in the crowd, especially those from Johnson, Crook, Weston, and Converse counties. Payton said that posse members expressed "general bitterness" toward a few men "who seemed the objects of undisguised hatred." Still, it was "a remarkably orderly procession," he said, and the troops, who had expected trouble, were "pleasantly surprised."[30]

The accounts of some of the cattlemen about their treatment after the surrender contrasted sharply with the writings of Van Horn and Payton. Irvine, for example, wrote twenty years later that the posse members followed them, jeering at the invaders until they had almost arrived at Fort McKinney, over three hours later.[31] In light of the contemporaneous reports of Van Horn and Payton, however (as well as Sam Clover, who wrote that the march back to the fort "was accomplished without molestation from the rustlers"), Irvine's reminiscence is not credible.[32] On the other hand, there were several reports of ugly statements by the cattlemen. The *Bulletin* reported that the big cattlemen, "one and all, assert that though temporarily checked and under restraint, they will soon be at liberty and be back here to finish what they began."[33] George Dunning wrote that the invaders, being in fine spirits after the troops arrived, declared that "it would be but a short time when they would come back stronger than ever and would kill off every man that packed a gun against the mob at the T A Ranch."[34]

George Dunning was not among the men who marched to Fort McKinney on April 13. The man from Idaho concealed himself under the hay in the T. A. barn until the surrender proceedings were completed and everyone left for Buffalo. Then he emerged from the barn and walked, not away from the Johnson County seat, but directly to Buffalo.[35]

When the invaders were delivered at Fort McKinney, the posse disbanded.[36] Once the arrests were made, however, the work was just beginning for Sheriff Angus. The next day, April 14, Angus made a formal request that forty-four invaders held at Fort McKinney be turned over to him.[37]

Such a request was understandable and appropriate. Angus wanted to obtain custody quickly because custody was essential to pursuing the criminal investigation. Even in a small rural county in Wyoming in 1892, a sheriff knew something about effective methods of interrogation and plea bargaining.[38] Angus and his deputies most probably wanted to interview each of the forty-four men separately. He would also have looked for ways to house at least some of the men separately, so that the big cattlemen could not apply pressure or contrive stories or tactics to frustrate interrogation. Separate housing and interrogation would be very effective to split out men, such as the Texans, and, possibly, other hired men, who had no commitment to any great cause other than avoiding prison or hanging. If such interrogation techniques were employed, several of the less culpable men could have been offered plea bargains in return for telling the whole story. Only a few would need to have broken and soon almost all the hired men would have clamored to tell their stories. The big cattlemen would probably have found themselves isolated, with twenty or more men offering damning evidence against them.

Governor Barber, who may have understood these things also, undermined Angus's plan. Because of the actions of the governor of Wyoming, it would be more than two months before Sheriff Angus was allowed to interview his first suspect.

CHAPTER SIXTEEN

The Newspaper Wars

A public furor followed in the wake of the invasion, as the people of Wyoming grappled with an astonishing, unprecedented event. Wyoming newspapers presented a cacophony of conflicting reports and, at first blush, seemed to offer nothing but confusion. But some things were clear. One was that the big cattlemen were not about to capitulate. They were dogged and resourceful combatants who very soon concluded they had only lost a skirmish and their war against Johnson County could still be won. They just moved the struggle to new grounds, to battles over the facts, to the perceptions of the Johnson County invasion, and to the combat in the courtroom. The cattlemen quickly recognized that the public relations battle would very much affect the battle inside the courtroom. The conflict between newspapers was joined early and lasted for years, with big cattlemen and their supporters, and Johnson County residents and their supporters, vigorously presenting their wholly opposite views of the invasion and its backdrop.

Even while the invaders were still holding out at the T. A. Ranch, the first salvo on the new battleground had been fired, and, as in most wars, the first casualty was truth. The leading soldier for the cattlemen was Ed Towse, the Cheyenne journalist behind the Cattle Kate story. Towse had stayed at the Tisdale Ranch the night of April 9 with Governor Barber's friend Dr. Penrose and cattleman H. W. Davis of southern Johnson County when the remaining invaders set out for the KC Ranch. The next day,

April 10, the three men, although professing a desire to follow their friends, decided to leave the Tisdale place for Davis's ranch on the Powder River. They stayed there until April 11, and while there they heard from the area cowboys that Ray and Champion had been killed at the KC. They also heard that the cattlemen were besieged by several hundred men at the T. A. Ranch, and they knew that virtually all the residents were united against the invaders.[1] Dr. Penrose later wrote, with surprising candor, "We then and there gave up any hope of joining our friends. It would have been impossible, even if we had been anxious to do so, and we were not anxious."[2]

For the three men, it was a time of great uncertainty and fear, and their general nervousness made them all feel they had to do something. Davis decided to remain at his ranch—to protect it, he said. Dr. Penrose decided he should ride south, to Douglas, and Towse said that he would "go east and get out of the state into Nebraska."[3] Towse did go east, but instead of Nebraska, he rode to Gillette, arriving there probably late on April 12. The appeal of Gillette was that it had a working telegraph, and Towse could get his story out. At 1:30 A.M. on April 13—when the invaders were in desperate straits at the T. A. but had not yet surrendered—a "Special Dispatch" was wired to the *Sun*, almost certainly from Ed Towse.[4]

Towse's newspaper had already been actively supporting the big cattlemen's excursion, even in the absence of any facts about it. When Towse started sending in dispatches, he added a loud voice that strongly supported the *Sun*'s editorial stance. In his April 13 story, Towse provided only a general overview, which was about all he knew of the events, but in a story issued out of Gillette the next day, he went into considerably greater detail. The *Sun* headlined the story "A Graphic Account," and it was that, but much of it was creative writing, as Towse forwarded statements about which he could have had no information. For example, he wrote, "Sheriff Angus appointed about 200 deputies, providing all the rustlers with stars. He could do nothing with them, or claimed he was unable to command them." Towse embellished this point, saying that Angus had "appealed to the commander at Fort McKinney, acknowledging that his deputies were unmanageable."[5]

Towse had not been near the T. A. Ranch or Fort McKinney, so all he could have heard were rumors carried by horseback gossips, but that did not stop him from creating another set of assertions that were apparently sheer fiction. He began ringing a bell that would be sounded time and again in the next few days by big cattlemen and their supporters: "The depth of the acrimonious feeling of the rustlers is something horrible," Towse wrote, stating that many rustlers were for "burning and skinning the cattlemen alive." Towse wanted to attribute this sentiment to those besieging the T. A., but a careful reading of his story shows that he was only presenting idle talk among a few cowboys many miles from the fighting. He wrote about "Lee Moore and his gang of thieves" from Crook County, and the "thieves" from Converse, Weston, and Natrona counties, and he closed by declaring, "The rustlers, as I see it, are now in power. They at least cannot lose and every hoof but their own will be driven from the state."[6]

As Towse provided this story to the *Sun*, another story went out from Cheyenne to the *Chicago Herald*, Sam Clover's newspaper.[7] This story's origin was almost surely the *Sun*, but the author of the article was not identified. The first part of the story appears to be an amalgam of all the piecemeal information then available about the invasion, and the second part provided background information. The whole piece is unusually long, especially the second part. That second part is about three thousand words in length (about twice the length of the first part), and it was probably written before the invasion, because there is nothing within it that would not have been known before the invasion. It has all the hallmarks of the kind of journalism exhibited by Ed Towse in his earlier writings, and it is entirely possible that Towse wrote it before he boarded the invaders' train to Casper on April 5.

This second part of the story is headed "Long Suffering Ranchmen" and is a prototype of the kind of disinformation that would soon be disseminated throughout Wyoming and the United States by agents of the big cattlemen. The piece begins by stating that for up to ten years, the "reputable" cattle ranch owners and stockmen had "borne with an equanimity past belief" the enormous depredations by men who were not only thieves but committed "outrageous assaults on honest employees," who "in many cases were shot down in cold blood for remaining faithful to their trust." (In fact, no such events were ever reported by area newspapers, even by those friendly to big cattlemen, and, once again, such comments appear to be projections from the assassinations carried out by the cattlemen's own squads.) Despite the expenditure of vast sums of money for prosecution, the article went on, convictions were practically unknown, but this was to be expected because county officials "were in close league with the cattle rustlers," even "sharing in the profits of their nefarious business" and protecting the rustlers in court "when by some miscalculation the thieves were detected and captured."

The article went on in such similar vein, raging against the alleged lack of assistance from officers of the law and declaring that the lack of support from law enforcement was especially bad in Johnson County. Further, it was stated, all the cowboys were "of the same ilk" as the rustlers and would not interfere with attacks upon their foremen nor would they ever assist with prosecutions of cattle thieves.

The article said that the big cattlemen, as absentee owners and honest men, had no conception such terrible things could be happening, and could scarcely believe it. (The 1883 and 1884 activity of the Wyoming Stock Growers Association shows, to the contrary, that big cattlemen, almost from the beginning and irrespective of the evidence, believed deeply that all the small cattlemen in the state were thieves conspiring against them.) Finally, however, the big cattle owners realized that they were being "mercilessly" robbed, although "the truth was bound to be revealed when, year after year, the calculate increase continued to grow smaller in spite of easy winters and an abundance of feed." (The winter of 1886–87, with its 50 percent losses, was overlooked in this tale.)

The article trotted out Judge Micah Saufley's 1889 alleged statements about the impossibility of prosecuting rustlers, although adding considerable embellishment, even upon Fred Hesse's version. Then the article went on to praise at great length the wonderful law that created the Wyoming Live Stock Commission, providing a careful, almost lawyer-like justification of the confiscations by the commission. Then, after the great successes of the livestock commission, the article declared, the "balked bandits" did a Land Office business selling dressed beef to army contractors and railroad subcontractors, as well as shooting down "hundreds of steers" out on the range, or, if this killing did not amuse them, running off cattle "in bunches of fifty." (As with other such allegations, no supporting evidence was presented.)

Railing against the cattle rustlers who "violently denounced the live stock commission," the article said that a protest had come "from the head of the rustlers in Johnson county; from men who openly boasted of their thievery and who had given notice to the reputable stock men that they would not be permitted to make their annual round-up in that county." (This was evidently an allusion to John R. Smith and the local cattle association; Smith never "openly boasted" of thievery, nor did he declare that the large stockmen would not be permitted to conduct their own roundup.) This action, wrote Towse, "provoked the righteous indignation of every cattle man in the state, who . . . needed only this last straw to suddenly burst all bounds and determine by one grand coup to teach these rascals a lesson that should be remembered for all time."

The article also claimed that local sympathy was with the rustlers, because a few farmers had been driven from the land by big cattlemen and were bitter. The article claimed that these farmers would have otherwise been defeated by crop failure and starvation but nevertheless developed sympathy for the opponents of the big cattlemen. Because of this, Towse concluded, the "war of the rustlers" had support from a few men "who have been grievously wronged, and in this way commands a public sympathy which gives the struggle to some extent the aspect of a civil war rather than that of a straight contest between law and lawlessness."

All these points were backed by the enormous economic power of the big cattlemen, were disseminated throughout Wyoming and the nation, and were strongly supported by the Wyoming Republican Party, the predominant political party in the state. They carried frightening power. In fact, they were enormously effective in forwarding their purpose: to enable more than forty willful men to escape punishment for murder.

Ed Towse had the advantage of writing for a daily from Cheyenne, the state capitol and by far the largest town in Wyoming. Cheyenne was almost twice the size of the next largest town, Laramie, three and a half times Rock Springs, the third-largest town, and about six times the size of Evanston, the next largest. The *Cheyenne Daily Leader*, the *Cheyenne Daily Sun*, and the *Cheyenne Tribune* were all dailies printed in Cheyenne; all had been owned by big cattlemen, and in 1892, only the *Leader* was not. Every little town in Wyoming had a newspaper, usually at least two, but, except for those in Laramie, they were weeklies with little influence beyond the immediate vicinity of their towns. The Associated Press had been formed, but small locals were not served by the AP, and these hometown newspapers typically confined themselves to printing articles from other area newspapers, followed by comments about the articles and statements of area people. The small local newspapers could not undertake statewide reporting, as the Cheyenne papers did.[8]

The Johnson County War, however, was such a major event in the state that newspapers everywhere in Wyoming addressed the invasion, attempting to present the public with a different view from that of the Cheyenne newspapers owned by the big cattlemen. The regular publication date for the *Buffalo Bulletin* was April 14, but it was late by a few days. The editor wrote that he trusted no apology would be needed for those within Johnson County, and for those outside, "it might be well to say that the excitement of the past week made work so near the main thoroughfare of this city an impossibility."[9] When it did appear, the April 14, 1892, *Bulletin* showed that the people of Buffalo were angry and shocked, felt betrayed, were in disbelief, and were proud of themselves for standing up to an army of assassins. Maybe the best demonstration of their feelings is the set of headlines that accompanied the lead article about the events of the previous few days. It read:

BAFFLED!
MURDEROUS CRUSADERS
ROUTED

WITHOUT PARALLEL AND WITHOUT JUSTIFICATION

A MOTLEY GROUP OF ASSASSINS FROM THE SOUTH

ARE MET, CONQUERED AND HUMILIATED BY THE PEOPLE

THE GREATEST OUTRAGE ON AN AMERICAN PUBLIC.

RESENTED WITH WINCHESTERS AND DETERMINED HEARTS

The *Bulletin* wrote: "A band of armed men consisting of four classes, viz: Wealthy stockmen, suspected criminals, hired assassins and duped fools, invaded Johnson county and have committed murder and arson.

They were surrounded by the people of the county, captured by U.S. troops and shipped hence to the governor of Wyoming, care of Uncle Sam."[10] The plot was deliberately planned, stated the *Bulletin*, but "an allwise providence . . . frustrated the designs of this invading force." The article concluded, "The people of the county cry, not for vengeance, but justice."[11]

This editorial reads like some of Joe DeBarthe's writing, but most of it was probably written by G. E. A. Moeller, the musician and former deputy clerk of court. DeBarthe, the *Bulletin* reported, "has been and is now sick," and Moeller was acting as the editor for this edition. It appears that the conflict of the last few months had finally overwhelmed DeBarthe, and he had a mental breakdown, although Mayor Charles Burritt, the cattlemen's attorney in Buffalo, attributed the problem to whiskey.[12]

The *Bulletin* articles show that the involvement of local men in the invasion plot was what most rankled the people of Johnson County. Each of the Johnson County men in the invading force was listed and given a brief description in the *Bulletin*, and special comments were made about Fred Hesse and Frank Canton. The *Bulletin* excoriated Canton for his statement that all he was trying to do in the invasion was to serve warrants as a deputy U.S. marshal, asking rhetorically: "Was Frank M. Canton a deputy United States marshal last November, when at break of day, with four others he burglarized a dwelling, and without a word of warning shot at the head of the men he was presumed to want to arrest?" The article further stated that, next to F. M. Canton, the people of Johnson County blamed Fred G. S. Hesse as the "prime cause for the late attempt to shed the blood of their citizens." Referring to the marking of forty-two local citizens for murder, the *Bulletin* asked, "What excuse can Hesse give for deliberately and cowardly taking life?"[13]

Responding to Towse's April 13 *Cheyenne Daily Sun* article, the *Bulletin* defended Angus's control of the posse, branding the *Sun*'s criticism as "an unqualified falsehood." The sheriff's posse, the *Bulletin* said, "was completely under control and cheerfully obeyed all orders, no matter what hardships were involved."[14]

The newspaper battles were hottest in Cheyenne. The cattlemen-owned *Sun* and *Tribune* relentlessly trumpeted the big cattlemen's agenda, while the *Leader*, though late to the position, tried to set the record straight. The cattlemen were already angry with the owners of the *Leader*. After the newspaper started criticizing the livestock commission on March 22,

1892, they declared a boycott against the *Leader*.[15] H. B. Ijams, secretary of the commission, was reported to have said of the *Leader*: "The only thing left for us now is to knock out that damned outfit."[16]

The editor of the *Leader*, John Carroll, turned all this against the big cattlemen. Carroll was not a man to be bullied, and it seems that the harder the cattlemen leaned on him because of his refusal to follow their line, the harder he pushed back. Referring to "revival of the old spirit of intolerance of the Wyoming stock growers' association," the paper denounced the cattlemen's actions and published editions with large empty spaces where advertising had been. Heavy criticism of the boycott throughout Wyoming forced the big cattlemen to call it off.[17] The *Leader*'s continuing criticism infuriated them nonetheless, and it would not be long before the cattlemen would strike again at the newspaper.

For several days after the invaders were captured, the *Cheyenne Daily Sun* hammered the same points Ed Towse had earlier made, that the big cattlemen in Buffalo were in great danger because of the threat to them by Johnson County citizens. A raid on the fort was to be expected "at any moment," the *Sun* reported, by men who had poured into Buffalo "armed to the teeth." Meanwhile, the governor expressed deep concern because of the reported "great excitement" among Johnson County people.[18]

If the people of Johnson County were greatly excited—and after the invasion, who would not be?—vigilante action was hardly imminent. As the *Bulletin* pointed out, the posse had disbanded, and there had never been a lynching party in Johnson County. The *Bulletin* noted that one invader (probably Richard Allen) who had been in the Johnson County jail for six days had, upon the direction of the governor, been delivered to one corporal and one private of the U.S. Army on April 16, despite the presence of many men in town.[19] It was the *Cheyenne Daily Leader*, however, that gave the strongest rebuttal to the *Sun*'s statements. The *Leader*'s correspondent provided quite a different story on the condition of things in Buffalo. Contrary to Barber's claim of having received information showing great danger, the *Leader*'s special correspondent reported that "everything is now quiet and peaceful in that town" and that the people of Buffalo wanted only to be able to take legal action "when the proper time comes." To the *Leader*, this seemed a reasonable request. Besides, the invaders were held by a strong military force, the U.S. Army. The *Leader* said, "The people up there so far feel that they have simply upheld the law and defended their rights." The paper concluded that "the law should be allowed to take its course," meaning that the men should be kept in Buffalo to await trial.[20]

On April 16 the *Sun* complained that Angus had refused the governor's request that certain prisoners, including the teamsters, be turned over to military authorities, and the paper insisted (again), "The officers of that county are powerless to protect, and the confession of Sheriff Angus that he could not control the mob was a true index of the situation."[21] Angus had never "confessed" that he could not control "the mob" (his posse); the *Sun* had only its earlier unsubstantiated conclusions to cite as proof of the assertion.

The following day, April 17, the *Leader* issued a strong editorial, forwarding some simple truths that infuriated the big cattlemen and elated the people of Johnson County. The *Leader* first noted that irrespective of the social status or general influence of the big cattlemen, "nobody can be blinded to the essential fact that with a band of armed mercenaries they were invading Johnson county to do violence to its inhabitants and commit crimes against the laws."[22] This invasion, said the *Leader*, was "all that was necessary for the constituted civil authorities and the people of Johnson county to know." They then had a duty "to rise up en masse and repel the invasion," which they did with great skill. The *Leader* declared that "law and equity up to this writing, are entirely upon the side of the civil authorities," and it was "simply a piece of presumption" for the governor to demand that prisoners be turned over.

The *Leader* praised the Johnson County authorities, saying that they had acted with "coolness, common sense and a thorough grasp of the fundamental principles of the law." They had been provoked, said the *Leader*, by the "remarkable course pursued by Gov. Barber and his advisors." The editorial then observed, "The official actions have been such as to lead not only them but every disinterested man in the state to believe that a conspiracy is on foot to thwart justice. They hear threats of martial law being applied to a community which has risen en masse to uphold the law." Here the *Leader* was referring to the contention being zealously advanced by big cattlemen supporters that the elected authorities of Johnson County ought to be pushed aside and military law imposed upon the county. The *Leader* went on: "The people see inflammatory reports spread abroad in certain newspapers, the situation of affairs misrepresented so as to influence public opinion in favor of a proclamation of martial law in Johnson county."

The *Leader* closed the editorial with pleas to Governor Barber, stating,

> We do not believe that the people of Johnson County require anything more than a positive knowledge that justice will be done. So far they have every reason to believe the contrary. They believe the state authorities are leagued together to thwart justice. Let it be positively known before it is too late that this is not the case. . . . The governor should act vigorously and promptly not only for the sake of the captured stockmen and the people of Johnson county, but for the fair fame of Wyoming, already besmirched and again in the deadliest peril.

This was a powerful declaration, an appeal on behalf of the people of Wyoming for fundamental fairness. If state authorities were *not* "leagued together to thwart justice," it would have had a profound impact. Instead it became just one more reason why the big cattlemen despised the *Leader*, and hardly slowed Barber's determination to protect his friends.

The governor announced that the cattlemen were going to be taken to southern Wyoming. He vacillated at first—or at least he declared his great concern over making a difficult decision—but it was soon clear that all the prisoners would be taken by rail to Douglas and then to Fort Russell, near Cheyenne.[23] This news was not well received outside Cheyenne. Virtually all Wyoming newspapers, except the *Cheyenne Sun* and *Tribune*, condemned the invasion in unmistakable terms, and the governor's actions in refusing to turn over the prisoners to Sheriff Angus and instead taking them south lost him the few supporters he had.[24] The *Sheridan Enterprise* wrote that "no words of condemnation can be too strong for leaders and instigators of this diabolical attempt; nor for those state officials who have aided or abetted it either actively or quietly."[25] The *Laramie Boomerang* stated that, under the state constitution, people who levied war against the State of Wyoming were guilty of *treason*, and noted that "the situation is much more deplorable when the armed body comes from outside the state"—an apparent reference to the Texans hired by the big cattlemen.[26] The *Carbon County Journal* (Rawlins) spoke of the "merited criticism" of Governor Barber "for permitting the stock association to import an armed force to invade the state and murder our citizens," and the *Wyoming Derrick* (Casper) carried a story headlined, "THOSE ASSASSINS," which quoted Jones and Walker, the two trappers captured by the invaders.

Within the story, the *Derrick* stated that the invaders had compelled the two men "to witness one of the most degrading crimes ever committed in the state, the foul killing of Champion and Ray, by a mob of outlaws hired in Texas."[27]

Another group, perhaps surprisingly, declared their unequivocal condemnation of the invaders and support for Johnson County people. The *Bulletin* carried a column each week from Fort McKinney. One might think that the soldiers in the fort, living in Wyoming only temporarily, would not have strong feelings about its domestic disputes. Not so. The writer of the McKinney column seldom ventured into civilian matters, but on this occasion he revealed how the soldiers at Fort McKinney viewed the events, expressing a strong personal opinion. The writer first noted that those at the fort were watching the events "with as much interest as those actually engaged in this uncalled for war," and then stated: "It seems to us that law and order, not in Johnson county, but under the shadow of the Wyoming state capital is at a very low ebb . . . [and] it is about time somebody should overhaul the officials and state lawmaker for such breach of law and order." Observing that the campaign had been undertaken "for the purpose of driving out the rustlers and terrorizing that part of Wyoming in which the so-called rustlers reside," the writer left no doubt as to his opinion about the invasion: "In any civilized community, this could not have happened, and shows either one thing or the other; collusion, or inability to uphold the rights of the people and enforce the spirit of the law. Put the thing in any shape, it is deplorable and will go down in the history of Wyoming as an everlasting disgrace."[28]

The above examples are only a small sample of articles published throughout Wyoming that show the depth of alarm and anger. Three funerals were held in Buffalo on April 15, and they demonstrated the public's strong feelings. The first funeral was for Dr. John C. Watkins, who had died on April 12. Dr. Watkins was the county coroner and felt he should go to the KC Ranch and undertake an inquest regarding Nate Champion and Nick Ray. Watkins was not in good health, however, and he was stricken some thirty miles south of Buffalo with what was termed "apoplexy." He died on April 12.[29]

Nate Champion's funeral was the biggest event of the day. Frank Canton may not have seen Nate Champion as a hero, but the people of Johnson County certainly did. They knew that because of Champion's bravery, skill, and sacrifice, they were given the time to rally and protect their homes and their lives. To the citizens of Johnson County in April 1892, Nate Champion was a hero like Horatius at the bridge, and when they had the opportunity to honor him, they did so. About 500 people attended the funerals of Champion and Ray, about one-quarter of all the men, women, and children in Johnson County. The coffins of the two men were "beautifully and profusely decorated with flowers."[30] The small church where the funerals were held was "filled with ladies," and "large crowds of men stood on the outside." The procession past the coffins took eight minutes, and 483 people were in line.[31] The Methodist reverend Marvin Rader gave an impressive address, leaving most of those attending in tears. He closed his remarks by declaring that "these men have been sent to eternity, we know not why; they were not criminals." All business in Buffalo was suspended during that day.[32] The *Rocky Mountain News* commented, "It is doubtful if ten people here sympathized with the captured wealthy aristocrats, who committed the murders."[33]

During the time of the funerals, a coroner's jury was taking evidence. Indeed, the proceedings had begun on April 13, the day the invaders surrendered, although the coroner's report was not submitted until April 16.[34] The jury heard from several men who were in the thick of the events of April 9, 1892, starting with Jack Flagg and Alonzo Taylor. The two witnesses recounted their harrowing escape from the invaders on April 9 but also told the jury that Nate Champion and Nick Ray had been residing at the KC Ranch since about April 1. Taylor testified that he recognized Charles Ford, Frank Canton, Fred Hesse, and Phil DuFran among the men who surrounded the buildings at the KC; he also identified burned articles found at the KC as belonging to Nick Ray. Taylor had seen the body of Nate Champion and identified him, but said he was unable to identify the charred trunk that was supposed to be Nick Ray. Terrence Smith, the man who lived just four miles north of the KC, told the jury about the morning of April 9, 1892, when he had suddenly heard a barrage from the south, then snuck closer and saw men besieging the ranch.

Percy Brockway, a cowboy who had found himself at the T. A. Ranch on April 10, testified about the forty to fifty heavily armed cowmen who suddenly came into the ranch, and how they kept talking about surrounding a house and how they wished they had men as good as Nate Champion. He identified Will Guthrie, Charles Ford, Frank Canton, John N. Tisdale,

Major Wolcott, Billy Irvine, Fred G. S. Hesse, Mike Shonsey, H. W. Davis, Joe Elliott, Phil DuFran, and Lafayette Parker.

One of the teamsters who drove the invaders' supply wagons, William M. Colloum, testified at some length. He worked for Irvine and had joined the expedition at Casper. In his testimony he supplied a detailed list of the names of the big cattlemen, but he did not know many of the Texans. Colloum took his wagon to the KC Ranch, and he remembered men saying, "We have got one of them, but the worst son of a bitch got away." Then one man had said, "We have got the ranch afire," and some later came up and said, "We have got him."

Surprisingly, the testimony of George Dunning was not provided. Dunning was taken into custody by the Johnson County authorities soon after he arrived in Buffalo, which was probably late on April 13. He would have been an invaluable witness, filling in all the gaps and holes left open by other testimony. Dunning may have been deliberately kept under cover, though, perhaps because the Johnson County authorities became concerned about the governor's insistence that all prisoners be taken from Buffalo.[35]

The invaders were marched out of Buffalo by federal troops on April 17, the same day that Jim Dudley died at the hospital in Fort McKinney.[36] The occasion produced a frenzy of charges by the big cattlemen's supporters, seemingly based on nothing but fantasy, and Governor Barber led the chorus. Shortly before the cattlemen left Buffalo, the governor telegraphed General Brooke, the army commander over Fort McKinney, and his message can be viewed only as hysterical. Barber insisted that there was a great danger of sharpshooters on the march to Douglas, "that bodies of men are going north and that the Commander of Fort McKinney should be prepared to resist one thousand men before attempting to bring Wolcott party south." Then he added, "This is corroborated from other sources in all respects excepting the number of men who may be encountered, and my very best information is that a very large number of armed men are going into the country between Douglas and Buffalo."[37] Such a message supports Sam Clover's statement about Barber, that he was "a weak-kneed ass throughout, inept and overly smart."[38]

Governor Barber's version certainly was approved by the big cattlemen's Cheyenne newspapers, however. Ed Towse returned to Cheyenne on April 18 ("still breathing war") and immediately started turning out outrageous stories, two of which were printed in the *Chicago Herald*, Clover's newspaper.[39] An article to the *Herald* must have aroused Towse's interest, as it might gain national attention. He may also have been prodded by John Clay, a Chicago resident and president of the Wyoming Stock Growers Association, to "pour it on" for a major Chicago newspaper. Of course, Towse was also being paid to write such stories. Still, none of these factors would seem to fully explain the reporter's zeal in lashing out at his employer's enemies:

> The dead wire has been reduced by the thieves, who hope now, emboldened by their victory at the T. A. Ranch, to muster a sufficient force to take the prisoners of war from five companies of the United States army at Fort McKinney. More than a thousand rustlers and friends, including Angus' murderous deputies, are encamped about the post, and only fear of heavy loss in a collision restrains them from making a rush on Fort McKinney. They are willing to pay almost any price for the half-dozen unarmed men of Wolcott's command. At several ranches visited in riding from the country men were heard advocating the skinning and burning alive of the men on the list. The depth of hatred and vindictiveness is marvelous. This is not because Champion and Ray were killed especially, but is based on the broad and peculiar premise that there must be no interference with rustling.[40]

As with his earlier stories, Ed Towse was not at the scene he was reporting, and he had no basis for virtually any of the statements he published. For example, the assertion that one thousand men had gathered about the fort appears to be made out of whole cloth; this was more than twice the number at the height of the T. A. siege. Towse was not about to release his grip upon these fictions, though, even after the invading army left Buffalo with very little problem. In a story printed in the *Chicago Herald*, Towse insisted that five to seven hundred rustlers followed the army command and were expected to make an attack.[41]

The writings of more objective observers show that the departure was not of great moment. Major Fechet, commander of the escort, carefully planned the march, following strict formations, to ensure that if attacks came, the soldiers could efficiently and quickly protect their prisoners.

The command filed out of Fort McKinney the early morning of Monday, April 18. As the party left Fort McKinney, it passed a small hill overlooking the path of the march, and there some two hundred men gathered. Sam Clover reported that "farewell taunts" were flung at the departing big cattlemen, "but they offered no violence."[42]

After leaving Buffalo, there were no incidents at all—no shootings, no interference, not even any sightings of hostile men. The march to Douglas was not uneventful—the trek was a nightmare ordeal—but this was because of the hideous weather conditions, not because of any unfriendly action by "rustlers." The biggest complaint of the invaders was that the soldiers taking them south treated them rudely, almost like criminals.[43] Billy Irvine later wrote that "the only reason that the Army Officers of Col. [Major] Fechet's type were against us was that many of the rustlers were good spenders and hale fellows well met."[44] Irvine, so steeped in his own self-righteousness, apparently never considered that the soldiers were offended by the murderous expedition of Mr. Irvine and his compatriots.

Once the invaders reached Douglas, they boarded trains to Cheyenne, arriving there on April 23. There was no sign of "rustlers" on the journey to Cheyenne. The *Cheyenne Sun* never expressed any embarrassment, nor even provided any explanation why its predictions proved so wildly inaccurate.

The people of Johnson County, though they might not have been the bloodthirsty demons painted by Ed Towse and Governor Barber, were certainly unhappy that the invaders were being taken out of the county. They were satisfied with themselves for thwarting the invasion, but they had great fears that once the men who had been apprehended at the T. A. Ranch were sent to Cheyenne, it would be just the first step in a process leading to justice thwarted. They had good reason to fear. During the next few months a great travesty of justice would unfold.

CHAPTER SEVENTEEN

The Case—Part One

Despite the invaders having been sent to Cheyenne, Johnson County authorities were determined to pursue first-degree murder charges against all forty-five members of the invading army. Before formal charges were even filed, however, some of the invaders expressed contempt for the attempts to prosecute them for their attack on Johnson County citizens.

Within two weeks of the killing of Champion and Ray, newspaper reporters descended upon Cheyenne and interviewed the leaders of the invasion. A lucky reporter for the *Chicago Herald* found Major Frank Wolcott in Cheyenne on April 25, 1892. The major was in a relaxed mood, ready to talk openly.

"We have nothing to regret," pronounced Wolcott. "Blood was shed, it is true, but it was not the blood of an honest man. If an innocent man had been killed, the charge of murder would have been justifiable, but Champion and Ray were pirates, as the foremen of a dozen ranges can prove. We were forced to take the matter into our own hands, and we are willing to abide by the decision of the court as to whether we were right or wrong."[1]

When he read the *Chicago Herald* story based on the Wolcott interview, Willis Van Devanter was anything but relaxed. Any lawyer for a defendant charged with a serious crime cringes if his client makes a public pronouncement, and Van Devanter had to have been appalled to read his client's confession to murder in the pages of a major metropolitan newspaper.

Willis Van Devanter. Courtesy Wyoming State Archives, Department of State Parks and Cultural Resources.

Willis Van Devanter was a powerful force in the events of 1892, both as the attorney for the cattlemen and the right-hand man of Senator Francis Warren. Van Devanter had been in Wyoming only since 1885, but he soon stood out in the small town of Cheyenne. He was about five foot ten (taller than average in 1885) and was a vigorous man. Just twenty-five years old then, he was the oldest of eight children of an Indiana attorney and a recent graduate of the Cincinnati Law School. Van Devanter prob- *Lacey* ably came to Wyoming to follow John Lacey, who in 1884 was appointed chief justice of the Wyoming Supreme Court; Van Devanter was married to Lacey's sister, Dolly, and Lacey established a lucrative practice of law in Cheyenne. Cheyenne was probably attractive to Van Devanter for another reason as well. Wyoming has always been a magnet for men who love to hunt and fish, and Van Devanter, an avid hunter and fisherman all his life, hunted enthusiastically in Wyoming, including participating in some memorable excursions with Buffalo Bill Cody.[2]

Francis E. Warren was the territorial governor of Wyoming in 1885. He had arrived in Cheyenne from Massachusetts in 1868 (after service in the Civil War as an enlisted man) and had remarkable success as a

merchant and cattleman. One of the richest men in Wyoming, he controlled huge landholdings. He was a vastly ambitious politician. He and Van
Devanter quickly became allies, and in Van Devanter he gained early in
his political career an aide who would be of immeasurable assistance: Van
Devanter was a first-rate political operative.[3] More than that, Van Devanter
was a first-rate lawyer: intense, highly intelligent, highly disciplined, and
aggressive. He was as coldly realistic, tough, and flinty as any lawyer who
ever practiced law in Wyoming. Appointed chief justice of the Wyoming
Supreme Court at age thirty in August 1889, he served only a year, probably because his services as a private attorney were in such demand from
the monied people of Wyoming.[4] In 1890, "monied people" meant the
members of the Wyoming Stock Growers Association.

Contrary to Wolcott's posturing, Van Devanter wanted, above all, to
avoid a court ruling upon the merits of the charges against his clients.
This is most vividly shown by a June 27, 1892, letter from Van Devanter
to Wyoming senator Joseph Carey, who was suggesting tactics for Van
Devanter to use in his defense of the invaders. Van Devanter was having
none of it. Carey's comments about the probable success of a jury trial in
which the cattlemen defended their actions only irritated the hard-nosed
young Cheyenne lawyer.[5] A jury trial would not end favorably for his
clients, he declared to Carey. "It is all nonsense to say that these men
can be tried in any county. The most favorable one will undoubtedly
prove to be a dangerous place. This talk about saying that they were
excusable and letting them prove that they went up there to protect
their lives and property is all well enough but there is not one chance
in twenty of any such proof being admitted."[6] For example, Van Devanter
pointed out to Carey, "there cannot be a syllable of proof produced that
Champion ever wronged any of them or attempted to do so." In fact,
declared Van Devanter, there was no proof that Champion even stole a
calf. There was "some slight proof of direct thieving on Ray's part and that
is all." Appealing to Carey as a lawyer and a former judge, Van Devanter
reminded the senator, "You know absolutely that the commission of one
offense, where a very considerable time has elapsed, will not be any justification whatever of the commission of another, especially where the
second one was committed in pursuance of the most careful, complete
and deliberate arrangements." Van Devanter had no doubt that any judge
assigned to the case would do his duty fully, "and any expectation that

they will permit thoroughly incompetent and irrelevant evidence will meet with the greatest disappointment."[7]

Instead, Van Devanter wanted to frustrate the prosecution through means that completely avoided his clients' guilt or innocence. He wanted the murder cases removed from Johnson County, preferably to Cheyenne. Getting the cases moved dovetailed with twin strategies Van Devanter developed shortly after the invasion. The Cheyenne lawyer knew that Johnson County's very limited financial resources constituted its Achilles heel.[8] He also knew that, given the heated press reports circulated throughout Wyoming, Johnson County would have a hard time finding unbiased jurors, and many would be dismissed for cause. Then the large number of peremptory challenges (automatic challenges of jurors, requiring no cause) might allow the defense to finish off any remaining jurors, so that Johnson County could never seat a jury.[9]

Wolcott's interview with the *Chicago Herald* was not the only newspaper story Van Devanter had to worry about. Shortly after the invaders arrived back in Cheyenne, a reporter for the *San Francisco Examiner* managed to interview them in a gymnasium hall at Fort Russell, and several of them—Van Devanter's clients—made revealing and incriminating admissions.[10] The reporter spoke to the firebrands among the invaders—Canton, Wolcott, Irvine, Hesse, Ford, and Senator Jack (John N.) Tisdale. They were all "full of fight and breathing hatred against the rustlers" and "talked freely," so sure of their rectitude that they expected to be released within two weeks.[11]

The men interviewed also breathed arrogance, declaring that the siege could have lasted a month without harming them (but also saying that they were going to make a break for it the first dark night), and that they were only defeated because of the overwhelming numbers against them. They asserted that these "overwhelming numbers" came about only because the rustlers told "the wildest lies" about the expedition, such as that they "were going into Buffalo to hang the Sheriff and shoot down the citizens." In seemingly the next breath, however, the men admitted that "the sheriff wouldn't have been overlooked." The men bragged about how they had threatened to throw Deputy Sheriff Roles off the train carrying them from Douglas, and they asserted, "We were provoked into this thing. It was a righteous movement."

To demonstrate the righteousness of their movement, they declared that in the last four years, out of 180 indictments, there had only been one conviction in Johnson County. It is hard to fathom where this "180" figure came from, but different invaders always had some example to forward, none of which bore any relationship to the facts as shown by the criminal case files.[12]

The *Examiner* correspondent was obviously impressed by the invaders, stating that they "are a remarkable body of men." He continued, "The party is composed of Harvard graduates, politicians of great shrewdness and men who spend almost as much of their time in Chicago and New York as they do on their ranches. One glance at them would satisfy a person that all were men of iron nerve." The reporter closed with a remark that apparently reflected racial stereotypes of 1892: "Most of them are blondes and not one of them has dark eyes."

Those interviewed made a point of telling the reporter that when they killed Nate Champion, they killed the only witness left against Joe Elliott, crowing that Johnson County had thus lost the last remaining witness for the attempted murder of Champion and Gilbertson.

All in all, it was a most remarkable newspaper story and must have solidified Van Devanter's determination to avoid a trial on the murder charges at all cost. That determination was greatly assisted by the inside information he received from Buffalo.

During the invasion, Charles Burritt, Buffalo's mayor and leading lawyer, was in Cheyenne. When he returned on April 28, he was interviewed by the *Bulletin*. Mayor Burritt observed the great anger of Johnson County people and sought to distance himself from the invasion—and preserve the misguided trust of the people of Buffalo, which in turn preserved his usefulness to the big cattlemen. He "emphatically" made the following statement: "First, I knew nothing of the raid; Second, had I known of it I would have remained here and assisted in its suppression; third, I deprecate the movement and its objects and purposes; fourth, reports of interviews by me are unfounded; fifth, the men under arrest at Fort Russell must be tried by the civil courts and certainly will be."[13] Mayor Burritt's statement was misleading, as brazen a misrepresentation as Governor Barber's disclaimers; Burritt had already been retained by the invaders and was solidly in their camp.

Not a week later, on May 4, Burritt wrote Cheyenne attorney Walter R. Stoll (Stoll, Van Devanter, and M. C. Brown of Laramie were the primary attorneys for the invaders).[14] He explained to Stoll that it was "unsafe for anyone to express his real sentiments in this community" and it would

"take many months of skilled work to arrange things in such a way as
to even commence moving public opinion in favor of the stockmen."
Burritt slammed Joe DeBarthe, saying, among other things, that he "took
refuge in whiskey drinking" and that "DeBarthe has lost his caste with
the thieves and with the better element he never had any."[15] He referred
to Angus as "headstrong and bull-headed," a man who "spends much of his
time in bolstering up his weak-kneed associates." (Burritt was apparently
referring to the county commissioners, men heading the county, who
had the final say on finances.) Burritt assured Stoll, however, that he
would work to get the cattlemen away from Angus.[16] Burritt provided
Stoll with extensive and detailed information about the inner dealings
of the commissioners and Angus (mostly from conversations at which
he was present) and described to Stoll how he was working to undercut
the confidence of the anxious county commissioner Hogerson, although
it was hard, because, as he told Stoll, "there is as complete supression
[sic] of free thought and free speech as if we were living in a camp of
Italian brigands."[17]

Just two days later, Burritt wrote Walter Stoll with more information.
The Cheyenne lawyers were worried about George Dunning, a potentially
strong witness against them whom they had not been able to sequester
in Cheyenne; they apparently asked Burritt to locate him. Burritt responded,
"I have been unable to get at Dunning—I doubt if I can reach him at
all."[18] There had been press reports that Dunning was in Buffalo, but by
then, Dunning was being deliberately concealed by Johnson County,
keeping him from Governor Barber, who kept insisting that all members
of the expedition be turned over.[19]

Burritt continued to write letter after letter to the big cattlemen's
lawyers in May (nine to Stoll alone), providing inside information about
the sale of the *Buffalo Echo* to O. H. Flagg, as well as information about
virtually everything that happened in Buffalo relating to the prosecution
of the invaders. The sale of the *Echo* was significant because the newspaper
had been pro–big cattlemen, and if it sold to Flagg, he would certainly
change that editorial posture. In his letters, Burritt complained a great deal
about how he could trust no one and what dangers and oppressive burdens
he was laboring under.[20]

The letters showing Burritt's betrayal of the trust of the people of
Johnson County are troubling, but not as much as a May 8 letter from
Burritt to Judge John Wesley Blake, the district judge sitting on the cases

against the cattlemen. This letter was candid and gossipy, as if Burritt was speaking to an intimate friend; Burritt seemed to assume that Judge Blake was part of the defense camp. Burritt also told the judge about the sale of the *Echo* to Flagg, saying it showed "the real condition of things in Buffalo," apparently meaning that the owner of the *Echo*, Thomas J. Bouton, had been intimidated into selling. Noting that there were a "large number of so called rustlers in town" and that business was "practically suspended," Burritt commented that "the domination of stock thieves, the open and bold manner in which it is being done, calls for some active measures."[21] He further told the judge, "No one entertaining an opinion adverse to cattle stealing dare express himself in this community, and the only hope I can see is that the wrong doers, elated by their supremacy, will fall out and quarrel among themselves," Burritt stated his opinion that despite ample evidence available to prosecute a large number of men (apparently for cattle-related offenses), there was no disposition to prosecute anyone. Then he expressed the hope that "this entire cattle business can be kept out of politics," and he provided Judge Blake with juicy information about some of those involved in local feuds (referring to the physical assault of St. Clair O'Malley by Jack Flagg, and the nasty feud between *Echo* editor Bouton and *Bulletin* editor Moeller).[22] The most disturbing thing about the May 8 letter is not that Burritt was attempting to influence a sitting judge by providing him with improper information outside the presence of opposing counsel, which was bad enough. The more troubling fact is that Burritt wrote the judge as a confidant who already agreed with Burritt's extreme pro-cattlemen views (neither Blake's nor Burritt's views were known to the Buffalo community), and the judge, instead of repudiating Burritt, accepted these comments about Johnson County murder cases outside the presence of the prosecuting attorneys.

While Burritt had the open ear of Judge Blake (Burritt wrote him another chummy letter on July 8, 1892), Johnson County officials continued to be frustrated in their attempts to make contact with the invaders. After the cattlemen were delivered to Cheyenne, Howard Roles and E. U. Snider, sent to the state capitol as a special envoy by the county commissioners, were not even allowed to serve their warrants. The two continued to demand the custody of the prisoners but were not optimistic about their chances.[23]

Burritt persistently tried to worm his way into the confidence of Johnson County officials, in order to provide inside information to his

Cheyenne clients. Throughout almost all of his letters, he complained about how much danger there was to him from his efforts, to the point that in one letter he declared that if it got out that he represented "Wolcott and his party," he "would not be able to stay here another day."[24] He refused to send out telegrams or to have his secretary type any of these letters, and insisted that his legal business was being ruined (although at a later point, he wrote that he was more than making up his losses by the outside business).[25] Burritt began to send out "cipher letters," by which he apparently meant letters in code, wherein he would substitute animals for the names of men.[26] When Senator Warren sought a long, full statement from Burritt as to "the situation of affairs in this county," Burritt declined, saying he could not be sure that the letter would not be lost in the mails or "fall under the eye of any other person."[27]

For all his fears and caution, Burritt eventually did obtain what he was seeking—information supporting Van Devanter's goal of exploiting Johnson County's financial weakness. On July 7, 1892, Burritt wrote Van Devanter, telling him that he had been called upon "informally" by the Johnson County commissioners to advise them regarding the need to raise $12,000 for the murder trials.[28] In a letter the next day to Judge Blake, Burritt stated that he had told the commissioners he was retained by the defense, but this seems unlikely given Burritt's previous statement that revealing such information would mean that he would not be able to stay in Buffalo "another day."[29] It seems more likely that if Burritt said anything to the commissioners about his conflict, it was presented so as not to alarm them by making clear the consequences of their confiding in him.

Burritt told Van Devanter about the efforts of the county to raise adequate money to try the big cattlemen. The commissioners had been aware very early that Wyoming constitutional restrictions on county taxation meant that Johnson County had limited funds to spend on the trial—on May 5 the *Bulletin* announced that the commissioners were seeking contributions from citizens in Johnson, Sheridan, and Converse counties, since "the amount necessary cannot be raised by direct taxation under the law."[30] This solicitation obviously did not produce sufficient funds, and at the July meeting the commissioners had to directly address the financial demands of the trial.

John M. Davidson of Cheyenne was one of three attorneys specially hired to prosecute the case (the other two were E. A. Ballard of Denver and R. W. Breckons of Cheyenne), and he called on the commissioners

for $12,000 for the trial and expenses of the trial. This figure, greatly
more than the commissioners could raise by conventional taxation, represented about 60 percent of the total yearly budget of Johnson County
(approximately $20,000).[31] Davidson presented the commissioners with
a plan, though, saying that Judge Blake had advised him that they had
authority to issue certificates of indebtedness for the amount of money
required. This was the event that brought Burritt into the picture.[32]

Burritt reported all the details of the discussion to Van Devanter,
including the legal authorities considered; the opinion of county attorney
Alvin Bennett, who thought the prosecution ought to be dropped; and
the deep indebtedness of the county. It was as if Van Devanter had been
in the room listening to what everyone said.[33]

The next day, Burritt wrote another intimate letter to Judge Blake, still
the sitting judge on all the murder cases and then in the middle of a
crucial set of hearings setting trial arrangements. Burritt provided additional detail of the county commissioners' meeting, such as the arguments
Burritt had made to the commissioners as to why none of their plans
would work, and he carefully tested the judge's opinion about the financing
plan the judge had apparently endorsed to the commissioners.[34] Burritt
also wrote how terrible it was that some people were trying "to saddle
this county with a larger amount of debt simply to gratify the morbid
desires of a small minority of citizens for blood," and he told the judge
that the bank of which he was a member of the board of directors would
never advance money upon certificates of indebtedness. Finally, he assured
Judge Blake that the invasion had brought about a change in attitudes
such that people were now willing to convict defendants for theft of cattle.
(This common contention by the big cattlemen had small basis in fact,
for juries continued to convict or acquit on the strength of the case
presented.) Burritt's letter to the judge was apparently intended to be
surreptitious; he did not send copies to any other persons, certainly not the
attorneys for the prosecution.[35]

The July 7 letter to Van Devanter had to have been enormously
helpful to the defense attorneys, telling them the exact fund-raising tactics
of the prosecution so that, if necessary, these tactics could be undercut
by legal actions (such as a suit for an injunction); telling them about the
position of county attorney Bennett, a weak link in what should have been
a solid front by the prosecution; and, significantly, telling them how much
additional expense they had to add to prevent the trial. Even more

importantly, the information from Burritt showed that, despite the fervent hopes of Johnson County citizens, the prosecution of the invaders was not being effectively pursued. There was no clear leader of the prosecution and no clear plan for a winning court presentation—Johnson County was too preoccupied with the fundamental problem of paying for the cases. Of course, the people of Johnson County were not privileged to the correspondence of Willis Van Devanter and had no idea that the cattlemen also had serious problems with their case.

Burritt's breach of trust against Johnson County was not the only time Burritt breached the trust of one of his clients. In another letter, this one to Cheyenne banker and strong cattlemen ally Henry G. Hay, Burritt told of an arrangement with the First National Bank of Buffalo for a $1,500 note with the proceeds going to the special attorneys for the prosecution.[36] As with his other letters, Burritt provided great detail. He implored Hay to remember, however, that all this information was gained through Burritt's "official connection with the Bank as Director, Attorney and Chairman of the Finance Committee," and so was being communicated *"in Confidence"* (Burritt's emphasis) and was to be used "discreetly."[37]

By modern measure, Burritt's actions were a shocking violation of ethical standards, blatant conflicts of interest producing the most basic violations of trust. Such actions today would probably lead to disbarment. Even in 1892, however, they violated ethical norms. Rules governing the conduct of attorneys were sparse, but there were some, and one stated that an attorney guilty of deceit, with intent to deceive a party to an action, was liable to be disbarred.[38] It would be hard to feature clearer examples of deceit by an attorney than that practiced by Charles Burritt in 1892 against Johnson County.

While Johnson County struggled to find money to finance the trial of the criminal charges related to the invasion, the big cattlemen had no such problems. Instead of the floundering efforts of several public officials, the big cattlemen's financing devolved upon one highly competent man, John Clay, the president of the Wyoming Stock Growers Association.

Clay had left the United States in November 1891, and he was undeniably abroad in early April 1892, but though he maintained a low profile in 1892, he was in a unique position to be kept quickly and thoroughly informed about the invasion.[39] James T. Craig, who may or may not have been the frantic messenger warning the invaders about the public uprising against them (Milton Woods, John Clay's biographer, feels he was), was

John Clay. Courtesy of L. Milton
Woods.

certainly in the Buffalo area in April 1892, and Craig was Clay's most
trusted employee.[40] Another trusted employee, Robert Robinson, was
located at Belle Fourche, just across the South Dakota line, and had ready
access to a telegraph to Clay's Chicago headquarters.[41] The invaders'
cutting of the telegraph lines between Cheyenne and Buffalo in no way
affected Clay's ability to obtain prompt intelligence about the fate of
the invasion.

Despite their public pronouncements, it was not Wolcott or Irvine who
assumed damage control after the collapse of the invasion, but John Clay.
Clay rushed back to the United States during April 1892 and started
collecting the funds essential to defend the charges against the invaders.
Working with Henry G. Hay and George W. Baxter, Clay raised a huge
amount, $100,000, dwarfing the expenditures of Johnson County.[42]

A fundamental problem for the invaders was that there were witnesses
to their actions. In accordance with some of the customs of the day, the
big cattlemen had quickly moved to do something about the problem.

After the invaders killed Champion and Ray at the KC Ranch, Major
Wolcott, in a strange outburst of generosity, not only turned the two
captured cowboy trappers loose but passed the hat to compensate them

for some of their losses.[43] At that point, though, Wolcott, not anticipating the full extent of the disaster that awaited him and his men, never considered that the trappers, Billy Walker and Ben Jones, who had watched the entire chain of events the day Champion and Ray were killed, might be potent witnesses against the invaders.

After they were released, the two trappers had quickly gone south— away from the path of the invaders—and camped close to Casper on the evening of Saturday, April 9. They soon became local celebrities, though, and were interviewed at length for the next issue of the *Wyoming Derrick*.[44] With the surrender of the cattlemen at the T. A. Ranch, and the charges pressed by Johnson County, Walker and Jones suddenly became very important witnesses.

On May 4 they were taken from Casper to Douglas by Deputy Sheriff E. H. Kimball, who also happened to be the editor of the *Graphic*, a Douglas newspaper.[45] The two men were supposed to remain in the sheriff's office but did not. The exact sequence of events in Douglas is not clear, but it is fair to say that the men were taken against their will— kidnapped—by agents of big cattlemen. Thereafter they were spirited across Nebraska by railroad, triggering a wild sequence of court cases, writs, and competing warrants. Helena Huntington Smith refers to a battle of "legal shenanigans," and that it was. At the end of a five-day spree, the two trappers found themselves in a courtroom in Omaha, supposedly battling to be released from any legal compulsion to return to Wyoming. They were freed and almost immediately were put on a fast train eastward. The two men disappeared from public view, and there was much speculation as to what was done with them. It turned out that, unknown to the public, they were taken to Rhode Island and held there until their presence in Wyoming became irrelevant.[46]

The spiriting away of Jones and Walker produced harsh public reactions, and not just in Wyoming. D. H. Baber, in *The Longest Rope*, a book setting out the stories of Jones and Walker, wrote, "Omaha was all smoked up over the matter [the removal of the trappers] and seething with arguments about the way the cattle association was running the state of Wyoming. No matter where we went . . . all we could hear was the citizens giving the cattlemen hell."[47] These statements are certainly consistent with the comments of the *Omaha World-Herald*: "The plain case is that wealthy cattlemen have employed the process of law to spirit away witnesses needed to convict murderers of their crime. It is bad enough and serious enough as an offense to spirit away necessary witnesses, but when the processes of law are used as the instrument to do this thing the matter becomes a public disgrace."[48] The *Rocky Mountain News* (Denver) damned Governor Barber for the kidnapping of the two trappers, saying that the story "reads like the stories of the Greek banditti or the work of the mafia." The *News* added, "There will be no safety in northern Wyoming while such lawlessness is permitted to go unwhipped of justice."[49]

The big cattlemen did not care that newspaper comments following the trapper fiasco were harsh—they thought they had disposed of all the witnesses against them and that was all that counted. As Robert David wrote, without a hint of embarrassment, "With the witnesses out of the way, the invaders in Cheyenne had a fair chance of being acquitted at their trial for lack of evidence."[50] There was more evidence available to Johnson County than the big cattlemen knew—the testimony of George Dunning, for example, would have been especially strong—but the evidence of the prosecution was much thinner than it should have been. If a normal criminal investigation had been allowed, Johnson County would probably have been able to present the testimony of several invaders turning state's evidence.

A break came at last in late June, when Governor Barber allowed Johnson County to serve its warrants.[51] Fights among the prisoners brought the matter to a head. It was reported that the Texans and Irvine were armed, and they "had several fierce quarrels among themselves, and talked a great deal of escaping." It appears that Van Devanter became aware of this situation and reported it to the governor.[52] Barber then telegraphed Johnson County and asked that an officer immediately serve warrants and take the men into custody, although with the condition that they not be taken back to Johnson County.[53]

On July 5 the invaders were moved to Laramie. A hearing on a motion for change of venue was convened only two days later, on July 7.[54] Johnson County authorities apparently had access to their prisoners at long last, but the invaders shortly became aware of the potential problems of Johnson County over the expenses of a trial—after Burritt's July 7 letter to Van Devanter the invaders knew exactly what Johnson County's financial problems were. The invaders also knew that several matters were soon to be resolved, including a motion for a change of venue and bond arrangements. So, despite the recent friction, the leaders among them probably had little difficulty holding discipline among their men—keeping

The invaders at Fort D. A. Russell in Cheyenne in May 1892. Courtesy of Johnson County Jim Gatchell Memorial Museum.

them from turning state's evidence to save themselves—and could sustain that discipline for at least a short time.

On the same day the invaders arrived in Laramie, the attorneys for Johnson County and the cattlemen began their presentations to Judge Blake. The principal spokesman for the State of Wyoming was Davidson, and for the defense it was Van Devanter.[55] Two issues were addressed: the presence of prejudice against the defendants in a county, and the need to have a large jury pool. The northern counties of Sheridan, Johnson, and Natrona were quickly ruled out, and the parties discussed the counties of Uinta (Evanston), Carbon (Rawlins), Albany (Laramie), Sweetwater (Green River), Weston (Newcastle), and Laramie (Cheyenne); the prosecution objected to Laramie but had no objection to any of the others.[56] Further proceedings were held on July 7, the eligible counties were pared to three—Laramie, Albany, and Uinta—and the cattlemen presented their case against Albany County. It was agreed that the defense would present its case for Laramie County the next day.[57]

The first witness called by the defense in support of trial in Laramie County was a "Mr. Conroy," and when the prosecution began its cross-examination, Davidson and Van Devanter clashed. Davidson sought to establish that "the defendants wielded strong social, political and business influence at Cheyenne," and Van Devanter "strenuously objected" to the first cross-examination question that addressed this asserted influence.[58] The prosecution had a problem, though, as the inquiry upon the motion for change of venue was whether the *defendants* could get a fair trial, not necessarily whether the prosecution would be treated fairly. Still, Judge Blake ruled that the prosecutors could ask their questions of Conroy, and he would then "see about it."[59]

The prosecution was able to present a few good witnesses. One was Colonel P. Gad Bryan, from Cheyenne, who testified about the powerful influence of the cattlemen in Cheyenne and noted that the *Sun* and *Tribune* had "sustained the men" and that, in his opinion, the state could not "secure a fair and impartial trial in Cheyenne." Asa S. Mercer also testified, saying that "the sentiment in Cheyenne was favorable to the stockmen."[60] The files of the *Cheyenne Sun* and the *Cheyenne Tribune* were presented, and several editorial comments were read in open court. Judge Blake remarked that he believed these newspapers had exerted influence upon the public in Cheyenne.[61]

The defendants had an advantage in this series of hearings, however, in that their attorneys had a ready reservoir of witnesses from any county in the state. Members of the Wyoming Stock Growers Association and their allies could always be counted on to swear to the terrible prejudice against them in their counties. With regard to Laramie County, a large number of witnesses were ready to swear that a trial there would be immaculately fair. That advantage was in clear evidence on July 10, when the defense called only five witnesses, but each was a forceful advocate in favor of a trial in Cheyenne, especially the two called in the morning. Both these men, the Cheyenne City marshal and the Laramie County sheriff, were strong supporters of the big cattlemen's contentions. Indeed, perhaps these witnesses were too supportive, as it was apparent that they were in complete sympathy with the cattlemen. The marshal testified that he thought the defendants ought to be turned loose. The sheriff, A. D. Kelley, when asked if he knew Sheriff Angus, said he did not, but he believed that Angus was a rustler or sympathizer of rustlers and, further, that the invasion was justifiable.[62] Judge Blake expressed skepticism about the sheriff's claim that the *Sun* and *Tribune* "have not served as an index for public opinion" in Laramie County.[63]

The parade of pro–Laramie County witnesses continued on July 12. The defense presented seven witnesses who each asserted in the most positive terms that the big cattlemen would get a fair and impartial trial in Cheyenne.[64]

On July 13 the evidence had been completed, and the arguments, which went on all day, drew the largest crowd of all the sessions.[65] The custom in 1892 was to refer to any lawyer who had once held a judicial position as "judge," and the *Cheyenne Daily Leader's* story about this day referred to "Judge" Brown as having started the arguments for the defense, being countered by "Judge" Ballard for the prosecution, and then in the afternoon, "Judge" Van Devanter arguing for the defense, followed by "Judge" Davidson for the state.[66] The defense argued for a trial in Cheyenne, and the prosecution for Laramie. The defense seemed to have the stronger arguments, because many more witnesses had been presented who declared that a trial in Cheyenne would be fair and impartial than those few who said otherwise. Too, several witnesses had testified about strong negative sentiment against the cattlemen in Laramie.[67]

Judge Blake announced his decision on July 19. The judge was uncomfortable making the decision—he stated that it placed him in an embarrassing, perplexing, and difficult situation.[68] But the reason for his difficulty was probably not the abstract legal justification he set out in his written opinion. Blake was a judge of the Second District in Wyoming, meaning that although he would not have to face the voters of Johnson County, the people of both Albany and Natrona counties would vote for or against him, and he was probably sensitive to the apparent sentiment against the big cattlemen in both counties. Based upon the Charles Burritt letters to Blake and the confession of George Dunning, the judge had long since sided with the big cattlemen, but his several negative comments about their case would seem to indicate that he wanted to give his constituency the impression that he was fairly balancing the points for each party.[69] Even at the time of the announcement of his decision, however, it had already been determined that Judge Richard H. Scott of Cheyenne would try the case. The cattlemen had filed an affidavit of prejudice against Judge Blake. Perhaps they did feel that he was prejudiced against them—besides his comments during the change of venue hearing, Judge Blake had spoken out forcefully against the imposition of martial law[70]—but the judge clearly did not relish handling this most controversial of cases and perhaps he signaled the defense attorneys that he would welcome a motion to remove him. He certainly made no protest against leaving the case. From the standpoint of the big cattlemen, they would far rather have a judge from Cheyenne than a judge from a judicial district that was harshly critical of the invasion.

Whatever the behind-the-scenes politics, in his decision Judge Blake gave the cattlemen exactly what they asked, sending the trial to Cheyenne. He read his opinion from the bench and first made the valid point that it was clear there were strong feelings against the invaders in virtually every county except Laramie.[71] The problem with such reasoning, however, was that it gave an unfair advantage to the cattlemen. It meant that the counties that were offended by the atrocious actions of the invaders were trumped by the home county of most of the big cattlemen, a place in which the populace had been subjected to barrages of pro-cattlemen propaganda by newspapers owned by big cattlemen. Blake then made the point that the large number of defendants (he assumed forty-three) meant that the total number of peremptory challenges was 774 (eighteen per defendant), meaning that only Laramie County was a possible site for a trial, because Albany County would not have enough prospective jurors. He further concluded that even in Laramie County there could be only one large trial against all defendants, because the total jury pool would be exhausted after that trial.[72] In a case with a large number of defendants, however, it was a common practice to bring the first charges against only a few of those charged, usually those against whom the evidence was strongest. This was considered an appropriate exercise of discretion by the prosecution and was routinely allowed.[73] Judge Blake did not consider this possibility, although this option was apparently being discussed in the case—the prosecution was very soon to request an initial trial of only some of the defendants.

The stockmen were as "happy as schoolboys" with Judge Blake's decision; they regarded the setting of their trial in Cheyenne as "virtually amounting to an acquittal." It was reported that in light of this decision Johnson County was seriously considering "discharging the case against the quasi-prisoners."[74] That the stockmen had reason for their jubilation was shown in the first contested hearing before Judge Scott, held on August 6. The prosecution submitted a motion to begin the cases by trying only four defendants: Frank Canton, Frank Wolcott, Tom Smith (leader of the Texans), and Buck Garrett.[75] The obvious reason for seeking this arrangement was that the prosecution thereby had a chance to seat a jury, because there could be only 72 total peremptory challenges. Then, if there was a conviction of first-degree murder, which was probable, the prosecution could proceed against another group of men. The new group of men, however, would likely seek a plea agreement to avoid the death penalty. Van Devanter for the defense strenuously objected to the prosecution's plan. Neither court records nor newspapers report the grounds for the objections, but his obvious motivation was that a trial of all the defendants would mean an almost certain acquittal because of the inability to seat a jury, whereas a trial of only four men would probably result in a conviction.[76] The *Cheyenne Daily Sun* reported that Judge Scott, after "hearing the pros and cons, . . . decided that the collective information"—the May 1892 charging document against all forty-some of the defendants—"having been filed first, should take precedence."[77] And just like that, the Cheyenne judge undercut the last real chance for a conviction against any of the invaders, ostensibly basing his decision on the flimsy grounds of the sanctity of the order of the filing of informations. It was one more example of Van Devanter receiving everything he asked for from a Cheyenne court.

On August 6, Laramie County sheriff Kelley brought a matter before the district judge, and the ruling of Judge Scott further compromised the prosecution's case. Kelley was an ally of the big cattlemen and it appears that he was working to find a way to assist them. Indeed, it was Willis Van Devanter who presented Kelley's petition to the judge.[78]

Kelley, who now had custody of the prisoners, raised the issue of payment of the large expenses being generated for holding the defendants. He complained that Johnson County had not paid the money it owed to cover these expenses, and he further stated that if he had to cover the expenses, he was in danger of losing a large sum of money in light of the "insolvent condition of Johnson County."[79] Judge Scott took the petition under advisement, and on August 10 he made his decision. He observed that he could not force Johnson County to reimburse the sheriff, and so he decided to set all the defendants free on a $40,000 recognizance bond.[80] Such a bond requires no payment of money, but simply a promise to return.

All the defendants immediately signed their bonds and then scattered, the Texans back to Texas and the Wyoming defendants to their homes in Wyoming.[81] Johnson County thus lost any hope that it could cut a deal with any defendants by trading immunity for testimony.

It is hard to trace Van Devanter's influence on the events finally leading to the release of the prisoners, but his management of the situation seems to have been masterful, so manipulating the case that Johnson County never got the opportunity to undertake an effective investigation.

Judge Scott at first set the trial for August 22, but it was then reset for January 2, 1893, thereby taking the invasion away from direct public attention during the 1892 campaign and election. During the four-month delay, no formal proceedings would take place. Behind the scenes, however, the attorneys worked hard preparing their cases, and on the morning of January 2, all the opposing attorneys, their clients, and witnesses would descend upon Cheyenne and fervently resume the battle.[82]

CHAPTER EIGHTEEN

Martial Law

In the middle of all the court struggles, another conflict was being played out. Only days after their surrender, the big cattlemen started clamoring for a declaration of martial law, whereby all facets of the Johnson County government would be taken over by military authorities, as if it were conquered enemy territory. Legally, this was a bizarre demand, there being no actual war, and the authorities in Johnson County being quite able to exercise their proper functions. It is hard to pin down the motivation of the cattlemen in their advocacy for martial law, because their aims were confused and seemed to vary with the individual advocate. They had not thought through their goals and, at different times, seemed to want the abolition of the entire county to prevent criminal prosecutions, the replacement of all officials, or the abrogation of the votes of Johnson County citizens.[1]

A declaration of martial law in the United States in a time of peace was rare, and on those few occasions when martial law was imposed, such as with labor strikes, it was done at the request of local authorities.[2] But the big cattlemen and their powerful political allies still zealously pursued this all-out attack on the offending county. One obvious appeal was that it would label Johnson County as a criminal society, representing in the cattlemen's minds a complete, public vindication, and would, perhaps, stop everything the county was doing. A declaration of martial law might even allow the big cattlemen to force all the "rustlers" (by then a generic term referring to all their enemies) out of Johnson County. The sensational reporting by the big cattlemen's newspapers in Cheyenne, painting Johnson County in April as chaotic, was part of the big push, and the intent behind the stories was to provide support for politicians with the power to make a declaration of martial law. The *Cheyenne Sun* continued its shrill advocacy through May, so that on June 2 the *Bulletin* wrote: "That hyena of Wyoming journalism, the *Cheyenne Sun*, is howling itself hoarse to induce the proclamation of martial law in Johnson county."[3]

The *Sun*, as part of its campaign, had presented several people as martyrs, people who had supposedly taken a strong stand for law and order and had, as a consequence, been driven out of Johnson County. One of them was Thomas J. Bouton, who finally sold the *Buffalo Echo* to Jack Flagg, and another was H. R. Mann.[4]

In the summer of 1889 Mann had shown independence from the big cattlemen by writing strong editorials opposing some of their positions. He had strongly criticized the prosecution of a Buffalo entrepreneur, Henry P. Rothwell, stating that the case demonstrated why prosecutions under the stock laws had come into disrepute, and he blistered Asa Mercer's intemperate writings after the lynchings of Ellen Watson and James Averell. Even at that time, however, it seemed that his strong stands bothered him, and almost as soon as he made them, he tried to balance his criticisms with statements favorable to the large cattle owners. After 1889 Mann moved further away from his earlier positions against the big cattlemen. Indeed, it appears that he came under their influence, best shown by his involvement with the Northern Wyoming Protective Association in 1891 (the group that so conveniently identified "rustlers" for the Wyoming Live Stock Commission). The board of trustees of this association consisted of Fred G. S. Hesse, Frank Canton, Frank Laberteaux, Fayette Parker, and H. R. Mann, and the organization was obviously a front for big cattlemen. Of the five trustees, only Mann did not participate in the invasion; the four others all rode north with the invading army.[5]

The Johnson County invasion was big news, even in Salt Lake City, and a *Salt Lake Tribune* reporter sought out Mann, as a prominent resident of Buffalo, and solicited his views about the invasion. In light of his earlier writings, many of Mann's comments were startling. Mann provided a version of the invasion that closely tracked the line of Canton and Hesse, speaking of how brazen and widespread rustling was in Johnson County. Mann insisted that there was not "a word of truth" to the assertion that the big cattlemen were attempting to "freeze out" the small ones, insisting there was only the "best of feeling" between the big cattlemen and small ranchmen and that the only reason that the small ranchmen had opposed the invasion was intimidation and threats by the rustlers, who were "reckless and determined men."[6] Mann stated further that it was impossible to convict rustlers even when they pled guilty, because the jurors were all frightened of the rustlers' wrath, and that "the executive committee of the rustlers" had threatened to kill people who had committed the offense of visiting the prisoners at Fort McKinney. The interviewing reporter apparently did not ask what virtually any resident of Johnson County would have asked: What "executive committee"? What "rustlers"? As with so many of such pronouncements by the big cattlemen and their allies, no detail was provided and certainly no source for this highly dubious information.

The people of Johnson County must have been disappointed and angry with H. R. Mann. Gustave Moeller printed an article from the *Idaho Journal* (written by a former resident of Buffalo), which declared that Mann had made a "dastardly and unwarranted attack upon the people of his state" and added: "To call him in the interview referred to, a falsifier—willful, malicious and base calumniator is not too strong. He was too great a coward to stay at home and defend himself and his ideas."[7] Since Mann had traveled to Salt Lake City about a month before the invasion, (and so had hardly been driven out of the county), his example provided small support for the cattlemen's contention that the honest people of Johnson County were being forced out.

The big cattlemen and their allies first considered obtaining a declaration of martial law from Governor Barber. There were several problems with this tactic, however. Barber was already being heavily criticized by almost all the newspapers in Wyoming, as well as by citizen groups. There was even a question whether the state militia would follow an order declaring martial law. On April 20, 1892, the *Rock Springs Miner* ran a story announcing that the officers of companies D and E had resigned and harshly criticizing the governor for commanding the militia not to obey the requests of local sheriffs, thereby forestalling efforts by the state militia to stop "the invaders in their march of murder and devastation." The *Pioneer Press* of St. Paul wrote about the possible "dismemberment" of the Wyoming state militia, reporting that four officers had resigned and that many officers were asserting that the governor had used the militia "to aid his friends, the stockmen" and that "unless satisfactory explanation of his actions are made they will refuse to remain in the service."[8] Despite these problems, Governor Barber was apparently willing to declare martial law if he could get solid assurances that federal troops would be available to enforce his edict. Wyoming's senators, Joseph Carey and Francis Warren, however, were never able to obtain from federal authorities what Warren referred to as a "definite promise."[9]

Throughout the northern part of the state, citizens held "indignation meetings" wherein "resolutions of condemnation" were passed. In Story, Big Horn, Banner, Casper, Glenrock, and, of course, Buffalo, citizens met and made declarations they intended politicians to hear.[10] Their statements were not polite grumblings but the strongest kind of bitter complaints. The people of Big Horn, Wyoming, referred to the "gang of murdering miscreants who, led by hired assassins such as Canton and Hesse," had murdered their citizens. They denounced Governor Barber, saying that "words cannot measure our contempt and detestation for the perjured scoundrel who has proven false to his oath, recreant to his duty and a traitor to the people."[11] In Casper the people of Natrona County denounced the governor as "treasonous" and the invasion as "the greatest crime that could be committed against the people of the state." The Casper resolution was sent to several newspapers, the U.S. Congress, and the president, but not directly to Wyoming's congressional delegation; apparently the people of Casper felt that such a delivery would be a waste of time.[12] The *Lander Mountaineer* opined that Acting Governor Barber was criminally liable as an accessory, which may have made Barber nervous.[13] If Barber were to declare martial law, he would have had good reason to fear the response of Wyoming citizens.

In early May, however, just when some of the excitement over the invasion was dying down as the judicial proceedings were beginning, the big cattlemen got a break when someone murdered George Wellman. Wellman, who had just been appointed a deputy U.S. marshal, was the foreman of the local Hoe Ranch, having taken over for Frank Laberteaux, a member of the invading army now jailed in Cheyenne with the other invaders.[14] On the morning of May 10, near old Fort Reno, along the Powder River in far southeastern Johnson County, Wellman was riding north toward Buffalo while accompanied by Tom Hathaway, a Hoe employee, when they passed a low hill covered by sagebrush. Hathaway reported that someone in hiding suddenly started shooting at them, and after several shots, Wellman fell from his horse, dead. Hathaway rode in a panic to Buffalo and reported the incident to Sheriff Angus.[15]

Wellman had enough of a connection to the invaders that they could plausibly declare he had been killed as an act of vengeance by "the rustlers." Newspapers favoring the big cattlemen leaped at the opportunity to do so. "Of the hundred and odd men who have been warned to leave this section on pain of death one has been assassinated, and indications are that the rest will either promptly obey the rustlers' mandate or leave the country," declared the *Denver Republican*.[16] The *Chicago Herald*—Sam Clover's paper, which had run several stories highly favorable to big cattlemen—printed an article that opened by saying, "The recent cowardly assassination of George Wellman, foreman of the Hoe Ranch, in Johnson county, Wyoming, by the cattle thieves that infest that region proves conclusively, what the respectable cattlemen have long claimed, that the life of one of their number who in the pursuit of his business dared to enter that county without an escort was not worth a moment's purchase."[17]

There were flaws in these contentions, immediately recognized by Buffalo people. One was that Wellman was the first northern Wyoming man associated with the big cattlemen to be killed (other than Billy Lykins, when he tried to lynch Champion and Gilbertson, but the cattlemen never brought up Billy). As the *Bulletin* had noted earlier, on May 5, 1892,

> There is considerable said about threatening letters sent to stock-men by mythical rustlers, but as yet none of the cattle kings have suffered any personal harm. All the murders have been on the other side. The bloody scalps of Ella Watson, Jack Averill [*sic*], Tom Wagner, Tisdale, Jones, Ray and Champion ornament the belts of the stockmen, and the rustlers have nary a scalp to show. It is too much like the riots down south where the negroes have to furnish all the victims.[18]

Another flaw was that no one knew who shot George Wellman, and still another was that no one in Buffalo really objected to Wellman. Indeed, he was almost universally liked, and most of the people of the county seemed genuinely dismayed at his death. Johnson County people may have had their faults, but for the majority of the residents, disingenuous dissembling was not one of them. A reading of the *Buffalo Bulletin* shows a consistent expression of regret about Wellman's death and a desire to find and punish his killers. The *Bulletin* wrote about how unfortunate and unwelcome the news of Wellman's killing was, saying that Wellman was "a young man of sterling worth ... who had fewer enemies than almost any man in it." The newspaper also noted the sad fact that Wellman had just married, on April 12. The *Bulletin* declared that the crime must be solved and the guilty punished, and soon the paper was able to announce that the county commission was offering a reward of $2,500 for the arrest and conviction of the murderer or murderers.[19]

None of this affected one whit the big cattlemen's determination to turn the Wellman cause into a cause célèbre tarnishing the "rustlers" and showing the need for martial law. The invaders turned their local spy Charles Burritt onto the case, and he enthusiastically accepted his charge. Burritt wrote U.S. marshal Joe P. Rankin, imploring him to "spare no expense" to "pursue, discover and punish the murderers" of his deputy, and to bring to bear "the entire power of the U.S. Government."[20] Burritt also undertook a more extensive effort that involved Sheriff Angus. Burritt began to spend a great deal of time with Angus and then wrote letters to Cheyenne sneering at Angus's initial investigation. Angus had gone to the scene of the crime to investigate and soon charged Tom Hathaway with murder, but then made no further arrests.[21] According to Burritt, Angus had conducted a sloppy investigation (there was probably something to this) and had a completely wrongheaded and intractable notion that Hathaway had committed the crime.[22] Burritt, thinking he perceived the situation much more deeply and accurately than Angus, came up with quite a different theory. But a bit later in the investigation, when Angus imprudently confided in Burritt, it turned out that Angus was pushing the case against Hathaway only because he believed Hathaway could provide more information than he had thus far, and Angus's opinions as to the probable perpetrators were not that far from Burritt's.[23] Indeed, when the crime was finally solved, over forty years later, it turned out that Angus had more accurately identified the real killers than had Burritt.[24] The killers were three men who had never been identified as rustlers; they were just local thugs. Ed Starr shot Wellman, apparently for no other reason than a vicious streak and a general anger toward men wearing stars who were associated with big cattlemen.[25]

The problem for all the parties at the time was that the killers had not left many clues. It was a difficult case, and during the lifetimes of those who committed the crime, no one was able to solve the puzzle. Of course, none of this affected the cattlemen's opinion of Angus. To them, he was still the beastly enemy, and the scarcity of evidence in the case did not keep the big cattlemen from pushing charges in federal court involving Wellman's murder.

After the killing of Wellman, though, to the disappointment of the big cattlemen, nothing very startling happened in Johnson County. Burritt wrote Walter Stoll that the houses in the big ranches were being stripped. The *Bulletin*, however, denied these stories.[26] Burritt was prone to great overstatement during this time, but it would be surprising if Johnson County citizens had not taken some vindictive actions. For some reason, though, such actions, to the extent they happened, did not increase the notoriety of the county. In the middle of May the regular roundups began, and although the *Cheyenne Sun* could not restrain itself from negative speculation about difficulties with the roundup, there were no unusual problems.[27] And so, despite the furor over the murder of George Wellman, by the first of June the notion of having Governor Barber declare martial law was abandoned. Instead, Senators Warren and Carey started importuning President Harrison for a federal declaration.[28]

The president, though apparently giving courteous attention to the Wyoming senators' request, was uneasy with the whole notion of declaring martial law to remove duly elected county officials. Such a move would have been an awkward precedent, given widespread violations of the civil rights of former slaves by southern authorities. If the federal government were to take over law enforcement every time local authorities failed to fully enforce the law, it could be argued that federal troops should take up posts throughout the former Confederacy.[29] Another possible reason Harrison was bothered by the notion of imposing martial law in Wyoming was the several statements of outrage sent him by Wyoming citizens. The president even replied to the one from Johnson County, saying, "I could not know anything of the situation except as it was stated by him [Barber] and could not refuse the aid of troops to preserve peace." The strongly worded citizens' statements, reflecting deep and widespread feelings of the general citizenry against the invasion, the actions of Governor Barber, and big cattlemen's tactics in general, probably gave the president pause.[30]

Historian Lewis Gould wrote that it was clear by June 10, 1892, that "some other tack would have to be taken," although all actions were put on hold until the Republican National Convention was completed.[31] Harrison did throw his fellow Republicans a bone by sending some troops to Wyoming in early June.

About six hundred soldiers were dispatched to far southeastern Johnson County, along the Powder River, supposedly for "summer camp." Their presence was resented, and local citizens felt that this was just the first step toward martial law.[32] But even though serious trouble arose between residents of Suggs and some of the troops who were "buffalo soldiers" (African Americans), the situation was never viewed as insurrection. The trouble began as a quarrel over a woman and escalated; a skirmish ensued, resulting in the death of one soldier and the wounding of five others. The incident was apparently seen as being the fault of the troops.[33]

Despite the failure of all the schemes to bring about martial law, Senator Warren persevered. Even though he was not on the ballot in 1892, he did have a strong personal stake in Wyoming's 1892 political battle. After the Wyoming legislature selected Carey and Warren in 1890 as the first U.S. senators from their state, lots were cast in Washington and Carey was assigned a four-year term and Warren a two-year term. Warren was up for reelection by the Wyoming legislature in 1893, and if the legislature was not controlled by Republicans, he would lose his seat.[34]

Warren always insisted that he did not know of the invasion until it was well under way, and perhaps that was true. But whether or not he was directly involved in the planning for the invasion, he was a diehard supporter of the big cattlemen. Their cause was his cause, and he did everything humanly possible to support and promote their goals, starting with wakening President Harrison the evening of April 12, 1892, so that Harrison could order troops to rescue the invaders, followed by his close collaboration with Willis Van Devanter, who not only spearheaded the big cattlemen's case but throughout kept a watchful eye on the invasion's political consequences for Warren. Then Warren undertook the unsuccessful campaign to push President Harrison to declare martial law.[35]

When President Harrison proved to be much more principled than Senator Warren expected, Warren began to lobby for another scheme that he believed would have the same effect as a declaration of martial law.[36] The plan was to create an event that would justify the immediate assistance of federal troops, and the heart of the plan was to use the Wyoming U.S. marshal as fodder to force a federal takeover of Johnson County. It was a cleverly designed scheme, and it might have succeeded.

What undercut it was that Marshal Joe Rankin became wary, suspecting that he was being used for improper purposes. Rankin had been to Buffalo in the previous year, and he knew that the big cattlemen's outrageous stories about the outlaw community of Johnson County were lies. Months later, when he was forced to defend his conduct, his comments show that he had keenly observed what had actually happened in Johnson County, not what big cattlemen said had happened.

In the spring of 1892, Willis Van Devanter was not only defending the criminal charges against big cattlemen but also handling their civil cases. Van Devanter filed suit in early May in the federal district court for an injunction against the small cattlemen's roundup.[37] It was odd that the case was filed at all, because the Johnson County small ranchers had abandoned their roundup plans, and the roundup set by the Wyoming Live Stock Commission was proceeding as scheduled. It was also odd that it was filed in the federal district court rather than a state district court. The U.S. district court was probably selected because Van Devanter felt, based upon past success, that he could obtain anything he sought from a Cheyenne court.

All of these proceedings, though legally unusual, advanced Van Devanter's purposes. He obtained his injunction, although he supposedly had difficulty obtaining service against the defendants. During May a criminal case was also filed in the federal district court in Cheyenne, in which several men were charged with conspiracy to murder George Wellman. This was another odd proceeding; the Wellman murder would normally have been addressed only in the state district court. Willis Van Devanter, though a private attorney and not the federal prosecutor, was probably the guiding hand behind the proceeding. This federal criminal case provided another set of papers that had to be served; even better, arrests had to be made.

By the first of June, the cattlemen's plan was in place: U.S. marshal Rankin need only charge into Johnson County with a contingent of troops and deputies, produce a clash, and then call for more federal troops to enforce the law. At least, that is what Warren, Van Devanter, and the big cattlemen wanted and expected. But Rankin proved to be like President Harrison, surprisingly unwilling to compromise principles.

Rankin saw clearly that he was being used as a pawn. He noted that the settlers of Johnson County perceived, not unreasonably, that the true motivation of the big cattlemen was to keep out settlers.[38] He knew that the big cattlemen were probably behind the series of assassinations leading to the invasion, and he also knew that, contrary to the statements of the big cattlemen, the "war" at the T. A. Ranch was not between a small band of big cattlemen and a gang of thieves but between virtually the whole male population of Johnson County and a few wealthy cattlemen and their hired gunmen.

Rankin was sure that before the invasion he would have had little trouble serving papers, but many residents, already believing that the invaders had all been deputized during the invasion, were now convinced that U.S. officers and the big cattlemen were in league. Rankin determined that the big cattlemen and their attorneys really did not want action from him, except to drive men out of the country and create an incident. In sum, Rankin recognized that the big cattlemen had deeply and unfairly provoked the people of Johnson County and now were trying to use the agitation they had created as a pretext to complete their purposes. Rankin resolved not to bring on conflict but to do everything he could to avoid a clash.

Rankin's resolution created friction with the big cattlemen, their lawyers, and the politicians supporting them. Senators Carey and Warren had to work through President Harrison to force immediate action from Marshal Rankin, but Harrison continued to resist the push for aggressive action from troops, saying that Rankin should just take sufficient deputies to Johnson County and ask for troops only if he met violent resistance.[39] But through June and into July, Rankin kept finding reasons why he could not ride north, to the great frustration of Warren and Van Devanter. Rankin finally went to Johnson County in late July but found, he reported, that many of those singled out as rustlers had left the area and that "with very few exceptions the people have turned to their original avocations." Rankin concluded, "I do not look for any reorganized defiance of the United States authority."[40] The agitation of the people of Johnson had been exaggerated, but in any case, during the month and a half that Rankin procrastinated, the anger of the people of Johnson County further subsided, helped by their awareness of attempts to paint them as out of control in order to justify a declaration of martial law.

Senator Warren does not come off well in this episode, but it should be remembered that he was under enormous pressure from his supporters. The best example of that pressure is a letter, not from one of those supporters, but from the senator responding to what must have been an incredibly intemperate letter from Billy Irvine. Irvine's letter is not available, but based on Warren's response, it had to have been a hysterical rant.

On July 23, Francis Warren wrote to the Honorable W. C. Irvine in Cheyenne, "In your letter you accuse me either directly or inferentially, or both, of lack of friendship, hypocrisy, falsehood, double-dealing, selfishness, of being a political trickster, of desiring to promote myself by pulling down my best friends, of cowardice, etc. etc." In the letter, Warren disputed Irvine's claim that the senator was no true friend: "The best evidence in the world that I can offer of still being your friend is that I answer your letter at all, for I have very few friends on earth whom I would allow to pen such a letter [as yours], and none, that I would accept such a letter from, unless I believed the friend sorely pushed, suffering through happiness or misfortune and hardly in his right mind."[41]

Warren firmly denied that he had not supported Irvine and Irvine's friends: "I have been active, tenacious and aggressive in trying to obtain relief for the situation and bring about the delivery of the property of the northern country to the control of its rightful owners and to bring punishment to the depredators."[42] And, in fact, an overview of all of Warren's actions after the invasion fully supports his claim of zealous advocacy on behalf of his friends.

Warren's letter was remarkably temperate, almost sad, but he pulled no punches in telling Irvine how he was mistaken. Warren carefully explained that martial law applied only in rare circumstances, but never to stop thieving or any other crime not involving violence. He made the firm point that if anyone was to ask for martial law, it would be the sheriff of Johnson County, as "you would have been the people sought to be suppressed, because you were against the duly authorized officers, the county, the sheriff, etc." Further, Warren pointed out, if the president had proclaimed martial law after the T. A. Ranch conflict, "it would have been directed to your party to disperse."[43]

The letter was careful not to redirect blame, but Warren could not resist showing that there was a clear avenue to calling troops out, and that avenue was an allegation of "insurrection should armed men resist and attack United States marshals and deputies." He acknowledged that the delay "as to the marshal going north to arrest culprits" had been "vexatious," although he himself had been "zealous and industrious in having pushed the matter."[44] But, Warren noted, "you can lead a horse to water, but he won't always drink," and if Rankin were to be "resisted in arrests now, it is but to touch the wire through the Governor to secure all needed."[45] The primary purpose of the letter was to placate Billy Irvine, not to attack Rankin, but the letter certainly provides a clue to the later rage Warren directed at the marshal.

With Rankin's uneventful excursion to Johnson County in late July, the cattlemen's energetic campaign for martial law finally guttered out. The whole effort certainly alarmed the people of Johnson County, and at times, when Governor Barber or President Harrison seemed to seriously consider a declaration of martial law, the effort appeared perilously close to success. In the end, though, the chief effect of the cattlemen's crusade for martial law was to give the Democrats of Wyoming, already blessed with abundant grist for the political mill, even stronger points to present to the electorate.

CHAPTER NINETEEN

The 1892 Election

Eighteen ninety-two was an election year, meaning that voters engaged in debates throughout Wyoming about all the issues they felt important. The electorate obviously thought the invasion to be of the greatest importance, because the Johnson County War became the transcendent issue of the election. Voters expressed their opinions about every aspect of the invasion, and the November election results indisputably showed the verdict of Wyoming people about the assault on Johnson County.

The invasion presented the Wyoming Republican Party with a problem of the first order. The party was dominant in Wyoming after the 1890 elections, and in early 1892, before the invasion, it appeared its dominance would continue. But then, when the facts came out about the northern excursion and the support of Republican officeholders for the invaders, Republicans suffered the stigma of being the party of the cattlemen.[1]

The big cattlemen and their allies quickly took the position that the excursion into Johnson County had no political significance, or at least *should* have no political significance. The *Cheyenne Daily Sun* on April 17 condemned "blatant agitators" who were trying to blame Republicans for the invasion, and when Mayor Burritt wrote Judge Blake on May 8, he expressed the hope that "this entire cattle trouble" could be "kept out of politics," and he predicted that making the invasion political "would not change the general result in the state."[2] These supporters of the invaders sought to comfort themselves, hoping that the atrocious actions of their principals would somehow escape the notice of the voters. But their gestures were as futile as King Canute's command to the incoming tide to retreat.

The voters of Wyoming, especially those in northern Wyoming, were furious at the actions of Republican officials, and outrage increased as people watched justice being manipulated. Even worse for Republican hopes, a great many Wyoming people saw the ballot as their most reliable recourse. November 8, 1892, was Election Day, and the date was circled almost immediately. The *Buffalo Bulletin* mentioned November 8 in its first edition following the invasion, and the date was sounded time and again through 1892.[3] One of the reasons Johnson County citizens were alarmed at the prospect of martial law was that they saw it as an attempt to prevent what they foresaw as "the landslide this November."[4]

When they noticed Republican officeholders scurrying to lend aid to the big cattlemen, Wyoming people deplored their actions. At the beginning, most of the condemnation was aimed at Acting Governor Amos Barber, a Republican. His feeble attempts to justify his notorious preinvasion order to the militia and his decision to bring the big cattlemen down to Laramie County made things worse. As well, although Senator Francis Warren's steadfast support of the big cattlemen was not immediately apparent, it was not long before it became so, and soon he was tarred as a lackey for the big cattle owners. Indeed, when Warren wrote Billy Irvine on July 23, 1892, he rebutted Irvine's accusation that politics had governed his conduct, saying: "To begin with, my political future, if I had one before, has been ruined by this northern cattle business." He added that his known friendship for Irvine and his associates had "alienated all those opposed" to them, as was made clear "constantly by the outside press, and by letters, assertions, resolutions, speeches, talks, etc."[5]

In the public mind, Senator Joseph Carey, as a former president of the Wyoming Stock Growers Association and the owner of what was probably the second-largest herd of cattle in the state of Wyoming, was already irretrievably tied to the actions of big cattlemen. (The public perception was accurate; there is strong evidence that Carey was "deeply implicated in the planning of the invasion."[6]) In addition, Carey was not only a Republican senator but also, at the time of the invasion, the chairman of the Wyoming Republican Party.[7] A month after the invasion, Carey was to give a public address in Casper, the first time he had ventured into Wyoming since the invasion. He called off the speech, however, because of public indignation toward him. (Supposedly the purchase of rotten eggs by citizens caused Carey to change his mind.)[8]

Democrats within the state immediately accepted and embraced the linkage of Carey, Warren, and Barber to the invasion and all the associated shenanigans. After the apparent abduction of the two trappers, editor E. H. Kimball of the vigorously Democratic *Douglas Graphic*, demanded that Carey, Warren, and Barber return the men.[9] Kimball undoubtedly knew that these Republican politicians did not hold or control the trappers, but his demand was an effective device to tie Republican officeholders to the big cattlemen.

In early May of 1892, less than a month after the invasion, a Republican convention was held in Cheyenne, with Senator Carey acting as chairman.[10] Perhaps it was too soon for the party leaders to devise a politically effective way to respond to the event. They chose to say nothing about the invasion, apparently pretending that it never happened. This response, awkward though it was, was never improved upon; throughout 1892 the Wyoming Republican Party never did mention the Johnson County War. Individual candidates did, but the party fled from the grim reality until the disastrous end of the campaign. Republican politicians were inextricably connected to the big cattlemen, who were probably their strongest supporters, but in 1892 it was a bad bargain. One historian made an observation, well supported in the historical record, that "the Republicans also suffered from the gross stupidity of the invaders and their sympathizers, who showed themselves to be without the slightest understanding of the depth of popular feelings against them."[11]

Beyond straightforward political efforts, there was a big push to suppress those in the Wyoming press who wrote too critically about the invasion. The politically influential employed the services of highly effective attorneys—including Willis Van Devanter, who became the Republican state chairman in the summer of 1892—and took legal actions against newspapermen who were outspoken against the big cattlemen. E. H. Kimball, John Carroll, and Asa Mercer were each set upon by big cattlemen, and in each case, though unpleasant for the targeted newspaperman, the attack did more harm than good to Republican office seekers.

E. H. Kimball was the first of these Wyoming journalists to learn how much havoc could be wreaked by a man with power and money. Kimball wrote an article, published in the *Douglas Graphic* on May 31, 1892, in which he stated that seventeen Texans were camped at Fort

Fetterman and were going to work for former governor George W. Baxter (strongly allied with the big cattlemen). Kimball indicated that the populace might be faced with a new invasion.[12] After the April invasion, the people of northern Wyoming were very skittish, and rumors proliferated about the big cattlemen making another raid. These were harmless background noises during an anxious time, but Kimball's article gave Baxter the opportunity to strike at the Douglas newspaperman, who had been a dedicated adversary of big cattlemen. Baxter filed a criminal libel complaint against Kimball, and a warrant was sworn out for his arrest, which was permitted in 1892 for libel.[13]

Kimball was arrested in Douglas and jailed in Cheyenne, where the charges had been filed. He was placed on $2,500 bail, but the bond money was not posted, because Kimball and his lawyer feared that the editor would only be rearrested on another charge. In late June, Kimball's bail was reduced to $500, the amount was posted, but then, as expected, another big cattleman, A. B. Clarke, filed another charge. After some difficulties, another $500 was finally posted, and in early July, Kimball was able to travel back to Douglas.[14] Local Wyoming newspapers closely followed Kimball's treatment and informed their readers of these latest high-handed actions by big cattlemen.[15]

Former governor Baxter was also involved in another aggressive move against a newspaperman, John Carroll. Baxter and Frank Kemp, an Omaha cattleman with Wyoming interests, were minority shareholders in the company that owned the *Cheyenne Daily Leader*, and they filed suit, asking for the appointment of a receiver to take over the paper. Baxter and Kemp were represented by Walter R. Stoll, then the chairman of the Democratic Central Committee. The suit alleged that Carroll and Joseph A. Breckons— an owner of the *Leader*—had misappropriated the funds of the company, committed "conspiracy," had voted themselves into the offices they held with the company, and had used too many employees when publishing the *Leader*.[16] But the transparent reason for the suit was to force Carroll to change his objectionable editorial policy.[17] The suit was never likely to succeed, given that it was obviously aimed at silencing the *Leader*, but the incident provided yet another demonstration of bullying tactics by big cattlemen.[18]

Asa Mercer was the target of a third, literal assault upon a newspaperman. Mercer's journey from the most radical of supporters of the big cattlemen to their sworn enemy is a strange tale. When Mercer established his newspaper, the *Northwestern Live Stock Journal*, in Cheyenne in 1883, his principal patrons were the members of the Wyoming Live Stock Association, and he was a committed advocate for that group.[19] It was reported, albeit from the frequently unreliable *Cheyenne Daily Sun*, that in late April, after the invasion, Mercer had offered pro-cattlemen resolutions at a meeting of a regional stock growers association in Ogden, Utah.[20] But something happened between April and July, because on July 8, 1892, Mercer published an editorial in his newspaper that was unlike anything he had ever printed before. Instead of breathing fire against rustlers and advocating their mass extermination, Mercer wrote about his efforts to provide bail for E. H. Kimball. His reason for doing so, he said, was that a "brother quill driver" had been "deprived of his liberty and treated as a felon because he had the courage of his convictions and dared to say that murder was wrong and that murderers, their aiders and abettors, should be punished."[21] Mercer went on to describe how, as a result of his actions, he had been subjected to a boycott by the big cattlemen. He even listed and published letters in which these men withdrew their advertisements.[22]

Mercer's contradictory actions were and are a puzzle. For that matter, Mercer's whole life—ambitious, ardent, erratic, and flamboyant—was a puzzle. He had first come to public attention in the new Washington Territory, where he had prospered, becoming the first president of the University of Washington in 1861. He gained fame in 1864, as well as the deep gratitude of Washington men, when he and his brother, Captain William Mercer, imported marriageable women from New York to Seattle. But soon after this project was completed, he moved on to Oregon, where he stayed eight years. In 1876 he left Oregon for Texas, where he was the proprietor of four newspapers during the next seven years. And in 1883 he traveled north from Texas to Cheyenne, Wyoming, there starting the *Live Stock Journal*.[23]

There has been a great deal of speculation as to why Mercer suddenly refused to support his patrons. Lewis Gould opined that Mercer was in great financial distress and, forced to seek patronage from the Democratic Party, sought to ingratiate himself to Wyoming Democrats.[24] But Mercer's actions after July 1892, in which he actively supported the Democratic Party and the battles against the big cattlemen (and then sought political patronage), seem more likely a subsequent expedient to make a living. They do not necessarily show that Mercer moved away from his big cattleman sponsors in order to gain something from the Democrats. His July action more likely sprang from some angry disagreement back in May or June of 1892. There is no explanation in the historical record why Mercer so precipitously split from the big cattlemen; it is possible something about the invasion bothered him and, when he raised questions, he was punished in some form and rebelled. The big cattlemen behind the invasion brooked no dissent over the nobility of their April mission to Johnson County. Unfortunately, at least from the standpoint of getting at the truth, the defection of Mercer is clouded by emotional charges. Mercer presented himself as a man compelled to act on his conscience, but he never explained how he came to move from an opposite position that had not bothered his conscience at all. Whatever the reason for his change, the big cattlemen had an "irate reaction to the sudden defection of a kept agent."[25]

When Mercer committed to a cause, he did so with vigor, and he pummeled his former allies. In late August he wrote: "These are war times. There can be no fence riding. If your sympathies are with the constitution breakers and murderers, get into the republican ranks where you belong. That is the party of free-booters, land grabbers, and millionaires, and you will feel at home with them from the start. They are your kind of people."[26] Mercer kept up his attack. On August 23 he accused John Clay, president of the Wyoming Stock Growers Association, of supporting the invading force by lending his employees. C. A. Campbell, an employee of Clay's who had in fact joined the invasion, went to the office of the *Live Stock Journal* and confronted Mercer. Campbell, larger and younger than Mercer, struck him, breaking the newspaperman's glasses and inflicting deep cuts. The story of the attack was published in all the Wyoming Democratic newspapers and "evoked general outrage."[27]

The state Democratic convention was held on July 27 in Rock Springs. Walter Stoll, the state chairman, was in deep trouble with the great majority of his party, who had viscerally reacted against the invasion. The *Laramie Boomerang* had already called for Stoll's resignation, saying that he not only had represented big cattlemen but truly supported the purposes of his employers.[28] When Stoll gave the opening address to the convention, he removed all doubt as to his beliefs. In addition to attempting to justify the Johnson County War, he delivered a "bitter harangue" against the party members associated with the *Cheyenne Daily Leader*.[29] In so doing, he was "annihilating" himself and he knew it: Stoll crowned his address—which would certainly have been followed by his ouster—by resigning.[30]

Luckily for Republicans, only three statewide offices were open in 1892: the governorship, the congressional seat, and justice of the Wyoming Supreme Court. The governorship was the most hotly contested, probably because several men recognized that 1892 was a rare year of opportunity for Democrats in Wyoming, the minority party from the beginning of the territory. Four candidates vied for their party's nomination, and finally, on the thirty-seventh ballot, Dr. John Osborne, a physician from Rawlins, was chosen. Henry A. Coffeen and Gibson Clark, both of Sheridan, were selected as the nominees for congressman and justice of the Supreme Court, respectively.[31]

The Democratic Party platform did not hide from the Johnson County War. The platform declared in favor of strict enforcement of the Wyoming Constitution and the laws of Wyoming. In case any voter was unsure what this meant, it was spelled out. The Democrats held the "Republican administration largely responsible for allowing armed men to march in to Johnson County in open and armed defiance of the constitution and laws and in resistance of local civil authorities."[32] The platforms of the two parties thus provided a clear choice to Wyoming voters on the most important issue of the 1892 election. If they had no problem with the invasion of Johnson County, they were free to vote Republican. But if they were offended by the invasion, the Democratic Party welcomed them. Rarely in any election has the electorate been given such a clear option to express dissatisfaction with a political party.

The platform also set out other issues of the election, none of which resonated with voters as did the invasion. Probably the next most important issue was the Warren Arid Land Bill, and it gained much greater significance after April 1892. Senator Warren had been pushing hard for federal legislation that would turn Wyoming's public domain lands— still the overwhelming majority of lands outside riparian areas—over to state authorities. Even before the invasion, Democrats were skeptical of such legislation, feeling that it might result in more land going to big landholders, such as Warren himself. But after the invasion, this concern became an obsession. As shown by the Democratic platform, many Wyoming people were now convinced that the Warren land bill was a clever device to allow the big cattlemen to grab up almost all the land in Wyoming. They believed that men who held such great power that they could defy the land laws of the United States and literally get away with murder could easily seize control of all the important land in Wyoming. And the Democratic Party, which by and large was the party of those not holding such power, did more than dissent from Warren's legislation. They condemned the Warren Arid Land Bill as an "infamous measure, covertly designed to aid land sharks in obtaining control of large areas of land and thus defraud the people of their rightful heritage."[33]

There were other issues in the election, of course, such as an obligatory reference to precious metals (the Democratic Party thought that both gold and silver should be used for coinage in the United States).[34] "Bimetallism" had been a hot topic in previous years, but in the year of the war on Johnson County, the issue was drowned out. Other sub-rosa issues carried more weight, and they all went back to the invasion. Wyoming had just become a state, and many citizens were sensitive to the criticism that the country had erred when it allowed statehood for Wyoming. Such citizens could not have been comforted by a June 30 article in the *Buffalo Bulletin* that quoted the *Seattle Post Intelligencer*. The Seattle newspaper blasted the big cattlemen: "A more shameful spectacle has not been seen . . . than that of the governor of Wyoming refusing to support the sheriff of a county with the militia to repel a lynching party of wealthy cattlemen, and then appealing to the federal government for troops when he feared that the sheriff and his posse were likely to capture the lynchers in spite of his refusal to call out the militia." The really stinging remark, though, was the next one: "A state where the only warrant necessary to execute an accused man is the irresponsible will and posse of grisly Judge Lynch is a state only fit to be given over to the occupation of the land pirates and Kilkenny cats of civilization."[35]

The 1892 election became a referendum on settlement, another issue closely tied to the invasion. The *Buffalo Bulletin* printed part of an editorial from *Irrigation Age*, a journal published in Chicago that promoted the benefits of irrigation in the West. The editorial referred to statements of a "public official" who had said he wanted nothing to do with anything that would bring more people into Wyoming: "There are too many people here now—too many people and too few cattle." *Irrigation Age* noted that the man who made this remark was "a leader of the armed mob that went forth to kill the rustlers" and that although this official was willing to go to battle, "he came home in shame and defeat, and realized sharply that the day of frontier barbarism, both mental and physical, had gone." The piece concluded that "civilization is driving barbarism before it, just as the rustlers put this insolent champion of cattle on the run."[36] The "insolent champion of cattle" was probably Billy Irvine, who was a member of the Wyoming Live Stock Commission and was never shy about speaking his mind. It was one more example of a big cattleman helping out the Democratic Party in 1892 by expressing his intemperate beliefs.

Still another issue with ties to the invasion was the "Cheyenne ring." When Democrats used this loaded phrase, it meant Republican officials associated with the state capitol, especially Warren, Carey, and Barber, who were "controlled by the cattlemen's group."[37] That this issue mattered to voters was shown by an editorial in the April 28, 1892, issue of the *Wyoming Derrick* (Casper). The editor wrote that the Republican Party of the state had become "simply the party of the Cheyenne and cattlemen's clique," a clique that "has controlled the republican party of the state for ten years and will continue to direct its course until the party is routed and defeated."[38]

Back in Buffalo, all of these themes had been voiced in the strongest terms. All through May and June, new editor Gustave Moeller published numerous articles from newspapers around Wyoming and the region that criticized the big cattlemen and supported the people of Johnson County. By quoting from at least a dozen and a half newspapers of Wyoming and other states, including, of course, the *Cheyenne Daily Leader*, the editor of the *Bulletin* persuasively demonstrated how thoroughly the big cattlemen were being condemned in the region.[39] Moeller did not just use the words of other editors either; he added several of his own forcefully worded remarks. For example, on May 19, 1892, he responded to a comment from the *Laramie Sentinel*, asking how it was that twenty rustlers could have terrorized the four to five hundred people who rushed to their aid.

In a thoughtful and interesting response, Moeller offered what was probably the clearest expression of the feelings of the people of Johnson County about cattlemen, cattle theft, and the invasion. He wrote that the people of Johnson County were determined to resist oppression and that "the course of the cattlemen in their past dealings with the people has been one of injustice and oppression." He referred to the actions of the Wyoming Live Stock Commission and declared that some Johnson County people had been unjustly branded as outlaws and their property seized. "This is one act of oppression," stated Moeller. Another "act of oppression" was that men were hired to assassinate Johnson County citizens. He referred to the "first attempt," meaning the assault upon Champion and Gilbertson on November 1, 1891, and noted that it had "failed signally." But the second attempt had resulted in the deaths of two men, "one of them, [John A. Tisdale] a man of family and a man who was in no manner a rustler." Then, Moeller went on, the big cattlemen had invaded Johnson County, "bragging as they come that every suspect shall be made a lead mine or an ornament to a halter and deliberately kill[ing] and burn[ing] our fellow citizens." Moeller argued, "Should the people of Johnson county have quietly remained at home, not knowing who was to be the next victim? . . . Could a law abiding community do less than rally around our sheriff to vindicate the law so grossly outraged? We decline to denominate any man a thief until we know he is one. The presumption of innocence is the inherent birthright of every American." If there was evidence of theft, however, Moeller asserted that Johnson County citizens would convict.

Moeller declared that the worst scoundrels were the *Cheyenne Sun* and the *Cheyenne Tribune*, which had branded all of Johnson County as thieves and outlaws. But, said Moeller, repeating the theme underlying all of his editorials, just wait until November, when the people will set things right. Moeller recognized that there were some stock thieves in Johnson County, and he did not deny that cattlemen had been robbed of cattle. "Yet we reiterate," he continued, "that there is law in this free country, and to the law the stockmen must appeal and not to physical force." He then concluded:

> Johnson county did not rally at the beck of thieves to defend the sanctity of home and human life, but at the call of the sheriff, the county's executor of civil law. Johnson county citizens are not terrorized by thieves and will not permit themselves to be terrorized by them, but they are kept in constant agitation and terror by the reiterated threats of cattlemen to come again to finish the work so forcibly begun and so ignominiously interrupted.[40]

Through the spring and early summer of 1892, Moeller repeated how important it was to throw the Cheyenne Republican "rascals" out. On May 19, 1892, he wrote that the *Bulletin*, which had been a Republican newspaper since at least September 1888 (when Carroll H. Parmelee became the new editor), would not now commit to any party, having declared, "Those in high places who, regardless of their official oath, either actively or constructively assist in oppressing the people, will be handled without gloves by THE BULLETIN regardless of their political faith and party affiliation."[41] By June 16, Moeller had come to the position that because of the "grasping and grinding monopoly known as the Wyoming Stock Growers Association" and a governor "governed by a political ring of bad repute," all of rural Wyoming needed to unite behind the best men, whether Democrats or the Populists (the People's Party, which had gained political strength in 1892).[42]

Two weeks later, Moeller stated that every independent voter should remember that every Republican paper in Wyoming, except the *Cheyenne Commonwealth* and, to some extent, the *Laramie Sentinel,* "espouses more or less ably the cause of mob rule, the cattle barons' method of human extermination and the accidental governor's action or non-action in emergencies." He stated further that the voters held the power to consign all these Republicans to private life "and to place the government into the hands of men of the people."[43] On July 7, 1892, Moeller declared in no uncertain terms that the one and only objective of the coming election was to throw out the ruling elite from Cheyenne, and in this quest party loyalty mattered little: "No amount of soft soap or cajolery on the part of the republican press can bring back to unquestioned party loyalty the thinking republicans of Johnson county whom the actions of the present state government has estrayed from the party."[44] And, on July 14, Moeller declared: "Farmers, ranchmen and stock owners, if you want the public domain leased to syndicates of cattle barons to your own detriment, vote the republican national ticket."[45]

Moeller obviously felt that he was in the front of a crusade, that the overriding imperative was ridding the state of the Republicans who had provided such aid and comfort to the invaders. Based upon the results of the November election, Moeller and the people of Johnson County were exactly in step. But in his zeal, the editor apparently failed to notice that he was not in step with his employer, the owner of the *Bulletin,* who was a committed Republican. Abruptly and without explanation, on July 28, 1892, the tone of the *Bulletin* was altered. The lead article that day was a reprint from *Bill Barlow's Budget,* the Douglas newspaper that had become more supportive of the big cattlemen than even the *Cheyenne Sun* or *Tribune.* The article praised to the highest the Republican Party, "which has always been the friend and ally of the common people and supporter of the settler," and insisted that the common man would surely not listen to the old cry of "the ring" and the dishonest appeal of ambitious Democrats charging the Republicans with the invasion; the Republican Party was not to blame for the invasion, and Republicans should reject this "slander."[46]

On August 4, 1892, it became clear what was happening. That issue contained a short, sad, and somber note from Moeller, in which he explained that his tenure as editor of the *Bulletin* would immediately cease. Moeller said that he had taken the post of editor only "as a matter of personal friendship of the proprietor," C. M. Lingle. Apparently the friendship had soured: Moeller told the *Bulletin* readers that there was such a difference of opinion between him and the proprietor that they could only agree to disagree—Moeller's positions "being deemed too democratic to suit the republican patrons of THE BULLETIN." Moeller thanked all the people who had approved of his tenure as editor and assured his readers, "I will always be found ready to defend the rights of the people with my pen, and with my life if the occasion should arise."[47]

The next week, the new editor of the paper, A. McArthur, told the people of Buffalo how the *Bulletin* would be different:

> In coming before the people of Johnson county as editor of THE BULLETIN I wish to state that, during my connection with the paper, the same will be first, last, and all the time, in the interest of Republicanism. We feel as though there has been a lack of the proper spirit of politics in THE BULLETIN, but henceforth we will endeavor to redeem ourselves from the political standpoint and try and gain the confidence of our constituents and of the people in general.
>
> And now, in regard to the cattle question, we have this much to say: That we think it is bad enough as it is, without any further discussion. The readers of THE BULLETIN know that this question has proven very detrimental to Wyoming, and more especially to Johnson county, and the less said the quicker mended.[48]

The *Cheyenne Daily Leader* lamented the change, saying that, "The resignation of Mr. Moeller means that the methods and policies of the *Bulletin* are to be radically changed, and the paper, instead of representing the people, may represent the political clique which has tried to fasten anarchy on the state."[49] And, indeed, the change in the *Bulletin* was remarkable. True to his word, in subsequent editions the new editor said almost nothing about the invasion. The *Bulletin* went from a fire-breathing organ to one that would make a junior high school newspaper seem belligerent. All was mild and mellow; it was as if the most outrageous event in the history of Wyoming never happened. The new newspaper in town, however, the *People's Voice*, formerly the *Buffalo Echo*, which was owned and edited by Jack Flagg, took up the cause of the people of Johnson County versus the big cattlemen.

Flagg did not lack for topics to inflame his reader's ire at the big cattlemen. On September 3, 1892, Senators Warren and Carey moved against Marshal Joe Rankin, writing United States Attorney General William Miller to demand Rankin's resignation, asserting cowardice by Rankin in failing to charge up to Johnson County in May or June.[50] But like so many of the tactics of Republicans that year, their actions backfired. Rankin went to the press and soon there were stories putting the Republicans in a very bad light. The *Leader* had a field day, running one article after another about how the stockmen were "after Rankin's scalp." The newspaper correctly detected that the big cattlemen had tried to use Rankin as a pawn to produce a pretext for martial law, but concluded that "providence was on the side of the settler at this juncture and the scheme miserably failed."[51] The newspaper reminded the people of Wyoming about Rankin's heroic past, running a long article about young Joe Rankin's harrowing ride to Fort Steele in 1879 to bring help to 130 troopers besieged by Ute Indians at Meeker, Colorado.[52] The *Leader* also quoted comments by Joe's brother (a former Carbon County sheriff), and his statements probably represented what Joe thought but knew would be impolitic to say. Ex-Sheriff Rankin charged the leaders of the invasion—Major Wolcott, John N. Tisdale, and Billy Irvine—"with conspiracy to down him [Joe] simply because he would not make arrests by the wholesale in Johnson county upon trumped up charges."[53]

Marshal Rankin refused to resign and demanded an investigation.[54] The public resentment became so great that, as Lewis Gould wrote, "to repair this damage to their cause, Warren and Van Devanter adopted a pose of detachment." Gould observed that "Warren pretended that the justice department acted on its own, while Van Devanter assured restless Republicans of his earnest solicitude for Rankin's fate."[55]

But a much bigger blow against Wyoming Republicans was in the offing, and it was probably the greatest test of Willis Van Devanter's ability to suppress the truth in 1892. Asa Mercer printed the confession of George Dunning in the October 14, 1892, issue of the *Northwestern Live Stock Journal*.[56] In a long and detailed statement to the Johnson County authorities, Dunning set out the whole story of his involvement, starting with the first contacts by H. B. Ijams, which Ijams could not deny, because Dunning possessed two letters from the secretary of the Wyoming Live Stock Commission, foolishly written on the commission's stationery.[57] Dunning recounted several conversations with Ijams and, in Cheyenne, with R. S. Van Tassell, Ben Morrison, and W. H. Tabor. He had participated in the entire invasion until the point of surrender to the federal troops and recounted all the events from Cheyenne on April 5 to the T. A. Ranch on April 13. He told of the plans for killing men in Johnson and other counties, how he was informed of the involvement of Governor Barber, Senators Warren and Carey, Judge John W. Blake, and Joe Rankin (which, when related by Ijams, may have been overstatements), and all the arrangements for compensation for killing "rustlers."

Many years after Dunning's confession, the great majority of his statements were admitted by various of the invaders and their supporters, so that Dunning's statement does not now read as a radical paper. The admissions of Robert David and Dr. Penrose leave little question that Dunning's statements about lists of targeted victims and the active support of Governor Barber were correct. But in 1892 these contentions were strongly denied by cattlemen (and Barber), and even the *Cheyenne Daily Leader* was careful not to mention the victim list nor to make direct accusations against the acting governor. And of course the *Cheyenne Sun* and the *Cheyenne Tribune* put out a stream of stories full of denials and misrepresentations.[58]

In addition to stories forwarded to several big-city dailies, the big cattlemen had even managed to plant a story in a national magazine, *Frank Leslie's Weekly*. The article was contributed by an anonymous person from Cheyenne ("A. R. T.") and was dated May 17, 1892.[59] Of all the various articles coming out of Cheyenne and pushing the line of the big cattlemen, the story in *Frank Leslie's Weekly* may have been the most extreme. It spoke of how, in Wyoming, the thief became "a man of power," possessing "vast herds," even though thousands of cattle had been confiscated by the Wyoming Live Stock Commission. The article referred to a "secret society" in Johnson County that compelled participation on threat of immediate banishment from Wyoming and prevented any convictions by intimidation. The article had its own fantastic numbers for charges versus convictions; two hundred charges were supposedly brought for cattle and horse theft, resulting in only five convictions. The alleged comments of Judge Micah Saufley were again trotted out, only this time the judge was supposed to have declared from the bench, "Each of these four men who have been tried is guilty of the crime charged and it has been as clearly proved as in any case that has ever come within my knowledge, and yet the jury has in each case turned the prisoner free. I refuse to go on with any more of these cases; it might as well be understood that there is no protection for property in Johnson County." The article went on to praise the fine characters and sterling reputations of Wolcott, Irvine, and others. These men supposedly showed their "pluck" by refusing to surrender to the "thieves," and in fact "not all the men in Johnson County could have captured them," because they were "simply invincible." The author even praised Amos Barber, who "has manfully done his duty regardless of the criticisms of the newspapers, which have, singularly enough, taken the side of the thieves."

This article, though profoundly misleading, neatly encompassed what big cattlemen wanted the people of Wyoming and the United States to believe. It was probably written by Ed Towse or Edward Slack, who knew well the big cattlemen's take on the invasion. Through these kinds of articles, the big cattlemen had managed to obfuscate the facts sufficiently so that while most Wyomingites greatly disapproved of the invasion (as shown by the results of the election), many gave some weight to the big cattlemen's version of events. More than that, the actions of Governor Barber had prevented a proper investigation and the probable presentation of the testimony of twenty Dunnings (in which case, not even Barber and the Cheyenne judge could have resisted a full-throated demand for a trial on the merits). So when George Dunning's confession showing the full ugly truth was released through Mercer's newspaper, Van Devanter was able to paint it as a strange aberration and vigorously challenge it.

When the article first appeared, the editor, Edward Slack, was out of town, and so Van Devanter just took over the newspaper. He was then the lead attorney for the big cattlemen and the Republican Party's state chairman, and nobody questioned his authority to act. Van Devanter obtained and printed denials from Barber, Blake, and Attorney General

Charles Potter, and he composed a long editorial that railed against "the Stock Journal's slanders."[60] Beyond that, editor-lawyer Van Devanter filed suit against Mercer and closed his printing shop. Mercer, who had gone to Chicago, was arrested for criminal libel upon the complaint of John Clay, and he was thrown in jail in Chicago.[61] The Cheyenne postmaster held the issues containing the confession, asserting, according to Mercer, that they were "obscene."[62] But all these efforts also backfired against the Republicans. Mercer was soon released from jail, and "a goodly number of copies went out by express, so that the public got the information before it quite generally."[63] All of the furor and the harsh reaction to Mercer fueled the public's interest in Dunning's statement.

The people of Buffalo could closely follow all these developments if they read the *Voice*, but if their sole source of information was the *Bulletin*, they would have no idea any of these events had occurred. The editor of the *Bulletin* usually refused to be pulled into the fray, going only so far as to make smug observations about the coming election. On August 25, the *Bulletin* made the following comment: "From the present outlook there is no question but that the state republican ticket will be elected this fall. There has not been a prospective candidate mentioned but what would carry the state at an overwhelming majority. The most of the people are dissatisfied with the democratic ticket and the people's party can't expect to do anything."[64]

The *Bulletin's* mention of "the people's party" was a reference to Wyoming's Populist Party, which had, in the late 1880s, drawn some interest and support and seemed to be invigorated by the outrage over the invasion. Party loyalty was strong in the nineteenth century, and many Wyoming citizens, although offended by the Republicans' actions, were not quite ready to switch to the Democratic Party, and so found the People's Party a more comfortable half step. As the election neared, a great community of agreement between the People's Party and the Democrats became apparent. Most importantly, the two political parties apparently agreed wholly on the need for "the reformation of the present state government and the overthrow of ring rule."[65] Members of the two parties began to speak of "fusion," whereby they would join in a solid front against the Republicans. It is understandable why the Democrats would find this appealing—Wyoming Republicans had run roughshod over the Democrats for many years, and there was desperation within the Democratic Party. When the opportunity arose in 1892 to actually win an election, Wyoming

Democrats seemed to feel that it might never come again and that they had better do whatever was necessary to take advantage of it. So they took the risky step of endorsing fusion. Of course, they could not have known how poorly the experiment would eventually work out, but the Democrats should have recognized that, without fusion, most of the disgruntled Wyoming voters would probably have moved to the Democrats, if only to avoid wasting their votes on a third party that was unlikely to make much difference.

The People's Party held its convention in Douglas in late September, and the Wyoming Democratic Party chairman, A. L. New, appeared, appealing for the fusion of the efforts of the Democratic Party and the People's Party.[66] After vigorous discussion, the delegates resolved to accept a Democratic proposal, whereby Populist electors for the presidency would be substituted for Democratic electors and, in return, the Populists would accept the Democratic nominees for governor, the House of Representatives, and the Wyoming Supreme Court (John Osborne, Henry Coffeen, and Gibson Clark).[67] The formation of a fusion ticket to present to the voters was announced by W. T. O'Connor, the chairman of the People's Party, and he enthusiastically expounded the persuasive reasons why the arrangement was a good thing. His argument was that the two parties needed to unite to defeat a common enemy, the Cheyenne ring, and that they were in complete accord on all the important issues. Indeed, as O'Connor expounded upon the common agreement about the shameful actions of the acting governor, the "wicked" invasion that had so tarnished the reputation of Wyoming, and the atrocious Warren Arid Land Bill, it really did seem that the Democrats and the Populists were in complete accord and would work together in perfect harmony.[68]

The Republicans held their nominating convention in September and their candidates for governor, representative, and justice of the Supreme Court were Edward Ivinson, Clarence D. Clark, and Carroll H. Parmelee. When the *Cheyenne Daily Leader* criticized the omission of any mention of the invasion in the Republican platform, the Republicans responded that they had consulted with members of the convention from Johnson County and were told that the invasion was a "local issue," not a statewide matter, and therefore should be left out of state politics.[69]

On September 21 the *Leader* ran an article providing still another example of a "hellish" conspiracy against small stock owners by the big cattlemen.[70] Milo Burke, a ranchman from Ten Sleep (in the eastern

Big Horn Basin), shipped about one thousand head of cattle to Omaha, four hundred of which he had bought in Johnson County from different parties, including Robert Foote. The cattle were seized in Omaha, to be forfeited to the Wyoming Live Stock Commission, but Burke had anticipated this move and obtained an injunction against W. C. Irvine, stock commission inspector C. L. Talbot, and H. B. Ijams. Burke was able to show that his cattle had been seized on perjured affidavits, recovered his stock, and brought a separate suit against Irvine, Talbot, and Ijams for the damages he had suffered from loss of reputation.

In Johnson County, as a result of the fusion arrangements, the Democrats and Populists presented a joint ticket to the voters in late September, one in which members of the two parties were completely intermixed. There were fifteen local offices up for election in the county in 1892. Seven candidates—for state senator, county clerk, two county commissioners, sheriff, assessor, and clerk of the district court—were Democrats, and seven candidates—for two state representatives, surveyor, county treasurer, county attorney, superintendent of schools, and coroner—were Populists. One of the men named for the county commission was R. A. Waln, who was probably a Republican and was later also nominated by the Republicans, but he was apparently so well regarded that he was included in the fusion ticket.[71]

Another race in Johnson County was of special interest. Carroll Parmelee, who had been named as the Republican candidate for the Wyoming Supreme Court, was a Buffalo attorney. In a normal year, local pride would have assured him a big vote in his home county, but 1892 was not a normal year. Parmelee had acted for Governor Barber at the time of the invasion, and before that, he had ruled that there was no probable cause to bind over Frank Canton for the murder of John A. Tisdale. Jack Flagg took him to task in the *People's Voice* for the Canton ruling, but the *Bulletin* defended him, accusing Flagg of "personal malice" and saying that Parmelee could have made no other decision.[72] Parmelee was generally respected in Johnson County—Robert Foote, the Democratic candidate for the Wyoming Senate, had even stated that "no better man lives in Johnson County than Carroll H. Parmelee"— but Flagg may have struck a chord by reminding Johnson County voters of Parmelee's decision regarding Canton.[73] The election would reveal whether Johnson County citizens were willing to give Parmelee the benefit of the doubt or whether anger over the invasion transcended other considerations. The one fact that Parmelee could not avoid was that four months after he released Canton, Canton returned at the head of a gang of men invading Johnson County to kill its citizens.

To the last days of the 1892 campaign, the *Buffalo Bulletin* maintained its bland confidence that all this overemphasis on the invasion was wasted noise. On November 3, 1892, in the last issue before the November 8 voting, the *Bulletin* wrote: "The Republican party will go to the polls united as they have never been before and sinking for the time all personal feelings, will cast a solid vote against the piratical combination whose existence is a menace to the State and the county."[74] Other Republicans, though, were not so successfully self-deceptive. Senator Warren knew that Wyoming Republicans were in deep trouble, and toward the end of the campaign he became so frantic that he accused Democrats of originating and financing the invasion.[75]

Warren was right to be deeply worried, and the *Bulletin's* position proved to be a flight from reality—the editor shed his sugarcoated comments after the election and bitterly complained about how the voters had been deceived by the fusionists.[76] In Johnson County, all fifteen of the fusionist candidates won, most by margins of about two to one. There was only one remotely close race, and that was Jack Flagg (who was disliked by many in the county) versus W. P. Keays, the incumbent county clerk; the final count was 529 votes for Flagg and 453 for Keays. The only Republican who won was R. A. Waln, who had been endorsed on the fusion ticket.[77] For every other Republican candidate, the *R* next to their names proved to be the kiss of death. Even the Republican candidates for county surveyor and county coroner lost by tallies of 608 to 327 and 633 to 323.[78] It was probably the most lopsided loss by Republicans in a Northern Wyoming county in the history of Wyoming.[79]

The Republican Party was routed not just in Johnson County but throughout the state of Wyoming. All the statewide Democrats won, with John Osborne and Gibson Clark carrying virtually every county but Laramie, and even there the races were relatively close. The tightest contest was for representative, with the Democrat Coffeen winning, 8,855 to 8,394. The other two races were not so close; in each case the Democrat carried about 55 percent of the vote and the Republican 45 percent (Osborne had 9,290 votes versus 7,509 for Ivinson; Clark had 9,240 votes versus 7,671 for Parmelee). Carroll Parmelee was humiliated in his home county, losing to Clark by 685 to 284. And, unfortunately for Senator Warren, the fusion candidates for the state legislature made excellent showings, so that it appeared Democrats and Populists had gained a majority of state legislators.[80]

For this one brief time, there was good news for the people of Johnson County. The predicted landslide had happened. November 8, 1892 was probably the best day for Johnson County citizens in the whole sad and sordid history of the Johnson County War. Wyoming voters had hardly needed to be reminded of the April invasion; the delay in the trial of the invaders seemingly made little difference to the outcome of the election.

CHAPTER TWENTY

The Case—Part Two

After a gap of more than four months since the postponement of the trial of the invaders, the case of *State v. Frank M. Canton et al.* for the murder of Nate Champion resumed on January 2, 1893. The Johnson County authorities had never been able to conduct a proper investigation. As a result of the Governor Barber's machinations, the county authorities had only a limited opportunity to interrogate their putative prisoners, an opportunity with little meaning because it was obtained only a few days before all the prisoners had to be released on bail. The final resolution of the criminal charges against the invaders, however, came to pass for reasons quite different from the failings of the frustrated investigation.

By a prior ruling of the sitting district judge, Richard H. Scott, all of the defendants were to be tried at one time. It was a ruinous decision to the prosecution, meaning that no jury could be seated until hundreds of peremptory disqualifications were exercised. Indeed, the defense did not feel they needed the peremptory challenges of any of the Texans who participated in the raid. None of the Texans appeared in Cheyenne, not even their leader, Tom Smith. In Smith's case, though, his absence was not because he chose to stay in Texas; he had been shot and killed on a train in Oklahoma on November 5.[1]

All but two of the Wyoming cattlemen arrived at the trial. The two who did not appear were the Harvard men, Frederick O. de Billier and his ranching partner, Hubert Teschemacher. Back in July, when the invaders were held in Laramie, de Billier suffered a mental breakdown and had been allowed to return to his home in New York; it was predicted that the change would be "beneficial to his mental and physical condition."[2] Teschemacher's reason for not appearing was that his brother had suddenly died in Switzerland. Teschemacher's bond, as well as those of the Texans, was forfeited.[3] Of the forty-four defendants charged, twenty-three answered when his name was called.[4]

These twenty-three had gathered in Cheyenne, together with their lawyers, Willis Van Devanter and Walter Stoll. The prosecution was represented by John Davidson, E. A. Ballard, and R. W. Breckons. Witnesses also came to Cheyenne, including an especially important one for the prosecution, George Dunning, who was reported to have been seen on the streets of the town, accompanied by an officer; he was wearing two six-shooters, had grown a beard, and was "pale from his long confinement."[5] Defense witnesses arriving in Cheyenne included John Burkhart, George Sutherland, J. E. Chappell, E. E. Miller, St. Clair O'Malley (the Buffalo correspondent for the *Cheyenne Sun* and soon to become the editor of the *Buffalo Bulletin*), L. Simmons, James Huff, Fred S. Pettit, and Wm. Heygood.[6]

The availability of witnesses for the defense immediately became an issue, and the cattlemen sought a continuance until May on the grounds that important witnesses were not available but would be in May. Two important petitions were filed, each of which had to be addressed by the trial court. In one, the defense asserted that it had attempted to subpoena several witnesses, but the Sheriff of Laramie County had refused to serve the subpoenas because Johnson County had not paid service fees and, further, Johnson County owed the sheriff other money it had not paid.[7] It appeared that all the witnesses listed were allies of the cattlemen from Johnson County and included George Munkres (Canton's close friend) and George Sutherland (Fred Hesse's brother-in-law). But some of the defense witnesses had in fact already arrived in Cheyenne, and those who arrived declared that the rest of the witnesses "were ready to come at once if wanted." These men were all going to declare that Champion and Ray had threatened to kill the defendants and were part of "an organization of thieves" that had driven several of the defendants out of the country.[8]

The second petition stated that the defendants had just discovered, on December 19, that two witnesses who had important testimony to give were not present in Wyoming (the two men were now allegedly in Watertown, South Dakota, and "at some point in the state of Nebraska"). Supposedly these witnesses would establish that Ray and Champion had stolen a group of fifteen or twenty horses found near the KC Ranch.[9]

Judge Scott appeared skeptical at first. It is not uncommon for defendants on the eve of trial to hear rumors about helpful testimony and frantically insist that the trial be delayed so that the witnesses can be produced. Van Devanter's clients were certainly aware of their attorney's position that the defense could not prove theft by Champion, and they had probably scrambled to find something. Scott initially denied the petitions, saying that the defense had not shown sufficient diligence in trying to obtain the presence of the witnesses. The next day, however, the defense provided some supplemental affidavits to address this deficiency, and Judge Scott declared that "this representation" was enough to secure a continuance."[10]

It appeared that the trial was about to be put off again, this time to May. But a compromise was reached, based upon the prosecution's agreement to allow statements of the missing witnesses to be presented if they failed to appear. No transcript of this hearing is available, just a newspaper summary, which probably did not report all of Davidson's remarks. It seems likely that Davidson would have told Judge Scott that if the court otherwise found the testimony relevant, then written statements would be accepted. Whether or not he did, the action of the prosecution "left no further basis for the suit for postponement," and the judge decided that the trial would begin in just two days, on Thursday, January 5, 1893.[11]

The Cheyenne newspapers reporting on the trial, including the *Leader* and the *Sun*, provided excellent detail about the trial and were, by and large, surprisingly objective. The cattlemen had not foresworn all attempts to influence the public, though. On January 7, 1893, the *Chicago Herald* ran an article datelined Cheyenne and most probably written by Ed Towse; it addressed the trial of the twenty-three "men of means and education." The article praised E. W. Whitcomb as "tough, agile and spirited," the bravery of Frank Wolcott, the talent and means of the Tisdales, the intelligence and means of Fred Hesse, Frank Laberteaux as a "splendid fellow," W. C. Irvine as "game to the backbone," and on and on in similar vein about several other invaders.[12]

Voir dire, the questioning of prospective jurors, began in the morning of January 5, with Ballard acting for the state and Van Devanter for the defendants. It became immediately apparent, no doubt to the delight of the defense, that the men in the jury venire, the pool of potential jurors, did not want to sit on a jury for a controversial trial that would probably go on for months. The *Cheyenne Daily Leader* wrote, "Many [prospective jurors] didn't wish to serve and very cautiously but clearly created a belief in their bias and had their ability rewarded by the usual request to step down."[13] Some jurors also voiced an "anxious inquiry" about whether they would be paid. They were to be issued a certificate against Johnson County, which would be converted into a Johnson County warrant, but jurors had apparently read the news stories about Johnson County's not paying for charges relating to the trial.[14]

Under these circumstances, it was no surprise that the great majority of jurors called on that first day of jury selection were dismissed "for cause"; of the 53 potential jurors examined that first Thursday in January, 42 were excused for cause, and not a single peremptory challenge was exercised by any of the parties.[15] A "for cause" challenge can be made for any of several reasons; here, jurors were challenged because of business relations with defendants, official business, opinions formed from speaking to defendants, being on the jury panel in the previous term, being an exempt fireman, being physically disqualified, not being able to write the English language, not believing in capital punishment, and, by far the largest categories (over half those challenged), being biased or prejudiced or having reached opinions from newspapers that could not be laid aside.[16] The most significant feature of a challenge for cause was that it did not reduce the total number of peremptory challenges available. Theoretically, every member of a jury panel could be challenged for cause without a single juror being seated, and not one peremptory challenge would have to be used. In this case, a total of 414 peremptory challenges were available, and so in order to empanel a jury, 414 challenges would have to be exhausted and then 12 jurors seated, for a total of 426 men passed for cause. On January 5, 1893, only 11 jurors had been passed for cause.[17] The *Leader* noted, "If the present ratio of challenges is continued there will need to be nearly 2,500 jurors summoned, which is greater than the number in the county."[18] It was a very encouraging day for the defendants.

The next day went no better for Johnson County. "All day long juror after juror stood up only to be knocked down by a cross fire of questions from the attorneys employed in the case," the *Leader* wrote.[19] The attorneys went through about another 50 men, but none was added to the jury;

the state used 8 of its peremptory challenges, the defense none. The prosecution still had 130 challenges, and the defense 276.[20]

The questioning was dull and predictable, but there were side events of interest. At the beginning of the trial, the defendants seemed relaxed to the point of boredom (W. B. Wallace went to sleep). They "wandered listlessly" in and out of the courtroom, until Judge Scott gave a peremptory order that all defendants were to remain in the courtroom while the case was being heard.[21] At a recess during the first day, Davidson for the prosecution "complained that some of the prisoners carried pistols in court and misbehaved themselves in the city." None of the defendants admitted to carrying weapons, and they were not searched. Judge Scott was reported to have spoken to the defendants "kindly but firmly" and to have told them that "he would expect their conduct to be exemplary throughout the trial and believed that it would be."[22] The attorneys used up prospective jurors so quickly that the regular panel of fifty was exhausted in the first day, and the Laramie County sheriff was directed to find a "special open venire," which meant that the sheriff had to roam the streets of Cheyenne looking for jurors. The *Leader* reported that the "principal business of a number of city gentlemen for the past two days had been to dodge the bailiffs armed with an open venire," but that the bailiffs were usually able to "run them down in alleys or back yards."[23] Some of the original panel had not appeared and got into a bit of trouble with Judge Scott. Both Charles Riner and George W. Baxter were called before the judge and fined for not appearing. It turned out that neither was eligible, as Riner, a former Cheyenne mayor, was "too friendly" with some of the defendants, and Baxter, the former governor, had been on the petit jury panel for the spring term.[24]

Willis Van Devanter's questioning of one juror showed that the people of Cheyenne, while skeptical of the newspaper reporting, still gave the opinions of the *Cheyenne Sun* some weight, as if the paper was, at least to some extent, expressing a disinterested point of view. The juror was asked whether he read the newspapers, and he replied that he had read "both sides," both the *Leader* and the *Sun*. Van Devanter immediately challenged the man, saying, "You don't mean to say that anything appearing in either paper was inspired by the defendants?" The prospective juror immediately retreated. "Not by any means," he quickly answered.[25] Of course, the defendants had done much more than "inspire" articles appearing in the *Cheyenne Sun*. Virtually all of the *Sun's* articles about the invasion had directly presented the big cattlemen's line, and on at least one occasion Van Devanter himself had written the newspaper's articles.

On Tuesday, January 10, the quest for a jury resumed, with much the same results as earlier. Day after day, January 11, January 12, January 13, January 14, January 16, January 17, January 19, January 20, and January 21, the voir dire went on.[26] During many of these days, more than 100 men were examined, but each day, the vast majority of them were excused for cause. The defense did have to use some of its peremptory challenges, 69 by noon on January 21, leaving 207 remaining. The prosecution used 25 and had 113 remaining.[27] As of noon, January 21, 1893, the number of veniremen who had been examined totaled 1,064; only 11 men had been passed for cause and sat in the jury box.[28]

On January 8 a meeting had been held by Johnson County people in Cheyenne, and they discussed dropping the prosecution. Those attending were of two minds; on the one hand, outrage over the invasion persisted, but on the other, many argued that pursuing the case would bankrupt Johnson County and a conviction was doubtful. These people stated that the cattlemen had been sufficiently punished, observing that Johnson County "whipped the invaders, have had them in prison, made them suffer political defeat, great humiliation and loss of time and money." No resolution was made.[29] On January 15 the *Leader* ran an editorial in which it argued that although the invasion was a crime and the invaders richly deserved punishment, it made no sense to continue piling up a heavier burden of taxation if it became "self-evident" that the proceedings "must inevitably fail." The *Leader* noted, however, that the final decision as to how to proceed was in the hands of Alvin Bennett, the elected Johnson County attorney, who was not then in Cheyenne.[30]

On January 21, 1893, all these issues came to a head. Alvin Bennett had arrived from Buffalo and, in fact, was conducting the voir dire that morning; neither Ballard nor Davidson was present in the courtroom.[31] Twenty-seven veniremen had been examined, and only one was found competent. The court had recessed at noon, and when the trial resumed at 2:00 P.M., Laramie County sheriff Ira Fredendall made a statement to Judge Scott. He told the judge that he was unable to find any more men for jury duty in Cheyenne, that he had secured "every man possible out of the shops, business houses and in the streets," and he would have to go into the rest of the county, outside of Cheyenne, with attendant higher expenses. Most significantly, the sheriff told the judge that he had been bearing all the cost of finding veniremen and feeding the eleven who had not yet been excused. He said he had approached Johnson County officials but received no assurance of payment and that the continuing trial "would be attended by a vast deal of expense and he felt himself financially unable to meet it."[32] Judge Scott then called up Bennett and presented all this to him.

It was the crucial moment in the trial, and Alvin Bennett was not ready to meet it. He asked for time so that he could confer with his co-counsel. But neither Ballard nor Davidson, the two attorneys who had principally handled the jury selection, had yet arrived in the courtroom, and Bennett was unable to find them. He conferred at some length with some Johnson County people who were present. Bennett had long felt the case could not be successful and should not be pursued, but he obviously did not want the whole responsibility for the disposition of the cases to rest upon him. Finally, however, he had to act. Alvin Bennett stood up and moved to dismiss all the cases.

Willis Van Devanter had anticipated this motion and immediately opposed it. He argued that a dismissal before a jury was selected would still leave Van Devanter's clients at risk for future prosecution, and that if the state "would not offer anything better, he [Van Devanter] would insist on going on with the case."[33] Bennett conferred further; he again tried to locate Ballard and Davidson but was unable to do so. Bennett then offered to have a full jury impaneled and sworn, and then move for dismissal. One more juror was needed, and a man in the courtroom, a bystander by the name of Adam Adamsky, was spotted and was immediately taken to the last juror's seat, sworn, and accepted, without a question being asked of him. Bennett proceeded to address every charge, taking the defendants in groups of four and then moving for dismissal in each instance. Van Devanter still objected to the procedure, saying that the jury should be instructed to return with a finding of "not guilty," but his objections were overruled.[34] When it was all done, though, the defendants knew that the cases against them were gone and that none were likely ever to be resurrected. The *Cheyenne Daily Leader* observed that the defendants were "immediately surrounded by their friends" and that "much handshaking and many congratulations were interchanged."[35]

The sudden dismissals were a surprise to the public, but even some people from Johnson County were surprised and complained about the way in which the cases were handled. The *Leader* interviewed several of the Johnson County participants and reported their comments. The *Leader* agreed that it had been evident for some time that a jury could not be secured, but said it had been understood that the trial would be pursued "for the present" and not abandoned until it was absolutely clear that no jury could be obtained. The *Leader* reported that many Johnson County people felt that Bennett had not proceeded in good faith, even that "tangible influences" had induced him to act as he had. The newspaper did provide some defense of Bennett's actions, though, saying that he had been abandoned by Ballard and Davidson, the two men "on whom the weight of presenting the case" had fallen, and that these two lawyers had some explaining to do.[36]

Bennett defended his actions, saying that he had discussed the propriety of dismissing the case with several people and all thought the trial was a farce. His version was disputed by ex-sheriff Angus, as well as Jack Flagg, who said that Bennett had just assured all the Johnson County people that he would not dismiss the case "as long as there remained a possibility of doing anything." Robert Foote, who was also present, said he was "sick and mad," but other Johnson County men were more accepting, conceding that dismissal was inevitable.[37]

The cattlemen and their supporters crowed, and that must have been one of the hardest things for Johnson County people to stomach. The *Cheyenne Sun*, when writing about the celebrations and joy of the cattlemen, nevertheless insisted that "they have, it is true, never been in danger by any court proceedings that could be brought against them."[38] Then, in an editorial, Edward Slack wrote that "we will not at this time discuss the rights and wrongs of the 'invasion.'" He immediately declared, however, that the time would come when "there will be no difference of opinion as to the 'invasion' being the legitimate outcome of the reign of theft and terror which existed in the state prior to the cattlemen taking the law in their own hands and retaliating upon the men who had preyed upon their herds." Slack went on in this manner at some length and then closed his editorial with a smug adage that must have infuriated the people of Johnson County: "All's well that ends well."[39]

Thus the criminal cases against the invaders came to their dishonorable end. But the aftermath of the invasion was not nearly over.

CHAPTER TWENTY-ONE

1893

Throughout 1893, repercussions from the Johnson County War continued to be felt. At the beginning of the year, Cheyenne was full of new officials who had been elected because of their outspoken criticism of the invasion and how it was handled by their predecessors. They had come to office under pledges to do something about the Cheyenne ring. The public would watch closely whether they honored their pledges.

Dr. John Osborne was formally inaugurated on January 2, 1893, and he first spoke to the Wyoming legislature as governor of Wyoming on January 11. He boldly addressed the Johnson County invasion in his speech. Osborne first lamented that he was unable to follow precedent for a Wyoming governor to congratulate the state's citizens upon their "happy and prosperous condition." But, Osborne stated, within Wyoming in the last year there had been "few signs of prosperity," and the clear reason was that "the lawless invasion of the State by an armed body of invaders, with its accompanying crimes, ... has given our State an unenviable preeminence in reputation and grievously interfered with its material advancement." The new governor sharpened his point, saying, "The fact that this invasion was organized and assisted by parties high in official and social position, that our congressional representatives in Washington gave out to the country and national administration that lawlessness reigned in Wyoming, ... was sufficient to deter immigration, paralyze our industries and prevent the investment of capital from abroad." Osborne especially deplored that "it was thought necessary to wantonly slander our State to excuse the crimes of the invaders."[1]

Osborne also addressed the Wyoming Live Stock Commission: "One of the most oppressive and unjust laws upon our statute books, is an act providing for a board of livestock commissioners. The despotic powers assumed by the commissioners and their employees, under this act, including the seizure of live stock in transit, in or out of the state, . . . are powers clearly unconstitutional, unjust and abhorrent to every principle of justice." Osborne declared, "The enactment is a disgrace to our statutes and should be promptly repealed."[2]

Governor Osborne's prelude to his January 2 inauguration had been frenetic and harrowing, as he ran a gauntlet of political and legal challenges. For most newly elected Wyoming governors, the time between the election and the assumption of office is a quiet, busy period, in which the primary efforts are organizing the new office, hiring a staff, and preparing for the imminent legislative session. But Osborne's experiences were different from those of any other Wyoming governor, past or future.

In the days immediately after the November 8, 1892, election, it was clear that the fusionists—Democrats and Populists combined—had won the election by a sizable plurality, 1,500–2,500 votes (out of about 17,000 votes), and it was assumed this margin would translate into a clear majority within the state legislature.[3] Several races were close, however, and as the *Cheyenne Daily Leader* later observed, "it was one thing to win a political victory in Wyoming and another thing to reap the fruits of it."[4]

The difficulty reaping the fruits of the election arose because of Willis Van Devanter. From his home in Cheyenne, he closely watched the election results and looked for ways he could turn apparent defeat into victory for Francis E. Warren. Van Devanter's task was made especially daunting because his patron was one of the principal targets of all those newly elected officials. In 1893 the Wyoming legislature was to be composed of sixteen senators and thirty-three House members; the election of a U.S. senator required a majority of the combined membership, or twenty-five votes.[5] The 1892 election began with seven holdover legislative officeholders, all from the Wyoming Senate. There were six Republicans and one Democrat, and these holdovers were the only reason Republicans were not swept from power in both houses of the legislature.[6] There should have been eight holdovers, seven Republicans and one Democrat, but Johnson County senator John N. Tisdale, a member of the invading army, had moved to Salt Lake City in 1891, where he married a wealthy Salt Lake City widow. Tisdale sold all of his Johnson County property and began a wool commission business in Utah; he returned to Wyoming only to participate in the invasion.[7] Because of Tisdale's absence, candidates for the office of state senator were voted upon in Johnson County, and Robert Foote won handily.[8]

Opportunities were presented to Van Devanter. Four seats in the Wyoming House of Representatives were in dispute, two from Natrona and Carbon counties, one from Fremont County, and one from Converse County. Not counting the four disputed seats, twelve Republicans had been elected to the state House, twelve Democrats, and five Populists.[9] Given an expected plurality in the Senate of four votes, if three of these four House contests went in favor of the Republicans, there would be a Republican majority in the joint legislature and Warren's reelection to the U.S. Senate would become possible, despite the debacle of the Johnson County invasion. Van Devanter, acting as the Republican state chairman, first struck in Converse County, traveling to Douglas on November 15.[10]

The election officials in Converse County initially determined that the Republican, John Scott, had won the election by three votes, but then discovered there had been an arithmetic error of ten votes in favor of Scott. This error was corrected, and after some dissension, a majority of the county canvassing board declared Nat Baker the winner of the election by seven votes. But later that same day an alternate writ of mandamus was obtained from Judge Scott, apparently by Van Devanter (a "writ of mandamus" is a legal petition whereunder a court may command the performance of a legally required act by a public official). The writ directed the county board not to "go behind the returns." The county canvassing board responded to the writ of mandamus by immediately changing its decision; it declared that Scott was elected, implicitly accepting the arithmetic error in his favor.[11]

Wyoming Democrats, who had been luxuriating in their presumed win of the Wyoming legislature, were brought to full alert by the Converse County events. The *Cheyenne Daily Leader* "bitterly assailed" Republicans for trying to steal the legislature and "greeted Van Devanter's strategy as further proof of Warren's willingness to stop at nothing."[12] When Van Devanter made his next run at contested House races, this time in Rawlins on November 26, he was met by Democrats determined to resist any attempts to manipulate voting results, including A. L. New, Democratic

State Central Committee chairman and his lawyer, Gibson Clark (just elected to the Wyoming Supreme Court).[13]

In Carbon County the voting dispute involved the Hanna precinct. The Hanna return had been submitted to the Carbon County clerk without indication of the polling place, and the poll list had not been signed.[14] Van Devanter declared that these deficiencies were enough to throw out all the results from Hanna, the consequences of which would be that Hanna's strong vote in favor of Democrats would be lost, and the two Democratic candidates S. B. Bennett and Harry Chapman would lose their races for the state House. Van Devanter persuaded the Carbon County clerk, S. B. Ross, to disregard the Hanna return. He probably had little difficulty, because unless the Hanna return was thrown out, Ross would lose his office.[15]

But the county canvassing board had three members (at least, it seemed to have three members; Van Devanter would soon argue that it really had only one), and the other two were not so ready to throw out all the votes from Hanna based on a technicality. Finally, on November 30, after what one writer termed "a desperate fight," the canvassing board voted 2 to 1 in favor of accepting the results from Hanna, which produced the election of five Democrats and one Republican. Van Devanter did induce Ross, the Carbon County clerk, to issue a false certificate, one that misstated the decision of the canvassing board by omitting the voting results from the Hanna precinct.[16]

The big problem for the Democrats was that the vote from all Wyoming counties was subject to review by the state canvassing board, consisting of three Republican officeholders—the state auditor, the state treasurer, and the secretary of state, with Governor Barber acting in the last position. They were all allies of Senator Warren.[17] The problem was compounded because Wyoming had not enacted any statutory provisions for the canvassing of votes cast for state officers, seeming to give the state canvassing board open authority to act any way it pleased. There was great concern that the state canvassing board would engage in wholesale manipulation, seating Republicans if given any opportunity to do so and withholding certification of Osborne's election as governor until the legislative questions were all resolved in favor of Senator Warren.[18]

Osborne, as the governor-elect, and Gibson Clark, as a Supreme Court justice-elect, met with Acting Governor Barber and sought assurance that they would be able to monitor the proceedings of the state canvassing board. Their interview with Barber was not satisfactory, as he gave them no assurances that anyone would be permitted to be present at the canvasses.[19] This was an alarming development to Osborne and Clark. They looked at Barber as little more than a criminal in light of his aid to the invaders, and they deeply distrusted him and the whole Republican establishment.

During the period after the election, Democrats had discussed when the election of Osborne and Clark would become effective. Both men were chosen in special elections to fill vacancies, and, it was contended, in light of the lack of authorization to canvas votes cast for state officers, simple copies of the county abstracts of the votes cast should suffice to establish the election of state officers. The *Laramie Boomerang* asserted that the state officers filling a vacancy should assume their elected offices as soon as the abstracts were received from the county clerks.[20]

Swearing in Osborne as governor before the normal time of inauguration would resolve a host of worries. Osborne, as the governor receiving the returns from around the state, would have the statutory prerogative to issue certificates of election, thereby making sure that certificates were issued only to the people "who are actually elected."[21] In the early morning of December 2, 1892, he acted.

Osborne appeared at the capitol with an oath of office in his hand, signed before a notary public.[22] The janitor, under Republican orders, refused Osborne entry to the governor's office. Osborne managed to get into the office anyway, though how is not clear. (Warren said that he "broke in.")[23] Osborne insisted that the secretary of state accept his oath of office. Barber was ill that day, and the secretary of state's office was then under the control of Jack Meldrum. Meldrum refused to accept the oath, so Osborne left it on his desk.[24]

From the governor's office, Osborne issued a proclamation. He announced that he had been elected governor of Wyoming, that in the absence of statutory provisions for a state canvassing board the returns from Wyoming county clerks sufficed to establish his election. Later that day, Osborne issued another proclamation, setting a meeting of the state canvassing board on Monday, December 5, before him as governor.[25]

Osborne remained in the Capitol that first night, as did Amos Barber's secretary, Richard H. Repath, who refused to give the keys for the governor's office to Osborne.[26] The Capitol was locked after business hours, however, and the only way to provide food and bedding to Osborne inside the building was along a ledge and through a window into the governor's office. Republican newspapers tried to tar Osborne, with some success, by insisting that he had crawled in and out of the window to gain access to the governor's office. Of course, Osborne's actions caused a great stir and were closely covered by newspapers. There was a predictable, approximately equal, split: Republican newspapers deplored Osborne's actions, and Democratic newspapers approved them.[27]

Barber recovered his health sufficiently that on December 3 he issued his own proclamation, disputing all of Osborne's claims and stating that Osborne had taken the office through "stealth and fraud."[28] During the morning of December 5, when Osborne's canvassing board meeting was supposed to take place, Jack Meldrum locked all the doors to the secretary of state's office, thereby denying Osborne access to any of the election information received from the Wyoming county clerks. Meldrum stated that Barber had given instructions to lock the doors "for fear a raid would be made on the office."[29] Democrats refused to credit these statements, believing that the only purpose for the Republican actions was to steal the legislature and cover up incriminating evidence.[30] Still, without the returns, there was nothing Osborne could do to force a meeting of the state canvassing board, and so he had to wait until Barber's meeting, on December 8.

On December 8 a crowd convened at the Wyoming secretary of state's office. Besides the canvassing board itself, representatives of the three parties were present (People's Party: I. S. Bartlett, E. A. Belcher, and James Talbot; Democratic Party: A. L. New, J. C. Thompson, and John F. Carroll; Republican Party: Willis Van Devanter, Jack Meldrum, and E. A. Slack), together with Sheriff A. D. Kelley and a dozen guards.[31] The proceedings before the state canvassing board showed that Wyoming Democrats had good cause to worry that Republicans would try to steal the election. The all-Republican canvassing board accepted every one of Willis Van Devanter's arguments; the only delay was so that the board was sure of getting Francis Warren's instructions right.[32] The board ruled that Osborne was not governor, that only Barber could issue certificates, that the board must accept the Carbon County clerk's certified abstract (meaning the Hanna returns were thrown out and the Democratic candidates for the state House lost), as well as the abstracts from Converse County (meaning that the Democrat again lost).[33]

These determinations if left unchanged meant that the Republicans would have a majority of votes in the combined Wyoming legislature when the Wyoming Senate and House convened in January 1893. The only remaining remedy for the Democrats was to bring a legal action before the Wyoming Supreme Court, another all-Republican group. The Democrats nevertheless moved in only a few days to ask the Supreme Court for a writ of alternate mandamus; they sought to compel the state canvassing board to perform its duty, which, the Democrats asserted, was to count the votes of the Hanna precinct. Van Devanter was quite confident at this point and believed it would be a simple matter for him to raise numerous issues to delay any decision by the Wyoming Supreme Court until the Republicans had already organized the legislature. He wrote Senator Warren: "We will make the opposition decidedly weary before they get any consolation or relief from the litigation."[34]

But then something happened that was strange and wonderful in the squalid chronicle of the Johnson County War: some public officials honored their oaths of office. The members of the Wyoming Supreme Court, Republican or not, recognized the importance of promptly deciding the election issues raised. And for the only time in the legal history of the Johnson County War, Willis Van Devanter met defeat.

The Supreme Court accepted and addressed all of Van Devanter's extra issues, but put the whole case on an expedited basis, scheduling two days of oral arguments in mid-December and issuing its decision on December 31, 1892.[35] The court ruled that the determination of the entire Carbon County canvassing board controlled and that the voting results from the Hanna precinct should therefore have been accepted by the state canvassing board. The Supreme Court rejected Van Devanter's argument that the vote of the county clerk was the only one that mattered when county voting results were canvassed. The court stated: "The rights of the people in choosing their officers are certainly safer in the hands of three persons, of different political parties when practicable, than in the hands of one man."[36] Regarding other election contests, the court ruled that these were to be resolved by the legislature, not the courts. The Court also ruled in a separate case decided on January 17, 1893, that John Osborne could not become governor until January.[37] In light of the other rulings of the Supreme Court, however, this determination had little practical significance.

The consequence of this decision by the Wyoming Supreme Court was that the Democrats and Populists, with the two members from Carbon County, would organize the Wyoming state House, and when so organized, this fusionist majority would decide the election contests from Converse County and Fremont County. And the consequence of these Democratic actions was that the Republicans would not have a majority of the joint legislature, and Francis E. Warren would not be returned to the U.S. Senate.

The decision of the Wyoming Supreme Court, however, welcome as it was by Democrats, hardly resolved all of the disputes between Wyoming Republicans and Democrats. Republicans did not take their election defeat graciously, and their first target was Governor Osborne. Republican newspapers throughout Wyoming lambasted him, and the *Buffalo Bulletin* was one of the leaders of this Osborne bashing. The *Bulletin* contributed a long editorial about Osborne's inaugural message, and it was a far cry from the soft approach of the newspaper before the 1892 election. The story never told the reader what the governor had said; it just condemned Osborne, seemingly in every way the writer could conceive. There was real fear and loathing in the attack, not just the mouthing of political slogans. The editorial referred to an "ill made hash of false and inflammatory campaign literature" and to the Governor's "feeble petulance" that was the product of "a small and vindictive mind." The *Bulletin* condemned the "spectacle of the highest official in the state openly traducing their chosen representatives in the councils of the nation, violently attacking a prominent and beneficent portion of its community, and showing himself in unmistakable terms, an offensive partisan of one particular section."[38] The Democrats and Populists, having been elected on promises of cleaning out the Cheyenne ring and suppressing the power of big cattlemen, saw the comments of Governor Osborne in quite a different light. It is little wonder that the 1893 legislative session was "bitter, faction-ridden and indecisive."[39]

The Wyoming House was controlled by the fusionists, and the Wyoming Senate by the Republicans, and party control was a wall never breached by either opposing political party. Custom called for the secretary of state to call the two houses to order. In the Wyoming House, however, it was not Amos Barber who rose to call the assembly to order but Johnson County representative E. U. Snider, who apparently deliberately acted to affront Barber.[40] The House moved quickly to solidify its power, acting in a matter of minutes to assign leadership posts and to create a committee on credentials. Within two weeks, that committee reported back and recommended that Baker rather than Scott be seated as the representative from Converse County (a matter of simple justice) and that Pickett rather then Okie be seated as a representative from Fremont County (a much more questionable action, seemingly a partisan step taken without regard to justice).[41]

The Wyoming Senate also acted quickly, but there the Republicans were in control. Amos Barber was not snubbed in the Senate, and he assumed his customary role, calling the Senate to order.[42] The Republicans, perhaps in response to the Democrats' actions in the House, decided not to acknowledge that John Tisdale had moved to Utah.[43] Robert Foote was not accepted as the Johnson County senator, despite strong evidence that John N. Tisdale was not then "an actual resident" of Johnson County. Later the Senate Democrats attempted to impeach Tisdale because of his participation in the invasion, but this move met the same Republican stonewall as the attempt to seat Robert Foote.[44]

The most important responsibility of the Wyoming legislature was to select a U.S. Senator, someone to represent the state in the federal upper house. Wyoming has never had more than one federal representative, so that within the state, this congressman has sometimes been perceived as having comparable standing to the two senators. Within the federal legislature, however, the lone Wyoming representative has usually been an insignificant figure, whereas a Wyoming senator wields substantial power, disproportionate to the size of the state, because the Senate is a much smaller body (just eighty-eight members in 1893) than the House of Representatives.[45] Selection to the U.S. Senate was highly coveted, the greatest prize the state of Wyoming had to bestow. The tiny population of the remote American outpost of Wyoming could send someone to Washington who would hold the same power and prestige as senators from New York, Texas, or California.

Political men in Wyoming were well aware of the significance of the selection to the U.S. Senate, perhaps too much so. As noble as the prize might be, the attempts to obtain it were correspondingly ignoble. The effort to select a Wyoming senator in 1893 was a travesty, surely one of the lowest points in the state's political history. The Republicans did everything they could to undercut the selection of a senator, but they would never have succeeded without the thoroughgoing political incompetence of the Democrats and Populists.

Voting for the U.S. Senate seat began on January 24, 1893. The first vote was split between sixteen candidates, but it was not unexpected that the first few ballots would be fragmented, as local politicians made gestures in favor of their favorite sons (and one favorite daughter).[46] But then the voting went on day after day, with no clear trend. It soon became clear to Warren that although he was receiving the most votes among Republican candidates, he could not command anywhere near the entire Republican delegation. Some Republican legislators had pledged, when in Cheyenne, not to support the Cheyenne ring. Warren was angry about this lack of support and blamed men who would later become governors of Wyoming— B. B. Brooks, Fenimore Chatterton, and DeForest Richards.[47] Warren's opponents in the Republican Party explored ways that one of them might be elected through the help of Populists. Warren noted that the Populists were well aware of their position of power, and he thought they were overly "inflated with their importance." But the soon-to-be ex-senator complained most bitterly about the actions of his Republican allies: "DeForrest [sic] Richards is sleeping with from one to four of the popu- lists, beseeching them on bended knees to accept him that he will be a populist and S. O. B. generally if they will do so. Others from our side are pressing them to their bosoms, and the democrats are, a part of them praying with them, some more sleeping with them, and still more clubbing them."[48]

The fusionists were certainly not taking advantage of the split in the Republican ranks, and Democratic newspapers started complaining, admonishing the legislature not to be factional. On February 2, 1893, the Democrats held a caucus and resolved that they would submit four names to the Populists, hoping that one of them would be acceptable, and pledged that each of them would have three unimpeded voting oppor- tunities. The four men were A. L. New (party chairman), W. H. Holliday (an old-line Democrat), George T. Beck (son of a Kentucky senator), and Samuel T. Corn (a lawyer, later a Supreme Court justice).[49] The most viable of these was New, but his candidacy created violent opposition, perhaps because he was able and ruthless, as was very soon demonstrated. Amazingly, the *Cheyenne Daily Leader* apparently favored George Baxter, who was one of the men behind the invasion and had sued the *Leader*, but the Populists would have nothing to do with Baxter.[50] The four-name proposal did not produce a consensus candidate, and in subsequent voting the pledged arrangements for three unimpeded votes were ignored.[51]

New, frantic to become a senator from Wyoming, concocted a scheme for his election. By February 4, New had lined up eighteen Democratic legislators to vote for him and, with five Populists, would control twenty-three votes. There was a problem, however, in that more than twenty-three votes were required to elect a senator; New's solution was to reduce the number of legislators so that twenty-three votes would suffice. In some manner, he connived to send one Republican state senator to Denver and then was apparently behind the poisoning or drugging of another state senator, James Kime, so that Kime would not be able to attend the next joint session voting on a senator.[52]

The effort failed because the Populists refused to accept New. The Kime incident gave the Senate Republicans a further opportunity to smear Democrats when they censured Democratic senator L. Kabis of Laramie County, the New supporter accused of administering a potion to Senator Kime.[53]

New finally recognized that he was not going to be selected, and on the twenty-first ballot he withdrew from the Senate race. As dismal as the proceedings had been to that time, however, it soon appeared that all would be salvaged. On February 15, 1893, a clear opportunity arose for the selection of a new Democratic senator from Wyoming. Four of the five Populists wrote a letter to the Democrats, stating that John Charles Thompson, a Cheyenne lawyer, was acceptable to them.[54] On February 15, Thompson was voted upon and received twenty-four votes, only one short of the number needed for election. One of those not voting for Thompson was a Populist, but another was a Democrat, the same Nat Baker whose election the Democrats had worked so hard to save in Converse County. The ultimate political prize from the state of Wyoming was within the Democrats' grasp.

But Baker, who had voted for George Beck, refused to change his vote to Thompson. The Democrats never could get Baker to vote for Thompson, despite his being "bitterly assailed." They were beside themselves with frustration and anger and suspected "Republican money as the cause of Baker's treachery."[55] There may have been something to the Democrats' allegation of a bribe. Back in November, when Warren was conniving to preserve his Senate seat, he wrote an ally, saying that if he (Warren) was able to hold the Republicans in a solid bloc, he could "then add the necessary votes from the opposition by persuasion, force or bribery."[56]

A bribe to prevent a Democrat from being sent to the U.S. Senate would have been in Warren's interest, because if he were not to be sent back to Washington as a senator, then the next best thing for him was to prevent the installation of a Democrat for a six-year term.

On the last day of the legislative session, Saturday, February 18, 1893, there was to be one final attempt to select a senator. But then, in a surprise move, a motion for adjournment of the joint session was made. Apparently, twenty-six legislators had gathered, and there was a majority of Republicans. To the immense anguish and frustration of the Democrats, the motion passed, cutting off the last chance for the Democrats to elect a senator.[57]

Still, there was possibly another way to rescue the situation. The Democrats assumed that Governor Osborne could appoint a senator even though the legislature had failed to select one. Osborne appointed A. C. Beckwith of Evanston. But this selection created another round of angry complaints by Democrats, and in the end, probably for political reasons, the appointment was not accepted by the U.S. Senate.[58]

One final opportunity arose for the appointment of a senator, when Governor Osborne announced that he would go to Washington in March to attend Grover Cleveland's inauguration. The Republicans quietly relished this announcement, because in the absence of Osborne, Amos Barber would again become the acting governor and he could appoint a Republican (who would presumably have been more acceptable to the Republicans in control of the U.S. Senate). But Osborne apparently realized the peril his absence might create and canceled his trip to the inauguration.[59]

For two years, during 1893 and 1894, Wyoming had only one U.S. senator, Joseph Carey, a situation that served the Wyoming Republican Party and Francis E. Warren well but was hardly good for the state. And the debacle over the failure to select a senator was not the only political failure by the Democrats. A bill to do away with the Wyoming Live Stock Commission failed, as did one addressing the use and occupancy of the public domain. A bill appropriating $23,000 for the expenses of the trial of the stockmen was actually passed by the Wyoming Senate, but then the Democrat-controlled House completely dropped the ball, adjourning before the final action of the Senate. The bill could not, therefore, be signed by the Speaker of the House in the presence of the House, as required by the Wyoming Constitution, and the bill failed to become law.[60]

Democrats rued the failure to provide Wyoming with a senator. The *Leader* admitted that the legislative session was "a dismal failure—the most pronounced in years." The *Leader* declared, "The Senatorial fight was the disturbing element from start to finish. It divided the delegations, broke up the legislature into factions and subordinated sound legislation to the expediency of party and individual ambitions."[61] Other newspapers were less measured in their criticism of the fusionists. The *Lander Clipper* implored, "May the good Lord deliver us from another reign of such base deceivers as they have proven themselves to be."[62]

Republican newspapers, on the other hand, were boisterously critical. The *Buffalo Bulletin* crowed: "Victory has proven more disastrous than defeat to the hybrid party. . . . With every promise broken, every trust betrayed, branded by the voice of their own allies in terms of measureless ignominy, without principles and without policy, the dismembered offspring of the demo-populist alliance in Wyoming presents a spectacle that may well give courage to the republican party for the future."[63] This highly partisan attack was blatantly unfair, but the reality was that the Democrats paid a higher political price than the Republicans for the disaster of the 1893 legislative session, if only because the Democrats had promised so much going into it. One historian perceptively wrote that the Democrats' "brave campaign promises of renewed integrity in government had become tarnished by the sordid infighting of the senatorial squabble."[64]

John Osborne was able to salvage something out of the legislative session, though. He used his line-item veto to strike down part of the appropriations bill that had provided $12,000 to the Wyoming Live Stock Commission, as well as $600 to reimburse H. B. Ijams for money Ijams paid for clerical employees. Cattlemen in Wyoming were livid. Apparently offended by suffering real consequences for their actions, many voiced bitter complaints to Francis E. Warren about Osborne's vetoes.[65]

The month of February 1893, when Senator Francis E. Warren had to return to Washington, D.C., to wrap up his affairs, was surely the winter of Warren's discontent. To Warren, it must have seemed that his comment in his July 23, 1892, letter to Billy Irvine was being thoroughly borne out, that his political future had "been ruined by this northern cattle business."

One thing that had deeply vexed Warren was the total failure of all his fervent attempts to punish U.S. marshal Joe Rankin, the man who, in Warren's eyes, had been far too timid toward Johnson County. Indeed, Warren did not fully abandon his campaign against Rankin until his term as senator ended in March 1893. Warren had hoped and expected that Rankin would be driven from his office in disgrace, but in the end, Rankin was completely vindicated.[66]

When Rankin wrote his defense to the Justice Department examiner in October 1892, he emphasized that it strongly appeared that the big cattlemen were setting him up in the spring of 1892 (after their invasion had so signally failed), demanding that he brashly create an incident in Johnson County that would further the imposition of martial law, all as part of an extensive scheme to "prevent small settlers coming in and taking up land."[67] The Justice Department examiner, F. B. Crossthwaite, followed up on Rankin's statements and interviewed Frank Wolcott and Billy Irvine. Crossthwaite addressed his discussions with Wolcott and Irvine in his final report, and he seemed to have been taken aback by their shameless candor; Wolcott and Irvine confirmed many of Rankin's contentions.

Crossthwaite stated that he considered Wolcott and Irvine to be "brave and fearless men," but that from his interview he was convinced "that they were impulsive and displayed a remarkable lack of good judgement in attempting such a foolhardy expedition as the one they conducted into Johnson County."[68] Crossthwaite underlined in his report what appeared to have most shocked him: "Mr. Irvine told me in person that he *hoped* and *expected* that, when Marshal Rankin attempted to serve the warrants for the arrest of the Rustlers in Johnson County; he would meet with the resistance threatened, namely, that they would die in their tracks before they would allow service to be made, thereby placing the marshal, if he lives, in a position to call for the assistance of the federal troops." Crossthwaite criticized the cattlemen's "motives purely selfish," noted Rankin's sterling past actions showing great courage, and concluded that Rankin's inaction had not been prompted in any part by lack of courage. Rather, Rankin, by the "exercise of good judgement," had prevented loss of life that would have occurred after the cattlemen incited Johnson County people to "the most intense hatred for all interested in the invasion."[69]

Both Carey and Warren had actively importuned Crossthwaite to punish Rankin, and Crossthwaite was initially inclined to do so. In fact, Crossthwaite made a kind of apology in his report, writing that he had not been able to contact Senators Carey and Warren to notify them that his views had undergone "a radical change."[70] In light of the report,

W. H. H. Miller, the U.S. attorney general, had no choice but to reject the Wyoming senators' demands. Joe Rankin was retained.[71]

In 1893 some loose ends from the war remained to be addressed, principally criminal cases against the big cattlemen's henchmen. Van Devanter succeeded in getting the venue of the cases against Canton, Elliott, and Coates transferred to Evanston (Uinta County) in the far southwestern corner of Wyoming.[72] During an odd interlude in early 1893, Charlie Basch appeared in Cheyenne and spoke to Deputy Sheriff Roles, who reported that Basch acted "a little queer." Then Basch just disappeared and was unavailable for the trial against Canton. It was reported, however, that even before Basch left for parts unknown, county attorney Bennett was going to dismiss the case against Canton.[73] Having Basch as the principal witness against Canton always made for a deeply impaired case, given Basch's initial testimony before the coroner's jury and in Canton's preliminary hearing. And an attempt by Basch to put a noose around Frank Canton's neck was always a strange exercise, given the history between the Basch and Canton families. Shortly before John Tisdale's assassination, Charlie Basch had saved the lives of Mrs. Canton and one of the Canton daughters by chasing down and halting a runaway team of horses carrying them to what appeared to be certain death. Canton, understandably, was said to have deeply appreciated Charlie's actions.[74] Forty years later, Basch gave a sad and pathetic interview in which he asserted with the greatest certainty (submitting implausible details not found in 1891 and 1892 interviews, such as a conversation with Canton) that it was Frank Canton he had seen the morning of December 1, 1891. Basch's 1933 interview is full of factual inaccuracies and cannot be given credence.[75]

The cases against Elliott and Coates were also dismissed, although it is not clear in what manner. Nate Champion was the last witness against them and, given Champion's murder, Johnson County had little choice but to let Elliott and Coates go.[76]

Another "loose end" case was the trial of Henry Smith for the murder of George Wellman, addressed in the federal court as conspiracy to deprive a citizen of rights. Smith pled "not guilty" in May, and in November he was tried in Cheyenne and acquitted.[77]

It seemed in May 1893 that all the killings by the big cattlemen and their agents were over. In truth, the list was already vastly too long, including Ella Watson, Jim Averell, Tom Waggoner, John A. Tisdale, Ranger Jones, Nate Champion, and Nick Ray. Two more names had been added in the fall of 1892, when Johnson County was so overwhelmed by the prosecution of the invasion that it hardly had the energy to address more murders. Two alleged horse rustlers from the Big Horn Basin, Dab Burch and Jack Bedford, while tied to their horses, were gunned down near Bonanza (east of the Big Horn River and along the Nowood River) by three range detectives. Before Johnson County could even arrest them, Otto Franc, a big cattleman from Meeteetse, Wyoming, spirited the men out of the state, and the Johnson County authorities were never able to pull them back.[78]

But there was one more name to add to the butcher bill. On May 24, 1893, Dudley Champion, one of Nate's several brothers, was shot and killed by Mike Shonsey. Champion had come to Wyoming, apparently looking for work, and had encountered Shonsey on a ranch fifteen miles from the town. Asa Mercer wrote that Shonsey had just suddenly shot down Champion without provocation and that it was a clear case of murder.[79] But a coroner's jury ruled that Shonsey killed Champion in self-defense, and Shonsey immediately left the country before any local officials could examine the case more closely.[80]

The killing of Dud Champion was the last death associated with the Johnson County War. There would be echoes and aftershocks from the invasion for years—there are reverberations in Johnson County still—but the worst of it was over by May 1893. What remained in Johnson County was the dull drip of seemingly countless years of lost ambitions and lost hopes. A place full of young people so ambitious and confident that they could not wait to bust into the future became a place full of people with broken dreams.

Epilogue

The years following the invasion were not kind to Buffalo. The Panic of 1893 was then the most serious economic decline in the history of the United States, and it hit Wyoming hard.[1] Governor Osborne felt that the invasion was the cause of the economic slump of Wyoming in late 1892, and perhaps it contributed, but the slowdown was more likely part of the national decline. Buffalo suffered further with the closing of Fort McKinney in 1894. As well, the cattle market slumped, and instead of going to Buffalo, the railroad extended to Sheridan, going around the Big Horn Mountains rather than through them; despite Buffalo's fervent hopes, that had always been the only topographically sensible route. Buffalo had to wait until 1915 for even a spur.[2] The population of Buffalo slumped from 1,087 in 1890 to only 710 in 1900, while Sheridan's population, helped by extensive coal mining, soared. Sheridan soon had about four times as many people as Buffalo, an advantage it still maintains.[3] Much of this probably would have happened regardless of the invasion, but the stain that the big cattlemen cast upon the community made its economic troubles more bitter.

The people of Johnson County had the consolation that they ultimately won the war against the big cattlemen. For all the taunts and braggadocio of the cattlemen and their henchman, they never dared return in anger to Johnson County. One who left was W. J. Clarke, referred to as the Water Commissioner, about whom it was said, "He emerges from the trial absolutely penniless, having lost everything as the result of the raid."[4] H. R. Mann apparently stayed in Salt Lake City; after 1892, he dropped out of sight within Johnson County.[5] Only two of the Johnson County cattlemen who participated in the invasion kept their ranches in the county. Surprisingly, one was Fred Hesse, probably because his efforts to sell his ranch were unsuccessful.[6] He did not return to the county for two years after the trial, and then he rarely came to Buffalo, where threats to kill him persisted for years.[7] Hesse's wife was highly regarded, so much so that her presence was probably a calming factor. Still, tragedy did not spare her family; in 1902, three of the Hesse children died from scarlet fever. But this calamity, certainly never forgotten by Mr. and Mrs. Hesse, had an unexpected consequence. Animosity toward Hesse eased. The deaths of his three children seemed to even the slate.[8]

The other invader who remained was Hard Winter Davis. Davis had been a reluctant combatant in the invasion. He was pushed by his cattlemen friends to join the expedition but was so bothered by his involvement that he wrote a letter to his wife, begging forgiveness for his actions. He rationalized his participation by arguing that perhaps he could stop the "unjust shedding of blood" and "prevent extreme measures of those guilty of nothing greater than sympathy for the rustlers."[9] But then as the invasion proceeded, it became apparent to Davis that he could not affect, much less repress the zeal of such men as Wolcott, Irvine, and Canton. He found a way to split off from the group before the fight at the KC Ranch, thereby inspiring the contempt of Billy Irvine, among others.[10] Davis and his family remained in Johnson County—at Sussex, twenty miles east of Kaycee—until shortly after Davis's death in 1923. One of his daughters, Dolly, married Mart Tisdale, the oldest son of John A. Tisdale; Helena Huntington Smith termed their marriage a "Montague-Capulet romance."[11]

John A. Tisdale's family struggled after his death. Kate Tisdale moved to Buffalo and started a restaurant in late 1892, "two doors south of the post office," but disputes quickly arose with her brother-in-law, Al Allison.[12] Embezzlement charges were filed against Allison (Martin A. Tisdale) on February 10, 1893, for his actions as the executor of the estate of John Tisdale, and about the same time, Kate Tisdale filed a contest against the Homestead Entry of Martin Tisdale, asserting that the homestead had been abandoned.[13] The embezzlement charges against Allison—that he had stolen from his dead brother's estate—were no doubt wrenching for Kate Tisdale. Her oldest son, Mart (short for "Martin"), was named after Allison, and Allison's betrayal must have added to the family's anguish. It is not clear whether Allison left Johnson County to avoid legal troubles, but in July 1894 he was killed in a gunfight in Glasgow, Montana.[14]

Even as a young boy, Mart Tisdale carried the burden of his father's murder. The Tisdale family was certain that Canton had killed John A. Tisdale, and there is a family story that when Mart was twelve, he planned to confront Frank Canton with a pistol when Canton made a return to Buffalo. It is not clear whether Mart intended to shoot Canton or if Lew Webb and Tom Gardner, waiting behind him, were going to do the job, but it became a moot point, because someone, perhaps Fred Hesse, tipped off Canton and he avoided the confrontation.[15]

Despite her troubles, Kate Tisdale raised all four of her children by herself and did a good job, beginning with Mart. His dispute with Frank Canton notwithstanding, Mart Tisdale developed into a remarkably mature young man. At a young age, he had to assist his mother with the care of the family, and before he was an adult, he ran the roundup for Webb and Gardner, who built substantial ranches and were considered solid citizens.[16] Mart Tisdale managed the ranch of his father-in-law, H. W. Davis, in the early 1920s, was a stock inspector in northern Wyoming for three years, and then was elected Johnson County sheriff in 1926. He served as sheriff for the next sixteen years and enjoyed a good reputation as a law enforcement officer.[17]

Mart had a son, Tom, and this child became caught up in the family saga. Tom Tisdale compiled an extensive collection of papers relating to the murder of his grandfather and to the Johnson County War—the Tisdale Collection, now housed in the Jim Gatchell Memorial Museum in Buffalo.

The Tisdale family engaged in long and deep discussions about their history, when family members frequently addressed the assassination of John A. Tisdale, and they kept recordings of many of these sessions. One cannot listen to the family tapes of these down-to-earth, likable people without being struck by how much the tragedy in 1891 still afflicted the whole family. They were haunted by the unjust killing of their father and grandfather. The Tisdales were not the kind of people to whine or complain about bad breaks, and they did enjoy one another, but this close family shared an understated, somber outlook on life and all its perils.

The uncertainty of life was also dramatically demonstrated in the results of the 1894 Wyoming election. After the Republican debacle of 1892, the response of many Republican newspapers was haughty outrage, scolding voters for their waywardness and gullibility. By all rights this posture should have assured Wyoming Republicans a long banishment to a political wilderness. But the Wyoming Republican Party was very, very lucky, and an eviction that should have extended ten to fifteen years lasted only two. When the Panic of 1893 visited the nation, voters all over the country did what democratic peoples always do in such situations; they threw out the party in power. The Wyoming Democrats in 1893 and 1894 were not only the party in power, but they had debased themselves by their incompetent and amoral behavior in the 1893 legislative session and their nasty bickering after the election.[18] The Democrats even lost their principal state newspaper in 1894 when John Carroll sold the *Cheyenne Daily Leader* to E. A. Slack; in September 1894 the *Leader* officially became independent. Further, the Populists in 1894 refused to agree to fusion, naively believing they could win on their own.[19] In the 1894 election, the Republicans swamped the Democrats, winning forty-eight of the fifty-five legislative seats.[20]

The invasion had proved to be a bigger problem than even Francis Warren and Willis Van Devanter could handle in the short term; it was certainly responsible for the loss of Warren's Senate seat. But Warren limited the invasion's political damage, and that surely helped his political resurrection. Warren was not one of those who heaped scorn on Wyoming voters for their anger about the invasion. He maintained support for his cattlemen friends, but he never justified their actions (at least publicly), and he even went to Johnson County to plead his case in October 1892. There the senator stated, "He who says I contributed one cent towards or had any knowledge of, or in any manner approved of that invasion, utters a lie as black as human tongue can articulate."[21] In later years he said very little about the invasion. Warren seems to have taken to heart the observation of the *Cheyenne Daily Leader* that Wyoming people would not tolerate shenanigans such as the Johnson County invasion.[22]

The 1894 triumph of the Wyoming Republican Party opened the way to the selection of two Republican senators in 1894. A consensus had evolved, though, that Wyoming citizens would tolerate only one senator from Cheyenne, and this was at first thought to be a handicap for Warren. Willis Van Devanter skillfully managed Warren's campaign, however; by Van Devanter's adroit handling of a threat from the nativist American Protective Association, the solid support of Laramie County was secured. Joseph Carey, Warren's rival, was then maneuvered out of any chance of a senatorship, and the joint legislative caucus named Warren by acclamation—marking the beginning of a bitter, twenty-five-year feud between Warren and Carey. Carey was completely pushed out of politics until 1910, when he was elected governor as a Democrat. Clarence D. Clark of Evanston was elected in 1894, over token opposition, as the second Wyoming senator.[23]

Warren's subsequent career in the U.S. Senate was legendary. He served for another thirty-four years—the longest tenure in the history of the Senate until Carl Hayden passed Warren's mark in 1964 and was chairman of the powerful Senate Appropriations Committee during his last eight years.[24] Warren rewarded Van Devanter by staunchly supporting his appointment to the Eighth Circuit Court of Appeals (President Theodore Roosevelt appointed him in 1903) and then the U.S. Supreme Court (President Taft's appointment in 1911). Van Devanter served until 1937, when he was persuaded to accept a generous retirement; he gained notoriety as one of the "nine old men" President Franklin Roosevelt harshly criticized.[25]

The active members of the Wyoming Stock Growers Association were not so circumspect as Warren about the Johnson County War. When John Clay gave his address at the annual convention of the Wyoming Stock Growers Association in 1893, he defended the invasion, asserting that circumstances justified it. Clay acknowledged that the invasion "ended unfortunately and gave rise to an almost interminable amount of bad blood politically and socially." Nevertheless, said Clay, a "spirit of admiration" had arisen for the invaders, and they were respected "for their manliness, for their supreme courage under the adverse fire of calumny and the usual kicking a man gets when he is down."[26] It was a masterful speech, showing solidarity with his comrades and almost seeming to justify the unjustifiable, but it was an exercise in vanity, uttered only to soothe battered egos. The speech did not suffice to soothe Billy Irvine's ego, though; he complained that he was tired of being "cussed" for doing the right thing.[27] Still, the oppressive reign of the Wyoming Stock Growers Association was almost over.

With a Democratic governor sitting in Cheyenne and the public having unequivocally condemned their actions, there would be no further invasions.

Governor Osborne's veto of the funding for the Wyoming Live Stock Commission effectively killed it, at least in its aggressive form. Milo Burke had shown the way to fight the confiscation of livestock, and cattle were no longer being seized in the wholesale way of 1891.[28] In 1893 the association was down to ninety-six members and was virtually broke. So the Wyoming Stock Growers Association reluctantly took the steps that would change the character of this feared group forever—it opened the organization to all of Wyoming's stockmen, some 1,500 of them.[29] In only a few years, the small stockmen became dominant in Wyoming, so that in 1905 Governor B. B. Brooks could say, "Today, our cattle are owned by 5,000 different cattlemen and farmers, instead of by a few hundred outfits."[30]

The actions taken at the 1893 annual meeting of the Wyoming Stock Growers Association, held in Cheyenne, must have pleased Governor Osborne, who no doubt read the proceedings. Osborne completed his term as governor and was even elected to the U.S. House of Representatives in 1896, serving one term. Dr. Osborne later was appointed as first assistant U.S. secretary of state (1915–17). In 1918 he challenged Francis Warren for the Senate. but Warren won, receiving about 57 percent of the vote. [31]

Osborne's predecessor, Amos Barber, remained in Cheyenne, the only place in Wyoming where he was not publicly reviled, and practiced medicine.[32] Barber's friend, Penrose, quickly left Wyoming in the fall of 1892.[33] During the time of the invasion, Dr. Penrose had left Hard Winter Davis's ranch by himself and journeyed south, trying to get back to Cheyenne. Unlike the two invaders who also rode south (after having been wounded by Nate Champion at the KC Ranch), however, Penrose was unable to get out of the state. Arrested in Douglas on April 14, the young doctor found himself in a highly uncomfortable situation, and he gave a confession that told some truths embarrassing to the big cattlemen.[34] Penrose was quickly rescued by Willis Van Devanter, though, who obtained yet another writ of habeas corpus. U.S. marshal Rankin seized Penrose in Douglas and returned him to Cheyenne, effectively putting him out of the reach of Johnson County officials.[35] Penrose left the practice of medicine in 1899 because of poor health. He died in 1925.[36]

Billy Irvine, who had worked with Penrose to write the doctor's memoir about the invasion, remained unrepentant about the invasion until his death. He was elected president of the Wyoming Stock Growers Association in 1896 and served until 1911. He ran as a Republican for Wyoming state treasurer in 1904 and was elected.[37]

Asa Mercer was probably the biggest thorn in the side of Billy Irvine and the Wyoming Stock Growers Association. In 1894 Mercer published a celebrated polemic, entitled *The Banditti of the Plains: The Crowning Infamy of the Ages*. Unabashedly critical of the Wyoming Stock Growers Association and all of its members who played a role in the Johnson County invasion, the book has been controversial from the day it first appeared. Debates have raged over Mercer's motivation, the book's accuracy, its effect, and the extent to which the stock growers association tried to suppress it.[38] Viewed more than one hundred years after its publication, the book has held up reasonably well. There were areas, primarily political, in which Mercer went beyond the facts, but most of his recitals have been confirmed through the years by the admissions of big cattlemen and their supporters. Mercer assisted Democrats during the election campaign of 1892, but after June 1895 he lost his job as the Wyoming state statistician and had no reasonable hope for further patronage. He took his family to the town of Hyattville, Wyoming, another community nestled close to the Big Horn Mountains—like Buffalo—except that Hyattville is in the Big Horn Basin, on the west slope of the Big Horns. Mercer died there in 1917.[39]

Most of the Johnson County people who were active in the events of the invasion stayed in Buffalo, at least for a few years. Robert Foote was again elected to the Wyoming Senate in 1894 (Johnson County still favored Democrats, although not as overwhelmingly as in 1892), and he was finally able to assume that office in 1895. His party was such a tiny minority, however, that he must have found his legislative service frustrating.[40] Foote survived a vindictive prosecution in the federal district court in Cheyenne for defrauding the government on a contract to supply grain to Fort McKinney; a jury acquitted him in May 1894.[41] But then things went wrong for Foote. Fire destroyed his large store in 1895, and "the family fortune dwindled until all its members moved to other parts."[42]

Foote's adversary, Charles Burritt, also left Buffalo a few years after the invasion. He continued to serve as the mayor until 1897 and he was elected to the state house in 1896 (Burritt and James Lobban got a bill through the state legislature to compensate Johnson County for the cost of the Invasion trials). Burritt left Buffalo in 1898 and traveled to the Philippines with Company C of the First Wyoming Volunteers. He returned to the United States in 1907 and began practicing law in Reno, Nevada. He died of pneumonia on June 1, 1927.[43]

Another enemy of Burritt's, O. H. Flagg, remained in Buffalo for only a few years. Flagg lost the 1894 election for county clerk (decided in a runoff when the vote at the general election was a tie) and an 1896 run for sheriff. In both elections he was accused of dishonesty; his defense was that he had paid all the diverted money back. Like Billy Irvine, Flagg remained a fierce partisan in favor of his side in the Johnson County War. In May 1895, Billy Irvine made a rare appearance by an invader in Buffalo and brought with him his bodyguard, "Quick Shot" Scott Davis, a participant in the invasion. Flagg accosted Davis in a Buffalo bar and challenged him to a fight, but a deputy sheriff separated the would-be combatants. Flagg sold the *People's Voice* in 1897 and began a series of jobs and other efforts to earn a living (apparently hampered by his fondness for drink); they led him to other parts of Wyoming, to Nevada and California, and then back to Nevada. He died in Reno in 1925.[44]

John R. Smith, the man in the middle of so much of the 1892 skirmishing, continued to run his ranch on Crazy Woman Creek south of Buffalo, which he expanded to 750 acres. Smith sold the ranch to his sons in 1903, when he and his wife moved to Idaho to be near their daughters. He died in 1930.[45]

Red Angus also remained in Buffalo for the next few years after the invasion, but his life was not without turbulence. In November 1893, Angus was involved in a confrontation with Arapahoe Brown, his ally at the T. A. Ranch. Brown had called Angus out over a bar bill. Believing Brown was armed, Angus secured a .32 pistol. The two men met in the street, and Angus shot Brown in the chest. Brown, surprisingly, was not seriously hurt, at least not so badly that he could not walk to a doctor's office for treatment. But it turned out that Brown was not armed, and so Angus was convicted of aggravated assault, but only fined.[46] Brown was murdered by two of his employees in March 1901.[47]

In July 1894, Angus's wife was adjudicated as incompetent, and he divorced her that same year, marrying Mary E. Bye a few months later—Bye had been charged with assault against Mrs. Angus in May 1894 and was fined $15.[48] In 1895 Angus moved to Great Falls, Montana, but he returned to Buffalo before 1909. He served then as a deputy clerk of court and was elected Johnson County treasurer in 1910, completing four years in that position. He was appointed as commandant of the Wyoming Soldiers and Sailors Home at old Fort McKinney in 1919 and served in that capacity for about a year, when he retired completely. Angus died peacefully in Buffalo in July 1922 at the age of seventy-three.[49] The Mayor of Laurel Avenue was a far more complex man than even the people of Johnson County knew when they first elected him sheriff in 1888, and he was seen differently by different people. Frank Canton hated Angus deeply and completely and could not say bad enough about him, but when Angus died, Jim Gatchell wrote an obituary that stated: "Mr. Angus was a man of forceful character, a true and loyal friend, an honest and upright citizen."[50]

Canton died five years after Angus, on September 27, 1927.[51] After leaving Buffalo, Canton led an eventful life, acting as a peace officer in Oklahoma, then Alaska, and then back to Oklahoma. One of the first things he did when returning to Oklahoma was to petition Texas governor James S. Hogg for a pardon. He presented a carefully edited version of his criminal past, and Governor Hogg awarded Joe Horner (Frank Canton) "a full, unconditional pardon."[52] In 1907 Canton was appointed adjutant general of the new state of Oklahoma, serving until 1916, apparently with distinction.[53]

Gustave Moeller lived the rest of his life in Buffalo. As he had before his tumultuous time in 1892 as editor of the *Buffalo Bulletin*, Moeller continued making music, organizing and leading choirs and playing the piano and the organ. Moeller bought the *Buffalo Voice* in 1898 and ran it until 1902. Then he became involved in the telephone business, managing the Buffalo office of the Bell Telephone Company after 1904, and was remembered as "a nice man to work for." He died in Buffalo in 1910.[54]

The Johnson County invasion was not the last extralegal violence in northern Wyoming. Until the 1890s the competition for the grass on the public domain was between cattlemen. But the battles between big cattlemen and small cattlemen were soon superseded by disputes between cattlemen and sheepmen. Cowboys staged raids all over Wyoming; several men and thousands of sheep were killed. Those raids culminated in the April 2, 1909, Spring Creek Raid, when seven local cattlemen shot to death three sheepmen. The bodies of two of the sheepmen were incinerated, dogs and sheep were shot, and wagons and gear were burned.[55] The raid occurred near the western slope of the Big Horn Mountains seven miles south of Ten Sleep, Wyoming (in an area that was part of Johnson County until 1897). Before 1909 no cowboy had ever been convicted of a crime in Wyoming in connection with a sheep raid.

The authorities in Big Horn County (the successor to Johnson County), including the district judge, were determined to stop this vigilante behavior. The governor of Wyoming, B. B. Brooks, made a quiet visit to the Big Horn County seat, Basin City, and met with county officials. The governor pledged full support for the efforts at prosecution and conferred at length with the district judge and the sheriff of Big Horn County about convening a grand jury.[56]

A grand jury was, in fact, convened, and developed strong evidence against the seven men who had conducted the sheep raid, all of whom were arrested. Two of the men turned state's evidence and with their testimony, as well as evidence developed from the sheriff's investigation and the grand jury proceedings, a powerful case was prepared by the prosecution. The charged cattlemen, though, knowing well the lessons of the Johnson County War and the Wyoming history of sheep raids, were supremely confident that there would not be a trial against them. Their allies attempted tactics that had worked well in 1892, such as launching vicious attacks against public officials by kept newspapers and intimidating witnesses.[57] This time none of it worked.

Big Horn County officials chose to try Herbert Brink first, believing that their strongest case was against him, and the prosecution deferred the trials of the remaining defendants. On November 11, 1909, the jury in the case of *State v. Brink* brought in a verdict of "guilty" of first-degree murder; Brink was sentenced to death.[58] Brink's codefendants stampeded to the Big Horn County prosecutors, seeking a deal in return for guilty pleas. Plea agreements were reached, and all five of the defendants were sentenced to terms in the Wyoming penitentiary. As part of the overall agreement, Brink's death sentence was commuted by Governor Brooks.[59]

The verdicts in these cases utterly squelched a brief but powerful vigilante tradition in northern Wyoming that had begun with the big cattlemen's 1891 assassination squad.[60] It was now clear to all the people in northern Wyoming that those who committed violent extralegal acts were going to suffer the hard fate of criminal prosecution and punishment. This triumphant result was greatly assisted by the presiding district judge. His attitude toward vigilantes and vigilante justice was well expressed in his charge to the grand jury that issued indictments against the Spring Creek raiders.

Condemning mob law, the judge made an impassioned and eloquent argument for the rule of law:

> No man or body of men, however wise or well-intentioned, may safely be entrusted to pronounce upon or redress public wrongs or private grievances outside of the forms of law. All acts of a mob give occasion for reprisal. The spirit of lawlessness grows by what it feeds on. And when one set of men or class of men on the one hand indulge in acts of lawlessness, it simply invites retaliation by like acts on the part of others. The example of a single mob is worse in a community than a pestilence.[61]

The district judge who made these pronouncements was Carroll H. Parmelee, and every word was equally applicable to the Johnson County invasion. Parmelee was tarred by his association with Governor Barber in 1892 and his ruling in the preliminary hearing of Frank Canton, and he was counted as a man on the side of the big cattlemen. His family insisted, though, with justification, that Parmelee was caught in the middle, that he was left with no legal choice but to act as he did in 1892. The Spring Creek Raid grand jury of May 1909 finally gave Parmelee a chance to express what he really believed about mobs and vigilantes; his charge to the grand jury stands as one of the most articulate condemnations of vigilante actions, including the big cattlemen's invasion of Johnson County. His rejection by Johnson County voters in 1892 must have hurt deeply, but Parmelee did not complain and continued to play well his role. It was surprising but fitting that Carroll Parmelee should have presided over the final death of the ugly specter of vigilantism in northern Wyoming. Parmelee served as district judge until January 1, 1917.[62]

For years after the invasion, books continued to be written about it, most of them by big cattlemen supporters, in which they built on the distorted historical record. Sam Clover wrote an odd book, first published in 1903, in which he told the story of the invasion through the person of Paul Travers, who was all too obviously Sam Clover.[63] Clover was not committed to willful fabrication, but he was faithful to his promise to get out the big cattlemen's story, and he uncritically accepted most of their contentions. Still another author who favored the big cattlemen, although his works were fiction, was Owen Wister, who was chummy with Frank Wolcott and other invaders and whose writings about rustling reflected the perspective of the big cattlemen.[64] Frank Canton wrote an autobiography, published in 1930, that was probably the most thoroughly distorted presentation, but Robert David's book, *Malcolm Campbell, Peace Officer*, first published in 1932, was hardly an objective chronicle either.[65] Helena Huntington Smith's 1966 book, *The War on Powder River*, provided a much-needed balance to these works of propaganda, but in 1971 John Rolfe Burroughs published an authorized history of the Wyoming Stock Growers Association that fully embraced all of the most extreme claims of big cattlemen since 1892. Scholars lamented the distorted and confused state of the historical record. Professor Lewis Gould wrote that historical accounts of the Johnson County War were "more distinguished for partisanship, incomplete research, and inaccurate presentation than for scholarly analysis and thoroughness."[66] Another historian suggested methods by which the truth might somehow be found.[67]

Worse than the disorder among scholars is that since the invasion, because of the high-decibel accusations of the big cattlemen, the general feeling in Wyoming has been that the cattlemen's denunciations had substance. People felt that although the invasion was not justified, the cattlemen probably had legitimate complaints. Big cattlemen supporters could and have argued that their intent was just to enforce the criminal laws that the Johnson County authorities refused to enforce. The people of Buffalo were never fooled by this twisted version of truth, however, and even today most people in Johnson County who consider the invasion have quite a different attitude. The Jim Gatchell Memorial Museum in Buffalo raised money for a life-size statue of Nate Champion, which was unveiled on June 27, 2009. The first sentence of the inscription reads: "In the exciting history of the Johnson County Cattle War, no one is held in higher esteem than Nathan D. Champion." Bumper stickers are available at the museum proclaiming, "Johnson County[:] We Haven't Trusted Cheyenne Since 1892."

The people of Johnson County have a valid complaint. Virtually all the independent evidence supports their view that their community was unfairly treated. Contemporary newspaper reports, land records and court records, the statements of Colonel Van Horn, and, probably most significantly, the admissions of big cattlemen and their supporters all demonstrate that, indeed, Johnson County was libeled shamefully. The big cattlemen's case was supported with a campaign of outrageous misrepresentations. When these are set aside, the only supportable facts are that the cattle rustling problem in Johnson County was a small, local problem. The 1892 view of the Johnson County commissioners, that the cattle barons carried out their actions against Johnson County residents in order to drive smaller stockmen off the range, was well founded. All the objective information is that the people of Buffalo and Johnson County in 1892, far from constituting a rogue society, were hardworking, ambitious, decent people—if anything, a moral cut above the usual run of human beings then in Wyoming. They were visited by a catastrophe not of their making, when big cattlemen, in deep criminal trouble because of their blundering assassination squad, chose to launch the invasion, seen as required because the abortive attempts to kill competitors made the killing of witnesses necessary. Through the whole nightmare episode, the people of Johnson County proved to be remarkably fair, brave, and resourceful. There should be a new page in Wyoming history according them the credit they deserve.

Wyoming people have long harbored a broad and deep streak of spit-in-your-eye libertarianism. The deepest mistrust is manifested toward the rich and powerful, and the Johnson County War was a large contributor to this attitude. After the invasion, Francis E. Warren's plan to move Wyoming's federal public lands to state ownership could never gain sufficient support to be enacted into law. The citizens of the state never held a consistent view as to what should be done with this land, though, just that the rich and powerful must not have it. Because Wyoming people could never agree on a specific plan, it was not until 1934, when a federal leasing system on the public domain was finally resolved upon, that the last ugly vestiges of physical competition over public resources were finally ended.[68]

The concrete effects of the war were mostly limited to the few years after 1892, but it was so built into the web of Wyoming experience that it resonated for many years more; the invasion became the benchmark by which people viewed their connection to Wyoming. In the grand jury proceedings leading to the 1909 Spring Creek Raid trials, questioning attorneys asked, as part of routine inquiry, when the witness had "come into the country." If the answer was near 1892, the invariable follow-up was something such as, "Two years after the invasion?" or "Just before the invasion?"

One could wish for a nobler, more edifying, and more inspiring event to so frame a state's perception of itself. This "most notorious" event, while it did bring out the decency and bravery of some Johnson County citizens, was neither noble nor edifying nor inspiring. For better or worse, however, for good or for ill, the Johnson County War is a profound part of Wyoming's heritage.

Diary of Nate Champion

Following is the diary of Nate Champion, according to "Regulators in a Trap," *Chicago Herald*, April 16, 1892, submitted by Sam Clover as the document taken from Nate Champion's body:

Me and Nick was getting breakfast when the attack took place. Two men here with us—Bill Jones and another man. The old man went after water and did not come back. His friend went out to see what was the matter and he did not come back. Nick started out and I told him to look out, that I thought, that there was someone at the stable and would not let them come back. Nick is shot but not dead yet. He is awful sick. I must go and wait on him. It is now about two hours since the first shot. Nick is still alive, they are still shooting and are all around the house. Boys, there is bullets coming in like hail. Them fellows is in such shape I can't get at them. They are shooting from the stable and river and back of the house. Nick is dead, he died about 9 o'clock. I see a smoke down at the stable. I think they have fired it. I don't think they intend to let me get away this time.

It is now about noon. There is some one at the stable yet; they are throwing a rope out at the door and dragging it back. I guess it is to draw me out. I wish that duck would get out further so I can get a shot at him. Boys, I don't know what they have done with them two fellows that staid here last night. Boys, I feel pretty lonesome just now. I wish there was some one here with me so we could watch all sides at once. They may fool around until I get a good shot before they leave. It's about 3 o'clock now. There was a man in buckboard and one on horseback that just passed. They fired on them as they went by. I don't know if they killed them or not. I seen lots of men come out on horses on the other side of the river and take after them. I shot at the men in the stable just now, don't know if I got any or not. I must go and look out again. It don't look as if there is much show of my getting away. I see twelve or fifteen men. One looks like [name is scratched out]. I don't know whether it is or not. I hope they did not catch them fellows, that run over the bridge toward Smith's. They are shooting at the house now. If I had a pair of glasses I believe I would know some of those men. They are coming back. I've got to look out.

Well they have just got through shelling the house like hail. I heard them splitting wood. I guess they are going to fire the house tonight. I think I will make a break when night comes if alive. Shooting again. I think they will fire the house this time. It's not night yet. The house is all fired. Good bye boys, if I never see you again.

Nathan D. Champion

Notes

The following abbreviations have been used for frequently cited works:

BB	*Buffalo Bulletin*
BE	*Buffalo Echo*
BHS	*Big Horn Sentinel*
CDL	*Cheyenne Daily Leader*
CDS	*Cheyenne Daily Sun*
CJS	*Corpus Juris Secundum*
LB	*Laramie Boomerang*

CHAPTER ONE

1. Larson, *History of Wyoming*, 283.

2. "Buffalo," *BE*, August 2, 1883; Larson, *History of Wyoming*, 99.

3. Larson, *History of Wyoming*, 129.

4. By my count, there are at least thirteen larger streams coming off the east slope of the Big Horns within what was early Johnson County: the Middle and North forks of the Powder River, three forks of Crazy Woman Creek, Clear Creek, French Creek, Rock Creek, Shell Creek, Piney Creek, Little Goose, Big Goose, and the Tongue River. The Little Big Horn might be included, but it flows northeast into Montana. Others have listed Prairie Dog and Wolf Creek. "Johnson County," *BE*, August 2, 1883.

5. Larson, *History of Wyoming*, 106.

6. "Fort McKinney—A Graphic History of the Post by General Brisbin," *BHS*, October 10, 1887. The fort was named in honor of Lieutenant John McKinney, who was killed by Indians on November 12, 1876, about thirty-five miles from the post.

7. "Buffalo," *BE*, August 2, 1883.

8. Bartlett, *History of Wyoming*, 1:522ff.

9. "Buffalo," *BE*, August 2, 1883.

10. "Buffalo, the Boss Burg," *BB*, July 30, 1891.

11. *BHS*, September 13, 1884; "Removal," *BHS*, October 31, 1885. There are published excerpts from editions of the *Echo* after August 2, 1883, and before September 1884, but to the author's knowledge, the August 2, 1883, edition is the only one for which an entire newspaper is available.

12. "Johnson County," *BE*, August 2, 1883.

13. "Johnson County," *BE*, August 2, 1883; Driskell, "History of Elias U. Snider," vertical file 3, Snider, Elias U. (Life of), Jim Gatchell Memorial Museum, Buffalo, Wyo. (hereafter "Gatchell Museum").

14. At age twenty-seven, he was measured at five feet, eleven and a half inches tall and weighed 138 pounds. DeArment, *Alias Frank Canton*, 44, 54. See also the discussion of Canton in chapters 2–4, infra.

15. Canton, *Frontier Trails*, 77. One of the important responsibilities of a sheriff is to serve legal papers.

16. DeArment, *Alias Frank Canton*, 70.

17. See "His Farewell Discharge," *BHS*, December 17, 1887, and "Down and Out," *BHS*, May 5, 1888.

18. Numerous newspaper articles show the warm relationship between Judge Blair and the people of Buffalo, including "District Court," *BE*, August 2, 1883; "The Last Republican Rose," *BHS*, April 23, 1887; "Local and Personal," *BHS*, December 7, 1887; "His Formal Discharge," *BHS*, December 17, 1887; *BHS*, December 24, 1887, 2, col. 5; *BHS*, February 9, 1893, 2, col. 1.

19. Editorial, *BHS*, December 24, 1887; "His Farewell Discharge," *BHS*, December 17, 1887. The five attorneys were N. L. Andrews (the first county attorney), Henry S. Elliott (his successor), Sam T. Lewis and J. D. Hinkle (practicing as Lewis & Hinkle; Lewis would soon depart the legal scene in Buffalo), and Charles N. Burritt.

20. *BE*, August 12, 1883, 1, col. 1. See also "Johnson County," in the same issue; and Buffalo's Centennial Book Committee, *Buffalo's First Century* (hereafter "*Buffalo's First Century*"), 6.

21. "City Nominations," *BB*, April 2, 1891; DeArment, *Alias Frank Canton*, 52; *Buffalo's First Century*, 5, 6. See the signature of Burritt reproduced herein.

22. *Buffalo's First Century*, 6;

23. Ibid.

24. Ibid., 4–6.

25. Ibid., 4, 5.

26. DeArment, *Alias Frank Canton*, 7. The discussion that follows is primarily based upon "Obituary," *BB*, August 3, 1922, written by Jim Gatchell, but I also used an article written by Bob Edwards in the *Sentry*, published by the Gatchell Museum Association (hereafter "*Sentry*"), October 2002.

27. DeArment, *Alias Frank Canton*, 7; Oliva, *Fort Wallace*, 45, 58, 59, 62, 63. In his obituary of Angus, Jim Gatchell reports that the fort was besieged by an overwhelming force of Indians

when the garrison contained only one company of soldiers and a few teamsters. The soldiers created dummy cannons (they only had two pieces of artillery), and women within the fort dressed as soldiers to give the impression of greater strength than the occupants of the fort had. "Obituary," *BB*, August 3, 1922.

28. "Obituary," *BB*, August 3, 1922.

29. Edwards, "W. G. 'Red' Angus," 1.

30. Ibid.

31. *Territory v. Angus,* Johnson County criminal cases 1 and 14; Johnson County Criminal Appearance Docket, vol. 1, pp. 1, 14.; Edwards, "W. G. 'Red' Angus," 1, 2.

32. "Buffalo," *BE*, August 2, 1883.

33. See Johnson County Clerk records, vol. 1, patents 1, 5, 7–9, 11, 12, 14, and 16–19.

34. See ibid., vol. 1, patents 2–4, 6, 15, 20–24, 26–28, and 30.

35. Ibid., vol. 1, patents 10, 13, 25, and 29.

36. The Fred G. S. Hesse claim was located about twenty miles south of Buffalo, on Crazy Woman Creek. He first made an entry on the land in 1883 (in the course of which he declared that he would become a U.S. citizen), but it was 1889 before he received a patent. See Declaration by Fred Hesse, Register's Final Certificate, and Deposition of Applicant, Desert Land Entry 485, U. S. Land Office, Cheyenne, Wyo., National Archives and Records Administration, RG 49, Bureau of Land Management, E2021A, Serial Patent files, 1908–51.

37. Fred G. S. Hesse Papers (hereafter "Hesse Papers"), 1880–85, accession no. 240-96-12-13, box 3, Wyoming Stock Growers Association Collection, American Heritage Center, Laramie, Wyo.; Smith, *War on Powder River*, 109.

38. Woods, *Moreton Frewen's Western Adventures*, 77.

39. Ibid., 20; Hesse Papers. Hesse's father manufactured barrels and was involved in related cooperage business.

40. Woods, *Moreton Frewen's Western Adventures*, 40.

41. "Passing of a Pioneer," *BB*, May 1, 1930. The age given in this article is sixteen, but that does not jibe with Smith's birth date.

42. Ibid.

43. Hanson, *Powder River Country*, 133–73, reprints of a series of stories by John R. Smith that were published in the *Buffalo Bulletin* in 1956.

44. "Passing of a Pioneer," *BB*, May 1, 1930.

45. See Smith's account of the Battle of Horseshoe Creek in Hanson, *Powder River Country*, 144.

46. Hanson, *Powder River Country*, 157, 158.

47. Ibid., 163; "Passing of a Pioneer," *BB*, May 1, 1930. See also Tanner, "Disposal of the Public Domain in Johnson County, Wyoming, 1869–1890," 113, 114, wherein the author commented on the farsightedness of Smith for riding all the way to Cheyenne to be sure he was first in priority for some sixty-four cubic feet of water appropriated on Crazy Woman.

48. "Johnson County," *BE*, August 12, 1883; Hanson, *Powder River Country*, 174. The two other men were T. W. Peters and Charles Farwell.

49. See "The Result," *BB*, January 14, 1892, in which an article from the *Washington (D.C.) Star* is reprinted and discussed. See also "Won't Budge an Inch," *BB*, March 3, 1892; and the discussion in later chapters, especially chapter 6.

CHAPTER TWO

1. *BHS*, May 30, 1885, 1; "A Terrible Weapon," *BHS*, June 6, 1885; *BHS*, August 8, 1885, 2, col. 1.

2. "Washington Letter," *BHS*, May 8, 1886; "Bloodshed in Chicago," *BHS*, May 15, 1886.

3. "This and That," *BHS*, March 28, April 18, and July 18, 1885; "News Notes," *BHS*, May 2, 1885.

4. "Horse Thieves Beware," *BHS*, October 11, 1884.

5. Two representative articles telling about the coming fair are "An Annual Fair," *BHS*, June 13, 1885, and "Coming! Coming!" *BHS*, June 27, 1885. See also the September 26, 1885, issue.

6. Specifically, the items within the categories included "cattle, horses, Swine, Poultry (Chickens, turkeys, ducks, pigeons and eagles), Mechanical (Shingles, Side saddle, Horse shoes, Toilet stand, Spring wagon, Two-horse wagon), Field Products (Field Corn, Clover, Miller, Wheat, Oats, Rye, Timothy, Sweet corn, Buckwheat, Spring rye), Vegetables (Pumpkins and squash, melons, cabbage, potatoes, turnip, beets, rutabagas, watermelons, Onions, Celery), Dairy products (butter), Cookery (sausage, preserves, rolls, cakes, pie, bread, jellies and vinegar, waxwork), relics and curiosities [Indian relics], gold quartz, stamps, petroleum, gypsum, fossils, corals, eggs, arts, needlework (silk tidy, pin cushion, knitting, knit spread, sofa pillow, mats, embroidery, crochet, calico quilts, rag carpets, knit lace, crochet scarves and towels)." "Premiums Awarded," *BHS*, September 26, 1885.

7. "Local News," *BHS*, February 21, 1885.

8. "Republican Meeting in Buffalo," *BHS*, September 13, 1884; "Republican Committee Meeting," *BHS*, September 27, 1884; "Local News," *BHS*, October 25 and November 25, 1884.

9. "Regulators in Court," *Chicago Herald*, January 9, 1893.

10. Clarke became the secretary and treasurer of the Johnson County Stock Growers Association in 1895, and Fred Hesse its president in 1986. They held these offices in the active organization for several years (along with several other important positions). See "Stock Growers Meeting," *BHS*, April 25, 1885; "Stock Association Meeting," *BB*, March 12, 1891; and "Officers Elected," *BHS*, April 16, 1887; as well as "Gives Entire Satisfaction," *BB*, January 22, 1891, quoting *CDS*. This last story was printed when Clarke was pushing for appointment as water commissioner, and Hesse declared him to be a "clear-headed, fair-minded" man. Regarding Clarke's activity with Conrad and Clarke, see "Local and Personal," *BHS*, August 8, 1885; and "Sheridan Shorts," *BHS*, April 24, 1886.

11. See *Territory v. Angus*, Johnson County criminal case 1, wherein Mann is listed as a deputy clerk of court.

12. The advertisement appears on page 2 of virtually every edition of the *BHS*. See also "Mount Hope Cemetery," *BHS*, February 14, 1885; and *BHS*, November 21, 1885, 3.

13. "Local and Personal," *BHS*, August 22 and November 21, 1885; February 5, 1887; and January 2, 1889.

14. "Commissioner's Proceedings," *BHS*, August 6, 1887. Mann was not an attorney, but his pursuits certainly extended into the normal work of lawyers; perhaps he was also reading the law in Hinkle's office and planned to become an attorney.

15. The primary source of this discussion is *Buffalo's First Century*, 151. In 1892, Moeller became well known to the public as the editor of the *Buffalo Bulletin*.

16. "Local News," *BHS*, October 18 and November 15, 1884.

17. Two of the items are in "Local News," *BHS*, January 24, 1885, one short piece and a longer article headed "Canton-Wilkerson: The Story of the Marriage of Frank Canton and Anne Wilkerson."

18. "Local and Personal," *BHS*, November 21, 1885.

19. "The Sheridan Hop" and "Our Dance," *BHS*, October 18, 1884.

20. "Local News," *BHS*, November 1 and 15, 1884.

21. "Local News," *BHS*, November 22, 1984.

22. "Local News," *BHS*, December 6, 1884.

23. "Local and Personal," *BHS*, August 29, 1885.

24. "Local and Personal," *BHS*, June 5 and August 14, 1886.

25. "Local and Personal" (two items), *BHS*, November 17, 1885.

26. "Local News," *BHS*, January 3, 1885 (infant son of Mr. and Mrs. J. B. Stroud died); April 11, 1885 (three-year-old Earl Braziel drowned); December 5, 1885 (infant child of Mr. and Mrs. Dave McFall died); February 13, 1886 (infant child of Mr. and Mrs. Drew Smith died); August 21, 1886 (six-year-old daughter of a county commissioner died of typhoid fever); September 25, 1886 (infant child of Mr. and Mrs. C. E. Drummond died).

27. "A Good Time Coming," *BHS*, January 17, 1885; "Pointers," *BHS*, March 15, 1885.

28. "As Others View Us," *BHS*, January 9, 1886.

29. The *Sentinel* is filled with articles showing Buffalo residents' unhappiness with Mrs. Hart because of her perceived greed and extreme litigiousness. The August 29, 1885, article "Playing the Sinche," is especially bitter, referring to "systematic robbery and extortion" by Mrs. Hart's agent. See also, for example, "Local and Personal," January 30 and February 27, 1886, and May 6, 1887; "Secure Title," March 13, 1886; "Turned a Deaf Ear," February 19, 1887; and "Buffalo Items," June 13, 1885.

30. "Open Your Eyes," *BHS*, December 5, 1885. See also "Playing the Sinche," *BHS*, August 29, 1885.

31. See "An Order from Sparks," *BHS*, April 10, 1886; and "Sparks Extinguished," *BHS*, April 17, 1886.

32. See "Buffalo," *BE*, August 2, 1883; "Inter-Continental," *BHS*, November 1, 1884; untitled article, *BHS*, February 14, 1885, 2; editorial, *BHS*, February 21, 1885.

33. "Local and Personal," *BHS*, July 25, 1885.

34. "The Civilizer," *BHS*, August 15, 1885; "Local and Personal," *BHS*, August 22, 1985; "Means Business," *BHS*, October 31, 1885.

35. See the records of the Johnson County Clerk of the District Court, criminal case nos. 1–100. Frequently, different cases are filed for what appear to be simply separate counts, which today would all be part of one file. Too, when a case was dismissed because of a technical deficiency, which happened at least a few times, a new proceeding became the basis for a new file. See, for example, criminal case nos. 3, 11, and 13 against Oliver St. Germain. It also seems that when a charge was reduced from a felony to a misdemeanor, a new case was filed. See *Territory v. Angus*, criminal case nos. 1 and 14.

36. The author is familiar with the administration of criminal dockets in many different courts and jurisdictions, ranging from special courts martial in Fort Lewis, Washington (I

was the courts and boards clerk for the special court martial of the First BCT Brigade from December 1968 until mid-April 1969) and special and general courts martial for Fort Leonard Wood, Missouri, and Fort Dix, New Jersey to justice (now circuit) and district courts in Sheridan County, Wyoming, and Hot Springs and Washakie County, Wyoming (I was the public defender for Hot Springs and Washakie counties for about four years). I am comfortable stating that for the majority of cases filed, resolution is not achieved by a guilty or not guilty verdict in the charging court. There is no reason to believe that the Johnson County District Court docket in the 1880s was different from more recent criminal dockets. See Johnson County criminal case nos. 4, 9, 10, 12, 15, 16, 19, 21, 31, 34, 35, 37–43, 46, 48, 52, 55, and 56.

37. Johnson County criminal case nos. 12 (Conrad) and 22 (Wright). The fornication charge against Wright was not because of her profession—she was a prostitute—but because she was living with a man without being married. Wright was also charged with other offenses, including larceny (case no. 15) and accessory to murder (case no. 19).

38. I have employed the word "about," because the records are not always clear as to the final disposition of a case. The court files in most cases show that a conviction followed a trial, but in some cases I made that conclusion from other sources, such as indications of a not guilty plea followed by evidence of transportation to prison. Most completed cases went to trial in the 1880s, but there were some pleas without trial, and so some of the sixteen convictions could have been had because of pleas rather than trials. I believe that among modern cases tried to verdict, about 80–90 percent result in convictions.

39. Regarding the acquittals for cattle theft, see case nos. 13 (*Terr. v. St. Germain*) and 50 (*Terr. v. Hartman*); for convictions, see case nos. 8 (*Terr. v. Felch*), 71 (*Terr. v. Riddell*), and 85 (*Terr. v. Samuel and Beaver*). Regarding the acquittals for a variant of horse or mule theft, see case nos. 61 (*Terr. v. Petty*), 72 (*Terr. v. Copsey*), and 83 (*Terr. v. Convey*); for convictions, see case nos. 44 (*Terr. v. Walters*), 45 (*Terr. v. Edenfield*), 47 (*Terr. v. Muldoon*), 57 (*Terr. v. Anable and Knight*), 59 (*Terr. v. Dunbar*; petty larceny but sent to prison under case no. 79), 92 (*Terr. v. Slack*), and 93 (*Terr. v. Lamb*). For the manslaughter acquittal, see case no. 88 (*Terr. v. Clair*), and for the murder conviction, see case no. 77 (*Terr. v. Booth*). For the acquittal of furnishing liquor to jail mates, see case no. 20 (*Terr. v. Simpson*); for grand larceny (stealing a saddle), see case no. 51 (*Terr. v. Enfield*); for the fornication charge, see case no. 23 (*Terr. v. Mitchell*); and for burglary, see case no. 68 (*Terr. v. Hinkle*).

40. There was a telegraph line between two army posts, Fort McKinney and Fort Fetterman, which townspeople could use to an extent, but it was frequently down. See "A Terrible Nuisance," *BHS*, June 12, 1886.

41. See criminal case nos. 1–50, Johnson County Clerk of the District Court records. See also the discussion of examples of crimes in the Big Horn Basin in Davis, *Goodbye, Judge Lynch*, p. 11 and chap. 2.

42. See Davis, *Goodbye, Judge Lynch*, 16; and "Horse Thieves Riding Bareback," *BHS*, September 27, 1884.

43. Davis, *Goodbye, Judge Lynch*, 16.

44. See criminal case nos. 1–100, Johnson County Clerk of the District Court records, especially those cases cited in note 32, this chapter. Canton served as sheriff in 1882 before being elected that fall, apparently having been appointed to the post; in July 1882, charges

were filed for the theft of twelve cows (criminal case no. 21). Also, in *Territory v. Bill Howell and Long John* (criminal case no. 52), an indictment was issued regarding the theft of four mules and five horses, but no further action was taken. Apparently these crimes became known to authorities, but the suspects escaped with their ill-gotten gains. For charges filed through 1892, with only one exception, these two cases (21 and 52) involved the greatest number of animals alleged as stolen in Johnson County. That one case, alleging the theft of twenty-nine horses, was *Territory v. McCauley* (117), filed in December 1986, immediately before Frank Canton finished his tour as sheriff. Only the indictment appears within the file; it is possible that the charges were filed in Johnson County in order to obtain a warrant in Johnson County regarding horses stolen in another county but being driven through.

45. "Official Vote Johnson County, 1884," *BHS*, November 22, 1884. The term "neat cattle" is from the criminal statute and refers to domestic cattle.

46. See Murray, *Johnson County*, 74; and records of the Johnson County assessor.

47. See the discussion in Murray, *Johnson County*, 74.

48. 1876 Compiled Laws of Wyoming, chap. 35, secs. 42–44. At the University of Wyoming College of Law, the students in criminal law were instructed that the reason for the very technical elements was that larceny was punishable by death in early England, and common law judges therefore insisted that the elements of larceny be defined very precisely, and each proven.

49. See Davis, *Vast Amount of Trouble*, 11; and "Territorial Wealth," *BHS*, August 21, 1886. The average horse in the 1880s was worth much more than $25, so conviction for the theft of a horse usually produced penitentiary time.

50. See criminal case nos. 3, 13, and 43, as well as no. 72 (in which H. P. Copsey was acquitted of a charge of stealing a mule whose owner was unknown).

51. "Editorial," *BB*, April 21, 1892.

52. See the discussion by the Wyoming Supreme Court in *State v. Hickenbottom*, 63 Wyo. 41, 178 P.2d 110 (Wyo. 1947), wherein the court reversed a conviction of the theft of sheep and granted a new trial because of the defendant's claim that he reasonably believed that the sheep he took were his.

53. The length of these periods varied, depending on how many cases had to be processed, but they usually lasted only two to three weeks.

CHAPTER THREE

1. See advertisements in, for example, *BHS*, May 29, 1886, 1, 2; and "Prepare to Receive Him," *BHS*, February 27, 1886.

2. "Local News" and "Justices and Constables," *BHS*, November 22, 1884.

3. "Local and Personal," *BHS*, October 10, 1885, and May 15 and July 10, 1886; "Local News," *BHS*, October 10, 1885.

4. "The Building Association," *BHS*, June 12, 1886.

5. "School Report," *BHS*, January 9, 1886; "Local and Personal," *BHS*, June 26 and September 11, 1886.

6. Hanson, *Powder River Country*, 233.

7. "Local and Personal," *BHS*, January 23, 1886; "An Explanation," *BHS*, February 6, 1886.

8. "Court Proceedings," *BHS*, July 3, 1886.

9. Whenever two separate charges were brought against a defendant, seemingly arising out of the same event, I counted them as one case. See *Territory v. Joseph Leightner* (criminal case nos. 104 and 107) and *Territory v. William Howell and Charles Stevens* (108 and 109). As noted in the text, the grand jury refused to issue an indictment against S. A. Iden; it also similarly refused regarding O. J. Rice (criminal case no. 106). Three of the remaining cases were dismissed by the county attorney, and in two it appeared that the defendant left the country. See criminal case nos. 100, 104, 105, and 107–17.

10. "Wyoming Stock Growers' Association," *BHS*, April 9, 1887.

11. "With His Boots On," *BHS*, December 5, 1885.

12. "Local and Personal," *BHS*, July 7, 1888.

13. Canton, *Frontier Trails*, 77.

14. In *BHS*, see, first, the "Local and Personal" columns for June 26 and July 17, 1886; then "County Politics," July 31, 1886, and "Local and Personal," August 21, 1886; then "The Outlook for the Sheriffship," September 11, 1886; then "Local and Personal," September 25, 1886; and, finally, ""Democratic County Convention," October 2, 1886.

15. See DeArment, *Alias Frank Canton*, 76, 77. DeArment asserts that the offer came only after it was clear that Canton was not running for office, but I believe that the events transpired in the reverse order, that Canton had been talking to the stock association (via Horace Plunkett, English ranchman) since about April 1886 and badly wanted the job, but he was unwilling to give up the chance of reelection until he was reasonably sure that a job offer would be forthcoming from the association.

16. See *BHS*, October 9, 1886, 2, col. 1, and several other articles discussing this attitude: "Political Indications," *Johnson County Republican*, October 23, 1886; *BHS*, October 30, 1886, 2, col. 3; and "The Official Returns," *BHS*, November 6, 1886.

17. "A Local Historical Society," *BHS*, November 13, 1886.

18. "The Result," *BHS*, November 6, 1886.

19. "Local and Personal," *BHS*, October 30, 1886.

20. Burritt edited the paper for six weeks after October 30, 1886.

21. Canton, *Frontier Trails*, 78.

22. "Local and Personal," *BHS*, November 13, 20, and 27, 1886; "Did Not Perish in the Storm," *BHS*, November 27, 1886.

23. "Local and Personal," *BHS*, December 4, 1886.

24. "Local and Personal," *BHS*, January 8, 1887.

25. "The Outlook for Range Cattle," *BHS*, January 8, 1887.

26. "An Unfavorable Outlook," *BHS*, January 15, 1887.

27. "Local and Personal," *BHS*, February 5, 1887.

28. "Local and Personal," *BHS*, February 12, 1887.

29. "The Safe Side," *BHS*, July 24, 1886, quoting *Grand Junction News*, which predicted that the coming winter was likely to be a "terror." Regarding the overstocking of the range, see Davis, *A Vast Amount of Trouble*, 3, 4.

30. "Local and Personal," *BHS*, February 12 and March 12, 1887; "Two More Victims of King Cold," *BHS*, February 26, 1887. The Stinking Water is now known as the Shoshone River.

31. *CDS*, August 25, 1888, 2, col. 1.

32. "Local and Personal," *BHS*, April 30, 1887.

33. "The Northwestern Range," *BHS*, July 28, 1888.

34. Burroughs, *Guardian of the Grasslands*, 133.

35. Clay, *My Life on the Range*, 248.

36. Burroughs, *Guardian of the Grasslands*, 133, 134.

37. Ibid., 134.

38. Ibid.; DeArment, *Alias Frank Canton*, 81.

39. DeArment, *Alias Frank Canton*, 81.

40. Clay, *My Life on the Range*, 247, 182. See also the discussion by Burroughs, *Guardian of the Grasslands*, 160, wherein the author refers to a "fundamental conflict of interest" between the two groups.

41. Brayer, "Range Country Troubles—1885," 171, 177.

42. Davis, *Vast Amount of Trouble*, 4.

43. See the discussion by the author in ibid., 2.

44. See the discussion in Rollins, *Struggle of the Cattlemen*, 207, 222–26. See also Gould, *Wyoming*, 84.

45. See "Local and Personal," *BHS*, May 9, 1885, and January 9, 1886; and "A Circular," *BHS*, January 16, 1886.

46. "The Fences Must Go," *BHS*, May 28, 1887.

47. Lindsay, *Big Horn Basin*, 142.

48. Ibid.

49. Smith, *War on Powder River*, 96.

50. Ibid., 97.

51. "Thom and Brock Families," as told by Margaret Brock Hanson, vertical file, Gatchell Museum.

52. Rollins, *Struggle of the Cattlemen*, 74.

53. See the discussion in Davis, *Vast Amount of Trouble*, 4.

54. Smith, *War on Powder River*, 114.

55. Ibid., 113, citing Frink, *Cow Country Cavalcade*, 135.

56. "Get Upon the Land," *BHS*, May 22, 1886.

57. "Wyoming Land Entries," *BHS*, October 16, 1886.

58. "Local and Personal," *BHS*, March 24, 1888.

59. "Local and Personal," *BHS*, July 16, October 1, and December 10, 1887; "Professional Cards," *BHS*, April 23, 1887.

60. *BHS*, March 19, 1887, 2, col. 1; "Local and Personal," *BHS*, May 21 and July 16, 1887.

61. "Local and Personal," *BHS*, April 23, 1887.

62. "Division Scheme," *BHS*, March 12, 1887.

63. "Food for Taxpayers," *BHS*, April 2, 1887.

64. "People's Ticket," *BHS*, October 22, 1887.

65. "The Bill Introduced," *BHS*, January 21, 1888.

66. "The County Division Bill," *BHS*, February 4, 1888; *BHS*, February 4, 1888, 2, col. 1.

67. "Local and Personal," *BHS*, February 4, 1888.

68. In the middle of all this heated emotion, one Buffalo merchant introduced some humor and sought an advantage from the topic of the day. He ran an advertisement in the

Big Horn Sentinel, headed "Division!! Division!! R. S. Hopkins Will Divide Profits For 30 DAYS to reduce stock. . . . Do not forget that HOPKINS wants MONEY. And to get money he will sell more and BETTER GOODS." *BHS,* February 4, 1888, 2. Loucks's conduct, while meriting criticism, was not unique. Big Horn County was formed out of Fremont and Johnson counties through the efforts of Colonel William Douglas Pickett, who was then a Fremont County state representative living in the Big Horn Basin. See Davis, *Goodbye, Judge Lynch,* 24. As well, Park County was carved from Big Horn County partially through the efforts of Charles Hayden, a Cody area resident who had been elected to the legislature from Big Horn County in 1908. See *House Journal of the 10th Wyoming Legislature,* 75, 192–93.

69. "Call Off Your Dogs," *BHS,* February 11, 1888.

70. "A Bad Policy," *BHS,* February, 11, 1888.

71. "Long to Be Remembered," *BHS,* March 10, 1888.

72. Ibid.

73. "Local and Personal," *BHS,* March 17, 1888; *BHS,* March 24, 1888, 2, col. 1.

74. *BHS,* March 31, 1888, 3, col. 5. See also "Local and Personal," *BHS,* March 31, 1888.

75. "Enjoined," *BHS,* April 21, 1888; *BHS,* April 21, 1888, 2, col. 1.

76. "Digging Their Own Graves," *BHS,* May 12, 1888.

77. "A Game of Bluff," *BHS,* May 5, 1888.

78. "The County Suit," *BHS,* July 7, 1888.

79. "The Fourth Volume," *BHS,* September 1, 1888.

80. Regarding the Johnson County commissioners, see *BHS,* December 19, 1985, 2, col. 1; and "Ignorance and Meanness," *BHS,* January 9, 1986. Regarding Edgar Wilson, the head of the Cheyenne Land Office, see "Rewarding Final Proof Notices," *BHS,* October 1, 1887; and "Our Side of the Question," *BHS,* October 8, 1887. Regarding Land Commissioner Sparks, see (among many) "Our Land Difficulties," *BHS,* November 6, 1886; and "Sparks Asked to Resign," *BHS,* November 19, 1887.

81. "Local and Personal," *BHS,* September 11, 1886; "Our American Cousin," *BHS,* December 8, 1888.

82. "Local and Personal," *BHS,* October 23, 1886.

83. "Local and Personal," *BHS,* December 1, 1888; "Recommendations," *BHS,* December 8, 1888.

84. The *Sentinel* was pitching hard for the Republican candidates in 1888 and criticizing the *Echo* because the editor "swallowed the Democratic nominations in their entirety." See *BHS,* October 13, 1888, 2, and November 3, 1888, 2.

85. All of the information in this discussion is taken from Johnson County criminal cases 118–53. See especially case nos. 129 (*Territory v. Snow*), 130 (*Territory v. Hunter*), 149, and 154 (*Territory v. Massey*); case no. 154 apparently was not tried but was dismissed for unstated reasons.

86. See *Territory v. McCauley* (Johnson County criminal case no. 117), which shows a December 13, 1886, indictment. Only the indictment and bench warrants are in the file. The horses may have been stolen elsewhere and were being taken through Johnson County.

87. *Territory v. Hopkins* (Johnson County criminal case no. 124). See also, Criminal Appearance Docket, District Court, Johnson County, Wyoming, vol. 1, p. 132.

88. Smith, *War on Powder River*, 119, quoting a letter from Canton to the secretary of the Wyoming Stock Growers Association.

89. "Secret Societies," *BHS*, September 14, 1889; "Resolutions of Respect," *BHS*, August 11, 1888.

90. "Menardi for Mayor," *BHS*, March 31, 1888; "Local and Personal," *BHS*, May 5 and 12, 1888.

91. "The Democratic Candidates," *BHS*, October 13, 1888.

92. "Republican Resolutions," *BHS*, October 20, 1888.

93. *BHS*, October 13, 1888, 2.

94. Ibid.

95. Bail bond, *Territory v. Gross* (Johnson County criminal case no. 148).

96. See the discussion in DeArment, *Alias Frank Canton*, 78. Canton made numerous comments in the years following 1888 that showed his attitude toward Angus and other Johnson County citizens, many being outrageous falsehoods.

97. "Official Returns," *BHS*, November 17, 1888.

CHAPTER FOUR

1. See "Local and Personal," *BHS*, December 5, 1885, and January 2 and June 12, 1886; "Johnson County Stock Meeting," *BHS*, March 26, 1887; "Pay Up Your Dues," October 29, 1887; "Local News," *BHS*, March 14, 1885.

2. "First Chronicles," *BHS*, October 10, 1885.

3. Larson, *History of Wyoming*, 184, 185.

4. Ibid., 183.

5. Burroughs, *Guardian of the Grasslands*, 53, 54.

6. See the discussions in Burroughs, ibid., 113, 158, 159.

7. Ibid., 100.

8. Ibid., 53.

9. Ibid., 104.

10. Ibid., 104, 105.

11. Ibid., 105.

12. O. H. Flagg, "A Review of the Cattle Business in Johnson County, Wyoming, since 1882," *BB*, May 5, 1892 (one of a series of articles by Flagg; hereafter "Flagg, 'A Review'"); Lindsay, *Big Horn Basin*, 141, 142. See also Burroughs, *Guardian of the Grasslands*, 106.

13. See ibid., 109, 117, as well as Dr. Charles Penrose to Robert Ralston, April 22, 1892, Tom Tisdale Collection. Dr. Penrose was new to the country, and his newfound compatriots, cattlemen from the cattlemen's exclusive Cheyenne Club, were almost solely his source of information. Penrose faithfully reflected the attitude of these men; anyone who disagreed with his friends was "siding with the rustlers."

14. Burroughs, *Guardian of the Grasslands*, 107.

15. See the discussion in Burroughs, ibid., 154. See also the February 18, 1889, letter of Thomas B. Adams, then secretary of the Wyoming Stock Growers Association, cited in ibid., 130.

16. Burroughs, *Guardian of the Grasslands*, 154.

17. Fred G. S. Hesse to Major Frank Wolcott, January 15, 1893, Hesse papers, accession no. 240.

18. Ibid.

19. See chapter 2, infra.

20. See chapter 4, infra.

21. F. M. Canton to WSGA, March 17, 1888, Letter File 1888, Wyoming Stock Growers Association Collection, American Heritage Center, Laramie, Wyo.; Canton, *Frontier Trails*, 78. Canton's statements in his book referred to the term of E. U. Snider, which was early 1887 to early 1889.

22. See, for example, the discussion by Lindsay, *Big Horn Basin*, 142–45.

23. Burroughs, *Guardian of the Grasslands*, 153.

24. DeArment, *Alias Frank Canton*, chap. 2, "The Outlaw, 1874–1879."

25. Ibid., 25. The discussion relating to the post office robbery and its aftermath comes from ibid., 23–26. Jacksboro is about seventy miles northwest of Dallas.

26. DeArment, *Alias Frank Canton*, 26–32.

27. Ibid., 31, citing Records of the Adjutant General, RG 94, National Archives.

28. Ibid.

29. See DeArment's discussion, ibid., 28–32.

30. Ibid., 31.

31. Ibid., 33.

32. Ibid.

33. Ibid., 34.

34. DeArment wrote that after September 13, 1875, Horner "would no longer be considered just another reckless cowboy, a little quick with a rope and a six-shooter, perhaps, but basically a decent fellow in a little legal trouble. From that day forward he would be an outlaw." Ibid., 31.

35. Ibid., 35, citing *San Antonio Daily Express*, February 4, 1876.

36. Ibid., 36, 37.

37. Ibid., 35.

38. Ibid., 36–38.

39. Ibid., 40. The charges against Canton back in Jack County (four counts of cattle theft and two of assault) were dismissed, a common practice by prosecutors when another jurisdiction convicts a defendant of a crime at least as serious. See ibid., 38.

40. Ibid., 41, 42.

41. Ibid., 42, 43.

42. Ibid., 43.

43. "Nipped in the Bud," *BHS*, December 5, 1885; "Another Attempt," *BHS*, January 2, 1886; "The Last Straw," *BHS*, February 6, 1886.

44. DeArment, *Alias Frank Canton*, 43, 44.

45. Ibid., 45, 46.

46. ibid., 46.

47. See DeArment's comments, ibid., 46.

48. See DeArment's discussion, ibid., 45.

49. See the discussion in Rollins, *Struggle of the Cattlemen*, 318.

CHAPTER FIVE

1. "Rah! for the Water Works," *BHS*, February 2, 1889.

2. "As Others See Us," *BHS*, April 20, 1889.

3. "Buffalo, Wyo.," *BHS*, July 20, 1889.

4. "Fatal Accident," *BHS*, April 6, 1889; "A Card of Thanks," *BHS*, April 13, 1889; "Local and Personal," *BHS*, May 11, 1889.

5. *BHS*, May 4, 1889, 2; *BHS*, May 11, 1889, 2; and June 1, 1889, 2.

6. Davis, *Worland before Worland*, 3, 4.

7. *BHS*, May 11, 1889, 2, col. 1.

8. *BHS*, May 18, 1889, 2, col. 1.

9. Advertisement, *BHS*, July 13, 1889, 4, and each subsequent edition until October 12, 1889.

10. *BHS*, December 17, 1887, 2, col. 1. In a September 18, 1889, letter to a Mr. Donnelly, Fred Hesse stated that $18 per head for range cattle was a fair price. Hesse papers, accession no. 240.

11. See *Territory v. McDermott* (criminal case no. 155).

12. See *Territory v. Gordon et al.* (criminal case no. 156; note that two cases are numbered 156); *Territory v. Carroll* (163); *Territory v. Coslett* (164); *Territory v. Rothwell* (165); *Territory v. Huff et al.* (166); *Territory v. Flagg et al.* (168, 172–78).

13. When, in the summer of 1891, four soldiers at Fort McKinney were accused of killing *one* cow, it was major news in the paper. See "Soldiers in Limbo," *BB*, August 27, 1891; and "Exact Justice" and "One Held," *BB*, September 3, 1891.

14. "His Farewell Discharge," *BHS*, December 17, 1887 (Jacob Blair); "Judge Saufley's Charge to the Jury," *Sheridan Post*, July 4, 1889 (Micah Saufley).

15. *BHS*, September 7, 1889, 2, col. 1.

16. Penrose, *Rustler Business*, 3.

17. Fred G. S. Hesse to his sister, Jenny, November 26, 1889, Hesse papers, accession no. 240.

18. There are good descriptions of Jack Flagg and his character by Helena Huntington Smith in her *War on Powder River*, chap. 17, and Sue C. Myers in her article "Jack Flagg Remembered."

19. Myers, "Jack Flagg Remembered," 1.

20. Flagg, "A Review," *BB*, May 5, 1892; Myers, "Jack Flagg Remembered," 1.

21. Burroughs, *Guardian of the Grasslands*, 112.

22. Flagg, "A Review," *BB*, May 19, 1892.

23. Myers, "Jack Flagg Remembered," 2.

24. Ibid. Hesse, in his letter of January 25, 1893, to Major Frank Wolcott, says, on the one hand, that Flagg "borrowed" considerable sums of money from the cowboys in the area, but then indicates that Tom Gardner and Billy Hill branded cattle with their own brand. Hesse papers, accession no. 240.

25. Myers, "Jack Flagg Remembered," 2; Smith, *War on Powder River*, 118.

26. Smith, *War on Powder River*, 118.

27. Smith, *War on Powder River*, 115.

28. See, for example, Hesse to Wolcott, January 25, 1893; Hesse to H. C. Plunkett, July 10, 1889; and Hesse to R. L. Glover, November 15, 1889, Hesse papers, accession no. 240.

29. Flagg, "A Review," *BB*, May 19 and June 2 and 23, 1892.

30. Myers, "Jack Flagg Remembered," 2.

31. See "The Hat Brand," box 1, file 10, Tisdale Collection.

32. See Flagg, "A Review," *BB*, May 26, 1892; Myers, "Jack Flagg Remembered," 2; and Rollins, *Struggle of the Cattleman*, 106.

33. Hesse was Plunkett's foreman in the Powder River Cattle Company and liquidated the stock from this company, as he (Hesse) was building up his own brand, the "28." In Flagg's writings, he does not make it clear who fired Spaugh, nor when, but George Baxter almost surely did it in the fall of 1888. By the summer of 1888, Plunkett's Frontier Cattle herds had been purchased by the American Cattle Trust, whose manager was George W. Baxter. See Woods, *Moreton Frewen's Western Adventures*, 195, 196; Hesse to Plunkett, July 10, 1889; and L. Milton Woods, interview by author, November 28, 2008.

34. Hesse to Wolcott, January 25, 1893.

35. Flagg, "A Review," *BB*, June 9, 1892.

36. See the comments of Smith, *War on Powder River*, 118.

37. See note 12, this chapter.

38. Ibid.

39. Hesse to Plunkett, July 10, 1889.

40. These acquittals were accorded huge, negative significance by big cattlemen, who indignantly cited them time and again as evidence that conviction before a Johnson County jury was impossible. It is a reasonable inference, therefore, that when the acquittals were first rendered, the big cattlemen were offended and angered.

41. Hesse was to comment about this event on numerous occasions, but apparently the first time he wrote an account was in his July 10, 1889, letter to Plunkett. I consider that if any of these versions are accurate, it is most likely the first one. There are several versions of the remark, but Fred Hesse seems to be the original source for each.

42. Hesse, in his July 10, 1889, letter to Plunkett, presents this statement as having been made by Saufley: "[Saufley] said he did not know what we would do to stop the stealing." But this does not ring right. If Saufley was confronted by angry men, as the author believes, the more likely scenario is that someone challenged the judge and hurled the question at him. This certainly fits with the refrain the big cattlemen sounded time and again: What are we supposed to do to stop all the stealing?

43. *Wyoming Reports*, 3:xxix; "Democratic State Ticket," *Sheridan Enterprise*, September 6, 1890; *Sheridan Enterprise*, October 25, 1890, 4, col. 1.

44. Burroughs, *Guardian of the Grasslands*, 130. The "sugan" referred to is also spelled as "sougan" and refers to a blanket or quilt for use in a bunk or on the range.

45. Five months later, the *Sentinel* reported that Elliott and Burritt, along with three other men, went on a ten-day fishing trip. "Local and Personal," *BHS*, December 12, 1885; September 11, 1886 (the Elliott and Burritt brick building was twenty feet by thirty feet and two stories high); April 7, 1888. This last reference contains two articles, one announcing the dissolution of the partnership and the other the appointment of Elliott as county attorney.

46. *BHS*, July 6, 1889, 2, col. 2. By "doing someone up," Mann apparently meant that the prosecution was finding a scapegoat to punish as an example.

47. Ibid.

48. "The Republican Primaries," *BHS*, October 6, 1888; *Buffalo's First Century*, 32.

49. Editorial, *BB*, April 21, 1892, 2.

50. Johnson County criminal case no. 166.

51. Sue Myers asserts that Frank Canton put together the cases against the Hat brand men, motivated by the $1,500 reward. "Jack Flagg Remembered," 3.

52. See Johnson County criminal case nos. 168, 172, 173, and 175–78, as well as vol. 1 of the Johnson County District Court Criminal Appearance Docket, including pp. 184, 186, and 194.

53. See Hesse to Wolcott, January 25, 1893. William C. Irvine recited another reason, which apparently came via Elliott and then Fred Hesse, for the refusal of Elliott to proceed with these cases. He stated that "some county attorneys, while admitting we had good cases, would refuse to prosecute unless we would agree to pay expenses of trial, although we were taxpayers in said county, giving as an excuse their counties were too poor to pay the expense." This passage indicates that the big cattlemen were putting heavy pressure on Elliott in the fall of 1891. Hesse was prone to overstatement. In the above letter, Hesse told Wolcott that in 1883, Eb Stewart had been arrested and tried for stealing some cattle and for branding maverick calves "and brought back with the strongest possible evidence," but he was turned loose. There is no record of any charges against Eb Stewart in Johnson County, Crook County, Albany County, or Laramie County. In 1883 it was not against the law to brand mavericks; that was the product of the law forwarded by the Wyoming Stock Growers Association in the 1884 territorial legislature. See Smith, *War on Powder River*, 117.

CHAPTER SIX

1. "Kate Maxwell Lynched," *BHS*, July 27, 1889.

2. "The True Story," *BHS*, August 3, 1889.

3. The primary source for the ensuing discussion is George W. Hufsmith's excellent work *The Wyoming Lynching of Cattle Kate, 1889*. Hufsmith, the composer of an opera about the lynching, developed a deep interest in the event. Over twenty years, he ferreted out independent, primary sources of information and was able to persuasively demonstrate that the version of the event forwarded by big cattlemen was untrustworthy, little more than propaganda. See Hufsmith, *Wyoming Lynching*, 9–15, as well as his discussion in chapter 15 of the same work. I also found chapter 11 of *Devil's Gate*, by Tom Rea, to be helpful, providing a somewhat different perspective from Hufsmith's.

4. See "What They Say," *BB*, June 30, 1892, citing a *Rocky Mountain News* article about newspaper ownership; and Hufsmith, *Wyoming Lynching*, 209, 210. The date of the lynching is not exactly clear from Hufsmith's text, but it must have been Sunday, July 21. George Henderson spotted Ellen Watson's calves on Saturday, July 20, informed Bothwell, then rode fifty miles to Rawlins and took a train to Cheyenne. After the lynchings, someone went to Rawlins and telegraphed Henderson. It would have been impossible to accomplish all this in one day. The first *Cheyenne Daily Leader* article confirms that the killings took place on Sunday. See Hufsmith, *Wyoming Lynching*, 11.

5. Hufsmith, *Wyoming Lynching*, 179, 211–21.

6. Ibid., 36–40, 54.

7. Ibid., 39–57, 152.

8. Ibid. 40–57.

9. See ibid., 39, 43, 136–42, wherein Hufsmith speaks of Ellen's trips to help out neighboring wives who were suffering from illness. See also Rea, *Devil's Gate*, 171. Of particular note is an incident that occurred in October 1887, when Ellen insisted that cowboys who had asked to sleep in her shed during a rainstorm instead used her spare bedroom. It was reported that "Mrs. Averill" said that, "No cowboy is going to make a bed in a cowshed while we have a house."

10. Hufsmith, *Wyoming Lynching*, 59–62. Perhaps when they met, they discovered that they had been born only 150 miles apart in Ontario, Canada, and that both of their families had then moved to the United States. Ibid., 59, 148.

11. Ibid., 60–65, 70–72. Johnson had killed a man named Charlie McLeod. See also Rea, *Devil's Gate*, 171.

12. Hufsmith, *Wyoming Lynching*, 74, 77, 78.

13. Ibid., 78.

14. Ibid., 80.

15. See the 2006 Official State Highway Map of Wyoming.

16. Hufsmith, *Wyoming Lynching*, 81–83, 86.

17. Ibid., 87–90.

18. Ibid., 92–94.

19. Ibid., 94.

20. Ibid., 131–34. Hufsmith takes the position that Averell and Watson were married, but I disagree. Marriage is a legal status, and until and unless all legal requirements are met, including performance of a wedding ceremony, there is no marriage. Wyoming does not recognize common-law marriages, and "living arrangements between a man and a woman must be formalized by the state before the traditional protections of the marriage relationship can be invoked." See *Kinnison v. Kinnison*, 627 P.2d 594, 595 (Wyo. 1981). See also 55 CJS *Marriage*, § 30.

21. Hufsmith, *Wyoming Lynching*, 134. This supposition is consistent with the statement of John H. Fales, who wrote that Averell and Watson were engaged and "were only waiting until she proved up on her homestead." Ibid., 144.

22. Ibid., 136. Regarding the log cabin, see ibid., 144, 145.

23. Ibid., 115; Kea, *Devil's Gate*, 182.

24. Hufsmith, *Wyoming Lynching*, 294, 298.

25. Rea, *Devil's Gate*, 182, 183. Regarding Spencer and Darwin, see ibid., 119, citing Hiram M. Chittenden. Regarding Bothwell as a promoter, see ibid., 116, 117. The photograph referred to is found in ibid., 114.

26. Rea, *Devil's Gate*, 182–85; Hufsmith, *Wyoming Lynching*, 181.

27. Rea, *Devil's Gate*, 183, 184.

28. Hufsmith, *Wyoming Lynching*, provides the statements of two men not directly involved in the 1889 conflicts, John H. Fales and Marc Countryman, verifying the sale. The significance of these statements is diminished because they are apparently not contemporaneous. Also, Tom Rea points out that no bill of sale survives. Still, both Fales and Countryman claim to have been present at the sale. Fales's statement is particularly persuasive

because of its detail (he drove the cattle from Independence Rock to Ellen Watson's place), and this evidence is certainly stronger than anything produced by the men who lynched Averell and Watson. Hufsmith, *Wyoming Lynching*, 143–47; Rea, *Devil's Gate*, 181.

29. Rea, *Devil's Gate*, 180–82; Hufsmith, *Wyoming Lynching*, 174, 175.

30. Hufsmith, *Wyoming Lynching*, 177.

31. The commissioners of the roundup were John Sun, John Henry Durbin, and Albert Bothwell. Rea, *Devil's Gate*, 186.

32. Hufsmith, *Wyoming Lynching*, 179.

33. Ibid., 181.

34. Ibid., 182.

35. Rea, *Devil's Gate*, 187.

36. Hufsmith, *Wyoming Lynching*, 182. The moccasins are on display at the Wyoming State Museum in Cheyenne.

37. Kea, *Devil's Gate*, 187; Hufsmith, *Wyoming Lynching*, 184.

38. Hufsmith, *Wyoming Lynching*, 185, 186.

39. Ibid., 185.

40. Rea, *Devil's Gate*, 188.

41. Ibid.; Hufsmith, *Wyoming Lynching*, 190.

42. Rea, *Devil's Gate*, 186 n. 6, 189; Hufsmith, *Wyoming Lynching*, 196.

43. Hufsmith, *Wyoming Lynching*, 180, 196, 258.

44. Ibid., 197.

45. Ibid.

46. Ibid., 206.

47. See Ibid., 328 n. 23.

48. Jack Cooper, a small ranchman, was shot about March 1, 1889, on the Sweetwater north of Rawlins. From stories reporting Cooper's death, it appears that newspapers sympathetic to the big cattlemen were working on smear techniques even before the killing of Averell and Watson. See *Sundance Gazette*, March 8, 1889; and "The Jack Cooper Killing," *Rawlins Journal*, March 16, 1889, copies of which were provided to me by Todd Guenther of Central Wyoming College.

49. See Hufsmith's discussion in *Wyoming Lynching*, chap. 17, and pp. 258, 263. John DeCorey was sent to Steamboat Springs, Colorado. Apparently, he was not considered as a witness, probably because of his age. Hufsmith, *Wyoming Lynching*, 259, 283; Rea, *Devil's Gate*, 189.

50. Hufsmith, *Wyoming Lynching*, 282; Rea, *Devil's Gate*, 189. Of interest is that an estate was established for Ellen Watson, and as part of it, a legal action was filed against John Durbin and Albert Bothwell for the value of the cattle taken on July 21, 1889, which the two men had appropriated; the result of the lawsuit is not known. Hufsmith, *Wyoming Lynching*, 253.

51. Regarding membership in the Wyoming Stock Growers Association, see Burroughs, *Guardian of the Grasslands*, 38, 124, 145. Galbreath is not mentioned in *Guardian of the Grasslands*, but based upon Hufsmith's discussion of him in *Wyoming Lynching*, 108–13, it seems highly likely that he was a member of the association. Regarding Bothwell and Sun, see Hufsmith, *Wyoming Lynching*, 291.

52. Editorial, *BHS*, August 17, 1889, 2, col. 1.

53. *BHS*, September 7, 1889, 2, col. 1.

54. Ibid.

55. Ibid.

56. Larson, *History of Wyoming*, 238.

57. Regarding the attitude toward statehood, see *BHS*, May 25, 1889, 2, col. 1, and June 8, 1889, 2, col. 1. Regarding the county convention, see *BHS*, July 13, 1889, 2, col. 1. When the counties voted on the constitution, a majority of Johnson County voters approved it, but by only forty-four votes. The state turnout was light, only about 45 percent of the turnout in the previous general election. See Larson, *History of Wyoming*, 256.

58. *BHS*, July 13, 1889, 2, col. 1; *BHS*, July 20, 1889, 2, col. 1.

59. Of the six nominated as delegates, Elliott received forty-seven votes, Burritt thirty-seven, and McCandlish thirty-three. Bouton, who received the next most votes, got only 15. *BHS*, July 13, 1889, 2, col. 1.

60. See "Instructions," *BHS*, September 28, 1889.

61. Burritt worked closely with Mead and Johnston, and the resultant constitutional provisions produced such a distinctive system of regulating water rights that William E. Smythe could appropriately declare that Wyoming "is recognized as the lawgiver of the arid region." See Larson, *History of Wyoming*, 254, quoting Smythe's *Conquest of Arid America*. Larson wrote of Burritt's eloquent pleading for the central concept of priority of appropriation. Larson, *History of Wyoming*, 255. The *Cheyenne Daily Sun* stated that "Burritt, of Johnson, is a power, and would be a leader in any convention" (September 21, 1889, 2, col. 1).

62. Wyoming Statutes Annotated, 1:257 (Lexis 2005).

63. Larson, *History of Wyoming*, 256.

64. Ibid., 259.

CHAPTER SEVEN

1. Burroughs, *Guardian of the Grasslands*, 138. Regarding complaints presented to Angus in 1890, see the discussion in chapter 8, infra. The livestock theft charges that were made in 1890 came from independent investigations of Sheriff Angus; no charges followed an investigation initiated by a complaint from big cattlemen. Violence involving cattlemen certainly still existed in Wyoming, as witnessed by the Sweetwater County killing of George Henderson (the John Clay cattle detective) at the hands of a cowboy named Jack Smith. It seems that Henderson's killing, however, arose from a pay dispute and friction between the two men rather than theft allegations, although Clay did refer to Smith as a rustler. See Woods, *John Clay, Jr.*, 105–109.

2. Woods, *John Clay, Jr.*, 118, 119.

3. Clay, *My Life on the Range*, 268. Clay was elected president of the Wyoming Stock Growers Association in the spring of 1890. Ibid., 116.

4. Ibid., 268, 269.

5. Woods, *John Clay, Jr.*, 117, citing *Miles City (Mont.) Stock Growers Journal*, August 30, 1890. Woods, Clay's biographer, describes the article as "obviously written by Clay himself."

6. See ibid., 118; and Stuart, *Forty Years on the Frontier*, xi. Regarding the Montana lynchings, see Burroughs, *Guardian of the Grasslands*, 160, 161.

7. Burroughs, *Guardian of the Grasslands*, 160, vi, vii.

8. "George Dunning's Confession," in Mercer, *Banditti of the Plains*, 158. Members of the Wyoming Stock Growers Association did not hesitate to use assassins (at least until a public outcry inhibited them), as shown by the writing of Dr. Penrose, *Rustler Business*, 37, 38 (discussing the employment of Tom Horn). Penrose also refers to "this secret, and personal or individual method of disposing of the thieves" when discussing the killings of Tom Waggoner, the attempted murder of Nate Champion, and the killings of John A. Tisdale and Ranger Jones. *Rustler Business*, 10. As well, the methodology used by the association was clearly set out by Penrose, following the statements of Irvine. Irvine spoke of arrangements whereby over a period of time H. B. Ijams presented evidence to the Executive Committee of the association, and that committee selected the names of men to be killed. Irvine was on the Executive Committee from sometime in 1883 until at least through the invasion. Penrose, *Rustler Business*, 13; Burroughs, *Guardian of the Grasslands*, 75, 127, 138.

9. Clay, *My Life on the Range*, 138; Burroughs, *Guardian of the Grasslands*, 56, citing a speech by Clay at the 1931 annual meeting of the Wyoming Stock Growers Association.

10. Burroughs, *Guardian of the Grasslands*, 56.

11. David, *Malcolm Campbell, Sheriff*, 133.

12. Regarding his military service, Wolcott was with the Twentieth Regiment, Kentucky Infantry; he entered the army as a lieutenant and came out as a major. This unit was formed out of the Lexington area in January 1862. The regiment was very active throughout the war, including at Shiloh, Corinth, and various other actions. Entry 519A, RG 94, National Archives, Military Records Branch. Regarding his alleged problems in the military, see "The V. R.: Mystery—Shadows . . . and Beauty," and Anonymous, *Alias, the Jack of Spades*, box 2, file 132, Tisdale Collection.

13. "The V. R."

14. Larson, *History of Wyoming*, 128.

15. "The V. R."; *Alias, the Jack of Spades*, 2.

16. Clay, *My Life on the Range*, 138.

17. Ibid., 134.

18. See "The Land Grabber," *Newcastle News*, May 14, 1892; *Alias, the Jack of Spades*, 3; "The V. R."

19. Pat Hall, introduction to *Alias, the Jack of Spades*.

20. "The Land Grabber," *Newcastle News*, May 14, 1892.

21. *Alias, the Jack of Spades*; "The V. R."

22. *Alias, the Jack of Spades*, 3.

23. The following discussion comes primarily from *Alias, the Jack of Spades*.

24. Hall, introduction to *Alias, the Jack of Spades*.

25. Ibid.

26. *Alias, the Jack of Spades*, 10–15 (Notes). A good part of these accusations appears in "The Land Grabber," *Newcastle News*, May 14, 1892.

27. Clay, *My Life on the Range*, 138, 139. Part of the reason for the delay in foreclosure was that the cattle business was in such deplorable condition that there was no benefit to a creditor for taking possession of his collateral. The reference to "supreme beauty" is from "The V. R."

28. One assumes that Wolcott and Irvine socialized, although in the early 1880s Irvine spent most of his time elsewhere. Irvine returned to Converse County in 1886, however, and in 1888 Wolcott and Irvine were part of a three-man committee from Converse County that was supposed to address "depredations" on the range. See Burroughs, *Guardian of the Grasslands*, 184; and "Stock Growers' Meeting," *BHS*, November 24, 1888.

29. Burroughs, *Guardian of the Grasslands*, 180–82. Regarding Irvine's size, see the photograph of the invaders in David, *Malcolm Campbell, Sheriff*, 158 and 209, intra.

30. Burroughs, *Guardian of the Grasslands*, 183, 184.

31. Ibid., 187.

32. See ibid., 187–90.

33. Ibid., 187.

34. "Local and Personal," *BHS*, August 18, 1888, and June 1, 1889; *BHS*, May 18, 1889, 3, col. 4.

35. Johnson County Clerk records, Book 17 of Patents, 494.

36. "Annual Meeting of Stockholders," *BB*, March 19, 1891.

37. Burroughs, *Guardian of the Grasslands*, 166.

38. Clay, *My Life on the Range*, 258.

39. Ibid.

40. Larson, *History of Wyoming*, 257; Burroughs, *Guardian of the Grasslands*, 140.

41. Hall, "Between the Lines," *SunDAY Magazine*, March 5, 1972.

42. "INIQUITOUS: The Law Creating the State Stock Commission; Every Honest Granger and Small Cattleman in the State of Wyoming Should Demand That the Law be Repealed," *BB*, February 25, 1892. When the dispute over the actions of the Live Stock Commission became very heated, the *Bulletin* printed the entire text of the live stock commission act, passed on January 25, 1891.

43. Ibid.

44. See "Honesty Demands an Answer," *BB*, February 4, 1892, as well as the discussion by Smith, *War on Powder River*, 137, 138.

45. See Smith, *War on Powder River*, 137, 138, wherein she refers to *Cheyenne Daily Leader*, February 24, 1892.

46. "Stockmen in Counsel," *BB*, May 14, 1891. Each man named as a trustee, except Mann, was to become a member of the April 1892 invading group.

47. Smith, *War on Powder River*, 138.

48. "Effective Work," *BB*, October 15, 1891.

49. "Exit the Sentinel," *BHS*, October 19, 1889; *BB*, November 20, 1890, 2, col. 1.

50. Smith, *War on Powder River*, 139.

51. "Newspaper Gossip," *BB*, October 29, 1891; *BB*, November 12, 1891, 3, col. 1.

52. "A Timely Topic," *BB*, August 13, 1891.

53. *BB*, August 20, 1891, 3, col. 1.

54. "Front Face," *BB*, September 10, 1891.

55. "Basin Items," *BB*, September 17, 1891.

56. "Newspaper Gossip," *BB*, October 29, 1891; *BB*, November 12, 1891, 3, col. 1.

57. "Forward March," *BB*, January 29, 1891.

58. "Enterprising Buffalo," *BB*, February 5, 1891.

59. "A Wyoming Town," *BB*, February 26, 1891; "Northern Wyoming," *BB*, August 27, 1891; "Johnson County Judged," *BB*, October 1, 1891.

60. *BB*, April 2, 1891, 3, col. 1.

61. "City of Buffalo," *BB*, August 27, 1891.

62. "The Model," *BB*, September 10, 1891.

63. *BB*, April 2, 1891, 3, col. 1.

64. "Buffalo, the Boss Burg," *BB*, July 30, 1891.

CHAPTER EIGHT

1. Penrose, *Rustler Business*, 12, 13.

2. Ibid.

3. In "Between the Lines," *SunDAY Magazine*, February 20, 1972, Pat Hall lists four men in the assassination squad—Billy Lykins, Joe Elliott, Fred Coates, and Frank Canton—and his conclusions are well supported in the historical record. Lykins was probably killed by Nate Champion on November 1, 1891, and Elliott and Coates were indicted by Johnson County for the assault on Champion and Ross Gilbertson (Johnson County District Court criminal case nos. 211 and 212). See Burroughs, *Guardian of the Grasslands*, 115; and T. F. Carr, interview by J. Elmer Brock, February 2, 1935, cited in Nanson, *Powder River Country*, 259. Carr lists the same men as did Hall, except that he referred to a "Woodbox Jim" instead of Fred Coates. "Woodbox Jim" was surely Coates. See also "Nathan David 'Nate' Champion," manuscript, p. 4, box 2, Champion file, Bob Gibbs Collection, Gatchell Museum (hereafter "Gibbs Collection"). George Dunning stated that the four men who attacked Champion and Gilbertson were Canton, Elliott, Tom Smith, and Fred Coats [*sic*], which was correct, except that he inaccurately substituted Tom Smith for Billy Lykins. Dunning also stated that the four were all employees of the Wyoming Stock Growers Association. Mercer, *Banditti of the Plains*, 172, 175.

4. DeArment, *Alias Frank Canton*, 81, 90, 93.

5. "The Powder River Case," *BB*, February 4, 1892; Hope, "Joe Elliott's Story," 156. When Coates was charged with the attempted murder of Champion and Gilbertson, he was defended by the law firm of Lacey and Van Devanter. John Lacey and Willis Van Devanter were the first team of lawyers for the association, and their representation is strong evidence that the association considered Coates an employee. See Johnson County criminal case no. 211.

6. Hope, "Joe Elliott's Story," 160; Burroughs, *Guardian of the Grasslands*, 115.

7. DeArment, *Alias Frank Canton*, 89.

8. "Lynched: Fate of a Weston County Horse and Cattle Rustler," *BB*, June 25, 1891, quoting an article in *Newcastle Journal*. See also the discussion by Smith, *War on Powder River*, 148–49.

9. Smith, *War on Powder River*, 148, 149.

10. Flagg, "A Review," *BB*, June 30, 1892.

11. "Lynched," *BB*, June 25, 1891, quoting *Newcastle Journal*.

12. Ibid.

13. Ibid.; Smith, *War on Powder River*, 149.

14. See Hope, "Joe Elliott's Story," 150–52, which is a transcript of a 1940s interview of Elliott. Regarding the identity of the three men, there is no indication that Frank Canton

was involved in this lynching, leaving the remaining three members of the assassination squad as the probable actors. Elliott and Coates were from the Newcastle area, and Elliott later admitted that he worked a great deal with Lykins. It is also possible that Tom Smith, a former Texas lawman, was one of the three, as George Dunning stated in his confession, but in another situation Dunning listed Tom Smith incorrectly. See notes 3 and 13, this chapter; and Mercer, *Banditti of the Plains*, 159.

15. See Penrose, *Rustler Business*, 17; and W. C. Irvine to Dr. Charles Penrose, December 6, 1913, in "An Era of Violence," comp. Ted Bohlen and Tom Tisdale, 184, in Tisdale Collection; Hope, "Joe Elliott's Story," 150, 151; "The Journal Misquotes Us," *BB*, February 18, 1892.

16. "George Dunning's Confession," in appendix of Baber, *Longest Rope*, 299, and in Mercer, *Banditti of the Plains*, 152–95.

17. Flagg, "A Review," *BB*, June 30, 1892.

18. See Hesse to Glover, November 15, 1889.

19. Al Allison's trouble back in Texas involved a shoot-out in which another man was killed. The Tisdale family was well aware of this. See taped interview of Martin Tisdale in the collection of interviews held by Martin Tisdale's granddaughter Lisa Anderson, Shell, Wyo.; and J. Elmer Brock, "The Hat Brand," box 1, file 10, Tisdale Collection.

20. Myers, "Jack Flagg Remembered," 3. It is not clear exactly how many cattle the Hat brand owned, because in his June 23, 1892, article in the *Buffalo Bulletin*, Flagg makes apparently inconsistent statements. He says that a total of 500 head were distributed to the Hat brand partners, but then he also says that about 80 animals were distributed to each of the five partners, which would total 400 head. It is impossible to know how many animals were traded or purchased locally from small cattle owners, as Martin Tisdale indicated was done by Lew Webb and Tom Gardner. Martin Tisdale was the oldest son of John A. Tisdale, was almost five years old when his father was killed, and as an adult he worked for Gardner and Webb for a few years, until 1910, and was Johnson County sheriff. He also indicated that some mavericks in the Hat brand herd had been taken. Martin Tisdale, taped interview by Johnny Tisdale, provided by Lisa Anderson, Shell, Wyo. See also "John Alfred Tisdale," p. 94, box 2, file 125, Tisdale Collection. There is no question that Al Allison would grab a maverick if he had the opportunity.

21. Hesse to Wolcott, January 15, 1893; Burroughs, *Guardian of the Grasslands*, 184; Martin Tisdale, interview by Frank Hinckley in about 1950, transcript provided to author by the Tisdale family.

22. "In $5,000 Bonds," *BB*, February 11, 1892. See also Mrs. Cash, interview, August 10, 1961, transcript, pp. 10 and 17, box 1, file 27, Tisdale Collection. Helena Huntington Smith found support for the statements of the paper. Smith, *War on Powder River*, 155. See also Mercer, *Banditti of the Plains*, 62.

23. Box 2, Champion file, Gibbs Collection; Hanson, *Powder River Country*, 268.

24. Smith, *War on Powder River*, 155; Flagg, "A Review," *BB*, May 26 and June 2, 1892. Regarding Mr. Spaugh, see chapter 5 of this book and note 33 thereof.

25. Willis Van Devanter to Senator Joseph M. Carey, June 27, 1892, cited by Gould, "Willis Van Devanter and the Johnson County War," 25. Van Devanter stated that he had no doubt that Champion has wronged his clients, but in my opinion this reflects only Van Devanter's empathy for his clients' fervent, but unsupported, hopes.

26. The Shonsey-Champion incident is taken primarily from the descriptions of Smith, *War on Powder River*, 152, 153 (which followed the writings of O. H. Flagg), and "Nathaniel David 'Nate' Champion," manuscript, Gibbs Collection.

27. Flagg wrote about this incident in "A Review," *BB*, June 30, 1992, and it is also addressed in the "Nathaniel David 'Nate' Champion" manuscript in the Gibbs Collection. As noted in chapter 7, infra, the author of *Malcolm Campbell, Sheriff* was Robert David, the son of the foreman for Robert Carey in 1892 (who was also cousin to Carey's wife). In my opinion, much of David's book is not credible. David somehow induced the Campbell family to allow him to write a biography of Campbell. It was published in 1932, when Campbell was ninety-two or ninety-three years old, and the story was much more David's product than that of this ancient peace officer. Instead of being a fair history of Campbell's life, the book was used as a kind of Trojan horse to forward the big cattlemen's version of the 1892 invasion one last time. The book is full of the kind of unsubstantiated and dubious allegations that have characterized the materials put out by the big cattlemen and their supporters, although there are some admissions against interest that can be credited.

28. Hesse to Wolcott, January 15, 1893. It should be remembered that Hesse's comments were written in January 1893, after the dispute between big and little cattlemen had erupted into open warfare and Champion was considered the enemy.

29. Flagg, "A Review," *BB*, June 30, 1892.

30. Smith, *War on Powder River*, 157. This cabin was known as the Hall cabin, and it has never been clear by what right Champion and Gilbertson occupied it. It has been assumed that it was abandoned when they decided to occupy it, but in any event there were no assertions that Champion and Gilbertson were there improperly.

31. "The Powder River Outrage," *BB*, December 17, 1891. Champion provided an account to the *Bulletin* in December, after the killings of John A. Tisdale and Ranger Jones, and this is the source of the statements in this paragraph.

32. Hall, "Between the Lines," *SunDAY Magazine*, February 20, 1972.

33. "The Powder River Outrage," *BB*, December 17, 1891.

34. Except as specifically noted, this account of the attempted murder of Nate Champion on November 1, 1891, is taken from Champion's own statement in "The Powder River Outrage," *BB*, December 17, 1891; T. F. Carr's account in Hanson, *Powder River Country*, 250; Hall, "Between the Lines," *SunDAY Magazine*, February 20, 1972; and Helena Huntington Smith's version in her *War on Powder River*, 158.

35. Interview of T. F. Carr, in Hanson, *Powder River Country*, 260. Burroughs, in *Guardian of the Grasslands*, 115, acknowledged that there was a "rumor" that Lykins was shot while attacking Champion and Gilbertson and that he had died in Missouri in late 1891 from the wounds he received. There are indications that a second man was hit, but nothing beyond an initial report. See "Dunning's Confession," in Mercer, *Banditti of the Plains*, 157, 172.

36. Smith, *War on Powder River*, 158.

37. "The Powder River Outrage," *BB*, December 17, 1891.

38. Ibid.; Flagg, "A Review," *BB*, July 7, 1892.

39. Smith, *War on Powder River*, 159.

40. There are numerous items of information available on John A. Tisdale. The sources on which this paragraph is based include Hanson, *Powder River Country*, 408–11; "An Assassination,"

BB, December 3, 1891; J. Elmer Brock, "Memories and Facts Regarding John A. Tisdale," box 2, file 125, Tisdale Collection; and "John Alfred Tisdale," box 2, file 125, Tisdale Collection; as well as newspaper articles published in the *Buffalo Bulletin* on December 3, 10, and 17, 1891. Regarding Tisdale's family in Texas, see "Made His Last Fight," *Valley County Gazette*, July 21, 1894. As to Al Allison, see note 19, this chapter. See also Burroughs, *Guardian of the Grasslands*, 73.

41. Smith, *War on Powder River*, 159, wherein the recollections of Johnny Tisdale, son of John A. Tindsale, are cited.

42. John Washbaugh indicates that Ranger Jones, like Tisdale, was killed because of what he knew about parties on the "other side," not for what he had done. See "The Murder of Orley E. Jones," statement by John Washbaugh, February 9, 1942, vertical file, drawer 2, Jones, Orley (Ranger) file, Gatchell Museum. All three men—Champion, Tisdale, and Jones—lived in the Hole in the Wall and were probably friends, with Jones living just downstream from Tisdale. See Hanson, *Powder River Country*, 408–11.

43. This paragraph is based upon the T. F. Carr account in Hanson's *Powder River Country* and the account in Smith, *War on Powder River*, 159.

44. There are two principal sources for this event. One is the writing of Helena Huntington Smith from the statements of members of the Tisdale family, and the other is T. F. Carr; their statements are consistent. See Smith, *War on Powder River*, 159; and Brock, "Memories and Facts Regarding John A. Tisdale." A supplemental source is Frank Hinckley's interview of Martin Tisdale in about 1950.

45. Smith, *War on Powder River*, 159; Brock, "Memories and Facts Regarding John A. Tisdale"; and Martin Tisdale interview by Frank Hinckley.

46. See Brock, "Memories and Facts Regarding John A. Tisdale." Flagg wrote that Elliott and Coates were later arrested because their horses and gear, found by Champion, had been traced to them and because Sheriff Red Angus—one of the few people in Johnson County who knew Joe Elliott—recognized him on the day of the attack and could also identify his horse. Flagg, "A Review," *BB*, July 7, 1892.

47. 801(d)(2)(E) of the Wyoming Rules of Evidence sets out this rule, which seems to be a universal rule of law. See 23 CJS *Criminal Law*, §§ 973, and cases cited therein.

48. "Attempted Murder," *BB*, November 5, 1891.

49. "'Small' Cattlemen," *BB*, December 24, 1891. See also *BB*, January 7, 1892, 2, col. 1; and "Who Did It?" *BB*, January 14, 1892.

50. Subsequent events would show a thorough investigation and the careful preparation of a case against those who tried to kill Champion and Gilbertson. See "The Crime Is Coming Home," *BB*, February 11, 1891; and Flagg, "A Review," *BB*, July 7, 1892.

51. "Local and Personal," *BHS*, December 15, 1888.

52. The criminal cases brought in 1889 were primarily the work of other men, including Frank Canton. As to the other charges brought in 1889, see Johnson County criminal case nos. 179–82. Regarding the 1890 criminal charges, see criminal case nos. 183–99. The livestock cases were *Territory v. C. C. Bugher* (192; killing one head of neat cattle), *Territory v. Oglander* (194 and 195; stealing a horse of a value of $75), and *Territory v. Robert C. Dalton* (196; unlawful branding).

53. All but one of the livestock cases was eventually dismissed, apparently because witnesses had left the state or the defendant jumped bail. This is puzzling, because at least two

of the cases had been bound over to the district court after preliminary hearings. "Make Haste Slowly," *BB*, November 19, 1891. The two cases in which the defendant was bound over were those against Bugher and McCarthy. There were other criminal cases in which the defendant was bound over, but Elliott never tried.

54. There were no spring term 1891 trials, apparently because of the ill health of the new county attorney, Bernard Foley, and the McCarthy case was tried by a newly appointed county attorney, Alvin Bennett. Regarding Foley's health problems, see "County Commissioners," *BB*, October 8, 1891; and "Another Man's Beef," *BB*, November 13, 1890.

55. "The District Court," *BB*, November 26 and December 3, 1890.

56. Saufley, in a similar case resulting in a conviction of petit larceny in 1889, had simply assessed a fine. See *Territory v. McDermott* (Johnson County criminal case no. 155).

57. The cattle cases were *State v. Durgin* (Johnson County criminal case no. 201) and *State v. C. H. Reynolds* (203), both for killing a milk cow, and *State v. Page* (204; killing one cow). The other charges referred to were *State v. Liddell* (202; breaking into the Occidental Hotel) and *State v. Sherman* (205; stealing property worth $2,000).

58. See the preceding note. Durgin and Reynolds were acquitted; Page was convicted. Liddell was convicted and sentenced to two years in the penitentiary, and Sherman to ten years. See "The District Court," *BB*, November 19 and December 3, 1891.

59. "No Jail Breaking Here," *BB*, March 5, 1891; "Local and Personal," *BB*, May 21, 1891; "Fire Chief," *BB*, June 4, 1891; "Lively Town," *BB*, October 1, 1891.

CHAPTER NINE

1. The following account of John A. Tisdale's killing is taken primarily from two December 3, 1891, articles in the *Buffalo Bulletin* entitled "An Assassination" and "Be Patient." Another article in the December 10, 1891, edition of the *Bulletin*, "Horrors Accumulate," was also helpful and authoritative. This third article is almost a transcript of the testimony in the preliminary hearing of Frank Canton, and the three articles taken together are excellent, primary sources.

2. Mart Tisdale, interview, tape 29, interview by Tom Tisdale, held by Lisa Anderson, Shell, Wyo.

3. "The Murder of John A. Tisdale," statement of John Washbaugh, Tisdale Collection. Washbaugh's account is of some value, but it was given many years after the event (a comparable statement by Washbaugh about Ranger Jones was not made until 1942; see "The Murder of Orley E. Jones"), and it followed years of discussing the event with Charlie Basch, so I have cited it carefully and only for statements that are consistent with other information.

4. "Be Patient," *BB*, December 3, 1891.

5. This is what was reported in the *Buffalo Bulletin*, but some of the testimony in the Canton hearing was that he left at about 7:00 A.M. In light of some of the other times given, 8:00 A.M. seems more accurate.

6. "Arrested and Acquitted," *BE*, December 12, 1891 (testimony of Samuel Stringer). Stringer was the mail carrier who made this route almost every day, and so his estimate of time should be given special weight. Stringer testified that he overtook Tisdale between 9:00 and 10:00 and that he later met Basch at about 10:00.

7. "The Murder of John A. Tisdale," Washbaugh statement. See also "An Assassination" and "Be Patient," *BB*, December 3, 1891.

8. Basch's identification was to become a key point of contention later. See "Horrors Accumulate," *BB*, December 10, 1891, for the testimony of Basch at the Canton hearing.

9. "An Assassination" and "Be Patient," *BB*, December 3, 1891.

10. "An Assassination," *BB*, December 3, 1891.

11. When preparing for the invasion in Cheyenne in April 1892, George Dunning was told that "the mob would do all witnesses up that knew of any facts that would tend to criminate [*sic*] any of the parties who had been in the employ of the association for the purpose of killing off the rustlers." Mercer, *Banditti of the Plains*, 173, 174. On another occasion in Cheyenne, Dunning was part of a group of several big cattlemen and their employees. Dunning stated that "there was a good deal of talk about the necessity of killing off all men who were witnesses against Elliott, Canton, Tom Smith and Fred Coats." Ibid., 175. After the invasion, when the invaders were brought back to Cheyenne, a reporter from the *San Francisco Examiner* came to Fort Russell—where the invaders were held—and then reported that, with the killing of Champion, the Johnson County authorities had lost their last witness against Joe Elliott. His only source for such information was the men interviewed. "Slayers of the Rustlers," *San Francisco Examiner*, April 25, 1892, 71.

12. Unless otherwise noted, the following discussion is taken from "Horrors Accumulate," *BB*, December 10, 1891; "The Murder of Orley E. Jones," Washbaugh statement; and Flagg, "A Review," *BB*, May 26, 1892.

13. See Smith's discussion, *War on Powder River*, 167.

14. Flagg wrote that there had to be at least two killers; Washbaugh said that he had been told on good authority there were at least three. See note 12, this chapter.

15. "Horrors Accumulate," *BB*, December 10, 1891.

16. Flagg, "A Review," *BB*, May 26, 1892.

17. "All Is Order," *BB*, December 10, 1891.

18. "McKinney Notes," *BB*, December 10, 1891.

19. "Horrors Accumulate," *BB*, December 10, 1891.

20. Ibid.

21. There are two very lengthy reports of this hearing, which closely track the testimony of each witness: "Horrors Accumulate," *BB*, December 10, 1891; and "Arrested and Acquitted," *BE*, December 12, 1891.

22. I estimate that Tisdale was killed about 10:00 A.M. The evidence is that it took about a half hour to go from Buffalo to the scene, riding hard. From there the killer tied his horse and walked one hundred yards to the road. There he spent "some time" at the scene before Tisdale drove through the gulch. I estimate the time from when the killer first arrived at the gulch until he shot Tisdale to be at least another half hour. After the killing, the shooter no doubt stopped the wagon and inspected Tisdale's body, to make sure he was dead. It is not clear exactly how the horses and wagon were then moved off the road, but they were probably tethered off the road and then the killer went back to his horse. In the middle of all this, he had to take some evasive action so that Basch did not see him. He rode back to the wagon and led the horses some eight to nine hundred yards down the gulch, where he shot them (the shots that Basch heard). Apparently after he had killed the horses

and moved westward away from the main road, he discovered that Tisdale's dog was following him and he killed the dog. I estimate that these actions also took about a half hour, which was followed by another half hour back to Buffalo, producing a total time away from Buffalo of about two hours.

23. I am referring to the witnesses George W. Munkres, Dr. Park Holland, James G. Craig, I. N. Pearson, St. Clair O'Malley, Frank H. Eggleston, Robert Dunn, and Dr. John Lott.

24. Parmelee was appointed to the district court bench later in his career, and some of his judicial actions are well known. His handling of the Spring Creek Raid cases (1909) was impressive. Despite a deep conviction that the vigilante actions of sheep raiders had to be suppressed, he addressed every matter presented to him with great fairness, compassion, and integrity. See Davis, *Vast Amount of Trouble.*

25. "Arrested and Acquitted" *BE,* December 12, 1891 (Justice Parmelee's decision).

26. Hiram B. Ijams told George Dunning, "Our men got Tisdale and Jones all right." Mercer, *Banditti of the Plains,* 157. I have no evidence to show this, but I believe that Canton was considered the leader of the assassination squad. In the hierarchy among the participants, Canton was by far the most prominent member.

27. Regarding the possibility that Canton was involved in the Jones killing, see Smith, *War on Powder River,* 168. Smith also writes about a "scrap of local tradition" regarding a feud between Jones and Hesse (161), but the most intriguing observation is that of Dr. Charles Penrose, the invader's physician, who wrote that Jones's death "was credited to Fred Hesse of the cattlemen's party." Penrose, *Rustler Business,* 10. Mercer also indicates that a few persons thought that Hesse was guilty of killing Jones. Mercer, *Banditti of the Plains,* 26. None of the information regarding Jones and Hesse seems authoritative.

28. John Washbaugh stated, "Mr. Jones, Mr. Tisdale, Mr. Nate Champion were not killed for what they had done. They were murdered because they knew too much about other parties that were on the other side." Hanson, *Powder River Country,* 262.

29. One of the persistent contentions of the big cattlemen was that all the honest people of the county agreed with them and that hooligans intimidated them from saying so. One does not have to go far to rebut that position, however. For example, the remarkably one-sided Johnson County election results in the fall of 1892 show that in late 1891 and most of 1892, the *Buffalo Bulletin* was faithfully reflecting the attitudes of an overwhelming majority of people in the county.

30. "Our Position," *BB,* December 17, 1891.

31. Ibid.

32. See chapter 7 of this book and note 53 thereof.

33. "Our Position," *BB,* December 17, 1891.

34. "'Small' Cattlemen," *BB,* December 24, 1891; *BHS,* May 25, 1889, 3, col. 4. See also Smith, *War on Powder River,* 160.

35. "The Powder River Outrage," *BB,* December 17, 1891.

36. "Press Comments, *BB,* December 17, 1891, citing both "A Deplorable Condition," *Rawlins Republican,* and "Take It Home," *CDS.*

37. "Press Comments," *BB,* December 17, 1891, citing both "We May Still Hope," *Carbon County Journal,* and "Hurtful to Wyoming," *Rawlins Republican.*

38. "Press Comments," *BB,* December 17, 1891, citing "The Real Cause," *LB.*

39. "'Small' Cattlemen," *BB*, December 24, 1891.

40. *BB*, January 7, 1892, 2, col. 1; "Who Did It?" *BB*, January 14, 1892.

41. Not only Hesse but other members of the Wyoming Stock Growers Association resided in Buffalo as well, such as Clarke, Holland, and Murphy, and no doubt subscribed to the *Bulletin*. Even if they did not, employees and sympathizers, such as Canton and Burritt, would have informed Irvine, Wolcott, and Ijams of the statements in the *Bulletin*.

CHAPTER TEN

1. David, *Malcolm Campbell, Sheriff*, 151.

2. See Smith, *War on Powder River*, 175. Basch told several different stories through the years, providing great detail about his identification of Canton, but any such later testimony would have been severely compromised by the contrary statements he made just a few days after the Tisdale assassination.

3. "Misrepresentation," *BB*, February 4, 1892.

4. *BB*, November 19, 1991, 3, col. 1; "Death from Diphtheria," *BB*, January 21, 1892; *BB*, January 28, 1892, 3, col. 1. The paper reported that Ruby had died and that Helen survived, but the opposite was true.

5. "The Result," *BB*, January 14, 1892.

6. Ibid.

7. DeBarthe referred to telegrams coming out of Cheyenne but made no comment as to who was behind them. Ibid.

8. Smith, *War on Powder River*, 180.

9. "To Protect Settlers," *BB*, January 21, 1892.

10. "Honesty Demands an Answer," *BB*, February 4, 1892; "A Question of Ownership," *BB*, March 3, 1892.

11. "Honesty Demands an Answer," *BB*, February 4, 1892.

12. "A Public Sentiment," *BB*, February 11, 1892.

13. "Won't Budge an Inch," *BB*, March 3, 1892.

14. Ibid.

15. Ibid.

16. "The Toploftical Commission," *Lusk Herald*, cited in *BB*, March 3, 1892.

17. "Good Logic," *BB*, March 10, 1892, quoting *Douglas Graphic*.

18. Yoshida, "Wyoming Election of 1892," 33. See also Smith, *War on Powder River*, 138.

19. "Time to Call a Halt," *CDL*, reprinted in *BB*, March 31, 1892.

20. "Leader v. Commission," *BB*, March 31, 1992.

21. Ibid.

22. "The Powder River Case," *BB*, February 4, 1892; "In $5,000 Bonds," *BB*, February 11, 1892.

23. "In $5,000 Bonds," *BB*, February 11, 1892.

24. "The Powder River Case," *BB*, February 4, 1892; "Something Going to Drop," *BB*, quoting *Gillette News*, February 4, 1892.

25. "Bail Furnished," *BB*, March 10, 1892.

26. Hope, "Joe Elliott's Story," 156.

27. From the investigation of the Tisdale murder, it appears that the killer returned to Buffalo after he shot Tisdale.

28. See chapter 8 in this work, note 46.

29. In 1892 the automatic penalty for first-degree murder was death; §§ 870, Wyoming 1887 Statutes and §§ 4710, Wyoming 1899 Statutes. See Davis, *Goodbye, Judge Lynch*, 70. First-degree murder is established by proof of premeditation, and a direction to kill Tisdale would certainly have proven premeditation.

30. Hope, "Joe Elliott's Story," 157.

31. Smith, *War on Powder River*, 158. In "The Stock Association," *BB*, October 4, 1894, it is stated that the proceeds from the sale of Ross Gilbertson's cattle were held up for a short time. Gilbertson was not as important a witness as Champion, in that he could apparently make no identifications, but he would probably have been helpful to corroborate Nate's testimony.

32. "Ono Oddities," *BB*, March 17, 1892.

33. "Two Remarkable Documents," *BB*, March 24, 1892. See chapter 17, infra, regarding Charles Burritt, who was probably one of the sources of the things Judge Blake heard.

34. Ibid. In his last sentence, Bennett is apparently referring to the actions of Angus in heading off any attempts at lynching.

35. "Sensational! O, No," *BB*, March 31, 1892.

36. See *BB*, March 31, 1892, 2.

37. "Four Bad Men," *BB*, March 31, 1892, from *Chicago Blade*, March 22, 1892. There are two articles about the Champion family in the Jim Gatchell Memorial Museum, one a 1992 paper by Bonnie Neal-Smith; both are found in box 2, Champion file, Gibbs Collection.

38. "Four Bad Men," *BB*, March 31, 1892, from *Chicago Blade*, March 22, 1892.

39. "Comment Unnecessary," *BB*, April 7, 1892.

40. Ibid.

41. "More Murder Promised," *BB*, March 17, 1892, citing the *Big Horn County Rustler*.

42. David, *Malcolm Campbell, Sheriff*, 151.

43. Just seven months later, Dunning was to set out in exhaustive detail the entire exchange with Ijams. Dunning's statement can be found in Mercer, *Banditti of the Plains*, 151–95.

44. The following discussion directly follows the confession of George Dunning in ibid., 151 et seq.

45. See the editorial in *BB*, March 31, 1892, 2, wherein DeBarthe described the "Four Bad Men" story in the *Chicago Herald* as a fair example "of the rot that finds its way to the eastern press from Cheyenne" and further observed, "It is almost needless to add that the whole story originated in the brain of the most accomplished liar whose residence is at the state capital."

46. "Very Inconsistent," *BB*, April 7, 1892. It is not clear to which persons DeBarthe is referring, but one of them was certainly Frank Canton and another probably St. Clair O'Malley, the *Cheyenne Daily Sun* correspondent in Buffalo.

47. Ibid.

CHAPTER ELEVEN

1. This discussion of the background of Drs. Penrose and Barber comes from McGreevy, "Amos Barber, Charles Penrose, and the War on Powder River," 632–38; and Penrose, *Rustler Business*.

2. See Roberts, "Cowboys Form a Health Cooperative," 63–69.

3. Penrose, *Rustler Business*, 3, 11.

4. Ibid., 7.

5. The admissions of David are especially telling because his sources included W. E. Guthrie (a prominent cattleman who was one of the leaders of the invading group), Mike Shonsey, and, of course, David's father.

6. David, *Malcolm Campbell, Sheriff*, 151.

7. Ibid., 152; Mary S. Watkins letter, in "Those Assassins," *Wyoming Derrick*, April 14, 1892. The idea that it would be acceptable in democratic America to assassinate elected public officials and replace them by people selected by the killers is a staggering, stupendously misguided proposition. Different sources have given different numbers for the total on the death list, such as Ijams (thirty—"Dunning's Confession," in Mercer, *Banditti of the Plains*, 160) and Irvine (nineteen; Penrose, *Rustler Business*, 13), but I considered the admissions of David, Guthrie, and Shonsey to be the most probable. I believe the differing numbers can be reconciled since Ijams was referring only to Johnson County and Irvine's statement apparently also only refers to killings within Johnson County, whereas David and others were referring to killings in three counties.

8. David, *Malcolm Campbell, Sheriff*, 167.

9. See "Dunning's Confession," in Mercer, *Banditti of the Plains*, 160, 173, 175. See also "Slayers of the Rustlers," *San Francisco Examiner*, May 25, 1892.

10. David, *Malcolm Campbell, Sheriff*, 152, 153; Penrose, *Rustler Business*, 11, 12; Mercer, *Banditti of the Plains*, 160, 175.

11. See David, *Malcolm Campbell, Sheriff*, 153, where the telegram is set out.

12. Ibid., 154, 155.

13. Ibid., 154.

14. Ibid.; W. C. Irvine to Penrose, February 22, 1914, in "An Era of Violence," comp. Ted Bohlen and Tom Tisdale, 187–97, in Tisdale Collection. As to the current value of $100,000 in 1892 dollars, by way of just one point of comparison, cattle in 1892 were worth about one-fiftieth of their cost in 2008.

15. David, *Malcolm Campbell, Sheriff*, 155.

16. Irvine to Penrose, December 6, 1913, 176.

17. "Dunning's Confession," in Mercer, *Banditti of the Plains*, 160. H. B. Ijams presented this information to Dunning and also stated that he, as well as "two officers of the association," were managing the venture. Ibid., 162. By "two officers of the association," Ijams surely meant Wolcott and Irvine.

18. Irvine to Penrose, December 6, 1913, 174. It is not clear from Irvine's letter exactly when this motion was made (or how many men were present), except that it was on or shortly after the early March meeting at which a plan was formulated.

19. Ibid.; Mercer, *Banditti of the Plains*, 35.

20. Irvine to Penrose, December 6, 1973, 175, 176; Penrose, *Rustler Business*, 11.

21. Penrose, *Rustler Business*, 12.

22. See ibid., 11, wherein Penrose mentions the involvement of Senator Carey's foreman, Ed David; and Mercer, *Banditti of the Plains*, 160, 176. Gould argues, with some merit, that Warren did not know of the expedition before it left Cheyenne; his position is not a majority view, though. Gould, *Wyoming*, 141, 142.

23. Mercer, *Banditti of the Plains*, 160, 176.

24. H. B. Ijams to George Dunning, March 16 and March 17, 1892. box 1, file 81, Tisdale Collection. The letterhead listed Ijams as secretary and the board members as J. W. Hammond (president), W. C. Irvine, and Charles Hecht.

25. Mercer, *Banditti of the Plains*, 166.

26. Ibid., 166–68.

27. Ibid., 169.

28. The .45-90 Dunning received was a Browning Brothers patent firearm and was most probably an 1886 Winchester model, a heavy, lever-action rifle. Jeffrey A. Donnell, interview by author, April 2, 2007. Judge Donnell is the sitting district judge in Laramie, Wyoming, and through a lifetime of studying, purchasing, handling, and firing late nineteenth-century rifles, is deeply knowledgeable about them.

29. Mercer, *Banditti of the Plains*, 173, 174.

30. Ibid., 176.

31. Ibid., 171–74.

32. Ibid., 175.

33. Ibid., 176, 177. Ijams reported to Dunning that the final approval was given at the April 5, 1892, meeting.

34. David, *Malcolm Campbell, Sheriff*, 157, 160, 161.

35. Ibid., 157, 158.

36. See *BB*, February 26, 1891, 3, col. 2; "Easily Settled," *BB*, April 16, 1891; and "Water Rights," *BB*, February 11, 1892.

37. *BB*, January 22, 1891, 2, col. 2.

38. "Stock Association Notice," *BB*, March 12, 1891; "Gives Entire Satisfaction," *BB*, January 22, 1891, citing *CDS*.

39. See the discussion in chapter 5 of this work and note 4 thereof.

40. Burroughs, *Guardian of the Grasslands*, 75.

41. Ibid., 21, 55, 119. It is not clear whether Guthrie was still on the Executive Committee in 1892.

42. Smith, *War on Powder River*, 185–89.

43. David, *Malcolm Campbell, Sheriff*, 158. See also "Regulators in Court," *Chicago Herald*, January 7, 1893; and "Slayers of the Rustlers," *San Francisco Examiner*, May 25, 1892.

44. "Stockmen Meet," *BB*, March 31, 1892.

45. *BB*, November 26, 1891, 3, col. 2; "Forging Ahead," *BB*, February 25, 1892; Smith, *War on Powder River*, 160.

46. "Stockmen Meet," *BB*, March 31, 1892; David, *Malcolm Campbell, Sheriff*, 150, 151.

47. See Smith, *War on Powder River*, 160.

48. Gould, "Willis Van Devanter and the Johnson County War," 20.

49. *BB*, May 12, 1892, 3, col. 1. See also Irvine to Penrose, February 22, 1914, n. 3; "An Injunction," *BB*, May 12, 1892.

CHAPTER TWELVE

1. "Dunning's Confession," in Mercer, *Banditti of the Plains*, 176–78. David states that 2:00 P.M. was the time of departure (*Malcolm Campbell, Sheriff*, 165), but his book was written

forty years after the event, whereas Dunning's recollection was only a few months after. Penrose, whose booklet was written more than twenty years after 1892, says the train pulled out at 5:30, close to the time stated by Dunning. Penrose, *Rustler Business*, 15.

2. David, *Malcolm Campbell, Sheriff*, 168, 169; Mercer, *Banditti of the Plains*, 178.

3. Irvine to Penrose, December 6, 1913, 176.

4. Ibid.

5. The entire night was required because trains of that era did not proceed at anywhere near the speeds they averaged in the twentieth century. Assuming a distance of 180 miles, which is the highway mileage from Cheyenne to Casper, the train averaged about 18 miles an hour to reach Casper at 4:00 A.M.

6. The *Bulletin* named them as W. J. Clarke, cattleman and water commissioner; F. H. Laberteaux, foreman for Henry Blair; F. M. Canton, U.S. deputy marshal; J. N. Tisdale, rancher elected state senator in 1890; H. W. Davis, cattleman; F. G. S. Hesse, cattleman; L. H. Parker, foreman for Murphy Cattle Company; Chas. S. Ford, foreman for Dr. Harris (owner of the T. A. Ranch); A. R. Powers, cattleman; and S. Sutherland, Hesse's brother-in-law. "Baffled," *BB*, April 14, 1892.

7. See the discussion in chapter 7 of this book.

8. "Baffled," *BB*, April 14, 1892.

9. See Smith, *War on Powder River*, 185–89.

10. Ibid. See also Clover, *On Special Assignment*, 230. This book is supposedly fiction about a journalist named Paul Travers, but "Paul Travers" is clearly just a pseudonym for Sam Clover, and Travers has experiences exactly like those of Clover.

11. "Dunning's Confession," in Mercer, *Banditti of the Plains*, 177.

12. Ibid., 178.

13. Smith, *War on Powder River*, 220; "Gone Up North, *CDS*, April 8, 1892.

14. Penrose, *The Rustler Business*, 15; Irvine to Penrose, December 6, 1913, 176.

15. Irvine to Penrose, December 6, 1913, 177.

16. Ibid. Irvine indicates that Wolcott may have provided an excuse for David to remain.

17. Ibid.

18. Penrose, *The Rustler Business*, 16.

19. Penrose, *The Rustler Business*, 16; David, *Malcolm Campbell, Sheriff*, 175; Smith, *War on Powder River*, 198.

20. "Dunning's Confession," in Mercer, *Banditti of the Plains*, 179; Irvine to Penrose, December 6, 1913, 178.

21. Clover, *On Special Assignment*, 239.

22. Penrose, *The Rustler Business*, 16; Irvine to Penrose, December 6, 1913, 178, 179.

23. Smith, *War on Powder River*, 201; Brayer, "New Light on the Johnson County War."

24. Brayer, "New Light on the Johnson County War." I agree with Helena Huntington Smith, who believed that stories about Shonsey's having spent the night at the cabin on the KC Ranch with Champion and Ray are not credible. See Smith, *War on Powder River*, 201, 203.

25. If Nick Ray was the "other person" present when Shonsey was forced to name the men who attacked Gilbertson and Champion, there was all the more reason for Wolcott and Irvine to go to the KC. Brayer, "New Light on the Johnson County War."

26. W. C. Irvine to Dr. Charles Penrose, December 16, 1913, in Van Valkenburgh, "Johnson County War," 179. The population of Cheyenne in 1890 was 11,690. Larson, *History of Wyoming*, 263.

27. "The Work of Extermination Begun," *Chicago Herald*, April 13, 1892. For possible sources of letters, see also David, *Malcolm Campbell, Sheriff*, 164, 179; and Mercer, *Banditti of the Plains*, 174, 175.

28. "Gone Up North," *CDL*, April 8, 1892.

29. See "To Weed Them Out," *Denver Times*, April 8, 1892; "To Protect Themselves," *Denver Republican*, April 8, 1892; and "The Expedition," *Denver Sun*, April 8, 1892.

30. Brayer, "New Light on the Johnson County War."

31. Ibid.

32. Ibid.; Smith, *War on Powder River*, 202.

33. "Gone Up North," *CDL*, April 8, 1892.

34. The descriptions by Clover (*On Special Assignment*, 242) and David (*Malcolm Campbell, Sheriff*, 188) are especially graphic.

35. Irvine to Penrose, November 2, 1913, in Van Valkenburgh, "Johnson County War," 157; David, *Malcolm Campbell, Sheriff*, 188.

36. "Dunning's Confession," in Mercer, *Banditti of the Plains*, 181.

37. Ibid.

38. This description comes from David's map (*Malcolm Campbell, Sheriff*, 193) and my visit to the scene.

39. Ibid., 190. See also "Dunning's Confession," in Mercer, *Banditti of the Plains*, 181.

40. "Dunning's Confession," in Mercer, *Banditti of the Plains*, 181, 182; David, *Malcolm Campbell, Sheriff*, 191–94.

41. David provides some self-serving speculation (*Malcolm Campbell, Sheriff*, 178) about those present, but I do not consider it credible. One of his sources, Shonsey, had his own reasons for favoring an attack on Champion and, thus, for exaggerating the situation at the KC.

42. "Dunning's Confession," in Mercer, *Banditti of the Plains*, 182, 183; David, *Malcolm Campbell, Sheriff*, 178.

43. "Dunning's Confession," in Mercer, *Banditti of the Plains*, 183.

44. Smith, *War on Powder River*, 204.

45. "Dunning's Confession," in Mercer, *Banditti of the Plains*, 184; David, *Malcolm Campbell, Sheriff*, 194–96.

46. Irvine to Penrose, November 2, 1913, 158. See also David, *Malcolm Campbell, Sheriff*, 197.

47. "Dunning's Confession," in Mercer, *Banditti of the Plains*, 185; Irvine to Penrose, November 2, 1913, 158; David, *Malcolm Campbell, Sheriff*, 197, 198.

48. Clover, *On Special Assignment*, 250.

49. The invaders always wanted to declare that they suffered no injuries, but David admitted these woundings in *Malcolm Campbell, Sheriff*, 198, 199.

50. This is one of those rare episodes in the Johnson County War for which all the accounts are relatively consistent. See ibid., 199–201; Clover, *On Special Assignment*, 250–52; and Flagg, "A Review," *BB*, July 14, 1892; as well as the testimony of Taylor and Flagg at the coroner's inquest. The testimony of Taylor and Flagg must be given the most weight. The discussion in the text directly follows the testimony recorded in the Coroner's Inquest Report,

Gatchell Museum. Flagg testified at the inquest that he was thirty-two. This conflicts with well-documented family records stating that he was born on February 26, 1863, but in "Jack Flagg Remembered," a reliable article by Sue C. Myers, his birth date is given as February 8, 1860. Flagg surely knew his age, and I can think of no reason why he would have stated "thirty-two" if he was actually twenty-nine, so I settled on thirty-two.

51. David asserted that Elliott yelled, "Shoot the scoundrel, that's Jack Flagg," but Elliott denied this, saying he did not know Jack Flagg. David, *Malcolm Campbell, Sheriff,* 200; Hope, "Joe Elliott's Story," 159. It was Irvine who made the observation about the bridge and the vegetation. Although he exaggerated when he claimed that crossing the bridge meant "certain death" from Champion, it is certainly plausible that the invaders were acutely aware of Champion's field of fire and it made them very cautious. See Irvine to Penrose, November 2, 1913, 157.

52. David, *Malcolm Campbell, Sheriff,* 201. Regarding the time, Flagg stated that it was about "15 to 20 minutes to three o'clock in the afternoon." See also Smith, *War on Powder River,* 206; and Coroner's Inquest Report, 8 (testimony of Jack Flagg).

53. Smith testified at the coroner's inquest, and this discussion directly follows his testimony. Coroner's Inquest Report, 4.

54. A story in the *Bulletin* states that Smith arrived about 7:30 P.M. "Baffled," *BB,* April 14, 1892. Mary Watkins, however, stated that Smith did not arrive until almost midnight. Watkins letter, April 14, 1892.

55. Irvine to Penrose, November 2, 1913, 159.

56. Ibid.

CHAPTER THIRTEEN

1. Several eyewitnesses gave accounts of the burning of the KC Ranch house—Irvine, Dunning, Canton, Clover, and David (through Guthrie and Shonsey). As well, Helena Huntington Smith, in chapter 8 of *War on Powder River,* describes at length the events of April 9. Surprisingly, in many instances, Billy Irvine's account seems to be one of the best. When he wasn't emotionally involved, Irvine had a fine eye for detail and was an excellent reporter.

2. Irvine to Penrose, November 2, 1913.

3. Smith, *War on Powder River,* 207; "Dunning's Confession," in Mercer, *Banditti of the Plains,* 186; Clover, *On Special Assignment,* 252–55.

4. Irvine to Penrose, November 2, 1913.

5. Clover, *On Special Assignment,* 254.

6. Smith, *War on Powder River,* 207; David, *Malcolm Campbell, Sheriff,* 203.

7. Descriptions differ as to where Champion came out of the burning cabin. Dunning says Champion ran out of the south end of the house (*Banditti of the Plains,* 186), David says the roof of a dugout (*Malcolm Campbell, Sheriff,* 204), and Clover says the rear door (*On Special Assignment,* 255). Helena Huntington Smith did not provide her own opinion but quoted Sam Clover at length.

8. Mercer, *Banditti of the Plains,* 186.

9. The description of the killing of Champion is taken primarily from David, *Malcolm Campbell, Sheriff,* 204. David's account contains good detail and is consistent with other evidence,

such as the examination of Dr. Park Holland, set out in the Coroner's Inquest Report, 6, and "Dunning Confession," in Mercer, *Banditti of the Plains*, 186. Whenever David found an opportunity to be critical of Johnson County people, he seized it zealously, so much of his writing must be taken with a large grain of salt. But when he provided a narrative with good detail and without apparent emotional involvement, and if his statements were otherwise consistent with more reliable information, I felt they were probably accurate.

10. David, *Malcolm Campbell, Sheriff*, 205.

11. Canton, *Frontier Trials*, 91, 92.

12. Clover, *On Special Assignment*, 255.

13. Irvine to Penrose, February 22, 1914, 190.

14. Smith, *War on Powder River*, 208, from ibid., 188.

15. Irvine to Penrose, February 22, 1914, 188.

16. "Regulators in a Trap," *Chicago Herald*, April 16, 1892. The story is datelined Edgemont, S.Dak., April 15, 1892. The same story was printed in the *Cheyenne Daily Leader* on April 19, with Clover identified as the author.

17. Clover, *On Special Assignment*, 269.

18. Clover to Henry Blair, May 15, 1892, quoted in Brayer, "New Light on the Johnson County War," 89.

19. Irvine to Penrose, February 22, 1914, 189.

20. See Smith, *War on Powder River*, 208. Besides concealing his active role with the invaders, other information shows Clover's tendencies. Helena Huntington Smith observed that Clover was "never notorious for his dedication to the truth" (*War on Powder River*, chap. 28, n. 11). Charles Penrose and Irvine complained that Clover took valuable property and never returned it. Smith, *War on Powder River*, 198.

21. "Bloodshed in the North!" *Bill Barlow's Budget*, April 13, 1892. This same statement was also published as "Nate Champion's Diary" in the *Cheyenne Daily Leader*, April 14, 1892, but its source may have been the same "special correspondent" referred to in the *Budget*.

22. Irvine to Penrose, November 2, 1913, 160; David, *Malcolm Campbell, Sheriff*, 208.

23. David, *Malcolm Campbell, Sheriff*, 209.

24. Clover to Blair, May 15, 1892; Smith, *War on Powder River*, 202, 208.

25. David, *Malcolm Campbell, Sheriff*, 209.

26. Irvine to Penrose, November 2, 1913, 160; Smith, *War on Powder River*, 210; David, *Malcolm Campbell, Sheriff*, 211.

27. This description of Flagg's actions after he left the area of the KC Ranch follows Flagg's testimony before the coroner's jury.

28. This passage primarily follows Smith, *War on Powder River*, 214, whose description seems well supported. Regarding Wolcott's assumption of command, see Irvine to Penrose, November 2, 1913, 160.

29. "Regulators in a Trap," *Chicago Herald*, April 16, 1892.

30. Regarding Dudley, see Mercer, *Banditti of the Plains*, 188; and Irvine to Penrose, November 2, 1913, 160. Regarding the rider, see Mercer, *Banditti of the Plains*, 188; Canton, *Frontier Trails*, 93; and Clover to Blair, May 15, 1892, 215. Canton stated that the rider was James Craig (with John Pierce), as did Irvine, but David said the man was Phil DuFran. David, *Malcolm Campbell, Sheriff*, 216.

31. David, *Malcolm Campbell, Sheriff*, 216; Irvine to Penrose, November 2, 1913, 162; Mercer, *Banditti of the Plains*, 189. I consider the Irvine account as the least reliable of these three, accurate in its general description but filled with improbable posturing.

32. Regarding the actions of Bessie and Omie Smith, see the topic "John R. Smith," in the proceedings of the Johnson County War Seminar, July 31–August 1, 1997, printed by the Johnson County Historical Society; and Mercer, *Banditti of the Plains*, 189.

33. Canton, *Frontier Trails*, 93. See also Clover to Blair, May 15, 1892, 213, in Brayer, "New Light on the Johnson County War."

34. Smith, *War on Powder River*, 214.

35. Ibid.

36. Ibid.

37. "Slayer of the Rustlers," *San Francisco Examiner*, April 25, 1892.

38. This was supposedly the proclamation of the man who rode in from Buffalo, delivering the warning to "turn back." Irvine to Penrose, November 16, 1913, 161, in Van Valkenburgh, "Johnson County War," 161.

39. Myers, "Memories of the Battle at the TA Ranch."

40. Mercer, *Banditti of the Plains*, 189. Percy Brockway, a cowboy who stopped into the T. A. Ranch just about the time the invaders arrived, testified at the coroner's inquest that Major Wolcott believed he could obtain assistance from the druggist "Eagleston" (referring to Frank Eggleston, who had been the county coroner) and from a man referred to by the incomplete name of "Munk" (almost certainly a reference to George Munkres, a Buffalo merchant and Canton ally).

41. David, *Malcolm Campbell, Sheriff*, 218.

42. Clover, *On Special Assignment*, 267.

CHAPTER FOURTEEN

1. See "Bloody Battle with Rustlers," *New York World*, April 13, 1892. The description found in this New York paper is particularly good, obviously written by a reporter who was on the scene. Part of my description is also based on my overnight stay at the T. A. in the mid-1990s; the original barn and log house are still there.

2. "Bloody Battle with Rustlers," *New York World*, April 13, 1892; Canton, *Frontier Trails*, 95; David, *Malcolm Campbell, Sheriff*, 219, 220.

3. Clover, *On Special Assignment*, 267.

4. Ibid.

5. Smith, *War on Powder River*, 213; Irvine to Penrose, November 2, 1913, 162.

6. Clover, *On Special Assignment*, 268.

7. Ibid., 271. This follows Clover's retelling of the incident and is probably more flattering to him than the actual event, although it is true that Clover did manage to extricate himself and gain the protection of Major Fechet.

8. Ibid., 273–75.

9. Ibid., 277.

10. "Baffled," *BB*, April 14, 1892; "War!" *Bill Barlow's Budget*, April 13, 1892; Mercer, *Banditti of the Plains*, 68.

11. "War!" *Bill Barlow's Budget*, April 13, 1892. See David's discussion in *Malcolm Campbell, Sheriff*, 12, wherein he criticizes Angus for not first soliciting surrender. But Flagg states that the first shots came from the invaders. Flagg, "A Review," *BB*, July 14, 1892.

12. Regarding Brown's indictment for aggravated assault and battery, see "Local and Personal," *BHS*, April 14 and December 15, 1888.

13. See *BB*, December 24, 1890, 3; and David, *Malcolm Campbell, Sheriff*, 232. I do not know whether Brown had military experience, but it would be logical that he did.

14. David, *Malcolm Campbell, Sheriff*, 236; Smith, *War on Powder River*, 217.

15. David, *Malcolm Campbell, Sheriff*, 237; Watkins letter, April 14, 1892, 1. Of the seven townsmen mentioned, only Robert Foote, Joe DeBarthe, and Angus were identified.

16. Watkins letter, April 14, 1892.

17. Dick Reimann, interview by Bob Edwards, Buffalo, Wyo., April 19, 2008, Gatchell Museum.

18. "Eager for Vengeance," *Chicago Herald*, April 19, 1892; *Buffalo's First Century*, 5.

19. "War!" *Bill Barlow's Budget*, April 13, 1892; David, *Malcolm Campbell, Sheriff*, 211, 223. See also "Caught in a Trap," *CDL*, April 13, 1892.

20. "Both in Casper," *CDL*, April 19, 1892; "Caught in a Trap," *CDL*, April 13, 1892.

21. David, *Malcolm Campbell, Sheriff*, 230.

22. "War!" *Bill Barlow's Budget*, April 13, 1892.

23. "A Quiet Day," *CDL*, April 9, 1892.

24. Ibid.

25. "Still No News," *CDL*, April 10, 1892.

26. "News from the Front," *CDS*, April 9, 1892; "A Battle Anticipated" and "False Reports," *CDS*, April 10, 1892.

27. "News from the North," *CDL*, April 12, 1892.

28. "An Embargo on News (The Wild Rumors)," *CDS*, April 12, 1892.

29. "Cleaned Him Out," *CDS*, April 12, 1892.

30. "Take a Stand," *CDS*, April 12, 1892.

31. *CDS*, April 12, 1892, editorial page, col. 2.

32. See "News from the North," *CDL*, April 12, 1892; and "The Militia under Orders," *CDS*, April 12, 1892.

33. Ibid.

34. David, *Malcolm Campbell, Sheriff*, 230.

35. Dowling's adventure is told in detail in ibid., 226, 227.

36. Ibid., 227.

37. Irvine to Penrose, November 2, 1913, 163. "Got the range" refers to sighting in at distance.

38. David, *Malcolm Campbell, Sheriff*, 234.

39. David, ibid., 235, states that twenty-six horses were killed, but this recollection is not as credible as Colonel Van Horn's contemporaneous statement that five horses were killed and several wounded. Colonel J. J. Van Horn to AG, Department of the Platte, April 13, 1892, box 1, file 42, Tisdale Collection.

40. David, *Malcolm Campbell, Sheriff*, 235.

41. Irvine to Penrose, November 2, 1913, 163.

42. David, *Malcolm Campbell, Sheriff*, 242. This is another rare admission by the invaders that some of their number were wounded, and I believe it is credible for that reason. David

made several such admissions, including many that acknowledged how desperate was the plight of the invaders.

43. Smith, *War on Powder River*, 215; David, *Malcolm Campbell, Sheriff*, 239, 240, 243, 245. The Covington Ranch was to the west about a half mile.

44. Irvine to Penrose, November 2, 1913; David, *Malcolm Campbell, Sheriff*, 244.

45. David, *Malcolm Campbell, Sheriff*, 245.

46. See ibid., 246, 247; and Hanson, *Powder River Country*, 316.

47. Donnell, interview, April 2, 2007.

48. David, *Malcolm Campbell, Sheriff*, 252.

49. Irvine to Penrose, November 2, 1913, 165; David, *Malcolm Campbell, Sheriff*, 257.

50. Smith, *War on Powder River*, 219; Clover, *On Special Assignment*, 278.

51. "War!" *Bill Barlow's Budget*, April 13, 1892. The idea has been attributed to Arapahoe Brown and E. U. Snider. See Mercer, *Banditti of the Plains*, 69.

52. "Baffled," *BB*, April 14, 1892.

53. See Irvine to Penrose, November 2, 1913, 170.

54. David, *Malcolm Campbell, Sheriff*, 245, 250.

55. Ibid., 250.

56. Irvine to Penrose, November 2, 1913, 174.

57. David, *Malcolm Campbell, Sheriff*, 251.

CHAPTER FIFTEEN

1. "Rustler War," *CDS*, April 13, 1892; "The Militia under Orders," *CDS*, April 12, 1892; David, *Malcolm Campbell, Sheriff*, 227.

2. "Rustler War," *CDS*, April 13, 1892.

3. Ibid. This telegram is a somewhat different version of one cited by David, *Malcolm Campbell, Sheriff*, 269, probably because Barber fired off more than one telegram to President Harrison.

4. See Smith, *War on Powder River*, 224. This is essentially Asa Mercer's version of what happened the night of April 12, 1892, in Washington, D.C., although Mercer was certainly not the only one to describe these events. Smith describes Grant as the "Acting Secretary of War," which had been true in January 1892, but Grant was the assistant secretary of war in April 1892. See Crockett, *Vermont*; and Mercer, *Banditti of the Plains*, 76. To my knowledge, Mercer's version was never denied by the big cattlemen.

5. Mercer, *Banditti of the Plains*, 75.

6. Ibid., 75, 76.

7. Smith, *War on Powder River*, 225.

8. Ibid. Smith used the word "country" for the wire, but Van Horn, in his April 12, 1892, letter to AG, Department of the Platte, used the word "county" when presenting the same phrase, and said further that the county's citizens were "determined to bring the regulators to justice."

9. Van Horn to AG, April 13, 1892.

10. Ibid.

11. Ibid.

12. Regarding the weather, see David, *Malcolm Campbell, Sheriff*, 269, who states that the moon shone for two hours the night before. None of the several accounts of the last day of the siege indicate that snow or rain was falling. Myers, "Memories of the Battle at the TA Ranch." Mercer, citing "a correspondent on the ground," states that the go-devil had traveled one hundred yards, the *BB* states two hundred feet ("Baffled," April 14, 1892), and George Campbell states "about half way down there" (Myers, "Memories of the Battle"). Even David acknowledges that that the go-devil "had moved to within close range" (*Malcolm Campbell, Sheriff*, 272). See also Mercer, *Banditti of the Plains*, 69. "Baffled," *BB*, April 14, 1892, states that the go-devil began its journey at dawn.

13. Van Horn to AG, April 13, 1892.

14. David, *Malcolm Campbell, Sheriff*, 267.

15. Clover, *On Special Assignment*, 283. There was no "Bertram" among the invaders; Clover probably got a name wrong.

16. Canton, *Frontier Trails*, 99.

17. "Surrendered," *CDL*, April 14, 1892. The correspondent was probably Edgar Payton. See Ewig, "E. T. Payton," 19.

18. Clover, *On Special Assignment*, 282, 283.

19. Van Horn to AG, April 13, 1892; "Would Have Used Dynamite," *Omaha Bee*, April 16, 1892.

20. "Surrendered," *CDL*, April 14, 1892.

21. See "The Northern War," *CDS*, April 16, 1892; and Clover, *On Special Assignment*, 282.

22. Van Horn to AG, April 13, 1892. Wolcott prepared a complete list of all of the weapons surrendered, and it makes fascinating reading. For an excellent article discussing this list, see Murray, "Arms of Wyoming's Cattle War," *Shooting Times*, July 1967.

23. The article "Would Have Used Dynamite" (*Omaha Bee*, April 16, 1892) noted that Alex Lowther was shot in the side, "'accidentally,' it was stated." On April 14, 1892, the *Cheyenne Daily Leader*'s special correspondent, who was on the scene, wrote that Lowther was "struck by a stray bullet." Floyd Bard, in *Horse Wrangler*, 44, wrote that, "The other one [Lowther] got shot in the belly while standing near a window in the TA ranch house." As to Lowther's death, see *BB*, May 19, 1892, 3, col. 1.

24. "Coming to Cheyenne," *CDL*, April 16, 1892.

25. "War!" *Bill Barlow's Budget*, April 13, 1892. See also Wolcott's comments in David, *Malcolm Campbell, Sheriff*, 275; Canton's writing in *Frontier Trails*, 101; and John Tisdale's comments in "Slayers of the Rustlers," *San Francisco Examiner*, April 25, 1892.

26. Van Horn to AG, April 13, 1892.

27. Ibid.

28. See chapter 10 of this book, note 21; "To Investigate," *CDL*, April 5, 1892.

29. See "Caught in a Trap," *CDL*, April 13, 1892; Ewig, "E. T. Payton"; and Smith, *War on Powder River*, 218.

30. This discussion is taken directly from Payton's article, "Surrendered," in *CDL*, April 14, 1892.

31. Irvine to Penrose, November 2, 1913, 165; David, *Malcolm Campbell, Sheriff*, 274.

32. Clover, *On Special Assignment*, 283.

33. *BB*, April 14, 1892, 2, col. 1. Jack Flagg made similar statements about the combative comments of the invaders, saying that many of the invaders were "abusive" and declared they would come back and kill a lot of men, the sheriff included. Flagg, "A Review," *BB*, July 14, 1892.

34. Mercer, *Banditti of the Plains*, 194, 195.

35. See Smith, *War on Powder River*, 227.

36. "Baffled," *BB*, April 14, 1892.

37. Mercer, *Banditti of the Plains*, 79.

38. Only a few years later, in Big Horn County (formed to include former parts of Johnson County), authorities effectively employed the technique of offering a plea bargain to a less culpable defendant in the 1902 murder case of *State v. Gorman*. See Davis, *Goodbye, Judge Lynch*, especially 43–45. Similar tactics were used in the 1909 Spring Creek Raid trials, when two sheep raiders were offered immunity for testifying against the remaining five raiders. Davis, *Vast Amount of Trouble*, 110–14, 190–98.

CHAPTER SIXTEEN

1. Penrose, *Rustler Business*, 24.

2. Ibid., 25.

3. Ibid.

4. See "Don't Remove Them," *CDL*, April 19, 1892, which quotes a *St. Louis Globe-Democrat* article stating that Towse, though "disabled early in the war," rode eighty-five miles in twenty hours to get to Gillette. See also "Cattlemen Besieged," *CDS*, April 13, 1892.

5. This discussion is based on "A Graphic Account," *CDS*, April 14, 1892.

6. Ibid.

7. "Wiping Out Rustlers," *Chicago Herald*, April 13, 1892.

8. "Buffalo, the Boss Burg," *BB*, July 30, 1891. Probably the best demonstration of the numbers of Wyoming newspapers in the late nineteenth and early twentieth centuries is Lola Homsher's *Guide to Wyoming Newspapers, 1867–1967*, compiled for the Wyoming State Archives and available there. Tom Rea has written an interesting article in which he discusses the conflicting Wyoming press coverage of the Ella Watson and James Averell lynching. "Dueling Newspapers: Versions of the Watson-Averell Lynching, 1889," www.tomrea.net/Dueling%20Newspapers.html.

9. "Baffled," *BB*, April 14, 1892.

10. Under the subhead "THE MURDERERS," each of the Johnson County men who were invaders was listed and identified. Ibid.; "The Latest Explanation of the Recent Filibustering Expedition," *BB*, April 21, 1892. The word "parallel" was misspelled in the headline.

11. *BB*, April 14, 1892, 2, col. 1.

12. See the discussions in *BB*, April 14 and April 21, 1892, both p. 2, col. 1; Charles H. Burritt to W. R. Stoll, May 4, 1892. All of the Burritt letters of May–July 1892 are in box 1, file 20, Tisdale Collection.

13. "The Latest Explanation of the Recent Filibustering Expedition," *BB*, April 21, 1892. See also note 9, this chapter. The reference to forty-two men on the invaders' list of targets in the article is puzzling, since several reliable sources state that seventy names were on that list. It may be that "42" referred only to the men in Johnson County who were targeted.

14. *BB*, April 14, 1892, 2, col. 1.

15. See Smith, *War on Powder River*, 138; *CDL*, March 22, 1892; "Leader v. Commission," *BB*, March 31, 1992; "Threatening to Kill," *Douglas Graphic*, April 2, 1892; *LB*, April 4, 1892, 1, col. 5.

16. "Time to Call a Halt," *BB*, March 31, 1892.

17. See Smith, *War on Powder River*, 138; "Time to Call a Halt," *BB*, March 31, 1892; and "The Leader Boycott," *BB*, April 7, 1892, citing *LB*.

18. "Demand by Angus," *CDS*, April 15, 1892.

19. *BB*, April 14, 1892, 2, col. 1.

20. "The Present Situation," *CDL*, April 16, 1892.

21. "Angus Refuses," *CDS*, April 16, 1892; "General Anxiety," *CDS*, April 16, 1892.

22. The following discussion is based upon the editorial "Time for Decided Action," *CDL*, April 17, 1892.

23. See "Coming to Cheyenne," *CDL*, April 16, 1892; "Don't Remove Them," *CDL*, April 19, 1892; Smith, *War on Powder River*, 238–41.

24. "Don't Remove Them," *CDL*, April 19, 1982; "From the North," *CDL*, April 16, 1892; "Kimball's Dispatch," *CDS*, April 17, 1892; "Cattlemen in Peril," *Philadelphia Times*, April 18, 1892. At first, *Bill Barlow's Budget* published anti-invader pieces, but its editorial stance soon shifted. See "WAR!" *Bill Barlow's Budget*, April 13, 1892.

25. "What They Say," *BB*, April 28, 1892, citing the *Sheridan Enterprise*.

26. Ibid., citing *LB*.

27. "Those Assassins," *Wyoming Derrick*, April 14, 1892.

28. "McKinney Department," *BB*, April 14, 1892.

29. "The Victim's Funeral," *Rocky Mountain News*, April 16, 1892; Watkins letter, April 14, 1892; Smith, *War on Powder River*, 230.

30. David, *Malcolm Campbell, Sheriff*, 292.

31. "The Victim's Funeral," *Rocky Mountain News*, April 16, 1892; "Baffled," *BB*, April 14, 1892.

32. "The Victim's Funeral," *Rocky Mountain News*, April 16, 1892.

33. Ibid.

34. The following discussion is based upon the "Coroner's Inquest on Nathan D. Champion and Nicholas Ray," box 1, file 48, Tisdale Collection.

35. See Smith, *War on Powder River*, 269; and "Time for Decided Action," *CDL*, April 17, 1892.

36. "Baffled," *BB*, April 14, 1892. See also "Sheriff Angus a Rustler," *New York Telegram*, April 13, 1892.

37. David, *Malcolm Campbell, Sheriff*, 290.

38. Clover to Blair, May 15, 1892.

39. "Notes," *CDL*, April 19, 1892. That the two articles printed in the *Chicago Herald* on April 20 and April 21 are Towse's is clear. Besides his unmistakable style, there is a reference in the April 20 article to the correspondent's ride from Powder River to Gillette, which was Towse's route when leaving H. W. Davis's ranch.

40. "Eager for Vengeance," *Chicago Herald*, April 19, 1892.

41. "May Fight the Troops," *Chicago Herald*, April 20, 1892.

42. Clover, *On Special Assignment*, 286.

328   NOTES TO PAGES 195–201

43. See Irvine to Penrose, November 2, 1913, 166, 168; "Slayers of the Rustlers," *San Francisco Examiner*, April 25, 1892.

44. See Irvine to Penrose, December 6, 1913, 181.

CHAPTER SEVENTEEN

1. "Gov. Barber Weakens," *Chicago Herald*, April 26, 1892.

2. This paragraph employs the "Willis Van Devanter" chapter of Van Pelt, *Capital Characters of Old Cheyenne*, 157–81, but relies primarily on May 29, 2008, interviews of Willis Van Devanter (the justice's grandson), Poolesville, Md., and Ethel Harris (granddaughter) of Chevy Chase, Md. Mrs. Harris recalls a stern old man who, when she was ten years old, treated her like a small adult, and she remembers how active her grandfather was as a hunter and fisherman, even into his old age. She also remembers the mounted head of a bull mouse in his apartment and references to a hunting trip with William F. Cody. See also In Memoriam to Mr. Justice Van Devanter, appendix 12, 86 L.Ed. 1786.

3. See Gould, *Wyoming*, 126, 128; Larson, *History of Wyoming*, 140, 175, 197; and Yoshida, "Wyoming Election of 1892," 65. Warren insisted that he personally owned only 500 acres, but the company he controlled owned at least 225,000 acres of land.

4. *Wyoming Reports*, 3:xxix. Van Devanter was born on April 17, 1859. Van Pelt, *Capital Characters of Old Cheyenne*, 157.

5. "Willis Van Devanter and the Johnson County War," 24, 25.

6. Ibid.

7. Ibid.

8. See the July 7, 1892, letter from Burritt to Van Devanter, in which Burritt provides invaluable inside information to attorneys for the invaders about the financial difficulties of Johnson County.

9. See "Their Faith in Barber," *BB*, June 2, 1892.

10. The ensuing passage follows "Slayer of the Rustlers," *San Francisco Examiner*, April 25, 1892.

11. In addition to the *Examiner* article, see David, *Malcolm Campbell, Sheriff*, 312.

12. See chapters 4 and 5 of this book. With regard to the number of cattle cases, 1889 was the most active year of the previous four; the dubious 1889 charges involved thirteen indictments against thirteen men for the taking or misbranding of twenty cattle. No cattle cases were tried in 1890 or 1888. Penrose referred to three hundred indictments in *Rustler Business*, 7; in one letter to Penrose (November 2, 1913), Irvine states that seventy cases were nolle prossed by "one stroke of the pen;" in another letter (December 6, 1913), the figure was seventy-five. There is no support among the court files for any of these assertions.

13. *BB*, April 28, 1892, 3, col. 1.

14. Burritt to Stoll, May 4, 1892; Yoshida, "Wyoming Election of 1892," 22, citing *LB*, April 25, 1892.

15. Burritt to Stoll, May 4, 1892.

16. Ibid.

17. Ibid.

18. Charles H. Burritt to W. R. Stoll, May 6, 1892.

19. "Justice, Not Vengeance," *Omaha Bee*, April 22, 1892.

20. See Burritt to Stoll, May 6 and 8, 1892; and Burritt to M. C. Brown, May 8, 1892.

21. Charles Burritt to Hon. J. W. Blake, May 8, 1892.

22. Ibid.

23. See "Demand the Accused," *CDS*, April 23, 1892; Yoshida, "Wyoming Election of 1892," 23, citing *LB*, May 11, 1892; and Charles Burritt to Hon. J. W. Blake, July 8, 1892.

24. Burritt to Henry A. Blair, May 14, 1892.

25. Ibid.; Burritt to Willis Van Devanter, May 15, 1892; Burritt to Henry G. Hay, May 23, 1892.

26. See Burritt's letters to W. R. Stoll, May 24 and July 3, 1892, and to Messrs. Lacey and Van Devanter, June 24, 1892.

27. Burritt to Hon. Francis E. Warren, May 17, 1892.

28. Burritt to Van Devanter, July 7, 1892.

29. Burritt to Blake, July 8, 1892.

30. "The Recent Outrages," *BB*, May 5, 1892.

31. See *BB*, April 28, 1892, 3, col. 1; "County Business," *BB*, August 4, 1892; Yoshida, "Wyoming Election of 1892," 22; and Burritt to Van Devanter, July 7, 1892.

32. Burritt to Van Devanter, July 7, 1892.

33. Ibid.

34. Burritt to Blake, July 8, 1892.

35. Ibid. As noted in chapter 8, the county officials obtained two convictions in late 1891, but during the later 1890s, acquittals continued to be common. See Davis, *Goodbye, Judge Lynch*, 33, 34. In late November 1892 there were charges against two men for cattle theft; one was convicted of a misdemeanor and the other acquitted, a result similar to many cases in previous years. "Legal Items," *BB*, December 1, 1892. See also *State v. Keiser*, criminal case no. 209, in which the prosecuting attorney dismissed a charge of killing horses, because the defendant mistook the horses for elk; and *State v. Brown* (case no. 232) and *State v. Benjamin* (case no. 245), wherein two defendants were convicted of killing and carrying away one head of neat cattle and each was sentenced to the state penitentiary.

36. Gould, *Wyoming*; Burritt to Henry G. Hay, July 2, 1892.

37. Burritt to Hay, July 2, 1892.

38. See sec. 6, chap. 80, General Laws, Memorials and Resolutions of the Territory of Wyoming, 1869, which appears to have remained effective through 1931.

39. Woods, *John Clay, Jr.*, 121–23.

40. Ibid.

41. Ibid., 125. As pointed out in chapter 16, the telegraph line out of Gillette, about seventy miles east of Buffalo, was open during the time of the invasion. See chapter 16, note 4.

42. Woods, *John Clay, Jr.*, 125, 127, 128. Woods reports that some $15,000 came from three Scottish companies Clay was managing, and caused a "tremendous howl" (128).

43. David, *Malcolm Campbell, Sheriff*, 208.

44. "Those Assassins," *Wyoming Derrick*, April 14, 1892.

45. See Smith, *War on Powder River*, 247–49.

46. See Irvine to Penrose, December 6, 1913, 182, 183; David, *Malcolm Campbell, Sheriff*, 320; and Baber, *Longest Rope*, 263.

47. Baber, *Longest Rope*, 259. In general, I don't regard this book as reliable authority, as it is full of unreliable statements such as invented dialogue, as well as many inaccuracies. But the reporting of the memory of Billy Walker about Omaha in May 1892 is probably reasonably accurate. This was something Walker probably reported; he was unlikely to forget it.

48. "The Prostitution of Law," *BB*, May 26, 1892, quoting *Omaha World-Herald*.

49. *BB*, May 19, 1892, 4, citing *Rocky Mountain News*.

50. David, *Malcolm Campbell, Sheriff*, 320.

51. Yoshida, "Wyoming Election of 1892," 26.

52. The following discussion is based on Van Devanter to Carey, June 27, 1892, 25.

53. Gould, "Willis Van Devanter and the Johnson County War"; Yoshida, "Wyoming Election of 1892," 26.

54. Yoshida, "Wyoming Election of 1892," 26.

55. "Cattlemen in Town," *LB*, July 5, 1892. In criminal cases the party bringing the case is always the state, regardless of the county in which the charges were brought.

56. Ibid.

57. "Cheyenne Tomorrow," *LB*, July 7, 1892.

58. "The Cheyenne 'Gang,'" *LB*, July 8, 1892.

59. Ibid.

60. Ibid.

61. "Slowly Progressing," *CDL*, July 9, 1892.

62. "Short and Spicy," *CDL*, July 10, 1892; "Nearing the Climax," *CDL*, July 14, 1892.

63. "Short and Spicy," *CDL*, July 10, 1892.

64. "Where Will It Be?" *CDL*, July 12, 1892.

65. "Nearing the Climax," *CDL*, July 14, 1892.

66. Ibid. See also "And Now for the Trial," *CDS*, January 5, 1893.

67. "Nearing the Climax," *CDL*, July 14, 1892.

68. "Trial at Cheyenne," *LB*, July 19, 1892.

69. See "J. W. Blake Is Dead," *LB*, February 25, 1895. Until 1893 the Second Judicial District included Albany, Natrona, and Johnson counties, but after January 1893, Johnson County became part of the Fourth Judicial District. See *Wyoming Reports*, 4:iii. Regarding the sentiment in Natrona and Albany counties, their leading newspapers had consistently sided with Johnson County, and in the 1892 election the two counties went Democratic. See notes 17, 26–28, chapter 16 of this book, and notes 70 and 71, this chapter. See also Mercer, *Banditti of the Plains*, 160.

70. "Judge Blake Speaks," *BB*, June 16, 1892. For a discussion of the big cattlemen's campaign for the imposition of martial law in Johnson County, see chapter 18, infra.

71. See "Trial at Cheyenne," *LB*, July 19, 1892, in which the entire opinion of Judge Blake is printed.

72. Ibid.

73. See, for example, the case of *State v. Brink*, in which the Big Horn County attorney began the trials against five defendants by presenting evidence against only Brink. Davis, *Vast Amount of Trouble*.

74. "To Join Their Cronies," *LB*, August 1, 1892; "The Cattlemen's Case," *LB*, July 20, 1892.

75. "Want To Try Four," *LB*, August 6, 1892.

76. Ibid. A letter from Willis Van Devanter to his father on January 4, 1893, shows that this was exactly Van Devanter's motivation. Gould, "Willis Van Devanter and the Johnson County War," 27.

77. "Cattlemen Were in Court," *CDS*, August 7, 1892.

78. "To Be Tried August 22," *LB*, August 8, 1892; Yoshida, "Wyoming Election of 1892," 27.

79. Ibid.

80. Yoshida, "Wyoming Election of 1892," 27.

81. "Stockmen Released," *LB*, August 10, 1892.

82. "To Be Tried August 22," *LB*, August 8, 1892; Yoshida, "Wyoming Election of 1892," 27.

CHAPTER EIGHTEEN

1. Probably the best demonstration of the cattlemen's confused thinking about martial law is the July 23, 1892, letter from Senator Francis E. Warren to W. C. Irvine, discussed later in this chapter.

2. See "The Situation Reviewed," *BB*, June 9, 1892; and "Judge Blake Speaks," *BB*, June 16, 1892. For a general discussion of martial law, see 93 CJS *War and National Defense*, § 48.

3. "Give Us a Rest," *BB*, June 2, 1892.

4. Regarding Bouton, see "Echo Suppressed," *CDS*, April 27, 1892. Bouton made himself enormously unpopular in Johnson County because his newspaper supported the big cattlemen. This *Sun* article is wholly one-sided, an opinion piece in all but name.

5. See the discussions in chapters 5–7 of this book.

6. "The Wyoming Cattle War," *Salt Lake Tribune*, April 23, 1892.

7. "The Ballot Is the Remedy," *BB*, May 12, 1892.

8. "Indignant," *Rock Springs Miner*, April 20, 1892; "Had Only Begun," *Pioneer Press*, April 23, 1892. It is not clear whether the two stories were referring to the same four officers.

9. F. E. Warren to Henry Hay, July 31, 1892, General Correspondence/Letterbook, Francis E. Warren papers, American Heritage Center, Laramie, Wyo.

10. See *Sheridan Post*, April 21, 1892, 2, col. 2; "Citizens Well Pleased with President Harrison's Message," and "The Big Horn Resolutions," *Sheridan Post*, April 28, 1892; *BB*, April 28, 1892, 2, col. 2; "Banner Briefs," *BB*, May 5, 1892; "Resolutions," *BB*, May 12, 1892; and Baber, *Longest Rope*, 187–90.

11. "Resolution of Condemnation," *BB*, April 28, 1892.

12. "Resolutions," *BB*, May 12, 1892.

13. "What They Say," *BB*, citing *Lander Mountaineer*, May 26, 1892.

14. "Killed by a Rustler," *Denver Republican*, May 11, 1892.

15. Ibid. See also Smith, *War on Powder River*, 255, 256.

16. "Killed by a Rustler," *Denver Republican*, May 11, 1892.

17. "Scoring the Rustlers," *Chicago Herald*, May 14, 1892.

18. *BB*, May 5, 1892, 2, col. 2.

19. *BB*, May 12, 1892, 2, col. 1; "$2,500 Reward," *BB*, June 9, 1892.

20. Burritt to J. P. Rankin, U.S. Marshal, May 17, 1892.

21. Brayer, *Range Murder*, 13. Regarding Burritt's very negative comments about Angus, see Burritt to Van Devanter, May 15, 1892.

22. Burritt to Blair, May 14, 1892; Burritt to Van Devanter, May 15, 1892.

23. Burritt to Hon. W. R. Stoll, June 15, 1892.

24. Angus provided Burritt with a list of six names, including Henry Smith, but when asked to state the three most likely perpetrators, he listed Charles Taylor, Frank Smith, and Ed Starr (ibid.). The names that Burritt listed were Henry Smith, Johnson Long, Clayton Crews, and Charles Taylor (Burritt to Hon. W. R. Stoll, May 22, 1892). The actual three killers were Ed Starr, Henry Smith, and Charles Denby (Brayer, *Range Murder*, 17). In his pamphlet *Range Murder*, Herbert Brayer persuasively demonstrated, by use of the discovery of Wellman's pistol forty-six years later, the identity of the actual killers. Unfortunately, Brayer's general comments about the Johnson County War and the Wellman killing demonstrate a thoroughgoing bias in favor of the big cattlemen.

25. Martin Allison Tisdale, "The Wellman Story," tape recording, December 1952, Tisdale Collection.

26. Burritt to Stoll, May 22, 1892; *BB*, July 28, 1892, 3, col. 3.

27. "After Angus and Rader," *CDS*, May 17, 1892; *BB*, June 9, 1892, 3, col. 1; "About Martial Law," *BB*, June 9, 1892.

28. See Gould, *Wyoming*, 149, 150.

29. See ibid., 150, 153.

30. *BB*, April 28, 1892, 3, col. 4.

31. Gould, *Wyoming*, 150.

32. Yoshida, "Wyoming Election of 1892," 25; "Troops Ordered In;" *BB*, June 9, 1892; *BB*, June 16, 1892, 3, col. 1.

33. Yoshida, "Wyoming Election of 1892," 26.

34. Larson, *History of Wyoming*, 266.

35. Probably the best demonstration of Warren's commitment to the big cattlemen's cause is his July 31, 1892, letter to Henry Hay.

36. Lewis Gould discusses Warren's plan in "Francis E. Warren and the Johnson County War," 131, and in *Wyoming*, chaps. 6 and 7.

37. Gould, "Francis E. Warren and the Johnson County War," 137.

38. The following discussion is based on the October 31, 1892, letter from J. P. Rankin to William H. Miller, Attorney General of the United States, box 3, Johnson County War file, Gibbs Collection.

39. Gould, *Wyoming*, 152.

40. Ibid., 156.

41. Warren to Irvine, July 23, 1892, 198–210.

42. Ibid., 200, 201.

43. Ibid., 202, 203.

44. Ibid., 205.

45. Ibid., 206, 207.

CHAPTER NINETEEN

1. Gould, "Willis Van Devanter and the Johnson County War," 19.

2. *CDS*, April 16, 1892, 2, col. 1; Burritt to Blake, May 8, 1892.

3. *BB*, April 14, 1892, 2, col. 1. See, for example, "Buffalo Will Celebrate," *BB*, June 23, 1892; and "The Solution," *BB*, July 7, 1892.

4. "Coming Events Cast Their Shadows Before," *BB*, June 9, 1892.

5. Warren to Irvine, July 23, 1892, 208.

6. Gould, "Willis Van Devanter and the Johnson County War," 24.

7. "The Heavy Owners," *BHS*, August 24, 1888; "Call for Republican State Convention," *BB*, March 24, 1892.

8. Baber, *Longest Rope*, 265, citing *Rocky Mountain News*, May 12, 1892.

9. "Some Real History," *Douglas Graphic*, May 21, 1892.

10. Yoshida, "Wyoming Election of 1892," 44.

11. Gould, *Wyoming*, 159. It should be pointed out that though the Republican Party received the blame for the invasion (richly deserved because of the party's support of the invasion), many of the invaders and their direct supporters were not Republicans, including, most prominently, George W. Baxter, Warren's 1890 gubernatorial opponent. Baxter, while firmly allied with the invaders, was a Democrat. See Larson, *History of Wyoming*, 263–65.

12. Yoshida, "Wyoming Election of 1892," 24.

13. Ibid., 24. See also *State v. Kimball*, Laramie County criminal case no. 3-365. "Libel" is a malicious publication.

14. Gould, "A. S. Mercer and the Johnson County War," 11.

15. See, for example, "What They Say," *BB*, June 23, 1892.

16. Yoshida, "Wyoming Election of 1892," 58.

17. Gould, *Wyoming*, 160.

18. See "What They Say," *BB*, June 23, 1892; and Smith, *War on Powder River*, 277. The suit was finally dismissed by agreement of the parties in December 1892.

19. Gould, "A. S. Mercer and the Johnson County War," 7.

20. The organization was the Inter-Mountain Stock Growers Association. Ibid., 9.

21. Ibid., 10, citing Mercer's editorial in *Northwestern Live Stock Journal*, July 8, 1892.

22. Ibid., 10.

23. Ibid., 7; Woods, *Asa Shinn Mercer*, 20.

24. Gould, "A. S. Mercer and the Johnson County War."

25. Ibid., 12.

26. Ibid., 13, quoting *Northwestern Live Stock Journal*.

27. Ibid., 13, 14.

28. "What They Say," *BB*, July 7, 1892, quoting *LB*.

29. Yoshida, "Wyoming Election of 1892," 38, 39.

30. See Ibid., 39, citing *CDS*, July 30, 1892.

31. Republicans in Wyoming had been greatly assisted by the continuous occupancy of the U.S. presidency by Republicans from 1868, except for a term by Grover Cleveland. The territorial governor was appointed by the president, and Republican presidents selected Republican governors. See Larson, *History of Wyoming*, 144; Yoshida, "Wyoming Election of 1892," 40, 41.

32. Yoshida, "Wyoming Election of 1892," 41 (summary of Democratic platform).

33. Ibid., 41, par. 5, n. 12.

34. Ibid., 41, par. 4, n. 12.

35. "What They Say," *BB*, June 30, 1892.

36. "What They Say," *BB*, May 26, 1892.

37. Yoshida, "Wyoming Election of 1892," 32.

38. "The Governor," *Wyoming Derrick*, April 28, 1892.

39. See *BB*, May 5, 12, 19, and 26 and June 2, 9, 16, 23, and 30, 1892. The newspapers were *Newcastle (Wyo.) Journal, Laramie Boomerang, Wyoming Derrick* (Casper), *Rocky Mountain News* (Denver), *Idaho Journal, Omaha World-Herald, Iowa Park Texan, Lusk (Wyo.) Herald, Lander (Wyo.) Mountaineer, Rock Springs (Wyo.) Miner, Laramie Sentinel, Irrigation Age, Wyoming Commonwealth, Laramie Times, Natrona Tribune* (Casper), *Seattle Post-Intelligencer*, and *Cheyenne Daily Leader*.

40. The following discussion is directly based on "How Is This?" *BB*, May 19, 1892.

41. *BB*, May 19, 1992, 2, col. 3.

42. "Looking Forward," *BB*, June 16, 1892.

43. *BB*, June 30, 1892, 2, col. 2.

44. "The Situation," *BB*, July 7, 1892.

45. *BB*, July 14, 1892, 2, col. 3.

46. *BB*, July 28, 1892, 3, col. 4.

47. *BB*, August 4, 1892, 2, col. 1.

48. "Introductory," *BB*, August 11, 1892.

49. *CDL*, August 10, 1892, 2, col. 1.

50. Gould, "Francis E. Warren and the Johnson County War," 141.

51. "After Rankin's Scalp," *CDL*, September 17, 1892; "Rankin's Resignation," *CDL*, September 18, 1892. See also "The Rankin Matter," *CDL*, September 18, 1892; "A Midnight Ride," *CDL*, September 20, 1892; and "The Plot Revealed," *CDL*, September 21, 1892.

52. "A Midnight Ride," *CDL*, September 20, 1892.

53. "Dismissed Because He Would Not Abuse His Authority," *CDL*, September 22, 1892.

54. Gould, *Wyoming*, 168.

55. Ibid., 167, 168.

56. Ibid., 168. Dunning's confession is printed in its entirety in Mercer, *Banditti of the Plains*, 152–95.

57. H. B. Ijams to George Dunning, March 17 and 18, 1892, box 1, file 81, Tisdale Collection. The letters are reproduced herein in chapter 11.

58. Regarding the denials by Barber and others, see "Are Prompt to Speak Out" and "The Governor's Statement," *CDS*, October 18, 1892.

59. "The Wyoming Cattle War," *Frank Leslie's Weekly*, June 2, 1892. The ensuing discussion is based upon this article.

60. Gould, *Wyoming*, 169.

61. Ibid.

62. Mercer, *Banditti of the Plains*, 151.

63. Ibid.

64. *BB*, August 25, 1892, 2.

65. "The People's Party," *BB*, September 1, 1892. Wyoming was not the only place that dabbled in the politics of "fusion" in the 1890s. See Ficken, *Washington State.*

66. Gould, *Wyoming*, 162.

67. "Fusion," *CDL*, September 27, 1892.

68. Ibid.

69. Yoshida, "Wyoming Election of 1892," 47–49.

70. The following passage is based on "A Test Case," *CDL*, September 21, 1892; and Yoshida, "Wyoming Election of 1892," 63.

71. *BB*, September 29, 1892, 2, col. 2; "The County Convention," *BB*, October 6, 1892; "Official Ballot of Johnson County," *BB*, November 24, 1892.

72. *BB*, September 29, 1892, 2, col. 3.

73. *BB*, October 6, 1892, 2, col. 4.

74. "That Corporal's Guard," *BB*, November 3, 1892.

75. Gould, *Wyoming*, 166; Yoshida, "Wyoming Election of 1892," 67. The two men who could most appropriately be credited with originating the invasion were Frank Wolcott and Billy Irvine, both Republicans during almost their entire adult lives. Regarding Irvine, see Burroughs, *Guardian of the Grasslands*, 186. As to Wolcott, see chapter 7 of this book, including the comments of John Clay quoted there (from *My Life on the Range*, 138). and "Wolcott for Governor," *CDL*, August 23, 1892, wherein the prospect of Wolcott as the Republican candidate for governor is discussed.

76. See "On Their Trial," *BB*, December 8, 1892.

77. "Official Ballot of Johnson County," *BB*, November 24, 1892.

78. Ibid.

79. I was the chairman of the Washakie County Democratic Party in 1974, when Watergate came to roost. That was the best year for Democrats in my lifetime. In my county we managed to elect a few Democrats, but most of Washakie County's officeholders remained Republican. Washakie County's experience was typical in Wyoming; there were Democratic gains, but Republicans still held on to most of the offices in Wyoming. The elections most comparable to 1892 were probably in 1932 and 1934, when Wyoming Democrats made their best showings, but the Republicans held many offices. See Larson, *History of Wyoming*, 462–66.

80. See Yoshida, "Wyoming Election of 1892," 74–79. Regarding the Supreme Court vote in Johnson County, see "Official Ballot of Johnson County," *BB*, November 24, 1892.

CHAPTER TWENTY

1. David, *Malcolm Campbell, Sheriff*, 344.

2. "De Billier Taken East," *LB*, July 8, 1892.

3. Smith, *War on Powder River*, 281; "Cattlemen on Trial," *CDL*, January 3, 1893.

4. "Cattlemen on Trial," *CDL*, January 3, 1893; *State v. Canton*, Laramie County criminal case no. 3-365. The men who answered the call were "Frank W. Canton, Joseph Elliott, William J. Clarke, Frank H. Laberteaux, Wm. C. Irvine, John N. Tisdale, Wm. E. Guthrie, Fred. G. S. Hesse, Michael Shaunsey, Chas. [C. A.] Campbell, Frank Wolcott, A. B. Clarke, Elias W. Whitcomb, Alexander D. Adamson, Chas. S. Ford, Benjamin Morrison, Lafayette H. Parker, W. B. Wallace, D. R. Tisdale, W. H. Tabor, A. R. Powers, W. S. Davis, and R. W. Allen."

5. "Cattlemen on Trial," *CDL*, January 3, 1893; Smith, *War on Powder River*, 270.

6. "Cattlemen on Trial," *CDL*, January 3, 1893; "Hunting a Jury," *CDL*, January 6, 1893.

7. "Cattlemen on Trial," *CDL*, January 3, 1893; "Hunting a Jury," *CDL*, January 6, 1893.

8. "Cattlemen on Trial," *CDL*, January 3, 1893; "Hunting a Jury," *CDL*, January 6, 1893.

9. See W. S. Davis Affidavit attached to the Motion to Continue in case no. 3-365.

10. "And Now for The Trial," *CDS*, January 4, 1893.

11. Ibid.

12. "Regulators in Court," *Chicago Herald*, January 7, 1893.

13. "Hunting a Jury," *CDL*, January 6, 1893.

14. "It Starts In Tamely," *CDS*, January 6, 1893.

15. Ibid.

16. See David, *Malcolm Campbell, Sheriff*, 347.

17. "It Starts In Tamely," *CDS*, January 6, 1893. Only men served on juries in Wyoming at this time. Although Wyoming established woman suffrage when the territory was established in 1869, and several women had served on petit and grand juries in 1870 and 1871, the practice had been discontinued. Larson, *History of Wyoming*, 84, 85.

18. "Hunting a Jury," *CDL*, January 6, 1893.

19. Ibid.

20. "Eight Challenges Used," *CDS*, January 7, 1893.

21. David, *Malcolm Campbell, Sheriff*, 346.

22. "It Starts In Tamely," *CDS*, January 6, 1893.

23. "Still After a Jury," *CDL*, January 7, 1893.

24. "Eight Challenges Used," *CDS*, January 7, 1893.

25. "Hunting a Jury," *CDL*, January 6, 1893.

26. See the list of Defense and State Peremptory Challenges, Laramie County criminal case no. 3-365.

27. See ibid.; and David, *Malcolm Campbell, Sheriff*, 347, 348.

28. "A Sudden Stoppage," *CDL*, January 22, 1893.

29. "May Let Cattlemen Go," *Salt Lake City Tribune*, January 9, 1893.

30. "The Invaders' Trial," *CDL*, January 15, 1893.

31. The following discussion is drawn from "It Was Very Peculiar" and "A Sudden Stoppage," *CDL*, January 22, 1893; and "The Legal Curtain Drawn," *CDS*, January 22, 1893.

32. "A Sudden Stoppage," *CDL*, January 22, 1893.

33. Ibid.

34. Ibid.

35. Ibid. Davidson stated that the cases involving Champion could not be refiled, since they had originated in Cheyenne, whereas those for the killing of Ray might be.

36. "It Was Very Peculiar," *CDL*, January 22, 1893. Ballard and Davidson's responses were essentially that they did not think anything of significance would come up that day, that efforts to find them could not have been very extensive, because they were in the area, that they were surprised of the dismissals, but this decision was, in any event, up to Bennett, the Johnson County attorney. "Judge Ballard Explains," *CDS*, January 24, 1893.

37. "A Sudden Stoppage," *CDL*, January 22, 1893. With the dismissals, the forfeiture of defendants' bonds was set aside, meaning that no monies were assessed.

38. "The Legal Curtain Drawn," *CDS*, January 22, 1893.
39. "The Trial Over," *CDS*, January 22, 1893.

CHAPTER TWENTY-ONE

1. "An Able Document," *CDL*, January 12 1893.
2. Ibid.
3. Yoshida, "Wyoming Election of 1892," 74, 75, 79, 80.
4. "Happily Ended," *CDL*, January 1, 1893.
5. Gould, *Wyoming*, 173.
6. Yoshida, "Wyoming Election of 1892," 79.
7. "A Scandalous Proceeding," *CDL*, January 19, 1893.
8. "Official Ballot of Johnson County," *BB*, November 24, 1892.
9. With regard to the disputed seats, Bennett and Chapman were the Democrats from Carbon County, and the other races were Pickett (D) versus Okie (R) in Fremont County and Baker (D) versus Scott (R) in Converse County. See Gould, *Wyoming*, 173–77, 184.
10. Yoshida, "Wyoming Election of 1892," 80.
11. Ibid., 81; Gould, *Wyoming*, 175.
12. Gould, *Wyoming*, 175.
13. Yoshida, "Wyoming Election of 1892," 82. When a case involving 1892 election disputes came before the Wyoming Supreme Court in 1893, Clark recused himself and was replaced by another judge. See *In Re Moore*, 4 Wyo. 98, 115 (1893).
14. Gould, *Wyoming*, 176.
15. Ibid.
16. Yoshida, "Wyoming Election of 1892," 83.
17. Gould, *Wyoming*, 177.
18. Ibid.
19. Yoshida, "Wyoming Election of 1892," 76; Gould, *Wyoming*, 177.
20. Yoshida, "Wyoming Election of 1892," 79, citing *LB*, November 14, 1892.
21. Gould, *Wyoming*, 177, 178.
22. Yoshida, "Wyoming Election of 1892," 84.
23. Gould, *Wyoming*, 178.
24. Yoshida, "Wyoming Election of 1892," 86.
25. Ibid., 85.
26. Ibid.
27. Ibid., 85, 86.
28. Ibid., 85, citing *LB*, December 3, 1892.
29. Ibid., 86.
30. Ibid., citing *LB*, December 5, 1892.
31. Ibid., citing *CDL*, December 9, 1892.
32. Gould, *Wyoming*, 180.
33. Ibid., 179, 180.
34. Ibid., 180, 181.
35. See *State ex rel Bennett v. Barber*, 4 Wyo. 56 (1892).

36. Ibid., 78.

37. *In Re Moore*, 4 Wyo. 98 (1893).

38. For articles criticizing Osborne, see "The End in View," *BB*, citing *Laramie Republican*, December 22, 1892; "That Mare's Nest," *BB*, citing *Laramie Sentinel*, January 12, 1893; and "The Governor's Message," *BB*, January 19, 1893.

39. Gould, *Wyoming*, 183.

40. Yoshida, "Wyoming Election of 1892," 94.

41. Ibid., 94, 97, 98; Gould, *Wyoming*, 184.

42. Yoshida, "Wyoming Election of 1892," 94.

43. The exact timing of the resolution of election challenges is not clear, but it appears that the House first acted and then the Senate did so. Gould, *Wyoming*, 184.

44. Yoshida, "Wyoming Election of 1892," 97.

45. The obvious exception to this generality was Richard Cheney, later to become secretary of defense and vice president of the United States. Despite his high competence, though, I do not believe that Cheney, while in the House of Representatives, ever wielded the influence that Warren or Alan Simpson did in the U.S. Senate. Wyoming was the forty-fourth state admitted into the Union, and Utah, in 1896, was the forty-fifth.

46. Yoshida, "Wyoming Election of 1892," 98, 99.

47. Ibid., 9; Gould, *Wyoming*, 184–87.

48. Gould, *Wyoming*, 186, citing Warren letters.

49. Yoshida, "Wyoming Election of 1892," 99; Gould, *Wyoming*, 185. Gould states that Holliday and Beck were "hacks."

50. Gould, *Wyoming*, 185.

51. Yoshida, "Wyoming Election of 1892," 99.

52. Ibid., 99, 100; Gould, *Wyoming*, 188, 189. Gould states that Russell went to Denver "ostensibly on business but with strong indications that his trip had been subsidized."

53. Yoshida, "Wyoming Election of 1892," 100; Larson, *History of Wyoming*, 288.

54. Yoshida, "Wyoming Election of 1892," 101; Gould, *Wyoming*, 189. Thompson was the son of a former U.S. senator from Kentucky, John Burton Thompson.

55. Yoshida, "Wyoming Election of 1892," 101; Gould, *Wyoming*, 189.

56. Gould, *Wyoming*, 173, citing Warren to J. D. Woodruff, November 16, 1892. See also Larson, *History of Wyoming*, 288.

57. Yoshida, "Wyoming Election of 1892," 101.

58. Ibid., 107–109.

59. Gould, *Wyoming*, 190.

60. Yoshida, "Wyoming Election of 1892," 102.

61. Ibid., citing *CDL*, February 19, 1893.

62. Gould, *Wyoming*, 190.

63. *BB*, March 2, 1893, 2, col. 2.

64. Gould, *Wyoming*, 190.

65. Yoshida, "Wyoming Election of 1892," 105.

66. Gould, *Wyoming*, 168, 190.

67. Rankin to Miller, October 31, 1892.

68. F. B. Crossthwaite to W. H. H. Miller, December 22, 1892.

69. Ibid.

70. Ibid.

71. Gould, *Wyoming*, 168.

72. See "Will Not Prosecute," *BB*, March 30, 1893; Johnson County criminal case nos. 211–13 (*State v. Coates, State v. Elliott,* and *State v. Canton*).

73. "Livestock," *CDL*, March 8, 1893; *BB*, 1893, 3, col. 1.

74. "Livestock," *CDL*, March 8, 1893. See also Smith, *War on Powder River*, 147; and Basch, interview by J. Elmer Brock, May 11, 1933, transcript, box 1, file 2, Tisdale Collection.

75. Basch interview, May 11, 1933, 0003, 0004. In a 1935 interview by J. Elmer Brock, Basch went so far as to say that Tom Horn was involved in the murder of Tisdale. DeArment, *Alias Frank Canton*, 141, quoting from interview transcript available at the Gatchell Museum. There is strong and reliable evidence that Tom Horn did not appear in Johnson County until May 1892 at the earliest. See Irvine to Penrose, February 22, 1914, 191.

76. See Hope, "Joe Elliott's Story."

77. "Refused to Plead," *CDL*, May 12, 1893; Smith, *War on Powder River*, 258.

78. Davis, *Vast Amount of Trouble*, 6, 7; Davis, *Goodbye, Judge Lynch*, 30, 31. See also Woods, *Wyoming's Big Horn Basin to 1901*.

79. Mercer, *Banditti of the Plains*, 140, 141.

80. "Shonsey Let Off," *CDL*, May 24, 1893; Mercer, *Banditti of the Plains*, 140, 141.

EPILOGUE

1. Murray, *Johnson County*, 124; Larson, *History of Wyoming*, 295, 296; Gould, *Wyoming*, 193.

2. Murray, *Johnson County*, 122, 124; Larson, *History of Wyoming*, 296.

3. The official population of Sheridan in 2000 was 15,804, and that of Buffalo, 3,900.

4. "Wyoming's War Ended," *Chicago Herald*, January 29, 1893.

5. After 1892, Mann's name does not appear in the area newspapers nor in the censuses.

6. F. G. S. Hesse to Messrs. Windsor, Kemp & Co., May 2, 1892, and Frank Kemp to F. G. S. Hesse, May 7, 1892, Hesse papers.

7. Smith, *War on Powder River*, 284.

8. Mrs. Hesse was born Isabelle Ross Sutherland in London, Ontario, in 1860. She came to Johnson County in 1881 and married Hesse in 1884. Fred G. S. Hesse (biographical details), Hesse Papers.

9. Edwards, "'Hard Winter' Davis," 2.

10. Ibid.

11. Ibid., 4; Smith, *War on Powder River*, 283.

12. *BB*, December 10, 1892, 3, col. 1.

13. See Johnson County criminal case no. 254 (*State v. Martin A. Tisdale*); "Contest Notice," *BB*, February 16, 1893.

14. "Made His Last Fight," *Valley County Gazette*, July 21, 1894.

15. DeArment states that it was the boy who was supposed to shoot Canton, and Gardner and Webb would finish him off only if Mart failed. DeArment, *Alias Frank Canton*, 241, 242. A granddaughter of Mart Tisdale, however, believes that the story is that Gardner and Webb were only using the boy as a decoy and they intended to shoot Canton. Lisa Anderson, interview by the author, Shell, Wyo., February 11, 2008.

16. "John Alfred Tisdale," p. 91, box 2, file 125, Tisdale Collection; *Buffalo's First Century*, 162, 65; Hanson, *Powder River Country*, 408, 409.

17. "John Alfred Tisdale," 3.

18. Lewis Gould provides an excellent discussion of the Democratic disaster of 1894 in *Wyoming*, chap. 8.

19. Ibid., 215, 217, 218.

20. Ibid., 223.

21. *BB*, October 20, 1892, 1, col. 5; "Pretty Mean," *People's Voice*, 1892.

22. "End of the Trial," *CDL*, January 22, 1893.

23. Gould, *Wyoming*, 225, 206–11; Larson, *History of Wyoming*, 447. Regarding the Warren-Carey feud, see Larson, *History of Wyoming*, 292, 320.

24. Larson, *History of Wyoming*, 316–18, 448.

25. Ibid., 318.

26. "Stockmen in Session," *CDL*, April 4, 1893.

27. Burroughs, *Guardian of the Grasslands*, 167.

28. See "The Stock Association," *BB*, October 4, 1894; and "The Stock Meeting," *CDL*, April 4, 1893.

29. Burroughs, *Guardian of the Grasslands*, 176; "Stockmen in Session," *CDL*, April 4, 1893.

30. Gov. B. B. Brooks's message to Eighth State Legislature, January 11, 1905.

31. Larson, *History of Wyoming*, 401, 402.

32. Dr. Barber testified as a physician in the 1902 trial of Tom Horn. Krakel, *Saga of Tom Horn*, 73.

33. McGreevy, "Amos Barber."

34. See Penrose, *Rustler Business*, 11, 17, 26; "Dr. Charles Bingham Penrose, One of the 'Regulators,' under Arrest," *Rocky Mountain News*, April 15, 1892; David, *Malcolm Campbell, Sheriff*, 253, 254.

35. Penrose, *Rustler Business*, 27.

36. McGreevy, "Amos Barber."

37. Van Valkenburgh, "Johnson County War," 13; Burroughs, *Guardian of the Grasslands*, 187.

38. See, for example, the foreword to the 1954 University of Oklahoma Press publication of the book, which is in stark contrast to Professor Lewis Gould's writings about Mercer, such as "A. S. Mercer and the Johnson County War," 5.

39. Gould, "A. S. Mercer and the Johnson County War," 20.

40. "Unofficial Ballot," *People's Voice*, November 10, 1894.

41. "Acquitted," *People's Voice*, May 26, 1894.

42. *Buffalo's First Century*, 5.

43. "A Memorial to the Members of the Constitutional Convention of Wyoming, Johnson County," *Annals of Wyoming* (July 1940): 176; *Buffalo's First Century*, 6, 213.

44. The comments about Flagg come primarily from Myers, "Jack Flagg Remembered." Regarding the 1895 confrontation with Scott Davis, see "Dismissed," *People's Voice*, May 11, 1895.

45. Vertical file 3, John R. Smith folder, Gatchell Museum.

46. *People's Voice*, June 30, 1894, 3; *BB*, November 16, 1893, 2, col. 2. Angus was fined $250 plus $100 court costs.

47. "Arapahoe Brown Murdered," *Sheridan Post*, March 4, 1901.

48. Edwards, "W. G. 'Red' Angus," 3; *People's Voice*, May 26, 1894, 3, col. 3.

49. Edwards, "W. G. 'Red' Angus," 3.

50. "Obituary," *BB*, August 3, 1922.

51. DeArment, *Alias Frank Canton*, 306.

52. Ibid., 153–58.

53. See ibid., chap. 12.

54. *Buffalo's First Century*, 151, 152.

55. See Davis, *Vast Amount of Trouble*, 9, 10, 46. The discussion about the Spring Creek Raid generally follows my writings in *A Vast Amount of Trouble*.

56. Ibid., 140.

57. See the discussion in Davis, *Vast Amount of Trouble*, chaps. 7–17.

58. Davis, *Goodbye, Judge Lynch*, 227.

59. Ibid., 232.

60. But it did not stop lynching in Wyoming. See Guenther, "List of Good Negroes," 2, where the author writes of five African Americans being lynched after 1909.

61. Ibid., 142.

62. Parmelee served as the district judge for Wyoming's Fourth Judicial District from January 2, 1905, until January 1, 1917. *Wyoming Reports*, vols. 13 and 24.

63. Clover, *On Special Assignment*.

64. See Payne, *Owen Wister*, 113, 114, 205. Wister first met Frank Wolcott in 1883 and was Wolcott's guest at the VR Ranch during that summer (82). Payne lists Hesse, Irvine, Teschemacher, de Billier, Canton, and Dr. Penrose as Wister's friends (125, 127).

65. Canton, *Frontier Trails*.

66. Gould, *Wyoming*, 138.

67. McDermott, *Writers in Judgment*, 20.

68. I am referring to the 1934 Taylor Grazing Act, 48 Stat. 1269.

Bibliography

ARCHIVES AND PUBLIC RECORDS

Coroner's Inquest Report, April 16, 1892. Jim Gatchell Memorial Museum, Buffalo, Wyo.

Driskell, Mabel Snider. "History of Elias U. Snider." Vertical file 3, Elias U. Snider (Life of). Jim Gatchell Memorial Museum, Buffalo, Wyo.

Gibbs, Bob. Collection. Jim Gatchell Memorial Museum, Buffalo, Wyo.

Hesse, Fred, Declaration by, Register's Final Certificate, and Deposition of Applicant. Desert Land Entry 485, U.S. Land Office, Cheyenne, Wyo. National Archives and Records Administration, RG 49, Bureau of Land Management, E2021A, Serial Patent files, 1908–51.

Hesse, Fred G. S. Papers. Wyoming Stock Growers Association Collection, American Heritage Center, Laramie, Wyo.

Johnson County Clerk. Records. Buffalo, Wyo.

Johnson County Clerk of the District Court. Records. Buffalo, Wyo.

National Archives and Records Administration, Military Records Branch, Washington, D.C. Records of the Adjutant General's Office, RG 94.

Tisdale, Tom. Collection. Jim Gatchell Memorial Museum, Buffalo, Wyo.

Warren, Francis E. Papers. American Heritage Center, Laramie, Wyo.

Wyoming Stock Growers Association. Collection. American Heritage Center, Laramie, Wyo.

BOOKS AND ARTICLES

Anonymous. *Alias, the Jack of Spades.* With introduction by Pat Hall. Cheyenne: Powder River Press, 1971.

Baber, D. F. *The Longest Rope.* Caldwell, Idaho: Caxton Printers, 1953.

Bard, Floyd C. *Horse Wrangler: Sixty Years in the Saddle in Wyoming and Montana.* Norman: University of Oklahoma Press, 1960.

Bartlett, I. F. *History of Wyoming.* Vol. 1. Chicago: S. J. Clarke Publishing Co., 1918.

Brayer, Herbert O. "New Light on the Johnson County War." In *The Westerners Brand Book.* Chicago, 1953.

————. "Range Country Troubles—1885." In *The Westerners Brand Book.* 1952

————. *Range Murder: How the Red Sash Gang Dry-Gulched Deputy United States Marshal George Wellman.* Evanston, Ill.: Branding Iron Press, 1955.

Buffalo's Centennial Book Committee. *Buffalo's First Century.* Buffalo, Wyo.: Buffalo Bulletin, 1984.

Burroughs, John Rolfe. *Guardian of the Grasslands: The First Hundred Years of the Wyoming Stock Growers Association,* Cheyenne, Wyo.: Pioneer Printing and Stationery, 1971.

Canton, Frank M. *Frontier Trails: The Autobiography of Frank M. Canton.* New ed. Norman: University of Oklahoma Press, 1966.

Clay, John. *My Life on the Range.* Norman: University of Oklahoma Press, 1962.

Clover, Samuel Travers. *On Special Assignment.* New York: Argonaut Press, 1965.

Crockett, Walter Hill. *Vermont: The Green Mountain State.* New York: Century History Co., 1921.

David, Robert. *Malcolm Campbell, Sheriff.* Casper, Wyo.: Wyomingana, 1932.

Davis, John W. *Goodbye, Judge Lynch.* Norman: University of Oklahoma Press, 2005.

————. *A Vast Amount of Trouble.* Niwot: University Press of Colorado, 1993; reprint, Norman: University of Oklahoma Press, 2005.

————. *Worland before Worland.* Worland, Wyo.: Northern Wyoming Daily News, 1987.

DeArment, Robert K. *Alias Frank Canton.* Norman: University of Oklahoma Press, 1996.

Edwards, Bob. "'Hard Winter' Davis." *Sentry,* April 2005.

————. "W. G. 'Red' Angus." *Sentry,* October 2002.

Ewig, Rick. "E. T. Payton: Savior or Madman?" *Annals of Wyoming* (Winter 2007).

Ficken, Robert E. *Washington State: The Inaugural Decade, 1889-1899,* Pullman: Washington State University Press, 2007.

Frank Leslie's Weekly. "The Wyoming Cattle War." June 2, 1892.

Frink, Maurice. *Cow Country Cavalcade: Eighty Years of the Wyoming Stock Growers' Association.* Denver: Old West Publishing Co., 1954.

Gould, Lewis Ludlow. "A. S. Mercer and the Johnson County War." *Arizona and the West* (Spring–Winter 1965).

————. "Francis E. Warren and the Johnson County War." *Arizona and the West* (Summer 1967).

————. "Willis Van Devanter and the Johnson County War." *Montana: The Magazine of Western History* (Autumn 1967).

————. "Willis Van Devanter in Wyoming Politics, 1884-1897." Ph.D. diss., Yale University, 1966.

————. *Wyoming: A Political History, 1868–1896.* New Haven, Conn., and London: Yale University Press, 1968.

Guenther, Todd. "The List of Good Negroes." *Annals of Wyoming* (Spring 2009).

Hall, Pat. "Between the Lines." Column in *SunDAY Magazine* (Cheyenne, Wyo.). Available in the Tisdale Collection, box 2, file 113. This newspaper magazine was published during the early 1970s by the *Cheyenne Tribune* and the *Cheyenne Eagle.*

Hanson, Margaret Brock, ed. *Powder River Country: The Papers of J. Elmer Brock.* Cheyenne, Wyo.: Frontier Printing, 1981.

Homsher, Lola. *Guide to Wyoming Newspapers, 1867–1967.* Cheyenne: Wyoming State Archives, 1971.

Hope, B. W. "Joe Elliott's Story." *Annals of Wyoming* 45 (Fall 1973).

House Journal of the 10th Wyoming Legislature. Laramie, Wyo.: Republican Printing, 1909.

Hufsmith, George. *The Wyoming Lynching of Cattle Kate, 1889.* Glendo, Wyo.: High Plains Press, 1993.

Krakel, Dean. *The Saga of Tom Horn.* Laramie, Wyo.: Laramie Printing, 1954.

Larson, T. A. *History of Wyoming.* Lincoln: University of Nebraska Press, 1959.

Lindsay, Charles. *The Big Horn Basin.* Lincoln: University of Nebraska, 1932.

McDermott, John D. "Writers in Judgment: Historiography of the Johnson County War." *Annals of Wyoming* (Winter 1993–94).

McGreevy, Patrick S., M.D. "Amos Barber, Charles Penrose, and the War on Powder River." *Surgery, Gynecology and Obstetrics* 136 (April 1973).

Mercer, A. S. *The Banditti of the Plains.* Norman: University of Oklahoma Press, 1954.

Murray, Robert A. "The Arms of Wyoming's Cattle War." *Shooting Times,* July 1967.

———. *Johnson County; 175 Years of History at the Foot of the Big Horn Mountains.* Buffalo, Wyo.: Jim Gatchell Memorial Museum Press, 2003.

Myers, Sue C. "Jack Flagg Remembered." *Sentry,* October 2005.

———. "Memories of the Battle at the TA Ranch." *Sentry,* August 2001.

Oliva, Leo E. *Fort Wallace.* Topeka: Kansas State Historical Society, 1998.

Payne, Darwin. *Owen Wister: Chronicler of the West, Gentleman of the East.* Dallas: Southern Methodist University Press, 1985.

Penrose, Charles B. *The Rustler Business.* Buffalo, Wyo.: Jim Gatchell Memorial Museum Press, 2007.

Rea, Tom, *Devil's Gate.* Norman: University of Oklahoma Press, 2007.

———. "Dueling Newspapers: Versions of the Watson-Averell Lynching, 1889." www.tomrea .net/Dueling%20Newspapers.html.

Roberts, Phil. "Cowboys Form a Health Cooperative." *Montana: The Magazine of Western History* 44 (Summer 1994).

Rollins, George Watson. *The Struggle of the Cattlemen, Sheepmen and Settlers for the Control of Lands in Wyoming, 1867–1910.* New York: Arno Press, 1979.

Smith, Helena Huntington. *The War on Powder River.* Lincoln: University of Nebraska Press, 1967.

Stuart, Granville. *Forty Years on the Frontier.* Lincoln: University of Nebraska Press, 1977.

Tanner, Francis Henry. "The Disposal of the Public Domain in Johnson County, Wyoming, 1869–1890." Master's thesis, University of Wyoming, 1967.

Van Pelt, Lori. *Capital Characters of Old Cheyenne.* Glendo, Wyo.: High Plains Press, 2006.

Van Valkenburgh, Lois. "The Johnson County War: The Papers of Charles Bingham Penrose in the Library of the University of Wyoming with Introduction and Notes." Master's thesis, University of Wyoming, Laramie, 1939. Available in "An Era of Violence," comp. Ted Bohlen and Tom Tisdale, in Tisdale Collection.

"The V. R., Mystery—Shadows . . . and Beauty." Available in the Tisdale Collection, box 1, file 96.

Woods, L. Milton. *Asa Shinn Mercer: Western Promoter and Newspaperman, 1839–1917.* Spokane, Wash.: Arthur H. Clark, 2003.

———. *John Clay, Jr.: Commission Man, Banker and Rancher.* Spokane, Wash.: Arthur H. Clark, 2001.

———. *Moreton Frewen's Western Adventures.* Boulder, Colo.: Roberts Rinehart, 1986.

———. *Wyoming's Big Horn Basin to 1901.* Worland, Wyo.: High Plains Publishing, 1991.

Wyoming Reports. Vol. 3. 1893.

Yoshida, John K. "The Wyoming Election of 1892." Master's thesis, University of Wyoming, 1956.

NEWSPAPERS

Big Horn (Wyo.) Sentinel

Bill Barlow's Budget

Buffalo (Wyo.) Bulletin

Buffalo Echo

Cheyenne (Wyo.) Daily Sun

Chicago Blade

Chicago Herald

Denver Republican

Denver Sun

Denver Times

Douglas (Wyo.) Graphic

Johnson County (Wyo.) Republican

Laramie (Wyo.) Boomerang

New York Telegram

New York World

Northwestern Live Stock Journal

Newcastle (Wyo.) News

Omaha Bee

People's Voice

Philadelphia Times

Pioneer Press

Rawlins (Wyo.) Journal

Rock Springs (Wyo.) Miner

Rocky Mountain News

Salt Lake Tribune

San Francisco Examiner

Sheridan (Wyo.) Enterprise

Sheridan Post

Sundance (Wyo.) Gazette

Valley County Gazette (Glasgow, Mont.)

Wyoming Derrick

Acknowledgments

The Johnson County War is so familiar to Wyoming people that one would expect the story to smoothly flow from the mind of any Wyoming author. It certainly did not flow smoothly from the mind of this Wyoming author, however. Nor was it done quickly; it has been almost seven years since I first started my research. The story is extraordinarily complex, involving hundreds of people. It is filled with anomalous twists and turns and, on seemingly every important point, has been the subject of at least two contrary versions. Without the assistance of many people, I could not have written this story, smoothly or otherwise.

Once again, I found myself thankful to be living and writing in Wyoming. I've dealt with local officials from virtually every state of the Union, and while most have been courteous and helpful, nowhere are they as consistently courteous, helpful, and friendly as in my home state. I was surprised sometimes by how far Wyoming folks went to help this stranger (although if it's one Wyoming person to another, are there any strangers?). Here it started with the people at the Johnson County Library, as I was given a complete tour of their substantial collection of Johnson County War documents and writings. Nancy Jennings performed some prodigious feats of research at my request, to the point that I began to feel guilty, but I certainly did appreciate her hard work.

The people at the Jim Gatchell Memorial Museum enthusiastically opened to me all the great body of information the museum holds. I relied especially on Bob Edwards, who was always responsive to my questions, even those that were sometimes off the wall. I especially appreciated a tour with Bob of southern Johnson County, in particular the beautiful Hole in the Wall country. There is an old saw among lawyers that an attorney should never try a case without having been to the scene. Likewise, any author writing about Wyoming history must visit the scenes of his topic, and Bob Edwards saw to it that I visited all the classic scenes of the Johnson County War.

To my great good fortune, my editor on this project has been Charles "Chuck" Rankin. Writing for Chuck Rankin is not for the fainthearted, however. Chuck is a tough editor—not English-major tough but Marine Corps drill instructor tough. Nevertheless, every time I worked through his criticisms and suggestions, it was inescapably clear that my manuscript had been improved, sometimes dramatically. A writer can put up with a lot of tough criticism if he sees that an editor is consistently making his manuscript better.

The research and investigation for any book has high points and low points. For me the highest point occurred during my inquiry into the personal life of Willis Van Devanter, the only Wyoming lawyer to sit on the United States Supreme Court. One day in May 2008 my secretary gave me a message; "Willis Van Devanter is on the line." It was not Justice Van Devanter (long since dead) but his namesake and grandson, Willis Van Devanter of Poolesville, Maryland. I had delightful conversations with Mr. Van Devanter and his sister, Ethel Harris, of Chevy Chase, Maryland, who graciously shared their seventy-year-old memories of their distinguished grandfather.

My secretary, Pam Gaulke, was of great assistance, not only because she is such a good shepherd of my office's computers but also because she was such a great help when completing the last details for the publication of the book. And, of course, my wife, Celia, was indispensable, acting as chief proofreader, sounding board, critic, and all-round adviser.

Index

Beach, Sumner, 84, 85

Beaver Creek Canyon, 103

Beck, George T., 264, 265

Becker, E. H. (first editor of *Sentinel*), 19, 20; leads fight against division, 39–41

Beckwith, A. C., 266

Bedford, Jack, 270

Belcher, E. A., 260

Bennett, Alvin (Johnson County attorney), 108, 112, 113, 125, 126, 204; prosecutes invaders, 252–54, 269

Bennett, H. A., 22

Bennett, S. B., 258

Big Horn, Wyo., 19, 218

Big Horn Basin, 6, 26, 27, 37, 91, 244, 270, 277

Big Horn County, 280

Big Horn County Rustler (newspaper), 129, 130

Big Horn Mountains (Big Horns), 5, 6, 26, 100, 147, 161, 271, 277, 279

Big Horn River, 6, 26, 56, 270

Big Horn Sentinel, 19, 42, 47, 90, 301n13

Bill Barlow's Budget (newspaper), 155, 156, 237

Bimetallism, 234

Blair, Jacob (judge), 9, 290n18

Blake, John W. (judge), 63, 106, 126, 127, 201, 202, 204, 210, 211, 212, 213, 227, 240, 241, 332&n69

Bonanza Rustler (newspaper), 91

Bonanza, Wyo., 270

Booth, Bill, 53

Bosler brothers, 86

Bothwell, Albert John, 71–76

Bouton, Thomas J., 202, 216

Bouquet County (Johnson County), 9

Bozeman Trail, 6

Brannan, Tom, 84

Brayer, Herbert, 36

Breckons, Joseph A., 123, 230

Breckons, R. W., 203, 248

Brink, Herbert, 280

Brock, Albert, 37

Brock, J. Elmer, 31, 60, 171

Brooks, B. B. (governor), 86, 264, 276, 280

Brooke, John R. (general), 174, 175, 193

Brown, Arapahoe, 164, 165, 170, 177, 278

Brown, M. C., 200, 211

Brown University, 9

Brockway, Percy, 192

Bryan, Colonel P. Gad, 210

Buchanan, Frank, 74–76

Buffalo, Wyo., 142, 14, 145, 146, 158, 159, 161, 164, 166, 168, 188, 191–93, 195, 199–201, 203, 206, 217–19, 223, 238, 271–73, 277, 283; early years, 5–14, 17, 18; description in *Washington Star,* 120

Buffalo Bulletin, 89, 90, 105, 106, 110, 111, 115, 117, 122, 128, 131, 138, 140, 165, 178, 179, 186, 187, 188, 191, 200, 201, 203, 216, 219–21, 228, 262, 279; election of 1892, 234–39, 242, 244, 245, 248, 267

Buffalo Echo (newspaper), 7, 13, 42, 201, 202, 216, 239

"Buffalo soldiers," 222

Buffalo Voice (newspaper), 279

Burch, Dab, 270

Burke, Milo, 243, 244, 276

Burkhart, John, 248

Burritt, Charles H., 9, 10, *10,* 33, 38, 45, 63, 78, 112, 123, 124, 136, 185, 200–205, 208, 220, 221, 227, 277, 278, 306n61, 334n24; director of building and loan association, 30; justice of the peace, 25; marriage, 22

Burroughs, John Rolfe, 50, 81, 82, 87, 88, 282

Bye, Mary E., 278

Calhoun (wounded invader), 156, 169

Campbell, C. A. (invader), 138, 143, 145, 232

Campbell, George, 159

Campbell, John A., 83

Canton, Frank N., 21, 35, 43, 47, 50, 53, 54, 58, 60, 77, 89, 104, 106, 119, 125, 136, 137, 139, 144, 145, 148, 149, 154, 158, 159, 165, 177, 187, 191, 192, 199, 213, 216, 218, 244, 245, 247, 269, 272, 273, 281, 290n14, 296n14, 296n15, 299n96, 300n34, 300n39, 303n51, 315n26; Oklahoma

Middlebury College, 9
Miles City (Mont.) Stock Growers Journal, 81
Miller, E. E., 248
Miller, William H. H., 239, 269
Moeller, Gustave Ernest Albert, 21, 202,
   217, 279; as editor of *Buffalo Bulletin*,
   187, 235–38; as justice of the peace, 25
Moore, Lee, 61, 183
Morrison, Ben, 136, 137, 139, 140
Muddy Creek, 111
Munkres, George W., 113, 248, 324n40
Murphy Cattle Company, 62
Mynett, Jeff, 154

Natrona County, Wyo., 210, 212, 218
New, A. L., 243, 257, 260, 264, 265
Northern Wyoming Farmers' and Stock-
   growers' Association, 139
Northern Wyoming Protective Association,
   89, 216
Northwestern Live Stock Journal, 76, 231,
   232, 240
Nowood River, 270
Nutcher, William, 62, 65

Occidental Hotel (Buffalo), 7
O'Connor, W. T., 243
Ogden, Utah, 231
Okie, J. B., 263, 339n9
Omaha, Nebr., 207, 244
Omaha Bee, 92, 115, 116
Omaha World Herald, 207
O'Malley, St. Clair, 202, 248
Oregon Trail, 7
Osborne, John, 233, 243; serving as governor,
   255, 256, 258–62, 266, 267, 271, 276

Panic of 1893, 271, 274
Parker, Lafayette, 89, 139, 193, 216
Parmelee, Carroll H., 38, 174, 236, 315n24,
   343n62; Governor Barber's aide-de-camp,
   168, 176; presides over Brink trial, 281;
   presides over Canton preliminary hearing,
   112–14; as editor of *Sentinel*, 41–45; as

school principal, 31; as candidate for
   Wyoming Supreme Court, 243–44
Parrot, George "Big Nose," 69
Payton, Edgar T., 178–79
Pearson, I. N., 114
Pease County, Wyo., 5–7
Penrose, Charles, 58, 82, 132–34, 136, 143,
   156, 181, 182, 240, 276, 299n13
People's Voice (newspaper), 239, 242, 244, 278
Peremptory challenges, 247, 250, 252
Peterson, George, 62, 64, 116
Pettit, Fred S., 248
Pickett, William Douglas, 263, 339n9
Piney Creek, 14
Pinkertons, 178
Pioneer Press, 217
Plunkett, Horace, 61, 99
Populists (People's Party), 237, 242, 243,
   262–64, 274
Potter, Charles, 242
Powder River, 6, 26, 182, 218; Middle Fork,
   101, 147; Red Fork, 102, 115
Powder River Cattle Company, 14, 62
Powers, A. R., 138
Pollock, Captain Edwin, 6
Prairie Dog Creek, 12
Public domain, 14, 283

Rader, Marvin (Methodist minister), 192
Railroad, prospects for in Johnson County, 24
Rankin, Joe P. (marshal), 92, 220, 223–26,
   239, 240, 276; attempts to drive from
   office, 267–69
Rawlins, Wyo., 69, 257
Ray, Nick, 103, 145, 158, 159, 164, 167, 175,
   191, 192, 196, 198, 206, 207, 219, 248,
   269; besieged at the KC Ranch, 148–52
Red Cloud, 6
Regulators (vigilantes), 176
Reimann, Joseph (justice of the peace),
   123, 165
Repath, Richard H., 259
Republican Party, Wyoming, 185, 222, 227–29,
   235, 237, 245, 264, 274, 335n31